W9-CKQ-470

HITLER'S COMPROMISES

NATHAN STOLTZFUS

Hitler's Compromises

COERCION AND CONSENSUS IN NAZI GERMANY

Yale UNIVERSITY PRESS

NEW HAVEN AND LONDON

Yale University Press books may be purchased in quantity for educational, business,
or promotional use. For information, please e-mail sales.press@yale.edu (U.S. office)
or sales@yaleup.co.uk (U.K. office).

Set in Scala and Scala Sans types by Westchester Publishing Services.
Printed in the United States of America.

Library of Congress Control Number: 2015959240
ISBN: 978-0-300-21750-6 (hardcover : alk. paper)

A catalogue record for this book is available from the British Library.

This paper meets the requirements of ANSI/NISO Z39.48-1992 (Permanence of Paper).

10 9 8 7 6 5 4 3 2 1

For Maria, φυσικά

CONTENTS

I BEGAN PLANNING this book as I thought about how to guide a new generation's learning about Hitler's dictatorship. I discovered that many in the classroom took the unfathomable brutality expressed in the Holocaust as characteristic of Nazi methods in all places; Hitler's dictatorship must have had the same cold-blooded approach to ruling the Germans at home. Some students were well aware of the unrestrained and brutal ways the German Army conquered and ruled populations during the war of annihilation in the East, but they mistakenly thought that this brutishness was typical of Nazi leadership within the Reich. While Hitler worked with a range of tactics, in search of consensus within the Reich, this book focuses on his willingness to compromise with the German people when the political stakes were high enough.

Nazi ideology held that providence had granted the German "race" a mandate to dominate all others. That was absolute. But Hitler and his circle did not suppose that they could beat eighty million Germans into accepting and carrying out all the implications of this ideology. Nazi leaders, especially Hitler as the people's Leader, wanted the Germans to work together to build up the strength and unity of a Nazi "national community." Except for a tiny fraction of the population, consisting of Jews, political dissidents, social outsiders, and the congenitally "incurable," National Socialism strove to bring all Germans into line with the thinking that they should be the master of others. The effort to extract the maximal effort of the people in conquering the continent and killing millions outright was conducted with concern for the "German-blooded" people. Nazi propaganda directed German women to become the mothers of the nation through appeals to love of Nazi leaders and heroes, as well as for their own children. The National Socialist People's Welfare (NSV) was an enormous agency dedicated to benefiting productive, racially valuable Germans. A basic impulse for the dictatorship to change its method of genocide in the summer of 1941 was the perceived effects that the mass shootings of Jews were having on the killers, according to Hitler's master planner of genocide, Heinrich Himmler. Himmler's observation of mass murder by shooting in mid-August 1941 supplied a decisive motivation for the dictatorship's decision to slaughter large numbers of people by gas instead. Observing the shooters, Hitler's trusted adjutant fretted that mass shootings were creating "neurotics" or "savages" out of loyal Nazis. At the outset of Nazi "euthanasia," Hitler reportedly asked about the most humane way to kill Germans who were an incurable burden to the fulfillment of Germany's historical mission; he too must have been thinking about the perpetrators, not the victims.[1]

As Himmler coached his SS men on how to kill, at Posen in October 1943, the architect of genocide presented a world populated by Germans and those they exploited. "Always be clear about it: [the enemy] is a beast. . . . One basic principle must apply: we must be honest, decent, loyal and comradely to those of our own blood and to no one else. . . . Whether the other peoples live well or whether they die from hunger is important to me only in so far as we need them as slaves for our culture." The result, Himmler said, was a class of humane mass murderers: "Most of you know what it is like when 100 corpses lie side by side, when 500 or 1000 lie there. To have experienced this and yet—aside from exceptions due to human weakness—to have remained decent, that has hardened us."[2]

In Nazi theory, the Germans together would perpetrate the terror and commit the horrible crimes for which Hitler's regime is known, only against all others. No German was required to commit murder, although the elite class was expected to do this with great aplomb, and one would have to keep one's mouth shut if one disapproved. This was a terrible price to pay for some, who could avoid being caught up in the persecuted fringe only by the terrible repression of their freedom to speak and act as they wished. It must be said that on the whole, however, Germans were grateful for the sense of security and stability that Hitler seemed to bring and were willing to give up their freedoms for it. Such a tradeoff is not at all uncommon in history, and the Germans had particularly strong reasons for feeling insecure. Germany had not been a democracy but still could have made the transition to it had it not been for the historical circumstances of World War I and its aftermath. In Europe, Germany's enemies, Britain and France, had the decisive advantage of winning that war. The war took on its own dynamic, demanding that new lives be sacrificed to give the many dead a reason for having died. When this justification of war sacrifices through victory did not happen for Germans, they were too easily convinced that they had been stabbed in the back and were beholden to refight the war to avenge the old loss.

Pursuing vindication, the Germans were able to advance so far during World War II only because they had liquidated the Jewish "saboteurs" and "agitators," Himmler said. Hitler's ideological war in the East was a civilizing mission because the Germans, unlike the Russians and Slavs, maintained their superior nature while exterminating masses of people. This ideal is pictured in the Auschwitz album of carefree killers joking and posing for the camera as if it were just another happy moment together. The ideal of Germans supporting each other as the instrument of mass murder helps explain why the wife of Auschwitz commandant Rudolf Höss, who lived with the family in a villa at Auschwitz within sight of the camp from 1940 to 1944, thought of her life there as "paradise," where she had wished to live "till I die." In photographs her young children smile happily while at play in luxury in the shadow of infinite cruelty, and Höss's daughter remembers him as the "nicest man in the world" who was "very good to us."[3]

Rochus Misch, Hitler's bodyguard who died in 2013, said that Hitler "wasn't a monster" but "a perfectly normal gentleman" who "spoke kind words to me." Then he asked a key question that lingers with us today: "If Hitler really did all the terrible things people *now* say he did, how could he have been our Führer," the German Leader?[4] This book aspires to address that question. The Germans have earned high praise for facing the crimes of their past, showing more reluctant countries how to do it. Still today there are signs of a retrenchment among some historians, as well as in the official commemorations in Germany, in the comforting belief that Hitler ruled his own "race" of people by intimidation and terror more than by incentives and rewards, that the Gestapo crushed all opposition, and that the dictatorship set its course according to its ideology and proceeded in a straight path toward it, steamrolling any obstacles with brute force. Many today are inclined to believe such an argument. The history of popular protests during the Third Reich was repressed by the regime, and the remaining evidence of them has too often been routinely overlooked in the commemorations of the courageous and the rescuers. Although public social opposition without punishment was possible, such resistance by ordinary persons is easily construed as a rebuke to the vast, overwhelming majority who did nothing, a mechanism illustrated by the decades-old reluctance of the Federal German Republic to rehabilitate the outstanding men sentenced to death by the Nazis for "undermining German morale" or refusing to fight the criminal war.

Only healthy, productive "German-blooded" persons experienced the methods and the timing of Hitler's dictatorship in the ways that some scholars today describe as characterizing "soft" dictators (see the introduction). Hitler's dictatorship was reassuring to most Germans for about nine of its twelve years, and there were many who believed, like Hitler, that the Reich would prevail in the end if the Germans only remained united and willing to fight to the death. Many believed with Himmler that "we will win the war. It is a law of nature."[5] Even as Hitler hastened toward catastrophe, many were also happy to live well on the plunder from Germany's Jewish victims and the spoils of war. This book casts the compromises of Hitler's rule of his people in sharp contrast to the ironclad ruthlessness with which the Nazi elite murdered and exploited those outside the Nazi Reich.

HITLER'S COMPROMISES

Introduction

Like a Roman emperor Hitler rode into this medieval town at
sundown today past solid phalanxes of wildly cheering Nazis who
packed the narrow streets. . . . For the life of me I could not quite
comprehend what hidden springs he undoubtedly unloosed in the
hysterical mob which was greeting him so wildly. . . . I got caught
in a mob of ten thousand hysterics who jammed the moat in front
of Hitler's hotel, shouting: "We want our Führer." I was a little
shocked at the faces, especially those of the women, when Hitler
finally appeared on the balcony for a moment. . . . They looked up at
him as if he were a Messiah. . . . As to [Hitler's] proclamation, it
contained such statements as these, all wildly applauded as if they
were new truths: "The German form of life is definitely determined
for the next thousand years!"

—*American journalist William Shirer writing on September 4, 1935,
about the annual Nazi Party rally in Nuremberg*

WE KNOW A lot about what happened during the Nazi dictatorship and
World War II. Yet we still puzzle over why Hitler was not stopped earlier. Why did the most literate of nations, well known for its poets, phi-
losophers, and composers, jump on the bandwagon as Hitler sped
impatiently toward Armageddon? There are clues to this puzzle in the
methods Hitler used to manage dissent at home in the Reich. The
strength of the Hitler Cult, together with the regime's terror and its
efforts to present itself as conforming to the popular will, normally
preempted social dissent. But to protect the myth that Hitler was a most
powerful and benevolent leader, the dictatorship responded to social

dissent with significant compromises, by adjusting its timetable or methods, particularly if widely practiced traditions provided the force behind dissent. To safeguard his prestige and the willingness of Germans to follow him, his dictatorship made compromises with the people on a variety of important issues, and such compromises continued during the war for as long as Hitler held out hope that Germans would remain united and win. Like a malevolent dance partner, Hitler led the Germans across the dance floor, from their old ways to his imagined new Nazi order, moving as briskly as possible. If the people slowed or stumbled, he was willing to wait or even double back in order to maintain his position as their Leader.

During the early postwar years, the initial explanations for popular collaboration with Hitler's dictatorship were seductive in their simplicity: Hitler had forced the Germans into doing his will against their better judgment. Hitler the overlord held all the power while the German masses had none. But who were the people at Hitler's side, and why were they serving him? How did such a lowly outsider, who had spent his youth slinking around the down-and-out sections of Munich and Vienna, accumulate enough power to bully this nation, which had rapidly developed an industrial capacity beyond others on the European continent? Why was such a well-educated population so unarmed by the irrational claims of Nazi propaganda?

By the early 1960s, some historians were beginning to hold persons other than Hitler responsible for Nazi crimes. As ordinary Germans faced trial in West German courts for the mass shootings of Jews during 1941, historians widened the circle of accountability to include German elites from business, the bureaucracy, and the military; one enduring account holds that the Nazi dictatorship came to life within specific post–World War I circumstances, and the Holocaust occurred due to a "cumulative radicalization" of anti-Jewish policies powered by these elites, according to one prominent explanation. Their rivalry, as they one-upped each other in an unending competition for power, led to a spiraling escalation of evil, ending in an unprecedented genocide. In this conception Hitler appeared to be a "weak dictator," pushed forward by structures native to modern society and economy. While this model succeeded in challenging the common refrain of "Hitler did it, not me," many were unsatisfied because it seemed to write Hitler out of the history, depriving the story of a prime mover.[1]

By seeing only the elites as Hitler's shareholders in power, this theory made a mistake similar to that of the German elites who had helped Hitler into power in 1933. They imagined putting Hitler on their leash, pushing him "so far into a corner he would squeak," but they overlooked the power of the people behind Hitler.[2] Many of the elites hailed from Germany's still unbroken aristocracy and could not imagine having anything to do with the unwashed masses. On the other hand, Hitler was convinced that he could not lead with terror and brute force in his effort to win the people's support while shaping them into the instrument he needed to win wars and sustain Nazism. The Nazi concept of power, playing to the masses, was as far out in front of these elites as the *Blitzkrieg* model for fighting ground wars was advanced beyond the tactics of its enemies in 1939 and 1940. Hitler took for granted that in the twentieth century, the masses had entered the stage to play their role in state power, and he greeted them. He did not, however, take cues from the democratic structures that followed the British and French revolutions. Hitler's approach to power borrowed from his hero, Benito Mussolini, and to some extent from Bismarck's autocracy, but he devised his own goals that were as far removed from the course of human history as the most utopian science fiction.[3]

Blossoming in the 1970s, social histories "from below" took account of ordinary persons and everyday life, a perspective that dominated during successive decades. Some of these new histories looked at working-class resistance and collected actions of defiance by churchgoers and religious authorities to defend their religious practices. "Hitler drew back whenever he met public resistance such as on euthanasia [in August 1941] and the Church question," a leading German historian wrote in 1976.[4]

But this new perspective soon took a turn toward viewing "bottom up" forces as merely contributing to, rather than also weighing down, Hitler's quest.[5] The investigation of the range of popular responses to the regime, however, was being drawn to a close before all events of mass nonconformity, social unrest, and popular protest had been examined as a type of German defiance to which the regime responded in

appeasing ways that slowed its progress. True, the workers had not resisted much, and church authorities had on balance assisted the dictatorship more than they had hindered it. Still there was hindrance that
showed how Hitler ruled within the Reich, and it came from populations
beyond the "German-blooded" workers and the Christian churches. In
Hitler's conception and exercise of power, it was not just the elites that
mattered or the specific church and working-class sectors of the German
people that held the possibility of influencing the regime. Rather it was
his "race" of people collectively that he considered the basic cornerstone
of his power, and those people would also (in his pipe dream) pass
along National Socialism for generation after generation once they had
aligned their thinking fully with his.

Hitler did not think that he could achieve total state power without
forming a total society, although shaping the Germans into a Nazi society was beyond his powers. Nonetheless, in the context of the national
humiliation and dislocation the Germans experienced after World War
I, Hitler made surprising headway with brass-knuckled solicitations in
gaining unquestioning fealty. German elites and those at the tops of
organizations were brought quickly into alignment with his leadership,
within a matter of months, but aligning the people with his leadership
was an effort that would have to proceed in phases over decades, as Hitler
readily acknowledged. When challenged by a mass of people motivated
by their German traditions, he held himself, for the moment, to persuading them that National Socialism offered a better way. Although
the compromises resulting from this persuasion slowed his progress,
Hitler was unwilling to allocate increased time for the achievement of
his goals. In fact, as thoughts of his death began to weigh on him, he
began to imagine realigning German attitudes so that the German
masses acted according to Nazi ideals within the span of his own life-
time. Reaching to realize his insane vision, his early feats in diplomatic
and popular success urged him on toward an end that brought Germany
and Europe down to what Winston Churchill called "a rubble heap, a
charnel house, a breeding ground of pestilence and hate."[6]

PLACING NAZI TERROR: INSIDERS AND OUTSIDERS

How did Hitler secure the collaboration of the tens of millions of Germans as the base of his ability to cause destruction on such a gargan-

tuan scale? The study of Nazi Germany is driven by the Holocaust and the evil it represents. But the Nazis also set out to strengthen the German "racial national community" so that it could dominate the continent, committing—or at least accepting—genocide and mass murder as a means to that end. A basic goal was to persuade the people to see Germany's destiny as Hitler did, not only in order to achieve Nazi goals for the present, but also as a foundation for permanent National Socialism after Hitler was gone. Hitler established an unsteady "system" that precluded reaching any point of stability, but he hoped that the people themselves would pass along Nazi values. He aimed for a permanent National Socialism so that even after he no longer controlled the instruments of brute force, the people's national community would pass along Nazi values from one generation to another in the one-thousand-year Reich.

Just as Hitler was the ultimate judge of propaganda and the stories in Germany's periodicals and newspapers, he was also the ultimate expert on matters regarding movement leadership and popular mobilization. Crucial but delicate decisions about how to preempt or respond to the social dissent that threatened his progress rested on a judgment about the overall sentiment of the people, in light of Hitler's basic goal of sustaining the momentum of his mass movement, measured by popular support for Nazi causes. Was brute repression the best response to public agitation? Should the open dissenters be punished, or would this draw the attention of more Germans who might side with the dissent? As the German Leader, Hitler was compelled to intervene because his image was on the line, and the widespread belief in this image was the plaster that bound the Germans to his dictatorship. Thus a study like this of the regime's response to incidents of unrest within the Reich that were so publicly visible the regime could not ignore them focuses more on Hitler than a study of many matters relating to domestic policy.[7]

Hitler is known for his charismatic qualities. In propaganda, he embodied what "racial" Germans—"the people"—liked to think and feel and also delivered a succession of momentous feats where others had failed. His dictatorship also relied on terror, but coercion, propaganda, and charisma together cannot explain fully why so many Germans fell in line with Hitler. Among Germans within the Reich, the popular acclaim for Hitler was a more important force for national conformity than the concentration camps, and Hitler guarded it jealously. Also propelling Hitler's strength were his abilities as a shrewd politician or company manager. His leadership was strategic, and he resorted to whatever tactic suited the moment. Consistent with his overarching goal, Hitler related to his "German-blooded" people, or the Volk, as partners in power, and he acted strategically so that the people would throw themselves at his service, and eventually at the service of all Nazi goals, even when this overturned long-cherished traditions or customs of the private sphere.

While his dictatorship murdered millions in the name of ideology, Hitler managed the relationship with the Germans of the Reich in ways that place him among those whom scholars now identify as "soft" dictators, who prefer the tactics of persuasion, enticement, cooptation, and compromise to work their will. These scholars associate "soft" tactics with dictatorships of the twenty-first century by contrasting them in one fell swoop with caricatures so gross they characterize both Hitler's and Stalin's regimes. Like Hitler, Stalin did have a "strategic mind" and was something of a "people person" who learned from Lenin to maintain core principles while exercising flexibility in tactics. Yet in ruling the Soviet Union, Stalin relied on force to a far greater extent than Hitler did to rule the Reich. In ruling his polyethnic territory, encompassing a vast swath of languages, religions, and traditions, Stalin carved a record of purges unthinkable to Hitler, who accepted disagreements among his subordinates as long as the leadership appeared to be united in public and everyone acknowledged Hitler's superior authority. The degree to which Stalin relied on terror against his own people, as illustrated by the terror he unleashed to force the collectivization of peasants, resulted in the death of millions. Hitler did embark on a project that could be viewed as social engineering on a revolutionary scale, but a project to force a change in traditions as radically as those changed by Stalin's collectivization was inconceivable inside Hitler's Germany, where his populist rule promised to restore the glory of a single culture.[8]

Against homosexuals, unproductive "useless eaters," or other social aliens, Hitler's dictatorship took the most extreme and brutal course. Otherwise, Hitler had different goals for his own "race" of "German-blooded" people. In the short run, Hitler cultivated them to fight a war for the continent, and in the long run he wanted to shift their attitudes and values so that they formed a tightly unified national community, or

Volksgemeinschaft. By embodying Nazi principles as their conscience, the people would establish new norms and customs that would naturally push out all persons who were either biologically inferior or out of step with the masses.[9]

Had he not been aiming to reshape the Germans into a Nazi national community, with a new Nazi superego, Hitler could have relied more fully on terror. But he was convinced that the existing German mythos could only be replaced by edging it out with another ideology the people found acceptable. In Nazi practice, as Hitler foresaw it, force could be deployed to secure the people's worldview once a majority was behind it, as he continued toward winning all but the fringe. Hitler believed that he excelled in shaping opinion, illustrated by his perceptions of having changed the minds of Marxists while he lived in Vienna.[10] However, he expected the Gauleiters, the party leaders of regions *(Gaus),* to win the people over to National Socialism in their own regions and generally allowed them to pursue his goals in the way they saw fit. Across the Reich, the Gauleiters were charged with knowing how and when to substitute new Nazi practices for established customs in their districts without pushing too many into dissent. With each Gauleiter competing for Hitler's favor, the different regions around the Reich became laboratories of fascism, workshops on how to persuade the people. Even when the definition of "racial purity" was in question, the Gauleiters had wide discretion in their regions, and they also made up the front line in the struggle to strip Christianity of its influence.[11]

Despite this tolerance in the choice of tactics, Hitler was uncompromising in his ideology and goals. The Jews were blamed for Germany's defeat during World War I, and the next war would be against them. On the "Jewish Question" the regime's decision-making processes, evolving under changing circumstances, became increasingly murderous and extensive. The radicalization within the SS is well established, and in conquered territories the Nazi army and its allies repressed opposition by wholesale, sometimes sadistic, destruction and murder.[12] But the regime scrupulously observed the local popular response to the deportation of German Jews and made small exceptions for certain categories of Jews who had German-blooded family members. The experience of intermarried Jews illustrates how compromise sometimes trumped coercion as a means of uniting constituents behind Hitler. In choosing tactics to win the people's trust, the Nazi dictator was promiscuously opportunistic, allowing room for improvisations as circumstances changed. Similar to a "soft dictator," he recognized that coercion could sometimes be more costly than compromise and might alienate his supporters.

Within Germany, Nazi compromise and terror were not pitted against each other in toe-to-toe opposition but deployed in mutual support to manage the people's thinking and values. Upon coming to power, the Nazi Party jailed, tortured, and intimidated the leaders of rival political parties, a brutality that was not just tolerated but also encouraged by millions and millions of Germans, due to widespread popular anticommunism. Many Germans saw the Nazi terror against Jews and leaders on the Left as rightly targeting the nation's troublemakers, and the dictatorship also sought and received popular acceptance in ostracizing those it identified as social outsiders. The head of the Security Police and the Security Service (SD), Reinhard Heydrich, preferred Germans to perceive the Gestapo as an agent of security feared by its enemies. In turn, the population helped the regime create and victimize "aliens" within the "community."[13]

The soft side of Hitler's dictatorship was often on display in his efforts to sway social attitudes that determined behavior rather than merely changing behavior. Hitler had foreshadowed this attitude already during the mid-1920s by his decision to pursue office through a "legal course" rather than a coup d'état. Hitler had sought power through elections for strategic as well as propaganda reasons, and after taking power, his party was careful to maintain his image of popular legitimacy, by preempting social unrest among the people. Already within a few months into his dictatorship, everything about the new Leader was so much in demand that the regime had to ban the commercial use of his name and image. But at home he often preferred cleverness over direct confrontation with an adversary, and he sometimes compromised to maintain his image and a corresponding amount of moral suasion, which he used to guide his people further into Nazi practices.[14] Such accommodations with the people took a variety of forms, depending on the context and the needs of the moment, ranging from his delaying a policy until the people were ready to accept it, to redirecting a course already taken in response to popular dissent, to simply not punishing those who publicly opposed a regime policy.

Cases of social dissent and mass noncompliance so bold that the regime could not ignore them were not so common. But by November 1943 they had occurred often enough to prompt Propaganda Minister Joseph Goebbels to fret that the people were already sure that they could use these methods to assert their will on the streets: "The people know exactly where to find the leadership's soft spot and will always exploit it." Goebbels questioned whether the regime should use coercion to enforce its regulations, in this case for the wartime evacuation of civilians from cities threatened by Allied bombing.[15] Hitler decided that force was not the appropriate means of quelling unrest over evacuations.

During the war, Hitler stopped the escalating use of coercive measures in the persecution of the churches as well, rather than allowing the use of force to radicalize, as it did in the persecution of the Jews, due to the competition for power among his subordinates. To preempt social unrest and protect his image as a heroic leader, Hitler was constrained to intervene against some of his top agents to prevent the escalation of the use of coercion to control Germans of the Reich. As the people's Leader, collectivized dissent posed not only a threat, but also an opportunity for Hitler. It could threaten the myth of his infallibility, but it also gave him an opportunity to intercede for the people, supporting the legend that all problems would be solved "if only the Führer knew."[16] He scrupulously avoided making martyrs of dissenters. His first line of defense was the people's eagerness to protect him in their own minds by blaming other party officials for anything they did not like. It was the Cult of the Führer that drew the people toward him, and he sometimes conceded to social dissent to sustain the people's faith. Hitler engaged in this back-and-forth dance of negotiation with the people only to draw the people along as quickly as he could in his plot to fulfill what he saw as his historic mission. Nazi compromises were cold, pragmatic calculations in search of the least costly way of reaching Nazi goals quickly.

It is difficult to overstate the appeal of a two-dimensional portrait of Nazi power based entirely on brute force applied ruthlessly against the will of all people. This simplified version of the Reich is illustrated all around—in video games and college "study guides," for example.[17] But repressing overt dissent was never the entire objective for the Nazi Party. The regime wanted the people to buy into new social practices by rehearsing them daily in its organizations such as Strength through Joy, the National Socialist People's Welfare (NSV), or the Winter Relief Fund (Winterhilfswerk; WHW) collection drives. "Stew Sundays," for example, introduced a once-per-month practice of just one dish for Sunday lunch, with the regime encouraging the savings for this simplicity to the national treasury. The value of these regular one-dish meals was not so much monetary as it was one of communal practice since donating funds was not an acceptable alternative. The Nazi League of German Girls did not teach so much by indoctrination as by "living practice," including the practice of promiscuous heterosexual intercourse. For men, there was military service, and the war brought demands for a new level of fanatical willingness to sacrifice, with the dead forming "the voice of our national conscience."[18]

Building on values like nationalism and anti-Semitism, National Socialism was the agent of "a transition for our German people," according to Hitler, "a mobilization of human forces of hitherto scarcely conceivable dimensions." Hitler saw himself as the agent, assigned by fate, of an enormously transformative power. Still, the Nazi transfiguration of German society required calculations by the Leader about how to change attitudes most quickly, using a range of tactics. If terror and other manipulations and incentives did not prevent social foment, Hitler's regime was constrained to limit public awareness of controversial Nazi policies. In general, sustained, widespread unrest or mass noncooperation indicated that the regime's policies had moved ahead of people's willingness to follow. As Reich Justice Minister Franz Gürtner warned at a meeting in June 1934, new laws and customs could be introduced only after the attitudes of ordinary Germans had already changed.[19]

The Nazi Party's struggle for power, and its consolidation of power after 1933, reveals a pattern of flexibility. Compromises and deal making also characterized Hitler's foreign policy and military strategy. He did not become a Communist, for example, by signing the Nazi-Soviet Non-Aggression Pact of August 23, 1939. In its foreign slave labor practices, the regime displayed a pattern of compromise alternating with periods during which policies were aligned more closely with ideology; when the German Army was advancing, Reich leaders brought policies more in line with Nazi ideology; when it faltered, the regime made compromises reflecting the increased pressures of the war economy, which forced millions of racially inferior Slavs, or *Ostarbeiter,* into hard labor. This flexibility is illustrated elsewhere within the Reich, notably in Hitler's reluctant compromise of Nazi ideals as he ordered women into the workforce in January 1943, following Germany's defeat at Stalingrad.[20]

These and other examples illustrate how Hitler shared power with the German elites of the military, industry, and government bureaucracy. Particularly in the increasingly brutal eugenics and genocide programs, these elites deciphered from Hitler's general statements what he wanted and forged policies to reach his goals. The people, on the other hand, were the raw material for the permanent national community Hitler envisioned. Hitler aimed to accomplish a "social revolution," an internal transition of individual and social attitudes, while recognizing that such "human conditioning" would take time.[21]

Much work was to be done to reshape the Germans into a self-perpetuating Nazi national community. But Hitler never bothered to square the otherworldly dimensions of his goals with his short and shifting time frame for achieving them, as his rapid successes reinforced his predilections to think that destiny had chosen him to establish permanent National Socialism.[22] Initially he figured that the "process of transformation" for uniting the people in a Nazi national community that they "understood and realized completely" could take "many generations." In August 1932 he was imagining a more shrunken time frame, saying that "only after a movement has been under way seventy or eighty years will it have developed the historic background and traditions that would enable it to carry on without a strong leader."[23] In February 1934, Hitler downsized his time frame yet again for accomplishing the same unrealistic goals, instructing his assembled Gauleiters that Nazi ideas must be put into effect "at once." Nevertheless, his conditions for translating ideology into policy remained etched in stone: "There must be no orders and plans beyond what could be put across to the people and actually carried into effect!" Six years later, following Germany's victory over France in June 1940, Hitler placed the French province of Alsace under Gauleiter Robert Wagner's authority, earnestly allotting him ten years to win the Alsatian people "to the ideas of National Socialism."[24]

CHRISTIANITY AND NAZI SUBSTITUTES

The challenge the Nazis faced was represented in the task of convincing the Germans to abandon their churches without alienating them. The churches, under the popular authority of bishops, were direct competitors with Nazism for the total allegiance that National Socialism required. Hitler aspired to co-opt all popular allegiances, but the churches commanded a loyal following, along with a creed requiring a lifestyle that in some ways challenged Hitler's ideology. They were also led by bishops, men with committed followings who represented authority in the style of "people leadership" (of *Menschenführung*), which the Nazi Party idealized: the ability to mobilize zeal and popular opinions. In June 1937 Hitler ruled that even his highest, most trusted lieutenants were forbidden to take measures against the clergy without receiving explicit permission from him. He complained that Nazi ideologist Alfred Rosenberg allowed himself to be provoked into a verbal battle with the Catholic Church even though "he had absolutely nothing to gain from it."[25]

Hitler calculated that to reach his goals and sustain the popularity of his movement, he could not take something as important as religion away from the people without offering them an acceptable replacement. Only "fools or criminals" would remove a people's religion before a substitute that was "visibly better" could be offered, he wrote in 1924. He repeated this sentiment in 1941 while contemplating the difficulty of displacing Christianity: "Nobody has the right to deprive simple people of their childish certainties until they've acquired others that are more reasonable."[26] In March of 1942, after a reversal of fortunes in the war, Hitler declared that if his own mother were still living, she would still attend church. Goebbels expressed the sense of what the Leader was saying as, "One must have respect for the naïve faith of older people, and not come at these people, entrenched in the Christian religion, with National Socialist propositions." If some older folks were too entrenched to change, Germany's youth would be Nazis fundamentally, Hitler thought.[27] At least until Germany had won the war, Hitler's lieutenants hoped to slip the rug of traditional practices out from under the people subtly, substituting a belief in Nazism reinforced by a sense of communal-national belonging.

Hitler's effort to found a national "Reich Church" was an early test of the Nazi effort to establish a National Socialist institution that would meet the popular needs previously serviced by the churches. Nevertheless, the sustained and mounting protests of Protestants in southern Germany convinced the Führer in October 1934 to set aside this ambition for the moment. Hitler had wanted to remain aloof from the problem of openly expressed protest by southern Protestants against merging their churches with the new Reich Church. But when it became clear that he was the only one who could resolve the matter, competing regional officials urgently called for his intervention. Several months earlier, Hitler had consolidated his support with stark brutality, during the lawless murder of the leadership of the Storm Troopers (the SA), known as the Night of the Long Knives. In that case, the wave of complaints against the unruliness of these SA men provided further evidence that the majority welcomed selective terror.[28] The great majority of the southern Protestants who refused to join the Reich Church in 1934 almost certainly approved of this murder purge as well, just as they almost certainly did not expect the regime to launch a purge against them in the same way.

In contrast with the brute force he used against the unpopular SA, Hitler met the southern Protestants with compromise, in order to achieve the same goal of consolidating his power without alienating a key constituency. Hitler wished to align the churches with his cause within a new Reich Church, but he did not think that he could do this by force alone. The Nazi Party must secure the future of Germany by uniting the people in a common struggle, but "this could not be done by some monarchy or other." Indeed, "every attempt at fighting a view of life by means of force will finally fail, unless the fight against it represents the form of an attack for the sake of a new spiritual direction," Hitler wrote in the mid 1920s. "Only in the struggle of two views of life with each other can the weapon of brute force, used continuously and ruthlessly, bring about the decision in favor of the side it supports."[29] In Nazi theory coercion could best be used to enforce the regime's will after a majority already appeared to be on the bandwagon. Generally, Hitler's preferred method for counteracting popular reluctance was not force but great feats that unified the people in deference.

Of course, the Nazi Party shared many values with existing German traditions, advancing and transforming old prejudices against Jews while promising the restoration of German values of family, gender roles, decency, and predictable state-provided order. In addition to nationalism, the hatred of Marxism and the Versailles Treaty also providing basic footholds for Nazism's growth, not to mention age-old incentives like material wealth. But Nazi leaders dreamed of changes on a scale comparable to those brought by Christianity itself, and Reichsführer SS and Chief of Police Heinrich Himmler agreed that it was necessary to use persuasion to change social lifestyles in ways that police work could hardly achieve. Himmler moved tactfully against the churches lest he alienate the people, even though he arguably saw destroying Christianity as the ultimate goal, more fundamental and challenging than annihilating Bolshevism and the Jews, for the success of Nazism.[30]

For a regime seeking some fundamental changes in German attitudes, popular reluctance and opposition were signals of how quickly it could advance and which methods were effective. Popular opposition showed the regime that its pressures had reached counterproductive levels for the moment or that better camouflage was necessary. To achieve spectacular feats, Hitler gambled recklessly to promote an image of himself as the near-superhuman Leader who deserved to be followed without any question. For example, he risked the remilitarization of the Rhineland in March 1936 even though his satraps and military advisers, who were not capable of such fantastic conceits as Hitler, urged him against it. The degree to which Hitler was willing to gamble to embody the great popular Leader he wanted to appear to be was ultimately suicidal and guaranteed that his Reich would never come to any point of lasting stability under his leadership.

EMBODYING NAZI LAW IN THE PEOPLE

A further illustration of the importance, in Nazi plans, of the people collectively was a new concept of the law. Hitler sought to redefine law by replacing established legal norms with what he viewed as the "healthy sentiments" of the people, which he saw as a raw, "primitive human instinct . . . just plain, sane herd instinct." The effect would be to drive "degenerates" away from the herd. A meeting on June 5, 1934, of high-level party officials, judges, and racial theorists considering reform of the criminal code took account of the importance of the people's sense of morality. Roland Freisler, the fanatical Nazi who later served as president of the notorious People's Court, opined that "the focused strength of the people" after "the state and the people had fused" would be comparable to the "concentrated firepower that could stop a tank attacking the front lines." Freisler's boss, Justice Minister Gürtner, concluded that new legal texts would not resolve the problem of mixed races until the people felt an "obligation to preserve [their] racial purity."[31]

Hitler envisioned shaping society like a social straightjacket of conformity, so that under party leadership it would automatically cast out elements that did not fall in line. In Hitler's fantasies, the people themselves would serve as a cornerstone of permanent National Socialism after he was gone. He saw the people (once they had been Nazified) as a bulwark against resistance, telling the Gauleiters in early 1934 that by the time his successor took power, Nazism must permeate Germans so thoroughly that anyone considering resistance would recognize that opposition was impossible.[32]

It would not be sufficient for Germans merely to passively accept the dictatorship's scorn for some existing norms. Instead they should take action themselves to defend Nazism by ostracizing enemies of the people, humiliating them in public. In 1938, following Hitler's great triumph of annexing Austria, the dictatorship launched a test case to see whether the Nazi movement was already strong enough—and the popular sentiment "healthy" enough—to ostracize a troublemaking Catholic bishop, Johannes Sproll of Rottenburg. The regime hoped to remove the bishop through a strong, continuous, and disciplined display of united popular opinion exhibited on the streets, in much the same way that southern Protestants had successfully opposed the Reich Church in 1934. Could the people be used to expel the bishop in this case, or would they rally to the side of their traditional institutions and in opposition to the Nazi initiative?

The demonstrations to ostracize Sproll were placed under the watchful eye of no less a figure than the head of the Security Police Reinhard Heydrich, although Gauleiter Wilhelm Murr, of the bishop's Stuttgart region, represented the regime's public face. By the time the government prosecutor for the Stuttgart region filed an indictment against Bishop Sproll for treason in early 1938, he had built up a record of the bishop's publicly opposing official programs that had violated church practices and ethics for a half-dozen years. The prosecutor admitted that the bishop was something of a hero for his recalcitrance, a challenge for a regime that often preferred to socially isolate a high-profile figure before sending in the police. In April 1938, the dictatorship seized an opportunity to paint Bishop Sproll as an outsider and an enemy of the people because he had declined to vote in the Nazi plebiscite on Germany's annexation of Austria, an extremely popular longtime goal for many on both sides of the border. Over the course of several months, thousands of demonstrators marched in front of the bishop's palatial residence in Rottenburg, accusing him of treachery and demanding an authentically German bishop in his place.

The dictatorship's plans were thrown off track when up to two hundred demonstrators turned violent, despite the admonition of Nazi officials. This level of disrespect began to stir counter street demonstrations on the bishop's behalf; the people were not yet united sufficiently to make a display of disciplined, collective opinion, as if speaking the official will with one voice, despite a Nazi terror system bristling in the background. With opinion openly divided, officials called for the demonstrations to end. But as the Reich Chancellery reported, only Hitler had the authority to order them to stop.[33] The ultimate arbiter of how to manage these public scenes was the Führer himself, since a decision required a judgment about whether the use of force would be counterproductive during any given phase in the Nazi movement toward a national people's community that embodied the new law with its practices. Hitler did stop the demonstrations, and weeks later, after arrangements had been made for Sproll there, the Gestapo took the bishop to the palatial quarters of the archbishop in Freiberg. A few months after these demonstrations failed to run the bishop out of his diocese, Heydrich noted that people were, however, acting as the regime's enforcers regarding its anti-Semitic laws. German Jews would not have to be concentrated in a ghetto, Heydrich said, because the "watchful eye of the whole population" kept them under control better than his uniformed agents could.[34] The Nazi interest in turning over "law" enforcement to the "healthy" people continued, although this aim would be subordinated to conquering the continent once Hitler launched war in September 1939.

MANAGING THE PEOPLE AS A CENTER OF POWER
DURING THE WAR

Hitler's image was the focal point of German consensus and had to be protected during war as well. In September 1938, when fear of imminent war caused hundreds of thousands of Germans to flee the French border, Hitler proved reluctant to put his prestige on the line by ordering regulations for the chaotic exodus of the people, despite the army elite's request. During September 1938, as Hitler threatened to invade Czechoslovakia, Germans feared that their ally, France, would attack. Wave after wave of Germans whose homes lay on the border with France flooded the roads as they streamed away from the path of an imagined invasion by the French army. This mass of German refugees hampered the Wehrmacht's ability to plan. Although the government had only informal ways of knowing where these Germans had settled, Hitler refused the requests of the most elite army leaders to issue orders regulating the civilian exodus. The following year the army general staff witnessed a similar massive disruption around the time of the Nazi attack on Poland. These massive movements of Germans were not demonstrations or political events, but the turbulence threatened Nazi propaganda in a similar way: masses were acting freely and without regard for their leaders. If hundreds of thousands of Germans were starting to move, Hitler should be leading them. In Nazi propaganda Germans were orderly and acted collectively under their Führer, while the French, on the other hand, were undisciplined. Nevertheless, in 1939 Hitler also refused urgent requests by his top army leaders to issue immediate orders that would regulate uncoordinated civilian movements that played havoc with military planning. When Hitler did order regulations—under cover of Germany's triumphal defeat of France the following year—many Germans ignored them, and, typical of such mass nonconformity, they were not punished.[35]

In these cases, the people's Leader weighed the needs of the people as if they comprised a power center against the demands of the army's top brass. Nazi leadership, especially Hitler himself, remained willing to compromise with the people in order to sustain his image as the hero and elicit full support for the war. During wartime, popular, open protests increased rather than diminishing; still Hitler and his satraps did not treat them more harshly than before the war. Even during the height of Nazi power, popular behavior persuaded Nazi leaders to accept some limits on their rule.[36]

Viewing the people as the primary foundation of his power, Hitler remained especially attentive to popular sentiments during war. He was a most fanatical Nazi, but Hitler sought to ingratiate himself with the people and was cautious about making demands on these constituents, especially during the war. Mobilizing for World War I, the autocratic German leadership recognized at once that a war of such dimensions could be fought only with the consent of the people; German local and civic institutions self-mobilized for the war. Hitler also saw the home front as the core of military strength on the war front, just as women comprised what he called the "small world" that formed the stabilizing core of the "big world" of men in war and politics.[37] Hitler blamed "defeatist" letters from women at home for poisoning the front line of soldiers. Like many Germans he was convinced that Germany lost World War I not because of the military but due to the treachery of Jewish Marxism, which had crippled the will of Germans on the home front to continue the fight, according to this myth. Avenging Germany's losses in World War I required killing those to blame—the Jews.[38]

This false memory of a "Stab in the Back" helps explain why the Führer continued to assert, into the very last months of the war, that Germany could still win as long as it remained unified. The simplistic belief that the unity and dedication of the German people were the decisive factors in war implied that even the declaration of war by the United States in 1917 had made no difference for the war's outcome because victory in war was purely a matter of national will. But the dictatorship did not think it could sustain morale and prevent a repeat of such a Stab in the Back through intimidation and force alone.[39]

There is some evidence, in fact, that Hitler and his circle were more reluctant to pressure segments of the population with terror if they were not delivering the victories of war Hitler had led Germans to expect, just as their willingness to compromise Nazi racial ideology by expanding the use of foreign labor within the Reich increased during military setbacks. During the summer of 1940, following the German victory over France, Goebbels confided to the Gauleiters that such spectacular triumphs afforded them more latitude for taking forceful action to govern the people. The churches, he complained, were using the funerals of soldiers who had died for Germany as propaganda for their own profit. For reasons of security, he wrote, party authorities had not yet stopped this opportunism, but following the victory in France these considerations no longer adhered, and Gauleiters were now free to clamp down.[40] It was easier to use force against a mere fringe of dissent, especially during periods of great consensus, and war victories allowed the dictatorship to bring the people closer together under its rule.

Hitler's leadership illustrates this relationship between fortunes at war and repression at home. During the war's first days, Hitler ordered the cessation of measures that might alienate either the Protestant or the Catholic Churches. Within weeks, as Germany quickly won its battles, Heydrich and Martin Bormann, head of the Nazi Party Chancellery, persuaded Hitler to resume attacks on the churches. Already in January 1940, however, Hitler reiterated that attacks on the churches would cause domestic strife and would be counterproductive until victory was certain. In early September 1940, the Führer evoked the mystique of a united people: "What makes the German soldier strong at the front is the awareness and knowledge that behind him stands an entire people united in iron determination and a fanatical will!" By September 1941, as it became clear that Nazi officials had underestimated the time it would take the Wehrmacht to reach Moscow, Heydrich on behalf of Hitler banned state actions that weakened institutions from which the people drew strength.[41]

Popular morale even formed the backdrop for the Führer's critical military decisions. As the Wehrmacht was poised to take Moscow in December 1941, Field Marshal and Army Commander in Chief Walther von Brauchitsch wanted to rest Wehrmacht troops with a tactical retreat by Army Group Center, but Hitler refused because he thought that such a retreat would undermine home front investment in the war. Goebbels claimed that the Wehrmacht would have taken Moscow if it had only had just 10 percent more troops, but Hitler replied that he had opposed adding troops because he had not "wished to inflict the burden of total war on the German people."[42] Up until the devastating defeat of Germany at Stalingrad forced his hand, in fact, Hitler's fear of alienating the people caused him to put off declaring "total war" and to shy away from ordering the enforcement of his "total war" decrees thereafter. This backing off stands in brilliant contrast to his frequent disregard for the army elites.[43]

The regime's anxiety about popular opinion continued as it conducted the murders demanded by its ideology. It used euphemisms and other deceptions to keep them secret, moving through a succession of phases until the people fully accepted such murders. In December 1940, the chief of Nazi terror, Heinrich Himmler, also bent to public pressure by closing a "euthanasia" killing center in the town of Grafeneck because, as he wrote explicitly, it had caused an aggrieved mood. The deportation of 7,500 Jews from Baden to the French camp at Gurs in October 1940 was a trial run to gauge the German people's reaction, and it is likely that popular opinion was also carefully monitored to the massacres of Jews in the Soviet Union by the Einsatzgruppen mobile killing units during the latter half of 1941, as a further test of popular response.[44]

In August 1941, the regime chose to accommodate the objections of the people rather than execute Catholic bishop Clemens August Graf von Galen for treason, because he condemned euthanasia, and Hitler again relented when the people refused to go along with a decree stripping religious symbols from Bavarian schools. At the same time, Hitler ordered Bormann to stop the confiscation of church property unless he had first obtained Hitler's permission. The reason for these compromises was the dictatorship's continuous concern about unrest in its most disturbing form: public, popular protest.

But the regime went beyond avoiding unrest by making compromises. It also harnessed the power of those powerful enough to erode its popular strength. Within weeks of Galen's treasonous condemnation of euthanasia, the Catholic bishops backed his call for Catholic men to throw themselves into Germany's war in the East, a cause he likened to Christian martyrdom, with equal rewards for eternity. The prominent Gauleiter Alfred Meyer wanted to execute the bishop and recommended this measure during an opportune moment when popular acclaim for a resounding Nazi war victory would muffle the outcry. But Hitler vetoed the clamor for an execution, preferring to partner for the moment with such a powerful voice of the people. In March 1942, instead of following the will of other government agencies to exact punishment, Hitler issued a "mercy pardon" to Brandenburg state judge Lothar Kreyssig, who also had a popular following and had also denounced the "euthanasia" killings of innocent Germans. With such a frightening terror complex behind him, the Führer could earn gratitude and appear magnanimous with the compromise of pardons.[45]

Hitler's willingness to compromise with the people, particularly when the people were drawing upon their traditions, continued up until some point very late in the war when he became convinced that Germany would be forced to surrender unconditionally. Naturally the people could not organize a meeting, decide what they wanted, and present it to the dictator in a street demonstration. But the regime did look on, for example, when the great majority of women sidestepped Hitler's total war decree of January 13, 1943, conscripting them into the labor force. Observing the strikes by Italian workers in March 1943, Hitler opined that bloody repression was not a solution because that would have "political consequences that could hardly be overlooked." During 1943 as well, Hitler preferred to appease rather than repress two spectacular street protests by women, even as the People's Court increased sentences for treason. By mid-1943, complaints and jokes about the regime leaders were so prevalent that prosecutors thought that singling one person out for punishment on such an offense was untenable, and the SD was concerned about an inner collapse on the home front. Even on its commitment to murder the Jews, the defining aspect of its ideology and an increasing focus of its mission as the war drew to a close, the regime compromised the number of Germans it persecuted and murdered as Jews. To focus its forces and avoid unrest within the Reich, the regime made a series of widening exemptions for German Jews with non-Jewish family members, beginning with the 1935 Nuremberg Laws.[46]

The Wehrmacht executed a frightening number of soldiers—some twenty thousand in total—for insubordination during the war, and death sentences issued by the judiciary did push somewhat higher in 1943 than in 1942, as the number of sentences for treason rose.[47] In contrast, at least through October 1944, Hitler prohibited even the soft forms of coercion that the Gauleiters wished to use to force masses of civilians to comply with plans for evacuating cities targeted by Allied air forces. Contrary to the increased use of force within the Reich elsewhere, Hitler judged "education" and not brute force to be the appropriate means in this case. "The frailest woman will become a heroine when the life of her own child is at stake," warned Hitler, whose goal was to unify Germans in the war rather than opening up another front at home.[48] It was this power of will that Hitler worked to summon all across Germany. Beyond the circle of competing elites that his dictatorship unleashed, Hitler remained dedicated to unleashing German energies in a hero's Volksgemeinschaft—a community that would form the strongest nation on earth.

It was very difficult to tell whether Hitler was merely pretending to believe the war could still be won, constrained as he was to convince the Germans to fight on, avoiding another Stab in the Back. Hitler's confidant and armaments minister Albert Speer wrote in March 1945 that Hitler was certain that "all thoughts that a struggle, behind which stands the entire fanaticism of a nation, could end in anything other than victory" must be repelled. As the German Leader, in January 1945, he solicited the people's support: "I would like to thank the countless millions of my racial [Volk] comrades. . . . I would like to ask them not to let up in the future either, to trust the leadership of the movement, and to fight this most difficult struggle for the future of our people with the greatest fanaticism." Even on February 24, 1945, Hitler took refuge in the fact that the home front had not revolted during the war.[49]

We do not know about all of the social dissent that was significant enough to draw the attention of regime leaders and prompt them to compromise, not only because many records did not survive the war, but also because the regime repressed evidence of dissent by crowds of ordinary Germans, lacing its records with deceptions. For example, in April 1943, when an unruly crowd of three to four hundred Dortmund civilians threatened a government representative, officials moved beyond repressing evidence to generating press releases and speeches that denied that this dissent had ever happened so that rumors of it could be plausibly denied.[50] Thus the evidence of popular mobilization in opposition to some aspects of the Third Reich is more restricted than the amount of protest itself because the regime was determined to control its image.

Taken separately, each instance of regime compromise might be explained as an exception that it made for specific sectors of Germans: workers, the churches, women. Taken together, the various cases of the dictatorship's willingness to compromise in ruling the people illuminate a pattern of response to social dissent, regardless of which group was dissenting. The regime's willingness to make concessions to the working class in order to assuage its dissatisfactions is well documented.[51] But it also preempted or ameliorated signs of sustained opposition in public by other social groups as well, an approach that is hardly surprising considering its earnest manipulation of demonstrations and rallies in an effort to influence opinion and "nationalize the people."[52]

Hitler was a villain second to none because he was able to use a range of tactics strategically to gain power in pursuit of breathtakingly atrocious goals. Behind the dictatorship's willingness to compromise was Hitler's intention not just to launch a political party, but also to be the unquestioned leader of a mass movement. He worked from the premise that he could not be the leader until the people recognized him as their Leader. Thus he had to accept that his power was constrained by how fast he could convince the German people to abandon familiar customs of the "private sphere." Hitler led the people in measured steps toward the goal of constructing a national community that would form a foundation for permanent National Socialism. As improbable as this goal was in the light of history, it led Hitler to take risks that initially attracted millions to him before its conclusion in catastrophe.[53]

Why did so many wait so long to see that catastrophe was in the making? Why did they choose to blame others for whatever went wrong, thereby protecting their image of Hitler as a brilliant and benevolent leader? Important clues lie at the beginning of the story, as Hitler schemed his way to power, using the "legal way," in the wake of the fragmented world of Germany after World War I.

CHAPTER ONE

The Strategy of Hitler's "Legal Course" to Power

LIMITING FORCE TO MAXIMIZE ITS EFFECT

> By acting constitutionally, on the other hand, I was in a position to restrict the activities of the Wehrmacht to its legal and strictly limited military function—at least until such a time as I was able to introduce conscription. Once that was accomplished, the influx into the Wehrmacht of the masses of the people, together with the spirit of National Socialism and with the ever-growing power of the National Socialist movement, would, I was sure, allow me to overcome all opposition among the armed forces, and in particular in the corps of officers.
>
> —*Adolf Hitler, May 21, 1942*

HITLER USED FORCE and terror to his maximal advantage. But to take power, he sometimes led with other tactics, committing the party to the use of any means that accomplished his aims. Although his decision to take the "legal course" to power made useful propaganda, Hitler also chose it because it enabled him to win massive popular support and to circumvent retaliation from the German Army. His choice of the legal course to attain power in 1933 foreshadows some of the approaches to his leadership as a dictator. He learned, for example, that he could prevent the SA's clamor for a second putsch before 1933 by relying on his ability to command loyalty without using the force of weapons.

Looking beyond his goal of taking power, Hitler aimed to form a permanent basis for a thousand-year Reich based on a productive, "racially pure" people who believed in the same Nazi myths. He did not think that even the most powerful leader—or even a set of political and religious leaders—could form as firm a foundation for permanent Nazism as a society totally committed to a Nazi way of life. Thus he aimed to persuade the people to embrace National Socialism rather than merely aiming to manipulate their outward behavior. He relished popular acclaim but sought it so that he could convince the people to serve Nazi purposes, even when the purposes clashed with some basic Christian values and the notions of "equality" and "liberty" from the Enlightenment and French Revolution. Facing this staggering challenge, Hitler claimed that the Nazi mythos was founded in the laws of nature rather than in the human imagination and that he was the agent of fate. He claimed to be unveiling the universal truths of biology while also launching a party to take political action. In power, the Nazi Party took firm control over state education and the media, while also seeking to channel the behavior of individuals and groups through the pressures of social mass conformity to Nazi practices.

Hitler's attempt to take power by a coup d'état in November 1923 was an impatient approach that he would later adamantly reject. His putsch in the Munich Bürgerbräukeller beer hall was a notorious failure that persuaded him to seek power as the legitimate heir of popular acclaim. In the arena of opinion, he had the advantage of sharing the perception across the Reich that the Versailles Treaty was treacherous and that the Weimar democracy had produced one bad experience after another. The SA, or Brownshirts as they were also called, reportedly pressured Hitler into mounting this improbable coup. Perhaps Hitler acquiesced to the SA lest he lose its support. But he would never again agree to SA demands for a putsch—although he did continue to make compromises for the sake of party unity.[1]

Had it not been for the SA's insistent desire to take power by a coup, Hitler may not have needed to establish the "legal course" as party policy. Writing in 1924, Hitler claimed to have been wary of a coup attempt, as if to blame the SA for his failure the year before. "We realized as early as 1919," he wrote, "that the nationalization of the masses would have to constitute the first and paramount aim of the new movement." Trying to accomplish such a nationalization with a coup, however, was a serious error. If it failed, the masses would see the defeat as a sign of an "uncertain" or "unjust" cause.[2] Hitler had surely noticed recent events in Germany that illustrated this observation, including General Wolfgang Kapp's attempted coup in March 1920. Seeking a military dictatorship, Kapp's army forces marched into Berlin, surrounded government buildings, and proclaimed the end of the republic. General Kapp had insufficient plans, although he did command loyal and skilled troops. He also had a considerable supply of artillery, machine guns, and planes. But Kapp failed because the Socialist-led Weimar government called a nationwide general strike that brought the economy to an abrupt standstill. Public trains ground to a halt, there was no gas for private cars, and there was no electricity to conduct business. An eerie silence settled over the empty streets of the city of four million. Within days Kapp fled for his life because it was clear that he had caused this shutdown and that he could do nothing to stop it because his authority was not recognized. The army was stunned, realizing that it would not be able to establish a military dictatorship. Army Commander in Chief Hans von Seeckt, in a potential lesson for Hitler, then proceeded to use legal means, under the cover of the constitution, to cleanse the army of Social Democratic influences, despite the opposition of the Socialist-led government itself. Contrary to Kapp's intentions, his rebellion provided a "decisive" boost to the army's enemies on the German Left. Within a year, however, the German Communists had also squandered this popularity in feckless attempts to assume control by armed attacks: the March 1921 attack of the German Communist Party (KPD) on police in Hall-Mansfeld alone cost the party two-thirds of its members, so the chastened party had turned to a "patient day-to-day" effort to win support. Yet the effect of collective action was signaled again in early 1923, when the Germans rebuffed the French and Belgian occupation of Germany's Ruhr area to commandeer German raw materials as war reparations. The Weimar government called for resistance, however, and the refusal of German people to produce and load German coal for the occupiers deprived the occupation of its goals, a victory celebrated by the Nazis.[3]

The results of the Nazis' armed insurrection at the beer hall were similarly dismal, especially when compared with the striking advances Hitler made through the press during his trial for treason in the weeks following the putsch. Radio and newspaper accounts splashed Hitler's testimony condemning the Versailles Treaty and the "November criminals" across the country, pulling him and his party out of their provincial obscurity. Months later, while in prison writing a major portion of *Mein Kampf,* Hitler calculated that Germany's existing democratic system provided the best available structure for achieving the first stage of a permanent Nazi movement. Formulating the so-called "legal course policy," he wrote that the party's "struggle will be fought out with legal means as long as the power which is to be overthrown uses such means." On January 4, 1925, shortly after his release from prison, Hitler told Bavarian minister president Heinrich Held that he would operate only within the bounds established by the Weimar Constitution from that point forward. He charted this course, which followed the letter if not the spirit of the constitution, in opposition to some party members who thought they would have to seize power by force in a putsch, especially if they were to carry out their radical aims.[4]

This course was an early sign that Hitler was a deft opportunist. Although he hated the democratic system passionately, and said so publicly, he determined that its arrangement of competing political parties would provide a framework for accomplishing the first stage of his vision. He would accrue the beginning stages of popular acclaim by emphasizing standards shared by his party and German society and follow the legal course to a constitutionally defined position of power. To be sure, this effort was to be nothing but a brief station on the way to a society that preferred Hitler's leadership above any constitution since, as Hitler anticipated, the uniform practices of an expanding popular movement would increasingly embody the new Nazi law.

NAZI TACTICS AND WEIMAR DEMOCRACY

While the Storm Troopers could hardly imagine doing away with the hated system without a bloody struggle, Hitler could have hardly advanced without the Weimar system to measure and bestow legitimacy on his party as it succeeded against the many others. This system required popular support, a road that Hitler was determined to take in any case; the constitutional system he despised provided all political parties with equal opportunities and entrusted power to them in proportion with their popular backing.[5] While he ridiculed the logic of parliament, Weimar's frequent elections provided detailed information about the demographics of his party's supporters and detractors, helping it to formulate its strategies for winning. As of 1929, by documenting the meteoric rise of Hitler's National Socialist German Workers' Party (NSDAP), poll results backed Nazi claims of their party's inevitable victory, lending the party critical momentum and adding force behind its propaganda slogan that victory was inevitable. As the Great Depression deepened, men of the SA, often culled from the great recesses of Germany's unemployed, were put to work in the menial labor of advancing the party in one election after another, as Nazi leaders asserted that the Germans should turn away from the failed parties to the Nazis.

To be sure, the radical changes in German politics and society caused by and following World War I set the stage for Hitler. Still, the Nazis exploited these critical circumstances deftly, calling on the police, for example, to protect liberties they found useful for their advancement at the moment but would later eradicate. Hitler's "legal" policy lent him firm footing for repressing the SA drive for a coup during the early 1930s, but the strength of Weimar itself helped him carry out his important decision to restrain the SA from another putsch after 1923. Another constitutional provision that played into the hands of the Nazi leadership was Weimar's exemption of party delegates serving in the Reichstag (parliament) from serving prison sentences. A further consequence of the "legal course" for Nazism was the tutelage it gave Hitler in exercising power through the force of the free exercise of speech, in person or through the media. Throughout the following decade he would continue to test and increase his ability to inspire loyalty, as a basis for the real power he sought rather than one merely based in force.

The mobilization of people and opinion through mass rallies was central to Hitler's "legal course," and under the Weimar Constitution demonstrations would finally be made legal throughout Germany. Before Weimar, Germany's Socialists primarily, but also German Catholics, had fought a decades-long battle to win legal protection for collective public action. Before the advent of television, German streets were an accessible venue for informing public opinion. Mobilizing crowds on the street was a near-fetish for the Nazi Party's primary enemy and fellow revolutionary party, the KPD. Rosa Luxemburg, one of Germany's most prominent Communist leaders during the first two decades of the twentieth century, celebrated the streets as the "essential space of political engagement." Hitler declared in 1926 that "We have to teach Marxism that the future master of the streets is National Socialism, just as . . . one day it will be the master of the state."[6]

The Nazis were as certain about their ideology as the German Communists were about theirs, but under Hitler's guidance they continued to use a range of tactics. During the 1920s the Nazis quickly mastered the new medium of radio, capable of influencing public opinion more readily than newsprint.[7] Writers such as Alfred Döblin and Stefan Zweig warned that the new mass media lent the pressures of mass conformity a ubiquitous and overwhelming presence, which in turn dictated norms for society that could stunt the growth of "the individual."[8] But the Nazi Party greeted these possibilities, seeing the chance to centralize its power, and it set to work to create a mass society that eagerly erased individuality.[9]

HITLER PUTS THE STORM TROOPERS ON
THE "LEGAL COURSE" LEASH

In prison for attempting a putsch with the SA, Hitler wrote a chapter on the "meaning and the organization" of that paramilitary Nazi organization. The old state—with its three pillars of monarchy, civil service, and the army—had disappeared, Hitler announced, before identifying the foundations that he sought for his power:

> The first foundation for forming authority is always offered by popularity. However, an authority that is based solely on this foundation is still extremely weak, unstable, and vacillating. Any supporter of such an authority, resting purely on popularity, must therefore endeavor to improve and to safeguard this authority by creating power. In power, therefore—that means in force—we see the second foundation of all authority. This is far more stable, more secure, but not always more vigorous than the first one. If popularity and force unite, and if thus combined they are able to last over a certain period of time, then an authority on an even more solid basis can arise, the authority of tradition. If finally popularity, force, and tradition combine, an authority may be looked upon as unshakable.[10]

Released from prison in late December 1924, Hitler focused on refounding the party by clearing the "fifty percent hurdle" of popular support—gaining "decisive majorities in the legislative bodies." Winning elections would create "the premise" for governing. Rather than building the SA for another coup, Hitler established a system of trustworthy NSDAP representatives throughout Germany and began to orchestrate his own public image more carefully in conjunction with propaganda that portrayed him as a super politician, always doing his utmost for the Germans. This "Hitler Myth" succeeded as more and more Germans responded positively to Hitler's claims to be the German leader, as he in turn became increasingly convinced that he was the nation's savior.[11]

Indicating the new subordinate position of the Storm Troopers, Hitler waited nearly two years after his release from prison to issue his so-called "First Order" to the SA. It was directed to SA leader Franz Pfeffer von Salomon on November 26, 1926, and charged the SA with winning over Germans to the Nazi movement, one by one. Far from planning a coup d'état, the SA now was ordered to avoid all appearances of conspiracy. Instructed to bring German views in line with National Socialist values, the SA was redefined as a support for other, more prominent party organizations. Otto Ohlendorf, the handsome young Einsatzgruppen leader who was hanged for mass murder in June 1951, recalled while on trial that in the mid-1920s he had persuaded local community people to join National Socialism by distributing papers and posters, participating in debates, and going house to house.[12]

Of course the SA would remain the party's strong-arm squad as well, although Hitler preferred that it learn tactics of wit rather than those of brute frontal assault. Hitler contrasted the new SA mandate to change attitudes at the grass roots with the methods of "dagger and poison or pistol":

> What we needed then and need now is not one or two hundred dare-devil conspirators but a hundred thousand devoted champions of our worldview. The work must not be done through secret conventicles, but through formidable mass demonstrations in public. Dagger and pistol or poison cannot clear the way for the progress of the movement. That can be done only by winning over the man in the street.[13]

While he remained clear that the SA must respond with violence against violent attacks, Hitler would reiterate the basic SA mandate of

November 1926 in various forms and directives. The SA continued to terrorize with violence, to be sure, and Hitler supported SA violence against Jews and the political Left.[14] But on the most critical issue— obedience to police bans on the SA and the suppression of SA desires to mount a coup—Hitler made sure that the SA painstakingly followed his "legal course."

GOEBBELS SHOWS THE SA HOW TO USE THE LEGAL COURSE

The Nazi exploitation of the Weimar legalities it intended to destroy was demonstrated early on by Joseph Goebbels in his role as the Nazi Party leader, or Gauleiter, of the German capital. Hitler entrusted him with this position in October 1926. The "little doctor" (Goebbels had earned a doctorate under the supervision of a Jewish professor) called Berlin "the reddest city in Europe after Moscow." His Berlin Nazi Party consisted of several hundred members, mostly SA men, in a city of some four million. Together Germany's two Marxist parties, the Social Democratic Party of Germany (SPD) and the KPD, received well over 50 percent of the Berlin vote in the May 1928 election, compared with 1.5 percent for the Nazis.[15]

Undaunted, Goebbels began an uphill struggle against the Left and the Jews. When the city media derided a speech Hitler gave on May 1, 1927, Goebbels trained his fire on what he called the "Jewish" press, denouncing the Jews several days later before a public assembly of two to three thousand in Berlin's Kriegervereinhaus. When a man, who by one account was a drunken Lutheran minister, contradicted Goebbels, the crowd took Goebbels's side. However, the following day, the Berlin police responded to SA violence by banning Nazi assemblies, parades, and demonstrations. The SA wanted to disregard the ban, but Goebbels thought this would be counterproductive, and he directed the SA away from armed confrontations with the forces of the state for strategic reasons.[16] The point for the short, twenty-nine-year-old propagandist who nursed a club foot was to win over the people since "whoever conquers the masses conquers the state along with them."[17]

With few resources and as the regional leader of a tiny party on the fringe, Goebbels taught the SA to use tactics of disruption. At the premiere of the antiwar film *All Quiet on the Western Front,* based on Erich Remarque's work and playing at the Mozartsaal Cinema, his SA men

began shouting, "Jews out!" Pandemonium broke out as the Brownshirts threw stink bombs and then released a swarm of white mice. The
police ordered the theater cleared, but the miscreants got away. Goebbels
followed through during the following four evenings by orchestrating
street demonstrations against the film. With more and more people gathering, the police blocked off sections of traffic near the theater in city
center Berlin, showing that the government and its police were straining
to maintain order.[18]

Goebbels calculated that he could challenge even the mighty capital's police vice president, Bernhard Weiss, who was a Jew, by denouncing him in public, using freedoms of the democratic system and rallying
German anti-Semitism in his cause. A member of Germany's Democratic Party, Weiss was a lawyer who had become a judge, then had
earned the highest medal for valor in the trenches of World War I. Following the war he rose quickly to the top within the Berlin police, quickly
capping a string of impressive successes. Goebbels attacked with a claim
that Weiss was not German at all but a Jew who cared only about protecting fellow Jews; one had to correspond in Yiddish with police headquarters in Berlin, Goebbels wrote, since that was the only language
understood there.[19]

Goebbels attacked Weiss on the assumption that he could pit mass
opinion against police force. He wrote that as a police chief, Weiss "has
the power to do what one wants, that is, if others let one get away with it!"
Goebbels set out to stigmatize Weiss, illustrating tactics of bullying with
the crowd. Through *Der Angriff,* a party newspaper Goebbels founded
in 1927 and by the orchestrations of local Storm Troopers on the streets,
Goebbels taught much of the Berlin public to know Weiss as "Isidor," a
name associated with Eastern Orthodox Judaism. When party members
met in public, they would break into a loud chorus of "Isidor, Isidor"
until a tumultuous crowd had formed, in an early foreshadowing of the
Nazi effort to endow "healthy" popular opinion with the force of law.[20]

Weiss sued *Der Angriff* and its editor in court more than two dozen
times, and Goebbels responded by mobilizing opinion. When *Der Angriff*
carried a cartoon of Weiss's face as the head of a donkey, Weiss sued
Goebbels for libel. Goebbels retorted that this was just a cartoon, while
insisting that Weiss's recognition of his face on the donkey suggested
that he held a poor opinion of his own appearance. Further sophomoric

jokes ensued when the judge ruled that it was obvious that the donkey had the face of Weiss. The court decided for Weiss, but the Weimar Republic exempted Goebbels from going to jail because he was a political party representative in the Reichstag.[21]

A chance for the Nazis to win favor for their legal course came in April 1929. Because he feared a bloody struggle among parties, Berlin's chief of police forbade all demonstrations on May 1, the traditional "International Workers' Day." The Nazis obeyed the police and stayed off the streets, as did the SPD. But the SPD's fellow workers' party, the KPD, was less tactful. Entrenched in dogmatic enmity with the police and leading with its paramilitary force, the Red Front, the KPD turned out for battle with the German police on May 1. The clash continued for two days and reached frightening proportions. In Berlin's working-class districts of Wedding and Neukölln at least 33 Communist demonstrators were killed, and 1,200 arrested. The Nazi press made great fun of Bernhard Weiss when, a few months later, he waded into a Berlin street struggle between police and Communists, trying to bring a resolution, and was soundly beaten by a young police officer.[22]

Had economic and political stability prevailed in Germany, the Nazi Party might well have staggered along between obscurity and marginality, unable to harm Weiss. As it was, Hitler's legal means were too often taken as an indication that his leadership would remain within customary bounds, especially considering the threat of the KPD, the other revolutionary party. The violence of the KPD became so pronounced by the early 1930s that some saw Nazi violence as less threatening, turned as it was against communism.[23] These violent KPD attacks on government institutions made it easier for Germans to believe that a revolutionary Communist plot was behind the destruction of the Reichstag building when a fire was set there four years later.

THE "LEGAL COURSE" IS MISTAKEN FOR A SIGN
OF MODERATE GOALS

Soon after the KPD's May Day battle with police in 1929, Goebbels sent out SA units to persuade men of the Red Front to switch loyalties and join the NSDAP. But some SA men, like the young Nazi rabble rouser and propagandist Horst Wessel, saw this recruitment effort as a pathetically passive role. Born in 1907, Wessel was an effective speaker who won some Communists over to the Nazis and quickly became the head of an SA squad in Berlin-Friedrichshahn. His poem "Die Fahne Hoch" was put to music, gained popularity around Berlin and then within the party generally, and ultimately became the Nazi Party anthem. But Wessel infuriated the Nazi rivals when his SA unit seriously injured four Communists in a pub brawl. Goebbels admired Wessel as a dynamic and idealistic youth but warned that if the Nazis "smashed up everything," the police would "happily ban us," adding that "we must first gather power."[24]

Hitler was showing that he could exercise power without resorting to force. During the early 1930s, SA agitation for revolutionary action challenged his capacity to hold the party together, putting his "legal course" and his ability to control the SA to a test. Some proceeded to court powerful support: already in 1930, for example, SA leaders including Franz Salomon discussed procuring support, or neutrality, from German Army officers, in case of a Nazi revolt.[25] Although the SA itself was the repository of Nazi armed force, Hitler was always able to dominate the SA leaders and their cadres by means of his personal authority.

Hitler also promised that he too would use instrumental force once in power, although he planned to do it with the backing of the people. When police broke up a demonstration by the Nazi Student Association, Hitler declared that the Nazi Party would one day "wield the rubber truncheon with exactly the same legitimacy as others do today." But as some in the SA continued to insist on overthrowing the state, Hitler's ability to enforce the "legal course" began to contribute to his image within the status quo as an acceptable German leader. It also pushed SA men into working for Nazi campaigns, within the very legal system they hated, by distributing pamphlets and posters or picture postcards and special newspaper editions.[26]

In the late summer and autumn of 1930, Hitler's authority as the party Leader was again challenged by a considerable segment of Storm Troopers. Prominent Nazi leader Otto Strasser accused Hitler of betraying the party's cause and was forced out, taking a number of others with him and aligning with another prominent Nazi rebel, prominent SA iconoclast Walter Stennes, who was a regional Storm Troopers leader in eastern Germany. Stennes had become a focal point for the many SA men ready for armed insurrection. Shortly before the September 1930 election, he declared that his men would refuse all further campaign work until the party met their demands. In a further assertion of independence, Stennes became a spokesman for SA men clamoring for better pay, and he openly accused party leaders of treating the SA poorly. Some SA quarters began to make an "avowal of violence" in direct opposition to Hitler's "legal course." Radicalized by the bitterness of unemployment and eager to throw themselves against the republic they blamed, much of the rank-and-file SA wished for a putsch. Contrasting his militancy with Hitler's "legal course," Stennes drew SA men to his group from outside his own region to build a "Stennes faction." Hitler's policy was to avoid conflict with the churches and entrepreneurs until the party had built up sufficient support to enforce its demands, but Stennes promoted anti-Catholic as well as anti-capitalist rhetoric.[27]

In August 1930, Stennes took his rebellion to Berlin, where he and about one-third of Goebbels's SA men in Berlin occupied party offices. Under rising pressure, Hitler was obliged to apply all his powers of persuasion in the service of his authority, unsupported by instrumental force. He made appearances in taverns to assure assemblies of SA men that he had their welfare in mind and followed up by ordering party dues raised by twenty cents for the benefit of the SA. Notably, and characteristic of his ability to draw support, those present swore an oath of loyalty to Hitler after hearing him speak.[28] He held the paramilitary SA in line, as it strained to break loose, with the force of his authority, the same way he planned to control the masses after he came to power.

In the Reichstag elections of September 14, 1930, Hitler's party scored heavy victories around the nation. The Nazi Party had suddenly become the second largest party, trailing only the SPD, a startling advance that garnered 18 percent of the popular vote. With the Great Depression permeating Germany with a sense that radical action was urgently needed, all other parties except the Communists saw their share of the national vote decline. But the big news story was the meteoric rise of Nazi popularity, and, again, the reputable democratic process signaled this impressive Nazi momentum in gaining popular backing like nothing else could.[29]

A key moment for the success of the "legal course" came that same month, as Hitler maintained before the Leipzig Federal Court on September 25, 1930, that he would take power only through legal means.

He appeared as the star witness for three army officers accused of subversive actions because they had proselytized on behalf of the Nazi Party. Under oath, with media coverage streaming around Germany, his testimony impressed on skeptical leaders of government that Hitler was actually interested in preserving important legal structures. To take power, he boasted to the court, "our movement has no need of force."[30] He rebutted accusations that he was not adhering to the "legal course," saying that he was more interested in seeing the German people "imbibe a new spirit" than in replacing the army with the SA. Hitler went on to promise—to thunderous applause—that "heads would roll" once he was in power. The "November Criminals"—those who had surrendered to the Allies in 1918—would finally have to pay. Questioned by the judge, Hitler provided a glimpse into his future concern about the appearance of legality. He would use the regular legislative process to create a national court that would condemn the criminals, Hitler told the judge, and thus executions would be accomplished legally. Hitler had once again exploited the legal process to commandeer national attention, magnified by the news media, as Goebbels enthused about the "magnificent echo" from Hitler's court testimony in the press.[31]

The court found no evidence that the party was planning a putsch, and important power brokers thought that Hitler's declarations on the "legal course" signaled trustworthiness. At the time of this Leipzig trial, General Kurt von Schleicher, the head of the German Army and a confidant of President Paul von Hindenburg, attempted to associate the NSDAP with illegal methods.[32] But in his Leipzig testimony Hitler's cautious promise not to interfere with the independence of the military led to the army leadership's new decision to trust Hitler's renewed commitment to the "legal course." Defense Minister Wilhelm Groener, noting that Chancellor Heinrich Brüning had decided to meet with Hitler, now rescinded the classification of the NSDAP as a "subversive" organization. This was a designation that had put the Nazis on par with the KPD, but now high government officials had been brought together by the fight against communism, and they backed Hitler's campaign against "cultural bolshevism."[33]

With the parliament system frozen in the grip of the Great Depression, Germany's political leaders were exercising much authority. But in obvious stark contrast to Hitler, they had very little popular backing.[34]

Hitler's new respectability, forged in the minds of high government officials by the legal course, began to open up the possibility that they would negotiate with him, just as the Nazis became the second most popular party in the elections of September 1930. This was a route to power wholly unavailable to the Communist leaders, who, like Nazi leaders, also had revolutionary aims but little tactical flexibility.

President Hindenburg, however, remained unconvinced; meeting Hitler for the first time on October 10, 1930, Hindenburg found the NSDAP leader uncouth and decidedly unfit for high office.[35] Perhaps the old president was also able to grasp that Hitler's "legal course" in no way delimited his goals. Hitler, as if warning listeners that they should not mistake his aims because he was using the "legal course," had stated to the Leipzig court that the party could strive to achieve its goals with constitutional means because "the constitution prescribes only the methods, not the aim. In this constitutional way we shall try to gain decisive majorities in the legislative bodies so that the moment we succeed we can give the state the form that corresponds to our ideas."[36]

But the "legal course" was not without its costs, particularly among SA members who could not imagine doing away with the Weimar Republic without armed struggle. As the new Reichstag met on October 13, 1930, the SA went on a rampage, smashing shop windows of Jewish stores but stopping short of battling the police. The party blamed the Communists, to make it appear as though the Nazis were following the "legal course," in stark contrast to the Communists. Some blamed the rebellious Stennes, but even Stennes's faction, comprising about one-third of all SA men, did not represent the full extent of anger in the party with Hitler's "legal course."[37]

The Communists hoped that Hitler's "legal course" would send droves of disaffected SA men into their camp, and Hitler was constrained to compromise carefully in order to limit the number of party men his course alienated. Richard Scheringer was among the Nazi Party members who began to rail against Hitler for betraying the armed revolt they thought of as essential. He was also one of the three army officers Hitler had defended with his testimony in Leipzig Federal Court in late September 1930 and was serving a sentence of eighteen months in prison, where he met with members of the KPD, as well as with Nazi leaders. In February 1931, while on furlough from prison, he even traveled in the company of Goebbels to Munich for a visit with Hitler. Goebbels considered him a marvelous youth with clarity and character and planned to work with him after his release.[38]

But the admiration was not mutual. Baffled and scandalized by Hitler's "legal course," Scheringer became convinced that he was really a Communist and not a Nazi since the KPD backed violent revolution. Upon returning to prison, the former Nazi penned a letter to the KPD announcing his conversion to communism, an immediate sensation. At the Reichstag, KPD Central Committee member Hans Kippenger rose to read Scheringer's letter triumphantly, showing the apostate's scorn for "Hitler the legalist." Scheringer's letter praised the KPD's "militarization of the entire working people for a prepared and militant German Red Army." Citing Lenin's claim that revolutionary war was necessary and praising the KPD as the most warlike party, Scheringer went on to confess the element he most despised about Nazism and admired about communism: "I reject . . . pacifism and take my place as a soldier in the ranks of the fighting proletariat!"[39]

Scheringer's conversion illustrates the way many Germans across the spectrum of class and social standing allowed Hitler's legal-way tactics to cloud their vision of his ultimate goals. Like many others, he assumed there could be no revolution without a bloody showdown and confused the rejection of violence for tactical reasons with the principled stance of pacifism. But he was right about the KPD, which was in fact revving up its violence in service of its revolution. Violence in the republic was primarily limited to street fighting and brawls with chair legs and beer steins rather than guns.[40] But as Nazi momentum increased, the KPD stepped up its attacks. It decided to stamp out Nazi growth by "armed struggle," focusing first on Nazi incursions into working-class neighborhoods, where political identity and struggle were so rife that public businesses and their customers alike aligned themselves exclusively with a political party. The Communists were incensed as the Nazis expanded their physical presence in Berlin's traditional working-class neighborhoods, Neukölln and Wedding. In the late summer and autumn of 1931, the Nazi Party became increasingly successful in establishing taverns as its new outposts, filling working-class taverns so completely that some became known among Communists as "Nazi Barracks." Escalating its militancy on Germany's streets, the KPD's political violence became "a terrifying fact of daily life" and threatened the ability of the police to keep order. Haunting the police now was the specter of a threat to national security: would the Red Front begin to act like an army?[41] In addition to intentionally murdering individual Nazis, the Communists rigidly viewed the police as an arm of the oppressor and continued violently attacking them. The NSDAP, on the other hand, "deliberately avoided confrontations with the police," preferring to appear to sympathize with the police "as victims of Communist aggression."[42]

THE "LEGAL COURSE" FENDS OFF PROVOCATIONS TO VIOLENCE

Despite Scheringer and others, more Germans continued to join than leave the Nazi Party, and Hitler retained control even as he further angered many in the SA by subjugating it further under other party agencies that were clearly loyal to him. When Heinrich Himmler, the head of the SS (which was subordinate to the SA), accused SA leader Salomon of training the SA to disobey Hitler, Salomon resigned. Hitler then named himself head of the SA.[43] Meanwhile, Ernst Röhm, who in 1928 had left the party in disgust because of the "legal course" to serve as a military adviser in Bolivia, returned to Germany and Hitler's service. Beginning in January 1931, he was the SA chief of staff.

The unruly Röhm initially helped Hitler to restrain the Storm Troopers. Playing the role of Nazi ambassador to the German Army, he wielded his influence to assure the status quo that Hitler was steadfastly committed to legal means. The army leadership became convinced, finally, to allow the SA to assist in the covert German rearmament. Röhm also reached an agreement with army leaders to lift army measures banning Nazi Party members from participating in army operations and border patrol units. Despite the public charges that Röhm was homosexual, Hitler was willing to keep him in his new high-profile position, even as prominent newspapers assailed Röhm. In a booklet titled *Out of the Brown Morass,* the famed World War I hero General Erich von Ludendorff scorned Röhm's homosexuality as well as Hitler's toleration of it. Hitler did remove the Hitler Youth from the SA and Röhm's authority in May 1932 but remained loyal to Röhm otherwise.[44]

SA insubordination was more troubling to Hitler than Röhm's homosexuality. During January 1931, the SA's assertion of independence around the Reich continued to pose potential risks. In southern Germany Walter Stegmann, head of the Franconia SA, threatened that his troops would join the KPD. Mutinous feeling and grumbling within the SA increased.[45] Hitler responded within weeks by embedding the SA deeper within party structures, subordinating SA units, region by region, under the leadership of the party Gauleiters. Hitler also banned the SA from carrying weapons and from public assaults.[46]

At the end of March 1931, SA indignation was greatly inflamed by a national Emergency Decree to "combat political excesses." The decree prohibited all political rallies that were not approved in advance by local police. Also banned were propaganda trucks, paramilitary uniforms, and sidearms—in other words, the daily activities of the SA. Violators were to be jailed for at least three months. SA members dedicated to violent uprising were incensed, and the question of whether Hitler could restrain them was once again pushed to the forefront and tested.[47] Goebbels recognized that the Emergency Decree fanned the desire for rebellion and posed the "worst crisis" to date for the party. If the SA turned "violent, radical, and rebellious," it "could embarrass the Party and alienate the middle class," a stronghold of Hitler's supporters.[48]

Hitler immediately ordered the SA to comply with the new Emergency Decree fully, carefully explaining that his order was in "the interest of the movement as a whole." His dedication to the "legal course" was due not to propaganda but a fear that his movement could be stymied otherwise. At the same time he sought to overturn the decree through Weimar's legal system.[49] The intent of the ban as Hitler saw it was to provoke the SA into an armed rebellion. On March 31, three days after the ban, Hitler wrote in the Nazi daily *Völkischer Beobachter* that the state was trying to move the party away from its more hardheaded approach of refusing to engage in a fight against the state and its superior armed forces. "In these days only one desire dominates the longing of the enemies of Germany: would it only work out that the National Socialists get agitated, so that their masses lose their nerves and break the laws," Hitler wrote. "The Emergency Decree must be obeyed by all Party Comrades and Party officials, SA and SS people in the most precise and thorough way."[50]

For Hitler, maintaining a calm, ordered response to the prohibitions was itself a defiance of the state's wishes.

Walter Stennes continued to go his own way, refusing Hitler's orders to receive approval from his superiors twenty-four hours in advance of holding rallies and demonstrations. The general German press stressed that Stennes wished to lead a putsch, while the party press played this down. On the whole, wishing to repress publicity about dissent, the party preferred not to draw attention to Stennes. When the Nazi leadership did charge Stennes with backing revolution, it characterized him as a rogue element favoring the violent uprising characteristic of the KPD.[51]

The Nazis regularly blamed violence on the Communists, but the question of taking control through violence was becoming a defining issue for them. Hitler ordered Stennes removed from his position, but Stennes refused and led a revolt by some SA units in Berlin and elsewhere in northeastern Germany on April 1, 1931. Goebbels made a call to the Berlin police to rid party offices of rebellious SA men, illustrating anew that the German democracy's most successful enemy was able to call upon that democracy's structures and resources to maintain its footing. SA insurgents once more demanded the end of the "legal course" because "the path to the people's community [Volksgemeinschaft] means struggle and not peace and order."[52]

Nevertheless, Hitler prevailed once again: on April 4, 1931, after Stennes was expelled from the party, all SA leaders were ordered to submit a declaration of loyalty to Hitler. Like a master of jujitsu, Hitler exercised a mastery that did not require him to match the brute power of his opponent. The resignation of SA leaders and the efforts of Stennes to form a rival organization did little damage to Hitler's authority within the party because so many of those who wanted a violent revolution remained loyal to Hitler nonetheless. "We will gain power only with the people, not against them," Goebbels wrote in April 1931. "They will join us when they feel as we do, when they are persuaded that what we want is correct."[53]

Hitler's concept of how to use the SA effectively was illustrated in mid-October 1931 by an enormous demonstration in Braunschweig that, according to Nazi sources, brought in some one hundred thousand SA men. The strict discipline against rabble-rousing that prevailed during the six-hour SA parade made a "powerful impression, particularly on the middle-class."[54] That same autumn continuing KPD violence served to highlight the image of law and order that Hitler wanted for his party. At a meeting with state police officials on November 17, 1931, Groener, who had become interior minister in October, explicitly sided with the Nazis against the Communists. He backed Hitler's assertion that SA men deserved additional police protection because they were the targets of violent attacks. The KPD, on the other hand, had to be put down because it posed a real threat of insurrection.[55]

Groener credited the Nazis for their "legal course." But within the party, at the helm of the SA itself, Ernst Röhm represented a grave threat. Röhm, by his own admission, was a poor strategist who liked to brawl. As "an immature and wicked man, war and unrest appeal to me more than good bourgeois order," he said.[56]

On December 14, 1931, a government report drew upon a range of Nazi sources to reveal that a rift had opened within the NSDAP over the "legal course" versus political violence. Again to his favor in the opinion of those governing Germany, Hitler was increasingly identified with the "legal course." The report pointed out that while Hitler's position was party policy, there was still a volume of opinion throughout the party ranks, as well as from some prominent Nazis, that opposed the "legal course."[57] The more the SA agitated for a coup, the clearer this distinction became.

In December 1931, Chancellor Brüning received unanimous support from his cabinet for an extraordinary new decree that banned all demonstrations and membership uniforms over the Christmas season. Brüning proceeded to make a clear distinction between the trustworthiness of Hitler and that of others prominent in the party. Although "the party leader of the National Socialists has emphasized [legal methods]," Chancellor Brüning said, "this stands in sharp contrast to the declarations of leaders who also think they have authority" and threaten "fratricidal struggle."[58] The ban reflected the chancellor's limited focus, betraying a sense that danger could be excised from the party: it applied to the SA but not to other Nazi Party members or agencies.

On January 7, 1932, Goebbels again pledged the party to the "legal course." Revolutionary violence, Goebbels explained to party members in Hamburg, was fruitless for the current stage of the movement. The propagandist pointed out that the Weimar Constitution itself held that "the people and not the party is of prime importance," adding that his party's definition of "legal" was "what the people wanted." Although the legal course was serving an important propaganda purpose, Hitler had selected it and remained committed to it because he perceived it as the most effective way, in the given context, for moving toward his goals. Goebbels too was expressing the party's real rationale for not risking all that it had successfully built up, in a mass movement, in one act of assault on the state. Popular support was the key. In the upcoming presidential contest between Hitler and Hindenburg, on March 13, 1932, Hitler restrained himself—if not other party leaders—from ridiculing Hindenburg because he was a popular hero. Hitler agreed not to slight Hindenburg because, "One should never deprive the people of their gods."[59]

Hitler had positioned himself to be the next "god" of the people, following Hindenburg's impending death. He did not aspire to succeed Hindenburg as president but as the people's god. This is why he chose to be called the Führer, or the Leader. "Leader" was not defined by the constitution or precedent and allowed for the open, unquestioning adoration from the people he sought and wanted to requite.

In the weeks before the German presidential election in March, the SA, once again, was conjoined to campaigning frantically for Hitler. But the Nazi leader lost to President Hindenburg, a defeat that triggered a depression throughout the party. SA violence escalated,[60] goaded on by another ban on the Storm Troopers, this one issued on April 13, 1932, by Chancellor Brüning. The new decree—"to secure state authority"—prohibited a range of activities that effectively shut down the SA.[61] Groener presented the ban as a logical response to data showing that the SA had become the major cause of street violence. This reproof was based on reports on SA activities from the most important German states, from conservative Bavaria to SPD-led Prussia and Hesse and including Württemberg, Baden, and Saxony. The new ban expressed the illusion, important for the further success of Hitler, that the problem with the Nazi Party was the SA; without it the NSDAP itself could be kept under control.[62]

Once again, Hitler issued an order demanding that the SA obey the latest ban. To aid compliance and emphasize its importance, a detailed list of the Emergency Decree's provisions was distributed among the Storm Troopers. Rather than fighting the police on the streets, the party (effectively) played the part of a martyr—a party struggling for Germany but singled out for unfair punishment by the ban. The result was that the ban elicited strong sympathy and support from German conservatives, an important victory for the "legal course." General Schleicher and President Hindenburg soon rescinded their support for the ban, and Hindenburg appointed a new chancellor, Franz von Papen, who lifted the ban in June.[63]

Anticipating the next Reichstag elections that Papen had called for on July 31, 1932, party propaganda promised that the NSDAP would come to power by winning an absolute majority.[64] Again SA energies were sublimated to frenzied electioneering, while Hitler, an enthusiast about motorization, took to modern technology by flying from one campaign site to another, making many more appearances possible.[65] The results were nothing less than stunning. The NSDAP received 37.3 percent of the vote, as much as Weimar's most popular party, the SPD, had received at the very peak of its popularity early in the republic. Now the NSDAP had eclipsed the SPD to become by far the largest Weimar party. Ominously for the republic, the combined vote for the two revolutionary parties, the KPD and the NSDAP, had risen to more than 51 percent.[66] Additionally, elections that month in Prussia, the largest German state, gave the NSDAP, together with the Communist Party, a majority, rendering a further coalition government impossible and resulting in the "Preussenschlag," a coup by Papen and Schleicher justified by the claim that the government had not been able to quell public unrest, a justification the Nazis would soon use to dominate states around Germany in early 1933. Nazi ascendancy in popular support now proved decisive in Goebbels's war with Deputy Police Chief Bernhard Weiss, who was out of office and soon fled for his life to London.[67]

NAZI NEGOTIATIONS AFFORDED BY THE "LEGAL COURSE"

The Nazi victory in July paled in the light of epic party promises, and many Storm Troopers were indignant that Hindenburg had refused Hitler's demand to be named chancellor, claiming this justified a coup. Otto Strasser's SA newspaper, *Die Schwarze Front*, encouraged a call to arms, as Strasser himself declared that the "legal course" had reached a dead end; loyal SA men who had fought so valiantly had been deceived and misused. "[It] is totally and clearly confirmed," he wrote, "the legal course cannot and will not ever lead to the National Socialist seizure of power." A number of German cities were swept with SA violence due to a "full-scale SA revolt." On August 21, *Die Schwarze Front* featured a call for revolution since "the Hitler Party managed to obtain only 37.3 percent of the votes," an insignificant gain over previous elections that "has proven to the most trusting SA man that the way of legality, that is to say, the way through the ballot box, can never lead to the National Socialist seizure of power."[68] By August, according to a close confidant of Ernst Röhm, the SA leader himself was prepared to stage a coup d'état were Hitler not to be appointed chancellor.[69] The struggle by parties for domination over streets and neighborhoods rose to such levels that the state appeared to have lost its monopoly on the use of force, and many feared civil war.[70]

Hitler had managed to restrain the SA from one crisis to the next, but it was clear that the party's conflicts with the SA were systemic. Socioeconomic disparities between party members and the Storm Troopers, along with differences in perspectives and goals, played off of each other and radicalized the conflict. Röhm grew increasingly restless. Revolutionary SA men could hardly proselytize in the sense of Hitler's November 1926 order because they did not share Hitler's wild, long-term vision, which required him to work so closely with the people in the effort to change their gods. Hitler, of course, aimed for a revolution too, if only a much more fundamental one beginning with a change of attitudes across society.

Buffeted as well by a dwindling treasury, Hitler rallied SA support by publicly backing SA men who had committed murder, justified as self-defense. In Altona on July 17, the KPD's Red Front ambushed a marching column of SA men, killing fifteen of them. In Silesia, regional SA leaders planned acts of revenge to "exert pressure" on the party leadership, and Hitler stood by the SA in its so-called "Potempa murder" of a Silesian worker. He had reassured SA men that they should respond in kind when attacked violently, and on August 22, 1932, as five SA men were sentenced to death for the murder, Hitler assured them in a telegram of his "unbounded loyalty."[71]

The balance Hitler was forced to maintain between playing to an SA itching for violence and rapidly broadening his party's popular appeal was beginning to show its limits. But police reports from September and October 1932 show that Hitler's willingness and ability to restrain the SA played well in general. The police credited him with the restraint of a violent SA putsch. According to a September 21 report from Stuttgart, the majority within the SA of the southwest region wished to take power with force but that they nevertheless were willing to follow Hitler. "There can be no mistaking the fact that . . . the SA men and SA leaders are waiting for a decision. The sentiment of a segment—which indeed is the majority—is 'to hell with the legal course.' Everywhere, however, there is the greatest trust in the Leader!"[72]

On October 10, the *Munich Post* indicated that SA chief Röhm was now promoting a violent takeover while trying to convince Hitler to abandon the commitment to legality. On October 21, in an analysis of the situation in Munich's neighboring Bavarian city of Nuremberg, the police reported a fundamental threat to Hitler's movement: Storm Trooper violence was alienating the voters. Party momentum had been halted by their public disorder, and even devotees of the movement were now rescinding their support. The police concluded that the Nazi Party would continue to lose support if the Brown Shirts were not contained. Within the party as well, some functionaries complained that militant SA behavior and revelations about Röhm's homosexuality were causing grave damage to the party's image and popularity.[73]

Industry leaders were alienated by SA violence as well. Reflecting their penchant for orderliness, conservative middle-class voters in particular found Storm Trooper violence repugnant (although many must have feared Communist violence more).[74] The police had articulated Hitler's reasoning in rejecting any effort to build his movement primarily with violent force: it would narrow the following, limiting it especially among large sectors of the bourgeois majority, and perhaps also inflame divisions within the party. Police reports also showed that Hitler was perceived as having the important ability to maintain public order.

The credit Hitler had accumulated for containing the SA had eaten away at notions that he lacked all qualifications for government office. This held not just among segments of the public but among those in office as well. Groener and Brüning had already drawn sharp distinctions between Hitler and the SA, while the police reports from Munich were now likely reaching others in Berlin at top levels. A police situation re-

port of October 15, 1932, that reached the republic's Interior Ministry—
and thus very possibly made its way from there to other national officials
as well—concluded that there had been no coup because the SA, like the
SS, was "firmly in the hands of the Leader." That same day, police in
Hamburg noted that disaffected SA men had joined the insignificant
"Stennes-Strasser movement" opposing Hitler's "legal course."[75]

The challenges Hitler faced intensified. But for the keepers of the Weimar government, the question of how to deal with Hitler's demands also
grew more pressing. The Nazi Party's towering popularity indicated that
he should be named chancellor. The declining Nazi fortunes in the
Reichstag election of November 6, 1932, must have sharpened Hitler's
interest in negotiating his way into power. The NSDAP lost some two
million votes and fell by about 4 percent. While some commentators
believed that this election had put an end to the Nazi danger, others associated their feelings of relief with Hitler's repression of an SA coup.[76]
The SA found compelling reasons for indignation in the election and in
the promises of party leaders, although Hitler still held to his "legal
course." On December 2, 1932, the day President Hindenburg appointed
Kurt von Schleicher as chancellor, the moderate weekly newspaper *Der
deutsche Weg* pronounced its conclusion that Hitler's party had "now totally rejected" the method of achieving power by violently overthrowing
the government.[77]

   But were the heads of government also influenced by Hitler's grip
on the SA? Some around President Hindenburg were asking whether
Hitler posed a "less risky course" than other options. Giving him power
was preferred over dramatic constitutional reform or military dictatorship.[78] The Nazi Party leader, now seen as head of the most potent
anti-Communist party, was on working terms with big business and
was certainly the best demagogue for mobilizing against the Versailles
Treaty and commitment to rearmament.

   It is telling that Hindenburg's government gave the Nazi Party a
massive propaganda boost on January 21, 1933, even as the Nazis ranted
against the republic and the Jews. The government granted the Nazis a
permit for a demonstration that day, while also refusing the KPD a permit
for a counterdemonstration. Under police supervision, about fifteen thousand Storm Troopers marched from Berlin's Bülowplatz to a cemetery

nearby for a dedication by Hitler of a memorial to Horst Wessel, the idealistic young SA man whom the Communists had shot and who was now memorialized as a Nazi martyr. Predictably, the KPD responded with force. Prepared for the melee, police met the Communists with brute force, arresting about seventy and wounding two with gunshots.[79]

Goebbels triumphed that the Nazi Party had won a major battle. As recently as the previous day, he had feared that the government would prohibit the Nazi demonstration. Now according to his information, the Defense Ministry itself had pushed the government to permit it. All in all, the scene that day "lent the Nazis an aura of respectability by aligning them with the forces of law and order against the Communists."[80]

The "legal course" made room for Hitler to negotiate his way to power within the high-level machinations of Franz von Papen. The great animosity toward communism and Hitler's towering popularity were also crucial, but the sense that Hitler might be trusted, forged by his legal course in relation to the SA, allowed for negotiations that would have otherwise been impossible. Chancellor Kurt von Schleicher, for example, thought that confining Hitler to the "legal course" would allow him the possibility of "converting the Nazi movement with its mass following into a prop of the existing government instead of a battering ram directed against it."[81] And Hitler must have finally made a better impression during his meeting with Hindenburg following the November election, for the meeting between the men seems to have effectively changed the president from foe to ally. On January 30 the president appointed Hitler as chancellor, and thereafter the eighty-six-year-old Hindenburg enabled Hitler's rapid ascension to dictatorship. The president's acquiescence to Hitler's major requests as chancellor indicates at least some trust in Hitler.[82] He authorized the February 28, 1933, "Reichstag Fire Decrees" gutting the constitution, agreed to the April 1 boycott of businesses owned by Jews, and a year later, in June 1934, signaled approval for Hitler's bloody SA purge.

It can be said with some irony that Hitler restored majority rule during 1933. His legal pledge had made good propaganda, but it had also played a key role in the rapid rise of his movement. In the sense that it cast Hitler's aims as milder than they really were, the pledge of legality was campaign propaganda. To the extent that the pledge suggested that Hitler was actually committed to the rule of law, it was a monumental lie, albeit one that was apparent from his repeated, readily available statements.

THE SA PURGE IN SERVICE OF A GROWING POPULAR MOVEMENT

In power, Hitler soon fulfilled his 1930 pledge that "heads would roll." As he had also predicted, he managed to align this effort with the letter of the law, which helped him maintain his bottom line: sustaining the momentum of growing popular support.[83] While Hitler continued his focus on building the mass movement of support, the SA marauded on the streets, especially against the Left and the Jews; public SA marauding reached a high point in mid-1933. The indiscrimination of SA violence is seen in American ambassador William Dodd's August 1933 account of an American doctor working in Berlin who was beaten unconscious for not raising an arm in the Nazi salute, as well as in pogrom-like attacks against Jews that injured non-Jews.[84]

While the Nazi terror system formed a backdrop for domestic social control, many Germans accepted Nazi terror as directed against those who deserved the punishment and necessary for maintaining order.[85] The public unruliness of the SA, however, did not correspond with the sense of orderly security the people wanted. In response, Hitler apparently tried to win Röhm's loyalty one last time. He campaigned personally across the Reich to win the loyalty of SA men, assuring them that they could share the prize of having won power—*if* they abandoned random violence and played their part in Hitler's long-term vision. In December 1933 he appeased an old SA grievance with a law granting Röhm membership in the Reich Cabinet. A few weeks later he addressed a letter to Röhm in tones of uncommonly frank intimacy, expressing gratitude for Röhm's "imperishable services" and assuring Röhm of his personal friendship. In addition, state pensions were now granted to members of the SA and others who had suffered injuries or illness.[86]

This was a considerable offering of concessions, but Röhm would not be persuaded so easily. In February 1934 he used his new cabinet position to propose that the SA would serve as the basis for an expanded army under a single minister, recommending himself as that leader. Hitler did not back this plan, and the army high command unanimously disapproved as well. By March, Hitler was informed that Hindenburg did not have long to live.[87] By February or March as well, Hitler had also decided against further efforts to persuade the SA leadership to relinquish its independent ambitions. On February 2, in a thinly veiled reference to the SA, Hitler confided to the Gauleiters that "those who maintained that the [Nazi] revolution was not finished were fools." There were "people in the movement," he added, "whose conception of revolution was nothing but a permanent state of chaos."[88]

On Hitler's orders and with the assistance of the army, the murders of the "Röhm Purge" were unleashed at the end of June 1934, a murder spree that revealed to all that Hitler was ruthless and that the Nazi Party would not tolerate threats to the regime, even from prominent public figures who had served Hitler so well. The important point from the dictatorship's perspective, however, was that the German people generally welcomed the terror rather than fearing it. In an implicit deal with the German people, the Nazis were free to use terror against outsiders who were not falling in line. Popular approval provided the teeth behind Nazi terror.

Germans generally greeted the brutal repression as a "long necessary act of liberation," according to police reports on opinion, a reception that represented an early realization of the new Nazi legal norms: the "healthy sentiment of the people," educated by the new regime, was already replacing the old codes, which condemned the purge as murder.[89]

Hitler had also persuaded Germany's eminent persons to give him great leeway. Seeking the cover of legality, he readily won approval from the cabinet ministers for a short paragraph known as the Law for the Emergency Defense of the State. Hindenburg signaled his approval, and following his death on August 2, 1934, the army offered an oath of allegiance to Hitler personally.[90]

Following Hindenburg's death, Hitler assumed the constitutional title of "president," although he preferred the new title of the Leader (der Führer), undefined by law. He had been the party Leader; now he was the people's Leader. He had used the legal course to both rule the party and come to power. Now he turned away from ruling the party to ruling the people. But he continued to search for popular legitimacy and continued to rely on the ideas behind his "legal course" strategy to exercise authority over his own "race." He continued to target the use of brute force strategically, to reinforce his popularity and prestige, just as he had restrained the Storm Troopers from another coup. After the murderous purge of June 1934, he told the Storm Troopers to stop rabble-rousing in the streets, promising that "just as we succeeded in conquering 90 percent of the German people for National Socialism, we will and must be able to win over the last 10 percent."[91]

The people comprised a force that Hitler trusted more than any other; only after he had introduced conscription was he certain that he would be able to prevail over any opposition from within the military. He did not gain this confidence when he became chancellor or when Germany became a police state following the Reichstag Fire. Nor was it sufficient, by his account, when each soldier swore an oath of allegiance to him personally in August 1934. This confidence had to wait until 1935, when conscription had swollen the military with half a million new conscripts, infused with the spirit of Nazism, backed by his movement's "ever-growing power."[92]

Following the Röhm Purge, Hitler had the backing of vast numbers of his people. But he was somewhat aware that in many cases this was merely a surface consent, pieced together by a sleight of hand that allowed Germans to think that they could hold on to all of their old traditions and follow their new Nazi Leader at the same time. Painstaking work still had to be done to carefully reveal the truths of Nazism that offended fixed norms. In 1934, Hitler was just beginning to feel his way forward, to see how quickly he could substitute new Nazi values and practices for any old German habits that got in his way. In some ways, Christianity and church practices lay in his way, but could he convince the people that what he offered was worth more than these old habits?

CHAPTER TWO

Contested Mobilizations

BISHOPS VERSUS NAZIS IN THE BATTLE
FOR THE PEOPLE

"THE PEACE OF WESTPHALIA MUST BE RESCINDED"

"This map here, listen to me . . . , is the religion map," Hitler said, addressing two SA leaders, Franz Pfeffer von Salomon and Otto Wagener, in early 1930 in their office. The SA men were perplexed by a map that revealed a heavier concentration of SA volunteers in northern, central, and eastern areas of Germany, the location of each unit of one hundred SA men marked with a single red pin. Awing the SA leaders with his perspicacity, Hitler pointed out that the current German settlements of Protestants and Catholics followed patterns designated by the 1648 Treaty of Westphalia:

> Can you see the Peace of Westphalia there? There are the
> territories of Münster, Bamberg, Würzberg, Bautzen. They are
> Catholic. . . . And northern Baden is Protestant! And that is
> why the SA is weak in the former areas and strong in northern
> Baden. . . . There you stand staring at the pinheads . . . and try
> with your human logic to penetrate the secret of this picture. . . .
> Where the Germanic breed predominates, the people are
> Protestants; where Romanism has left its mark, the people are
> Catholic. . . . The SA attracts the militant natures among the
> Germanic breed, the men who think democratically, unified

only by a common allegiance. . . . I shall send Himmler here. He must look at the map. I'll be back once more myself. No one else is to see it. It must be covered up. And from now on the concept of *a community of the people* must serve as a slogan throughout the entire SA and SS. The Peace of Westphalia must be rescinded. North and South and East and West must be forcibly fused. One Reich, one people—that must be our watchword. Otherwise we can never transcend the vestiges of past periods of history.[1]

This "religion map," passed down over centuries, displayed an enormous challenge for a leader who wished to seamlessly unify the country but could not merely sever the areas where "Romanism has left its mark"—including his native Austria. Hitler expected to make the Germans unconquerable by overcoming their many divisions and removing all independent sources of influence on German society. Above all, the Jews, as the biggest source of social unrest, had to be removed from the land. Then there was the problem of the churches, which threatened to interfere with Hitler's vision of unity. Churches divided Germans between Catholics and Protestants, and both claimed a higher authority. But they could not be exterminated because Hitler saw his power as resting on his people. He intended to unite the denominations around the "scientific" reality of "race," clearing the way for centralized power by stripping the churches of their authority.

Hitler had long dreamed of unifying Germany's twenty-eight independent Protestant dioceses in a new "Reich Church." His model was Henry VIII's forging of the Church of England on the eve of England's emergence as a world power.[2] A single national church was key to the centralization of Hitler's own authority, due to the churches' independence. But in 1934, the Protestants of southern Germany staged a bold protest that clashed with Hitler's ambition of dominating all German Protestants under a single bishop.[3] The Protestant opposition to joining its provincial churches in Bavaria and Württemberg to a Reich Church came to loggerheads with the regime directly following the bloody Night of the Long Knives purge, which showed that Hitler could quickly turn savage, even against Germans whom he had once esteemed highly. But was Hitler likely to deal with a bishop and his churches with the blunt force he used against Röhm's SA? Defanging the SA had consolidated Hitler's power and support, and the Protestant folk of Bavaria saw themselves on Hitler's side.

These Protestants in two southern provinces, however, were also defying the "German Christians," a Reich-wide organization working with the dictatorship by appearing to present a substitute for the traditional churches. Formed before Hitler came to power, the German Christian Movement helped garner quick-growing support for a Reich Church. By the end of the Nazi dictatorship's first half year, all but several of Germany's twenty-eight Protestant bishops supported this alignment of church leadership under Hitler.[4] In their neighboring provinces of Bavaria and Württemberg, Hans Meiser and Theophil Wurm worked in tandem with passionate churchgoers and lower-level church officials to lead a rejection of uniting their provincial churches under a national church headed in Prussia. Supporting them as well was a growing contingent of Protestant Germans who had become alienated from the German Christians under the unpopular "Reich Bishop" Ludwig Müller.

Bishop Meiser in particular demonstrated an extraordinary capacity for mass mobilization tactics resembling those of the party. Hitler had noted while serving time for treason that efforts to replace a worldview "[would] eventually fail" unless they were led by "a new spiritual direction." Bismarck had lost the battle against Marxism because he had relied too directly on force.[5] As the contest between the bishops and regional Nazi officials for popular support heightened, Hitler at first kept his distance, maintaining a sufficiently vague image that allowed Germans from all the different, sometimes rivaling, regions across the country to project onto Hitler a sense that he was their Leader who viewed what was "German" just as they did, in their own particular milieu.

HITLER APPROACHES THE CHURCHES

Coming to power, the Nazi Party encouraged the notion that Nazism and the churches could march hand in hand toward common goals. Hitler thought that Christianity would eventually be brought down by its own inflexibility but that some older Germans thoroughly rooted in Christianity might not be persuaded to give it up. Meanwhile, Christian dogma was sometimes compatible with Nazi dogma. Upon taking power in January 1933, Hitler continued to proffer signs of a truce to both the Christian denominations. The national government sees in both Christian confessions important bases for the preservation of our people, Hitler told the people in March 1933,[6] and it was not uncommon for church leaders to declare that the Nazi Party was inspiring a spiritual awakening and a national renewal.

Among the conservative elites who warmly welcomed Hitler's rule was a "particularly important segment" of Protestant bishops and other church leaders, including Bishops Meiser and Wurm. Meiser, appointed bishop of the Bavarian Protestant Church just two months after Hitler took power, had greeted the Nazi movement on Easter Sunday in 1933 by requiring the pastors across his diocese to read a glowing pledge of support: "A state which brings into being again a government according to God's Laws should, in doing so, be assured not only of the applause but also of the glad and active cooperation of the Church." This was a message in the true spirit of National Socialism—it was not at all sufficient to cheer the movement on from the sidelines; the dictatorship did not merely aim to suppress opposition but rather to engage the people fully in the daily practices of Nazism and its organizations.[7]

Along with others, Bishop Wurm also joined in expressing a common sentiment among church leaders that "the Leader of the new Germany" would renew Germany's "national and religious awakening." Even the famous Protestant resister, pastor Martin Niemöller, used the pulpit as late as the autumn of 1933 to praise Hitler's movement as a force for a great national revitalization, identifying "race and ethnicity" as key prerequisites. These numerous, generous pledges overlooked the new dictatorship's cruel policies separating Jews from other Germans. Church leaders as well as the laity greeted Hitler's party as a bulwark against the atheism of Marxism, and some saw the persecution of Jews as necessary for the eradication of communism.[8]

REICH BISHOP MÜLLER LOOKS TO THE GESTAPO

The German Christian movement, which called for a Christianity based on "blood and race," filled two-thirds of the Protestant church leadership positions across the Reich by July 1933. As of September 1933, regional church administrations had been pulled together under the new "Reich

Bishop," Ludwig Müller, with the backing of Hitler as well as numerous church leaders. At the same time, signs emerged that German Protestantism was too diverse to be united under a single Reich Bishop, at least not under the ham-handed Müller. In Berlin, Niemöller began in the late summer of 1933 to establish what in May 1934 became the Confessing Church, a basis of opposition for some Protestants. And in Bavaria, Bishop Meiser, an archconservative who also cared deeply about his regional state church structure, voiced hesitation about joining the Reich Church, expressing concern that Catholics had infiltrated German Christians and that the Reich Church would not be "sufficiently" Protestant.[9]

On January 25, 1934, Hitler met personally with the Protestant leaders in an effort to limit the controversy, chiding the church leaders for their "shameful" squabbles. He was sure, he said, that the disapproval expressed by some was not against the state itself but rather only against some of its measures regarding the church. The church leaders readily agreed with Hitler's prompting, agreeing that they endorsed Hitler's dictatorship itself. They also went further to assure the Leader that any criticisms by individual clergymen were isolated and not representative of all church leaders. Only two prelates summoned the will to raise their voices in the face of this overwhelming deference. When Niemöller expressed concern about prerogatives, Hitler retorted, "You leave concern for the Third Reich to me and look after the church!" Within the Nazi paradigm the expanding state required an ever-shrinking church presence in society. Bishop Meiser also proved capable of disappointing the Leader—and the majority that stood strongly behind him—by stating that the replacement of Müller as Reich Bishop would not be sufficient to gain his support for the Reich Church. Hitler then abandoned further inquiries about what might gain unified support for the Reich Church and departed by enjoining all segments of the church to reach accord. As if to model the way, he shook hands with each of the leaders present, including Niemöller.[10]

The meeting was a success for Hitler. Two days later the leaders who had been present at the summit agreed to swear their "unconditional fidelity" to Hitler and his Third Reich. Further, they wrote a collective statement of their sharp opposition to "all intrigues or criticism of state, people and movement." They added that "the assembled church leaders stand firmly behind the Reich Bishop and are determined to carry out his measures and decrees in the way in which he desires."[11] Only the Berlin pastor, Martin Niemöller, abstained from this collective fealty. But he did not have the popular backing that bishops had.

In return for the church leaders' agreement to eschew all matters related to politics, the party promised that it would not introduce religious matters or practices into party activities. Reinhard Heydrich, the head of the SD, directed the police in Bavaria, where Meiser was bishop, to avoid any actions that might disturb the movement toward the growth of a unified German Protestant Church.[12] This illustrated a tactic the regime would return to from time to time: calling a truce with the church when it wished to consolidate support among church leaders at any particular moment. When Bishops Wurm and Meiser requested a meeting with Hitler to inform him that they were reversing the support they had declared for the Reich Church just two months earlier at the January summit, Hitler urged the bishops to reckon with the certainties of "blood and race." Otherwise, he cautioned, developments within Germany would surely leave them behind. Meiser responded that "this leaves us no other choice than to become his most loyal opposition."[13] Reich Bishop Müller also voiced the belief that a revolution in attitudes was under way. Church leaders who withheld their support for Nazism were out of step with the new and must learn to "speak the speech of the present, the speech of everyday life, the speech of mother and child, the speech of farmers, workers, and the SA man!"[14]

But the self-censoring Müller, trained in Pietism as a youth, proved to be a poor tactician by Hitler's standards by quickly resorting to police force to confront the deep convictions of churchgoers. Complicating efforts to unify the Protestants under one bishop were clumsy tactics that alienated Germans rather than gaining their loyalty. Müller's "muzzle decrees" banning various forms of church expression evoked defiance from thousands of pastors speaking from their pulpits. His harassments, fines, and suspensions only escalated the conflict. As Müller's harsh tactics created solidarity for his position, Bishop Wurm of Württemberg wrote to regional Nazi officials at the end of April complaining that the German Christians were trying to have their way with the inappropriate *(ungeeignete)* means of force. In this important message,

Wurm appealed to the Nazi principle of unity, writing that the use of police tactics was the reason for the unrest among his churchgoers.[15]

Bishop Müller, however, could count on the backing of a far more powerful oppressor, Hermann Göring, who was the minister president of Prussia and founder of the Gestapo. Müller's deputy, August Jäger, a lawyer and the former commissioner for Prussian Church Affairs, fed the conflict by enlisting the SA's help to repress church dissent. Protests against this repression poured in to President Hindenburg, who expressed concern to Hitler that such suppression could lead to the destruction of "people and fatherland." In April 1934, the province of Mecklenburg's minister president, Walter Granzow, attempted to extend his political authority into church affairs by terminating Heinrich Rendtorff's tenure as bishop. Rendtorff turned to Hitler, who quickly reinstated him.[16]

Two months later, Hitler signaled his approval for the brutal purge of the SA, and he also signaled his renewed support for Bishop Müller as his point man for establishing the Reich Church. In June 1934, days ahead of the Night of the Long Knives, Hitler published an open letter praising Müller in the Nazi *Völkischer Beobachter*. He did so even though Interior Minister Wilhelm Frick, together with Foreign Minister Konstantin von Neurath, warned that Müller's strong-arm tactics were inciting condemnations, even from officials in other countries.[17] The following month, basking in popular and official approval for the bloody purge, Hitler met with Bishop Müller and Jäger. At the same time, in a pointed signal that his patience with Bishops Meiser and Wurm was growing thin, Hitler ignored their request for another meeting.

After Hindenburg's death on August 2 and due to the widespread acclaim for Hitler's leadership, political as well as church leaders were happy to see Hitler take the title of president along with that of chancellor. Hitler, who insisted on being addressed by the undefined title of "Leader," had reason to think that the overwhelming support for leadership would strong-arm the dissenting church leaders into conformity and that if he remained behind the scenes, any public dissatisfaction would be blamed on lower-level officials. On August 9, 1934, fifty of sixty delegates at a Reich Church synod voted to support the Reich Church under Bishop Müller's leadership. Expecting that Müller would have assuaged all dissent by then, Hitler now planned to honor Bishop

Müller for establishing a Reich Church, in a ceremony scheduled for late October 1934. Although Interior Minister Frick continued to accuse Müller of causing unrest with his blunt measures of repression, during his meeting with Müller in July, Hitler nonetheless endorsed the Reich Bishop's arbitrary decision to ban a church publication.[18]

THE BATTLE TO OSTRACIZE BISHOPS MEISER AND WURM

At the same time, party leaders and organizations mounted an expensive ongoing campaign to win support for the Reich Church from the wary Protestants in southern Germany. Already in the summer of 1933, Nazi officials and German Christian leaders had launched a series of mass public rallies for the Reich Church in Meiser's Bavarian diocese. Wielding the social pressures of conformity and exclusion, the bishop's opponents proclaimed that the entire Nuremberg clergy, with the exception of Meiser himself, would be participating in a demonstration on behalf of the Reich Church. The demonstration on July 17 turned out fifteen to twenty thousand participants, with national, regional, and local organizations marching in lockstep with the SA. Taking the stage, a German Christian leader said that "we want to become just one church; that is the will of the people." Following him was the main speaker, Karl Holz, a longtime close associate of Franconia Gauleiter Julius Streicher. Holz, a former editor in chief of Nazism's most sordid anti-Semitic propaganda rag, *Der Stürmer*, wore a tightly trimmed mustache resembling Hitler's and was following a rapidly rising trajectory of promotions within the party and the SA. Now, as Streicher's deputy for greater Nuremberg, Holz appealed to what he called the "historic faithfulness of Nuremberg," a direct challenge to Bishop Meiser's leadership. The event ended with Luther's hymn "A Mighty Fortress Is Our God," a Protestant stalwart that the party was assimilating as its own.[19]

All would have gone according to the Nazi schedule had the faithful in Bavaria and Württemberg not protested openly and continuously against the Reich Church. But the faithful might not have risen up so fervently had their leaders not prepared them so well. During the spring of 1934, Meiser and some of his congregational pastors began to anchor churchgoers as allies in the struggle to maintain their Bavarian independence. At the pulpit, the pastors began to wrest awareness of the church struggle from the restricted realm of the church leaders to make it a concern of the laity. Some of the Protestant pastors, particularly in southern and western Germany, condemned Reich Bishop Müller in a "declaration" read from the pulpits that was also printed in some newspapers, reported District President Hans Dippold of Middle and Upper Franconia. In June 1934 the government minister for Upper and Middle Franconia drew attention to this mobilization of opinion as damaging. Although the pastors were not directly attacking the state, this official wrote that they were nevertheless dangerous "from a political standpoint" because they might be *perceived* as political or might actually become political.[20] In any case, it would have been perilous to allow signs of disunity like this to fester.

The Nazi leaders, masters of manipulating perceptions, now saw their tactics of stirring up readiness for struggle deployed against them. In response, the regime attempted to repress church rallies, banning all published announcements about them. But this tactic proved unsuccessful, so that by late summer, Dippold, who was a loyal lieutenant of Gauleiter Julius Streicher of Nuremberg, warned anew that the open opposition to the Reich Church could easily be perceived as opposition to the Reich itself—or actually become that. Again the Nazi leader tried to ostracize Meiser by signaling that the trouble was primarily the work of the bishop. While nationally the church held true to the will of the regime, he warned, the majority of clergy and laity in Protestant Bavaria was standing firmly behind Meiser in rejecting the Reich Church.[21] Despite the overwhelming national support for a Reich Church under Müller, the synod of Meiser's Bavarian church continued its strong offensive on August 23 by unanimously rejecting a union with the Hitler-backed Reich Church.[22]

Hitler avoided association with the regional dispute, but his attention must have been drawn to the strength of the Bavarian Protestants opposing the Reich Church behind the "pulpit rallies." An order given "on instruction" of the Leader prohibited a pulpit rally Meiser had announced for August 24, 1934. This order was consistent with Hitler's function as arbiter of decisions about whether to use some form of coercion in the most delicately balanced contests for popular opinion. The Leader-backed ban was then issued against other pulpit rallies as well on grounds that they were "a direct attack on the cultural peace" and endangered the "public peace and security." Ten days later, the Reich Bishop's assistant, Jäger, followed up with an announcement that the Reich Church was assuming leadership over Meiser's and Wurm's churches.[23]

Official reports from the same weeks concerning church reactions to the ban on pulpit rallies would have drawn the Leader's attention for a further reason: as Bavarian Reich Governor (Reichsstatthalter) Franz Ritter von Epp stated to Interior Minister Wilhelm Frick, the struggle had escalated into a clear church-state confrontation, pitting party membership against church membership. Some churchgoers who "have counted and still count themselves among the most faithful followers of National Socialism" were offended by the ban. The state was alienating willing followers in what a Nazi report identified as a conflict between Reich Bishop Müller and Bavaria's Bishop Meiser.[24]

Even as state officials sounded the alarm about the "churching" of politics, Meiser struck back by saying his concerns were limited to the matters of the provincial church administration. He cleverly minimized what was at stake, refusing to agree with the official characterizations that the Nazi movement was endangered. Despite clear indications to the contrary, Meiser refused to cast his struggle as an opposition to Hitler and the myth backing him, but rather represented it as one the Leader would surely support. No doubt the great majority of Meiser's followers agreed, preferring to keep both Meiser and Hitler as their leaders. Also strategically important was the care Meiser and the Bavarian Protestants took to avoid provoking the police. The government officials interpreted this as a church decision to avoid any appearances of illegality that would undermine church authority—another tactic the Nazi Party had used.[25]

From September 4 to 10, the sixth annual Nazi Party Rally drew swarms of top party officials from across the Reich to the Bavarian city of Nuremberg, now also the scene of a continuous string of rallies for and against the Reich Church. Seizing the moment, Bishops Meiser and Wurm had begun a remarkably bold act of open civil disobedience on September 3. With overwhelming backing from his diocese, Meiser stated in the name of the Bavarian Church Council that "we do not recognize the validity" of August Jäger's order that the Bavarian and Württemberg churches were now under the leadership of the Reich Church. Bishop Wurm followed with a similar declaration. On September 7, Wurm grounded his stance in a poll of every pastor in his Württemberg diocese, showing that 82 percent supported independence over inclusion in the Reich Church.[26]

Facing opposition he was unable to dissuade, Müller impatiently turned to coercion. On September 8, 1934, acting on Müller's behalf, Jäger speciously accused Wurm of misusing church funds and removed him from all administrative duties. A propaganda offensive followed featuring these charges against Wurm. At the Party Rally, canonized by Leni Riefenstahl's *Triumph of the Will,* Hitler minced no words in calling for the collectivization of all provincial churches within a national church. The Leader also issued a continuing vote of confidence in Bishop Müller by posing for a photograph of himself shaking the Reich Bishop's hand.[27] Müller might have felt quite secure, although he was about to be reminded of the importance of popular mobilization in the Nazi model of leadership.

The following Sunday Bishop Wurm responded to Jäger's charges by encouraging the opposition it had stirred. "Everywhere, in many churches every day, confessional communities are collecting in ever growing numbers for evening services of intercession," he preached. One hundred thousand persons signed protests against the Reich Church action in just a few days before officials prohibited the further collection of signatures. Again resorting to decree, Müller on September 14 declared that Wurm was on a leave of absence, banning him from all further public utterances and placing him under house arrest for three days.[28]

Müller's disregard for the oppositional sentiment growing in Württemberg was met with increased signs of outright popular unrest under the banner of a "Wurm rebellion." Organized actions grew in size and proliferated in form, manifesting in rallies, petitions, collections, voluntary work, and ever more church services of intercession. Since masses of Germans disregarded the official bans on debates related to the church struggle and the church was able to communicate without press reports and leaflet distribution, the official bans were of limited value. At this point the Nazi officials turned to social mobilization as well, organizing social boycotts against Württemberg Protestants, a practice of shunning familiar to the region's Catholics at least since the Marpingen apparition pilgrimages decades earlier.[29] The notion that a Nazified people would succeed in expelling outsider elements simply through uniform ostracism was a Nazi ideal but still existed primarily in propaganda.

The German Christians, free to propagandize at will while their opponents were muzzled, enthused that "the battle for the Reich Church had now been won in Württemberg." This too was wishful thinking, despite indications that Hitler was backing Müller; in addition to Müller's photograph with the Leader at the Party Rally, a letter dated September 11 on behalf of Hitler and Reich Chancellor Hans Lammers ruled that Jäger's efforts to amalgamate the provincial churches were not illegal. Legality, however, was far from the heart of what mattered since it would not calm the protesting churchgoers. Asked by Müller whom he would suggest as a replacement for Bishop Meiser, Bavarian Minister President Ludwig Siebert cautioned that ousting Meiser would not be as easy as merely naming a successor.[30]

CRACKDOWN, POLICE FORCE, AND ESCALATED POPULAR DEFIANCE

As regional party leaders stepped up their public attacks on Meiser, the Protestants raised their opposition. On September 15 the *Fränkische Tagezeitung*, the daily newspaper of the Nazi Party leadership in Julius Streicher's Franconia Gau, published an article declaring of Meiser that "he is without honor," that he "commits treason," and that he had established a "Confessional Front." Meiser's refusal to confederate his Bavarian church with Müller's Reich Church, the article charged, constituted disloyalty to Hitler and the state. Copies of the article were immediately printed in the local newspaper and posted throughout the city in large numbers, particularly in the factories, shops, and other public places.[31]

This offensive, attributed to Streicher's deputy Karl Holz and the local community of the German Christians, initiated a new level of tension in the conflict, according to the provincial government's report. The Protestant loyalists attended meetings of protest and collected petitions, which they sent on to offices in Stuttgart, Munich, and Berlin. When a delegation of three pastors met with Holz shortly before midnight on September 15 to request that the anti-Meiser posters be removed, Holz made threats by claiming he had opinion on his side and that the people themselves might take action to harm or kill the outsider faction of Meiser supporters. "Very few parsons disagree," he claimed. "They will be strung up from the lanterns!"[32]

The events unfolded otherwise, however. Rather than masses rising up against Meiser's backers, the posters had been removed or blocked out by the following morning. In church services that Sunday, September 16, the Nuremberg pastorate read a declaration from the pulpit condemning the *Tagezeitung* article and explaining that "we stand in unshakeable trust behind" our bishop and "ask our communities to stand with us in the same loyalty for our church and provincial bishop." This opposition must have come as a shock to the Nazis of Nuremberg, who just a week earlier had witnessed the enthusiasm of seven hundred thousand Nazi stalwarts in town for the party rally. The battle continued the next day, as another article appeared on the front page of the newspaper proclaiming "Bishop Dr. Meiser Rebels!"[33]

That same day, September 17, Holz escalated his campaign from the papers to the largest square in Nuremberg, announcing that a "mass rally" would be held that evening on Adolf Hitler Platz. However, the police responded to his plans for a rally with alarm. Due to the "incredible agitation" within church circles, police authorities in the nearby city of Fürth consulted the Interior Ministry about measures for controlling the planned rally. The Interior officials, however, washed their hands of the matter, leaving it to the local police to consider whether they should ban the Nazi rally. In the end the police decided that a ban would be politically risky and that enforcing it, in the likely case that it was disregarded, would require more men than they had.[34]

Protestant solidarity, on the other hand, was boldly demonstrated through informal channels of church communication. Julius Schieder, the rector at the Nuremberg Protestant Seminary who used his position to direct counteractions, spread the news of Holz's planned mass demonstration. His students traveled through the city spreading word on foot and bicycle that "everyone is coming to the Main Square [now known as] Adolf Hitler Square" (many local authorities rushed to name important sites for the new Leader). Arriving on the square at 7:00 that evening, the parishioners were instructed by the police to leave (public assemblies not organized by the party had been banned since the earliest days of Hitler's rule). Consulting quickly, the clergy managed to direct the masses into three nearby church facilities so that they completely filled the cavernous St. Lorenz and St. Egidien Churches and the Heilig-Geist Hospital. Holz, who had taken the bully pulpit to lay out the state's case against Meiser, was left uneasy as those in attendance turned in droves to leave his rally as soon as they heard that Bishop Meiser was on his way to speak. Arriving promptly, Meiser addressed his faithful in one church after another. The bishop entreated calm in the face of what he now identified as "a new Luther period." As he left, the crowd saluted him with choruses of "Heil Meiser." Many lingered and were still present at 11:00. The police began efforts to clear the square but stood to attention as the people began singing the German national anthem, "Deutschland über alles." At this point, "the movement quickly took hold throughout Middle Franconia."[35]

The church had won the showdown with the party that day on the grounds of popular acclaim, as all could see. For the party, it could have been a disheartening reenactment of the myriad times it had stepped onto the streets in its early days to test its strength in numbers against the larger parties. Bishop Müller's response, however, was to redouble his threats. Giving a speech two days later in Hannover, he declared, "Whoever is not for me is against me. . . . Whoever cannot participate in the building of this church . . . should remain quiet or stand to the side. If he doesn't do this, then I will have to force him to." If the unrest did not stop, the state would stop it, he promised.[36]

Yet by September 20, there was evidence that social unrest had rippled across the country as far away as the Saarland, the essentially Catholic province on the French border that would soon vote (by provision of the Versailles Treaty) on whether to become part of Germany or of France. The Nazi leaders thought this vote had critical propaganda value, but here too, in substance as well as in tactics, Müller did not see the larger picture. When he publicly demanded "a Rome-free church" a Saarland paper retorted that Müller was declaring war on the German Catholics. Foreign Minister Neurath summoned Müller to his office, telling him that church politics dare not endanger German foreign relations in this way. Müller was characteristically dismissive, but Josef Bürckel, Palatinate Gauleiter and head of the German effort to win the Saarland plebiscite, was also alarmed. Hitler, however, held to the plans for a Reich Church and the ceremonial honoring of Müller in October.[37]

Efforts to suppress the grassroots movement fell flat, as Protestants continued to ignore the will of the regime. In response to a call from the

Protestant Church Council, a "great number of Protestant congregations from one end of the entire province to another" held worship services to alert all churchgoers about what was at stake in the struggle. Governor Epp continued the crackdown by banning further church demonstrations or reports on them in the Bavarian press.[38]

The first official compromise was not long in coming. When Meiser was denounced for maligning Gauleiter Julius Streicher, the regime slapped a ban on the bishop that prohibited him from keeping his scheduled appearances at two churches. Due to the threat of popular agitation, however, the officials decided to drop the allegations against Meiser and instead permitted him to speak to the throngs eagerly awaiting him. "The situation of the police," according to an official report, had become "precarious because of the great agitation and the holy zeal" of Meiser's supporters.[39] The police were greatly relieved and attributed the lack of violence at these meetings to the soothing words of Bishop Meiser.

The local police sometimes proved unwilling to take action against the churchgoers. In Schwabia, in the little village of Truchtelfingen, hundreds of parishioners gathered in front of the house of their pastor on a Monday evening to protest an official ban against a church meeting. The protest was organized to show solidarity with the pastor in full awareness that it was forbidden by current regional bans as well as by Reich law. When the Storm Troopers of Truchtelfingen refused to disband the crowd, officials called upon the SA and SS from the nearby town of Ebingen who were less likely to have family and community ties among the protesters. The pastor was then taken into protective custody and interrogated while a group of girls, who were also being detained, continued their protest by singing "Shall I Not Sing to My God?" A church deacon said that police and party officials preferred not to take further action because they had seen "with what elementary force loyalty to the church had been awakened and they were powerless against such things if they did not want the unrest to become universal."[40]

The Bavarian Protestants, like those in Württemberg, were experiencing an impassioned collective renewal. During the final days of September and early October 1934, numerous well-attended church services were held, sometimes three times in one day.[41] One witness in Nuremberg reported the following:

Enormous commotion going on in the town. . . . We only gave
out hand notices at twelve o'clock and in the evening sixteen
churches were full to bursting. . . . Similar favorable news is
coming in everywhere from the preaching trips which our
brethren are carrying out throughout the Franconia countryside.
Everywhere, often at the most inconvenient times, churches
are full. . . . The Gunzenhausen meeting was one single
exultant profession of faith in Meiser by thousands of Franconian peasants.[42]

The culmination of the struggle was close at hand. On October 6,
having lost the battle for opinion and faced with the refusals of Bishops
Meiser and Wurm to recognize his orders, Müller had Wurm put under
house arrest. Meanwhile, popular demonstrations of support for Bishop
Meiser pressed on. Proclaiming his allegiance to the Leader, attesting
to his followers' faith in the Leader and a belief that Nazism and the
church should be partners, Meiser and his entourage exchanged the
threefold "Heil Hitler!" bellow. At one stop Meiser addressed a crowd of
some three thousand on the subject of devotion to the church. Everyone
joined in singing the Lutheran standard, "A Mighty Fortress," which
was followed at once by the Nazi Party anthem. It might have passed for
a Nazi rally, except for the "Heil Meiser!" cry of the laity as their hero
took his leave.[43]

A day after Wurm's arrest, Gauleiter Hans Schemm of upper Bavaria
(Bayreuth) appeared before an assembly of the League of National Socialist Teachers (NSLB) to instruct the participants that bringing the
people into step with the Nazi dance could not be achieved overnight.
"Along the path that the National Socialist state will take, we consider the
two [Christian] denominations to be intermediate stages, not end stages.
We are on the way to God and cannot reject every position our forefa-
thers had as atheism!"[44]

Still there were Nazis who thought that the only learning aid necessary was brute force. Meeting in Munich at the "Brown House" headquarters of the Nazi movement on October 8, just two days after Wurm's
arrest, officials decided to arrest Meiser as well. The police were ordered
to suppress "the expected demonstrations" following the arrest. Jäger
met with Pfeffer von Salomon, a representative of Hitler's deputy Rudolf

Hess, who held the distinction of directing the Nazi Party's "Office of Religious Peace."[45]

Several days later, Jäger and several police agents forced their way into the offices of Meiser's Bavarian church to stop "the situation of mutiny and rebellion." The bishop was out, so they proceeded without him to pronounce an end to Meiser's term as bishop and the continuation of the Bavarian church as part of the Reich Church. Meiser responded in a sermon that evening by condemning the police for an "act of violence done to our church." Meiser decried police force deployed against the collective, popular will, in the style of leadership heeded by elite Nazi officials. Meiser declared himself "unwilling to give up the office of bishop granted by the church." In the name of "obedience to steadfastness" and "loyalty and allegiance," Meiser called deacons, pastors, and members of the church to collective civil disobedience. "Our Protestant church would cease to be Protestant, nor could it be named after Luther, if we were now in this situation to give in to this violence."[46]

Upon departing, Meiser, the hero who again and again was able to attract bigger crowds than any regional Nazi leaders, was greeted by throngs, "as far as the eye could see," who accompanied him home so enthusiastically that his car could wend its way only intermittently. Again, songs of the Fatherland mingled seamlessly with church hymns and cries of "We want Meiser!" The deacon for the city of Munich stated that he and all the pastors would follow Meiser "come what may!"[47] Upon refusing to sign a notice relieving him of his position, Meiser, like Wurm, was put under house arrest.

THE "CONFESSIONAL FRONT" REPUDIATES
THE ARREST OF ITS BISHOPS

When Meiser was arrested, the church communication office was closed, and its director was arrested. In its place, improvised underground channels of communications snapped into operation. An eyewitness to Meiser's arrest dictated a report and had it distributed in hand-addressed envelopes. Under arrest and upon reflection, Meiser reiterated that the state's use of violence undermined its legitimacy even as it stiffened his resolve. "What has happened to me and our church in these last days will not weaken my spirit but on the contrary it convinces me even more of the necessity of our struggle," he stated. "A capitulation under a regime of violence is not an option for me, even if I am held captive week after week." Throughout Bavaria it was above all the measures of violence and the handling of the Bishop that caused the greatest agitation and also rallied the greatest readiness for demonstrations of sacrifice and loyalty.[48]

Again, numerous Germans drew strength from imagining that the Leader was on their side. The government reports suspected, however, that some were ready for a more general condemnation of the regime itself. Again Dippold's office warned that "it is dangerous for the Protestant Church controversy to continue." Again the Bavarian political police resorted to prohibitions, issuing another "muzzling decree" suppressing church publications and a separate order banning the gathering of protesters, the distribution of pamphlets, and the symbolic ringing of church bells. Nevertheless, the protests did not stop, and the leaflets continued to be disseminated. Thousands signed petitions, and delegations of churchgoers—some fully committed to Hitler's rule—brought their protests to the regional authorities.[49]

The provincial authorities now frankly admitted that the measures of repression had not only failed, but they had also fanned the flames of more insistent resistance: "During the entire month of October the Protestant Church controversy dominated awareness in a way that made other events recede in comparison. . . . An extraordinary turbulence broke out among the population." Responding to an official denial of Bishop Meiser's request to attend a service on October 14, parishes held church services in front of the homes of both Bishops Wurm and Meiser. Delegations of children appeared at Meiser's home to bring him greetings. In parishes on that October day, hundreds of pastors across Bavaria read a declaration of protest by Meiser, appealing to Hitler: "We complain before God and the Community, we complain before the people and the state, we complain before the Leader of the Reich about the breach of trust and faith."[50] The churchgoers decided that until their bishop was released, the church meetings would be services of mourning. With press reports banned, the church members continued to improvise channels of communication, including an extensive distribution of flyers and announcements from the pulpit, actions that Nazi officials identified as "effective"; the government ban on official communications was counterproductive.

From his office in Ansbach, twenty kilometers west of Nuremberg, Dippold noted with consternation that the churches appeared to be girding for an even bigger struggle: "In Nuremberg, the Protestant clergy fortified itself through the gratification of evening meals taken in common, as if it were the outset of war!" Grassroots support for the cause was so widespread that each parish could be expected to organize its own petition drive protesting the arrest of their bishop, forwarded to Governor Epp and Bavarian minister president Siebert. Those in league with the church were overwhelming against the united efforts of the German Christians and the Nazi Party, and "some 95 percent of the protestant clergy" supported Meiser.[51] In direct contrast to Müller's intentions, his tactics had caused thousands to sign a petition not for the German Christians but for the establishment of another branch of the "Confessing Church" in Bavaria.

At the same time, the church leaders avoided statements of opposition to the regime itself. The entire theology faculty of the University of Erlangen, for example, wrote a letter of protest to Governor Epp, noting a common "wish to serve the German people and its Leader with the full gifts of the gospel!" But as Siebert and Epp reported, such collective noncompliance was essentially political within a regime based on a movement adhering to the beat of a single drummer, and it would have to be obliterated sooner or later. On October 15, hundreds of party members in possession of the Nazi Golden Party Badge (the party's highest decoration) assembled in Munich to rally against party interference in church affairs. Also on October 15, Gauleiter Schemm took his turn in urging the Protestants to stop protesting since, as he reasoned, there was no theological issue at stake. "The struggle being carried out today in Germany inside the Protestant Churches is that which brings unrest and times without peace. . . . Where and when, however, in National Socialist Germany has the confession been in danger? Not one pastor has been asked to preach in a way that changes the confession." The Gauleiter's tone grew more sarcastic as he claimed that some of the protesters "haven't been to church for years. For them this has nothing to do with the confession, but to the contrary, here they can express their opposition to National Socialism behind a mask." Indicating that church opposition was taking on political tones, a statement began to make its rounds that anyone in the

SA was a Bolshevik. An official communiqué found proof of the mistrust of government in the decline of contributions to the Winter Relief Fund and concluded that indeed "for some the church struggle will have also only been an excuse to hide their willingness to sacrifice."[52] The peer pressure among the people in support of the government was faltering.

In a different report to Minister Frick of October 15, Siebert repeated this alarm. Meiser's arrest was undermining support even within party offices; as Siebert had feared, the conflict was now openly passing from the parameters of a church affair into politics. His office was flooded with "mountains of telegrams" and "entreaties of every sort." Old party members, district party authorities, pastors who had long contributed heart and soul, together with supporters who had fought on the front during World War I, were now signaling that the struggle was having—or was about to have—serious consequences for the party. From Franconia a district leader wrote that his work now was almost entirely taken up with efforts to convince farmers not to leave the party.[53]

Christian commitment inspired a willingness to sacrifice everything, whether at the level of the laity or leaders, among the farmers as well as among the intellectuals. In Nuremberg Rector Schieder boldly refused orders to leave his position and turn over the keys. More than one thousand pastors signed a declaration of loyalty to Meiser. "The best of our congregations expect the courage of confession from us," the pastors stated. "Imprisonment is better than silence. We will refuse to obey the *new* Church regimen in every way."[54]

The departure of thousands of newly inspired individuals from the church services in the center of Nuremberg on October 16, a Tuesday evening, proved to be a turning point. As the services concluded, row upon row of impassioned faithful left the churches singing as they made their way to the main square. The spontaneous solidarity was so striking that the officials suspected that the clergy had organized the masses. A police investigation, however, concluded that the lines of thousands of people singing and heading to the square resulted from nothing more sinister than "departure from church." This was dismal news for those hoping to stop the trouble by finding someone organizing or inciting the crowds.

STREICHER CONCEDES TO A TRUCE TO PRESERVE HIS REPUTATION

Gauleiter Streicher at first complained that the police should have "locked up the entire church community" as it clogged Nuremberg's Hitler Square. But on the evening of October 17, he had decided that compromise was more sound strategically. At a meeting with the entire local pastorate, Streicher declared that he had neither written nor approved of the attacks Holz had published. When the pastors demanded that Streicher take their complaints directly to the Leader, Streicher was said to have answered in avuncular tones that the party would call off its attacks if the church did the same. "I understand that the church is infuriated, when its Bishop is arrested. I will throw everyone out of the Party who says anything against the church . . . stop the attacks on leaders of the Church from the [Party] organization."[55]

Concerned about his reputation and sensing the police were reluctant to interfere against the passionate crowds, the radical Nazi Julius Streicher called a truce, signaling a profound change in official tactics. District authorities warned Streicher that "so much doubt about the state and National Socialism has been conveyed to the population through the church dispute that, as local mayors have credibly assured me, *an election or plebiscite at the present time would show an absolutely devastating result!*" One pastor, long committed to the "movement," seemed to reaffirm the party's fear, musing that half of those among his flock who had just voted "Yes" in the recent national plebiscite, which confirmed Hitler as head of state, would leave the party as well as the church if Meiser were not reinstated.[56]

Yet the church authorities were eager to call off the struggle in exchange for the independence Streicher seemed to offer. Rector Schieder quickly seized upon Streicher's call for a truce, writing at once to the clergy of Franconia and requesting that in light of Streicher's promise, all cases of party interference in matters of religion or church politics should now be carefully documented and reported to Streicher's regional office. In turn, there were to be no more comments from the pulpit about Streicher. Schieder's quick action pushed Streicher to confirm or deny his proclamation, and two days later, on October 19, Streicher made his comments official with a public order stating that the disputes within the Protestant Church "have nothing to do with the NSDAP" and that the interventions by party offices in church affairs would be subject to the strongest penalties.[57] Further concessions followed: Streicher expanded freedom of expression for the church members who were also party members, declaring that they had the right to express their opinions on the church controversy outside of party activities.

The official turn to concessions now had momentum. On October 20, Siebert wrote again to Frick to say that the arrest of the bishops had only caused the crisis to continue to intensify. Some 95 percent of Franconian farmers supported their bishop, and the state absolutely had to gain control over the crowds if he were to "hold the farmers back from a rebellion." One delegation from Franconia had just made "the impression of religious fanatics," willing to "be stamped as martyrs." Epp as well as Siebert had received hundreds of declarations promising "united resistance to the last extreme." To head off "the most severe inner unrest," an immediate intervention *by the Leader* was needed, Siebert concluded. Epp, like Siebert, also opposed the further use of police force because it would set the party back.[58]

Notably, the officials were now referring to the church opposition in battle terms as "the confessional front." Dippold stressed the political significance in the fact that Germans were becoming more willing to express dissent *publicly:* "The vast majority of the Protestant population demonstrated that it stood behind provincial bishop Dr. Meiser and the confessional front not only in private but also was ready to represent their position publicly." As the "confessional front" grew, it threatened the Nazis' own mystique of exclusivity that lent them attractive force, although faith in Hitler continued. There was a widespread belief that if only Hitler knew the real facts, he would side with the bishops, and many pleaded with Foreign Minister Neurath to let the Leader know the truth.[59]

Bishop Meiser, who was kept under arrest in the hope that he would finally agree to his expulsion, instead sent an appeal to Hitler as "the highest guardian of the laws." Hitler did not answer, but Meiser's point of appealing to the Leader rather than opposing him was made clear again. The imperious Reich Bishop Müller, on the other hand, thumbed his nose at compromise and escalated the confrontation. He sent a "bishop," whom he had appointed in place of Wurm and Meiser, to take charge of a regular Sunday church service being held by a Pastor Schick. The new bishop arrived at the church bringing a small congregation of his own.

During singing he took the pulpit and declared, "I am holding the service here. I send pastor Schick to the vestry." Schick, backed by his congregation, ignored the new "bishop" until the imposter departed and held his service outside.[60]

The German people, in many cases uneducated peasants, proved capable of rejecting official propaganda. News reports claiming that the deposing of Meiser in exchange for a new church order had been " 'eagerly received by the broad masses of the population' had an effect opposite of what was intended, because they were obviously incorrect."[61] As popular response undermined Müller's authority, his position became increasingly insecure.

Nevertheless, belief in the Leader again proved impervious to the ire of the people, who cast the blame for offenses against their church on local and regional leaders. Hitler was for many a protector of all they held dear, while the regional authorities were openly condemned as unfit for office.[62] Some wanted their Leader to be informed at once so that they could continue with their usual practices, as he would certainly want. This call of the people for the aid of their Leader—whom hitherto they had viewed as so busy he did not yet know about their regional tormentors—transformed the struggle into a matter of national and not just regional concern. The practice of attributing the offensive policies to lower officials while imagining that the Leader would restore justice if only he could be informed is well demonstrated in the church struggle. It allowed the Germans to continue to believe in Hitler in other contexts as well.

The radicalized measures of Müller and his agents "awakened all sides of the Bavarian church to energetic action." Farmers increasingly took "matters into their own hands" without fear of consequences. Epp was reportedly moved to sniffles as a delegation of farmers confessed loyalty to National Socialism but added forcefully that they were ready to lay down their party membership if the struggle against their bishop continued. One farmer echoed Nazi avowals of the Fatherland and soil but tied it to his church: although his family had been on the same farm for twelve generations, if the church were taken, "our home and fatherland would be of no more value." Two days later another delegation of eight hundred Nurembergers took their protest to government offices in Munich to press for the release of Meiser.[63]

Nuremberg, the recent host of the party's annual glorification of Hitler, was now the "focus" of what district authorities referred to as "resistance," the "resistance [Widerstand] of the confessional front," which threatened to sap the Nazi movement. News of the struggle had spread not only through Germany but into the foreign press as well. Gauleiter Schemm, who had already asserted that the state had not impinged on religious services, now assured the people assembled in two public meetings, each filled to overflowing, that the Protestant Church would not be disturbed. Along with Gauleiter Streicher's truce, Schemm's public reassurances were among the few state measures that offset the struggle, according to regional authorities.[64]

HITLER COMPROMISES TO BRING THE PEOPLE BACK IN STEP

In Berlin, Hitler's deputy Rudolf Hess agreed with regional officials that *only* the Leader himself could make the decision to retract the bishops' arrest, a step that would dissolve the struggle. Hitler was the final arbiter on such delicate matters of coercion and consent, a role he would continue to play as long as his central authority held, and it was becoming apparent that he could hardly continue to remain aloof from the southern Protestant struggle. On October 16 Foreign Minister Neurath, who had been trying in vain to get Hitler to oust Müller for most of a year, met with Hitler. But despite Neurath's telling him that the church struggle was only making foreign relations more difficult and "endangering the execution of our rearmament policies," the Leader remained committed to his plans, including honoring Müller on October 23.[65]

The first sign of hesitation from the Leader came on October 19 as he ordered the celebration of Bishop Müller postponed for two days.[66] On October 22, Hitler met with Gauleiter Josef Bürckel, who already one month earlier had attempted to convey to the Leader the destructiveness of Müller's tactics for the upcoming plebiscite in the Saarland.[67] Also on October 22, Epp and Siebert in Bavaria tried continuously to reach Rudolf Hess in order to gain permission to have Bishop Meiser released, to appease the crowds. Although Hess refused to act without Hitler's directive, he promised to meet with Hitler the following day to discuss Epp's and Siebert's concerns.[68]

On October 23 Hitler held another meeting to discuss how to deal with the Reich Bishop. Goebbels, who was present at this meeting, opined that he was for dropping Müller and that the Leader was "also nearly there." Hitler finally took some concrete action the next day by canceling the ceremony to honor Bishop Müller. Two days later, as Epp and Siebert had requested, Meiser and Wurm were freed. Attempting to exercise power before he was recognized as an authority by those he pretended to rule, Müller had failed. Jäger resigned, and Müller remained Reich Bishop in name only. Rather than honoring Müller, Hitler met with Meiser and Wurm on October 30, recognizing them in their official capacity as bishops.[69] Four months earlier Hitler had shown during the Night of the Long Knives how readily he, as the Leader, could violate law in the most egregious way while still shoring up popular and government backing. Now it made sense to compromise to reach the same goals, by cutting loose his Reich Bishop, Ludwig Müller, in order to side with the Protestant bishops. Like the Night of the Long Knives, this compromise with the Protestants also served to protect Hitler's prestige and the party's forward momentum.

Hitler's reincorporation of Meiser and Wurm was a sharp reversal of his condemnation of these bishops, just a few months earlier, as "traitors to the people, enemies of the Fatherland, and the destroyers of Germany." The quest for a Reich Church did continue through a newly created Ministry of Church Affairs, which Hitler entrusted in mid-1935 to Hanns Kerrl, the Prussian minister of justice and close associate of Hermann Göring. Kerrl was supposed to convince church leaders that German Protestantism was compatible with National Socialism and should be placed under a single bishop reporting to Hitler. Hitler delivered only a faint hint of force in early 1936, saying that there was a Teutonic precedent for overcoming German tribalism by force and that force might again be used, if necessary, "to unite this stubborn German people."[70] That same month, however, Lothar Kreyssig, a Brandenburg state judge and leader of the Confessing Church, was not prosecuted for his public dissent (and eventually Hitler pardoned him despite the contrary wishes of the judiciary and Gestapo).[71]

By February 1937 it was evident that Kerrl too would fail to unite the Protestant Church under a Reich Bishop. Dealing with the churches was a delicate matter, illustrated by Hitler's decree in June 1937 that even his highest, most trusted lieutenants were forbidden to take measures against the clergy without first receiving explicit permission from him.[72]

Anyone who did so in a way that might harm the image of the party or the state without the Leader's express authorization would be "publicly disavowed" by the Leader. Hess then sent a memo on June 30 to the Gauleiters and Reich officials echoing Hitler's dictum: "Measures regarding church matters may be undertaken only according to orders of the Leader. This is in concord with an earlier directive of my own. . . . In the future, anyone who takes action in the area of the church . . . that would harm the prestige of the party and state, must expect to be publicly disavowed [desavouiert] by the Leader."[73] This order was important enough to merit its issuance from Himmler's office as well. The threat of a public disavowal by the Leader was sufficient to keep these powerful men in line.

Also in June 1937, Hitler authorized the arrest of a number of Confessing Church leaders, including Martin Niemöller, who alerted the faithful that the Nazi efforts to establish a national Reich Church were only salvos in a battle to do away completely with both Christian churches and Christianity itself. Angry that Niemöller "once again had delivered a rebellious sermon," Hitler ordered Niemöller's arrest following his sermon on June 27, 1937. This move made an impression at the time among church authorities that the "Nazi rulers hesitated for a long period before venturing to arrest Pastor Niemöller." According to Hitler's close associate Albert Speer, Hitler ordered the pastor imprisoned for life "since he had proved himself incorrigible." Hitler had given up hope that the Confessing Church leader might blunt his criticism of the regime, and of course he did not have a following as large as that of a bishop, whose protests might protect him, nor did he mobilize his followers publicly as Meiser and Wurm had done.[74]

Bishop Meiser in particular had proven himself a master at mobilizing the masses in the style Hitler had entrusted to the Gauleiters. After the failure of his Reich Church endeavor, Hitler continued the exacting process of winning church support by turning church leaders to his cause, or at least neutralizing them for the moment. Now regional leaders fought inch by inch together with Nazi proselytizers like Pastor Karl Steger, who preached that Hitler was sent by God to save Germany. Popular reluctance to surrender church practices was pitted against the appeal of Hitler's grand national accomplishments, which the Germans by 1938 would compare favorably with those of Napoleon.[75] Like so many

others, Meiser was enthusiastic about the defeat of German communism and the great expansion of German nationalism.[76] Although he
had demonstrated how well he understood the dynamics of Nazi power
and his own capacity to use them, Meiser did not join with fellow Protestant bishops to challenge the regime's assaults on church influence or
its so-called "Euthanasia Program," nor did he question the persecution
of the Jews. In fact, he never played a hand against Hitler again, publicly
backing the Leader's foreign policy and the war. Bishop Wurm did raise
objections occasionally during the following decade, especially regarding Nazism's "euthanasia," although he, like Meiser and the other bishops, generally expressed support for rather than opposition to the regime.

During the struggle to create a Reich Church in 1933 and 1934, Hitler
first encountered what would become a persistent pattern: Germans
were determined to maintain certain private spheres, holding on to traditions that were important to them. Hitler had finally tamed the SA
with one night of extreme violence, but he was not willing to govern by
overwhelming force in the face of protests backed by widely held traditions. He wanted first of all to avoid any display of unrest and disunity,
but he also wanted to reshape the Germans into a national community
strong enough to dominate all challengers. How could he persuade the
people to move in step with his leadership and without hesitation when
they were guided by contrary habits? One key was to encourage the popular belief that he always made things right as soon as he knew the
people were troubled. Hitler recognized that the party's trajectory would
at times have to bend to collective habits of the heart. Thus in October
1934, at the end of the pitched battle for popular allegiance among southern Protestants, he abandoned his Reich Bishop designee, whose power
was not grounded in popular acclaim, siding instead with the popular
heroes, Meiser and Wurm.

In the coming years the Nazi regime would make headway in under-
cutting church authority and practices, but would it remain on schedule
with Hitler's vision? Hitler and his party had taken power in a burst of
accelerating popular acclaim. But the dictatorship's early failure to
achieve the Reich Church flagged obstacles submerged in the people's
attachment to what they considered to be their independent religious
sphere. Such obstacles signaled an urgent need to convince the people
that the new Nazi ideology was better for them and Germany than

church traditions. So far, the party had won the acclaim of Catholics and Protestants by disguising its real aim of erasing church influence from the Reich. Now it would begin a concerted battle, waged in daily life across thousands of Germany's farming hamlets and cities, with a focus on the youth. From one corner of the Reich to another, Germany's Protestant and Catholic schools reflected the grip of the churches on popular culture, in a structure of public education that included church schools. Even the Socialist-led Weimar Republic had not made much progress in secularizing all of Germany's schools. These schools taught some allegiances and principles directly at cross purposes with Nazi attitudes and internalized what the Nazis saw as a venal division of the people. With Protestants generally more willing to change their schools to the new Nazi "community schools," the Gauleiters set to work to prod, deceive, and cajole Catholic leaders and families into letting go of their church-operated schools, if only one step at a time. Would the dictatorship meet less popular resistance in changing Germany's religious schools into Nazi "community schools" than it had found in constructing a Reich Church?

CHAPTER THREE

Germany's Confessional Divide and the Struggle for Catholic Youth

"WE DON'T NEED to always be telling the children: 'You are Catholic and you are Protestant,'" said Julius Streicher, the notorious publisher of *Der Stürmer* in 1933 as the Nazis took power. "Rather we must tell children, 'You are German.'" Like other Nazis, he viewed Germany's confessional schools as dividing the people and thus blocking the Nazi national community, or Volksgemeinschaft. But convincing German children that they were neither Protestant nor Catholic posed a monumental challenge, and as Hitler's deputy Rudolf Hess cautioned, it could not be accomplished in the face of general opposition. "In the long run the Church question is a question of the young people," Hess opined. "The less the parents' opposition is aroused on Church matters, the less they will inculcate in their children an opposition to the teachings of the Hitler Youth."[1] The school system could hardly be changed faster than the people themselves, Hess said. Nazism might have to wait for the passing of the older generations steeped in Christian education since childhood, while it invested hope in shaping the current generation of youth from its inception.

When the Nazis took power, the German education system was a patchwork of state and religious schools. The state still permitted both Protestants and Catholics to operate schools that met the requirements for public education. The Socialist-led Weimar Republic had not been able to rid Germany of these religious schools but had standardized training for teachers throughout Germany—with the notable exceptions of the strongly religious provinces of Württemberg and Bavaria along Germany's southern border.[2] Working toward the goal of doing away with church-operated schools, the dictatorship was forced into a series of compromises that undermined religious practices. It was slowly pressuring church influences out of German schools when Hitler ordered a stop to all unnecessary provocations of the churches in early September 1939, to maximize Germany's strength for fighting war.

The front line of the school struggle was in Catholic territories. German Protestants, especially in rural northern Germany, had provided earlier and stronger support for Nazism than German Catholics, and toward the Protestant Church, the historian Martin Broszat wrote, the "regime felt obliged to an astonishing degree to behave within acceptable limits."[3] But the solicitous Nazi approach was effective for sustaining Protestant allegiance even as the dictatorship eroded the Protestant collective identity. (This was especially visible in provinces like East Prussia, where solidarity in neighboring Catholic communities remained largely intact.) Some Protestants shared the Nazi goal of defeating "political Catholicism"—Catholic influences on public life. Catholic schools were not really German schools, teaching church holiness rather than national heroism and a Catholic rather than a Germanic "race." They instilled a pacifist character and promoted the church over the Fatherland.[4]

While some Nazi moguls like Alfred Rosenberg wanted to combat the churches with raw force at every turn, those who best understood Hitler's special relationship to the people used a range of tactics to persuade churchgoers to join the party. For the many who thought that their Christianity and Nazism were compatible, Nazi practices were to be introduced deftly and within an atmosphere pervaded by a sense of acclaim for the state so that even the people who were uncertain about following the new Nazi leadership would hardly notice that the carpet had been tugged away and replaced. The Protestant-Catholic divide within the Reich was considered so important that the Gauleiters generally came from the same denomination as the dominant one in their Gaus, or regions.[5]

GAULEITER LEADERSHIP AND THE SCHOOL STRUGGLE

Each Gauleiter was charged with directing the progress of the Nazi movement in his own cultural enclave, with its peculiar ways of being German. Hitler considered it "very satisfactory" that in each of the separate regions a "Gauleiter can lead the people forward step by step in the sense that we desire, according to the degree of emancipation acquired by the population of his Gau." Each of the several dozen Gauleiters (a group that expanded to more than forty during the war) selected methods to move his regional people toward unreserved belief in Nazism as quickly as possible. Each had the same general goals, set by ideology, but developed differing tactics and exercised tactical leeway in order to achieve compliance.[6] This Gauleiter prerogative illustrates the regime's preference for opportunistic improvisation over inflexible timetables and methods determined outside of specific circumstances.[7]

If Hitler had simply instituted the policies that matched Nazi ideology and then stood by to let the Gestapo clobber every sign of opposition, the role of the Gauleiters would have been considerably easier. As it was, the Gauleiters were charged with achieving some seismic changes in social attitudes *while avoiding conflicts with large segments of the people.* In contrast to Hitler's pattern of allowing competing chieftains in charge of the Jewish persecution to radicalize their methods, Hitler actually intervened to temper the methods of Gauleiters who were urgently attempting to relocate civilians from cities targeted by Allied bombing raids. The work of the Gauleiters was more complicated than that of the executors of the persecution because they were Hitler's regional agents for transforming Germans into Nazis, and preempting all signs of public unrest and social divisions among the people was a standard of their success.

Still, the competition among Gauleiters to be the first to reach the Leader's goals was fierce, just as it was among the executors of the Jewish persecution. These Gauleiters typically vied with one another to make their region the "model Gau," hoping to lead the way in achieving a goal shared by all of them. Hitler intervened in regional governance only when "basic decisions were at stake," as he told one Gauleiter in 1931. Gauleiter independence also supported Hitler's desire to appear disassociated from the domestic conflicts, especially one as visible as the church struggle. In turn, the success of Gauleiters in secularizing schools often depended on communities, parents, and teachers, who sometimes were called upon to use their own resources to meet party requirements. While the Gauleiters could resort to fines or police arrests, a favored Gauleiter tactic for eliminating church schools was the use of trumped-up plebiscites, claiming that a big majority favored the elimination of church-operated schools. In annexed territories, kindergarten teachers instructed children on how to behave at home and made home visits "to get the parents to the point that we are educating the children on a common basis."[8]

The Gauleiters experimented with a range of tactics to meet these competing challenges of maintaining quiescence while transforming religious schools into the new Nazi "community schools." This is illustrated in Bavaria, Germany's second largest province with a large Catholic majority. Gauleiters Adolf Wagner, Hans Schemm, and Julius Streicher were all Bavarian Gauleiters ruling regions of two million or more. Like all the most powerful Gauleiters, each of these men had portfolios beyond those of the typical Gauleiter: Wagner was the Gauleiter in Munich but also the interior minister of Bavaria; Schemm was the Gauleiter in Bayreuth and also the Bavarian minister of culture; Streicher ruled his Gau from Nuremberg and was also publisher of the crass *Der Stürmer*. They shared Nazi goals, but Schemm on occasion was more prone to begin by making an alliance with church leaders, the better to demonstrate the goods National Socialism had to offer.

Schemm's early tactics reveal the beginning of a trajectory for achieving Hitler's plan of winning the people continuously but gradually, making liberal use of deception and the incentives of party favors and the appearance of fitting in with new social norms. He also targeted Socialist and Communist leaders. On March 9, 1933, Schemm threw a rally in celebration of his party's new power in his home city of Bayreuth. He concluded the festivities by personally arresting dozens of leaders of the Communist and Socialist parties. This was good news for rival parties and the passionate anti-Left prevalent throughout the Reich. But Schemm also stifled Catholic Center Party leaders that he accused of mixing in matters of politics, procuring their agreement not to speak out, while ingratiating himself with Catholic leaders. Having stifled the leadership of his opponents, Schemm generally emphasized the aspirations he shared with his region. Nazism was the path toward goals on which everyone could agree, he emphasized, and attributed to Hitler his common refrain that "only the pure race can comprehend Christianity deep down."[9]

After also intimidating the Catholic political leaders in his region, Schemm encouraged the church to turn to him for assistance. In May 1933, when the SA imprisoned two priests, the Catholic bishops made an appeal to him, and Schemm had them released.[10] Launching his leadership of the Bavarian Cultural Ministry on March 28, 1933, Schemm issued a program that offered to "extend a hand in the Christian sense to both confessions for the common cultural work of building anew, in the service of all, for God and people, and thus in the struggle against the God- and people-destroying Marxism and Bolshevism." The Vatican's newspaper *Osservatore Romano* printed this program without commentary on the front page, as a sign of official "good-willed respect." In turn, when Schemm appealed to the conference of German Catholic bishops, they rescinded their earlier "general ban and warning" against National Socialism, urging loyalty to the new government instead.[11]

Schemm proposed that the Nazi struggle for control of the schools should be carried out at the deeper level of popular attitudes.[12] His plan was to leave the structure of the Catholic schools in place while introducing uniform training for teachers and a new Nazi curriculum. In his region's schools, Schemm worked to bring teachers in line initially, rather than firing them.[13] He allowed the Catholic Teachers League to continue, but its attraction dwindled, as he planned, with the increasing dominance of the Nazis. Even those teachers who had been members of the Socialist Party in Schemm's region were invited to keep their positions so long as they did not oppose the new regime.[14] In contrast, under the hard-line Gauleiter of the Hamburg region, each teacher was expected "at any time and place to prove himself a National Socialist in his entire behavior and self-expression," by the 1934–1935 school year.[15] Some Catholic teachers did hold out, although officials wrote this off to opportunism: the "passive majority is not so much against but also not so much in favor of National Socialism. Instead they are still waiting hour by hour to see who will gain a secure hold on power."[16] With the NSLB steadily gaining ground, a report from Alfred Meyer's Gau, dated October 30, 1936, recommended that the holdouts be treated with "education" rather than with punishment.[17]

Although the dictatorship cut off organized public criticisms and opposition with terror, it bristled with incentives that drew the people forward into the service of Hitler. Schools with at least 90 percent of their students enrolled in the Hitler Youth received an award. In this way, the regime rewarded those who formed an overwhelming majority, which then ostracized and bullied the remaining fraction, making it vulnerable to police actions that the vast majority would welcome. The schools with less than 90 percent stood out, and the pressure on the students to join the Hitler Youth was intense.[18]

Schemm died in March 1935, when upon lifting off, a sudden gust of wind tossed his airplane into a building. He might have initially taken exception to the harsher tactics of his neighbor Gauleiter, Adolf Wagner, whose methods pushed Catholic resistance to the surface. By the end of 1935, Wagner and other Gauleiters used plebiscites to back their secularizing policies. Plebiscites were an established practice for school decision making, and ostensibly they continued the tradition of giving parents jurisdiction over local school matters, although of course the regime manipulated the results.[19] Wagner, who was also the new director of Bavaria's Cultural Ministry, decreed that religious schools become secular, "community" schools and then launched a series of plebiscites showing popular approval. In Munich, official tallies claimed the number of persons voting for community schools had risen from 15.7 percent in 1934 to more than 90 percent in 1937. Such a trajectory, noted the London-based League for the Defense of Christianity, "will doubtless lead other Gauleiters to fall over themselves to be able to announce to the Leader similar or even more brilliant results." In an area of north Rhineland, the party organized displays of mass support for closing the denominational schools, followed by plebiscites. Wearing uniforms, proponents of the community schools went door to door in each neighborhood seeking signatures of support by speaking of love for the Fatherland and people's togetherness.[20]

Working with Western secularizing trends, the regime could count on the support of the many Germans who were in fact eager to dispose of the authority church leaders exercised and their presence in the schools. Given Nazi pressures and incentives, it was clear by the spring of 1937 that even in deeply Catholic Lower Bavaria, those opposing the secular trend would be outnumbered. By July 1937, when Vicar General Dr. Franz Riemer called for prelates and parents to stand up in solidarity for the continuation of confessional schools, church protest was muted. When protests did arise, however, Wagner was astute enough to order an immediate halt to pressures, as he did in December 1937, only to resume repression after protests died down. Like other Nazi leaders, he worked to isolate and then expose opponents. His decision to lift a coercive police measure banning the reading of a pastoral letter, and instead to appeal to Bishop Ludwig Sebastian of Speyer to voluntarily surrender the letter, was effective, for it revealed rifts within the church leadership between those who sided with the regime and those who did not.[21]

However, individual church parishes kept some church schools alive by insisting on tradition and announcing that their own plebiscites showed contrary results. Given the counteractions of the churches in mobilizing opinion and publicizing their own results, Security Police director Reinhard Heydrich gave instructions on May 27, 1937, that all plebiscites on the school question were to cease since they were causing unrest. As of April 1938, Gauleiters too were banned from sponsoring plebiscites, and a year after that, Bormann ordered that the denominational schools be formally redesignated as community schools.[22]

THE CRUCIFIX DECREE STRUGGLES

Catholic opposition and its fate, before the war, was illustrated in the struggles at various points in the Reich, including in newly annexed Austria, where anger culminated in public protests in August 1939. Spontaneous opposition flared up in response to decrees removing crucifixes and replacing them with Hitler's portrait. There were few subtle ways to remove the dominant icon of Catholic faith, but Gauleiters tried—by first moving the crucifixes to various new places on the wall or by using only portraits of Hitler that pictured him cozying up with children.[23]

Pervasive conflict over the display of crucifixes in the provinces of Oldenburg (which included the city of Oldenburg) and East Prussia exemplifies the struggle for the allegiance of Catholic youth. The Catholic bishops for Oldenburg and East Prussia, like their Protestant counterparts in the 1934 southern German struggle, demonstrated the value of mobilizing the laity to defend its church practices, even though there was a general opposition to such tactics by the bishops of both denominations. Parents, backed by their church leaders, proved sufficiently resistant to replacing crucifixes with Hitler's picture to stymie the complete success of the dictatorship's campaign to eliminate religious influence in schools, at least into 1938, the year before war caused Hitler to downgrade efforts to push the churches aside in favor of popular unity.[24]

Clemens August von Galen was the bishop for Oldenburg's Catholics, and the city of Münster was the seat of his diocese. Münster was also the capital city of Gauleiter Alfred Meyer's region in north-central Germany. The Münster region was hardly big enough for both Meyer and Galen, and because of Galen, it soon proved to be the Gauleiter's most challenging terrain. Galen's diocese was a center of "political Catholicism," with church influence extending beyond church walls and rituals.[25]

When Meyer arranged for his close associate and ally, Alfred Rosenberg, to visit Münster, Galen encouraged the laity to show its disapproval. Galen had welcomed Hitler, but he denounced Rosenberg as an advocate of "neo-heathenism" and wrote in protest to Gauleiter Meyer about Rosenberg's scheduled appearance. Rosenberg appeared nevertheless on July 7, 1935, and gave a public address in Münster's main square, near Galen's residence. After a big party rally following the speech, Hitler Youth marched up and down in front of Galen's residence chanting insults. The following day, in a counterdemonstration, nineteen thousand joined the annual Catholic procession for the Corpus Christi feast. The procession had attracted only about seven thousand in previous years.[26]

In the days and weeks following Rosenberg's speech, police reports revealed a wide discrepancy between the Catholic response and the claims made in Gauleiter Meyer's press that "Münster Shouts Approval for Rosenberg." The government reports of April 1935 observed that "wide segments of the population" disagreed with the "behavior of the state in the 'church question' and overtly express their dissatisfaction." The Catholics in general decidedly disagreed with "the state and the movement on religious questions."[27]

Meyer's response showed he was well aware that any repression would have to stop short of measures that would push the Catholic people too quickly. He promised swift retaliation against prelates who threatened the prestige of the Nazi Party but told the press that "we have no interest at all in manufacturing martyrs," a particular anxiety of party leaders.[28] Outright suppression of Galen risked reversing the mass movement dynamics that were working in favor of the Nazis, at least within the bishop's diocese at that time, as the Oldenburg crucifix struggle would soon reveal.

During the summer of 1936 the removal of religious images from the schools in Meyer's Gau led to agitation among parents. Government officials received many letters and petitions with long lists of signatures, particularly from farmers. Though those closest to the German soil, whether in Franconia or Oldenburg Provinces, had made an alliance with Nazism, they also showed a particular readiness to endure the hard sacrifices required to stand up for their biblical beliefs. Appealing to the dictatorship's concern about popular mood, Galen brought to the attention of Reich Minister for Church Affairs Hanns Kerrl the negative impression Meyer's office was making by demanding the removal of religious symbols. Reflecting the Nazi policy of choosing battles with the church carefully, Kerrl directed Meyer to distance himself from "small matters" that "offend the religious feelings of the people and in Catholic areas bring out justified ill feelings." Consequently, Meyer shifted blame for opposition away from Galen to the county adviser for schools and began to provide conciliatory funds for schools to buy "good decorative art," including religious pictures.[29]

A little more than five years later, Meyer was present among the small group of elite Nazis at the Wannsee Conference, planning unbounded brutality against the Jews of Europe. But he was also aware that inside the Reich, leading the people required attracting them while holding the line on opposition. "In my Gau many positions of authority would forfeit the trust of the people if the political leadership on the church question were to assume an unsympathetic and coercive position," Meyers commented in mid-1936. "The Westphalians in their stubborn style of holding tenaciously to the old ways can only be made into National Socialists with time! It would be wrong to try to make a change here with force."[30]

It was not Meyer, however, but another Gauleiter who faced the toughest Catholic opposition during 1936. This was Carl Röver of the Weser-Ems Gau, who ruled the Oldenburg area of Bishop Galen's diocese, a Catholic enclave in northern Germany surrounded by Protestantism. In November 1936, the Catholics in the Oldenburg counties of Cloppenburg and Vechta formed the front line in the Nazi effort to reform schools by rejecting an order for the removal of all crucifixes from the schools in Röver's Gau.[31]

The Catholics in Oldenburg Province, clustered in Cloppenburg and Vechta, were particularly pious, as well as unusually loyal to the Catholic Center Party. When the Nazi Party came to power with an absolute majority in Oldenburg Province in June 1932, it expressed a goal of ending the influence of the confessional schools so that the party itself "would gain access to the young generation through the schools and the teachers." Cloppenburg and Vechta represented a particularly tough challenge. They were part of "Black Münsterland," where Catholics collectively were accustomed to going against the grain of social as well as government pressures. Although their province became the first to give the Nazi Party a majority provincial vote, in Catholic Cloppenburg and Vechta the numbers voting for the NSDAP remained a minority. In March 1933, Oldenburg Catholics were still giving their vote to the Catholic Center Party in higher percentages than those of any other German region. In mid-1935, their Münster diocese still maintained "a large portion" of schoolteachers who belonged to the Catholic Teachers League rather than to the Nazi Party equivalent. For these reasons the area earned the epithet "Black Münsterland."[32]

Initially the church leaders in Oldenburg, as elsewhere, had cooperated readily with Nazi leaders. Large numbers of Catholics made peace with the new government following the Catholic Center Party's support in parliament in March 1933 for a four-year Hitler dictatorship and the Reich Concordat with the Vatican in July. In the spirit of the concordat, the state as well as church officials had warmly welcomed Bishop Galen's newly appointed representative for Oldenburg, Franz Vorwerk (vicar general of the diocese). Vorwerk responded in kind at the end of 1933, publicly stating, "We wish to approach the interaction of state and church authorities so that at this time state and church work loyally and peacefully together." The local paper, *Die Oldenburgischen Volkszeitung*, praised Vorwerk on December 6 as "well known throughout the most far-reaching circles in the land for his many years of social and welfare work," which had won him "a great deal of trust" among the Catholics and the non-Catholics alike. In the same newspaper the following day

Julius Pauly, Oldenburg's youthful director of the Ministry of Churches and Schools, hailed Vorwerk as a man "who is also thoroughly trustworthy in matters relating to the Fatherland, in short, one who is to be trusted in all matters."[33]

But by 1935, as Nazi officials pulled away the camouflage to reveal their real intentions for the church, Pauly and Vorwerk became entwined in a struggle over matters that had traditionally been determined within the church sphere for the control of Oldenburg's Catholic schools. Reflecting practice in other regions, Pauly's early steps to suppress church influence were piecemeal, including selecting and transferring teachers according to their acceptance of Nazism, along with increasing suppression of religious instruction in schools. Trouble erupted following Pauly's decree of July 4, 1936, curbing church oversight of religious instruction in schools. The Cloppenburg clergy rose to meet this new gauntlet, which they perceived as an intention "to pave the paths to undermining and eroding the heart of Catholic religion in its children." Claiming that the laity required a response, the clergy goaded Vorwerk into action. In Friesoythe, a Cloppenberg town at the center of southern Oldenburg's agricultural region, the clergy insisted that Vorwerk write a declaration to inspire public protest against Pauly's measure.[34]

On September 20, 1936, Vorwerk somewhat reluctantly took the novel step, for him, of addressing what the regime considered a political issue from the pulpit:

> The question is continuously being put to me about why the church does not take a stance on this or that article, speech, or event. All those asking this should for once think of this: there is a flood of hostility against Christianity coursing through our cities and villages. How is the church supposed to take a stance on all of these many issues? The pulpit exists for the preaching of God's word. In any case, the short time for the sermon does not allow sufficient room for taking a political stance. There is no newspaper at our disposal outside of the church paper, and this is censored in advance, which means the church no longer freely determines its content. . . . And whoever with open eyes observes things as they really are, that are playing out in the area of schools, whoever sees how the agitation against the

confessional schools grows from day to day, will question himself with concern: "when will the hour arrive when the crucifix will be removed from the school?"[35]

Vorwerk's appeal left little unsaid about the adverse circumstances facing Catholics. But while emphasizing that his individual power was limited, he closed his sermon with a call for the laity itself to take on a sense of responsibility for the education of its children, working with the church, the school, and parents. Having observed the regime's removal of crucifixes from schools in other regions, Vorwerk warned that this was likely in Oldenburg.

Barely six weeks after Vorwerk's sermon Pauly issued the order to remove crucifixes and pictures of Luther from Oldenburg schools on November 4. The directive banned the religious consecration of school buildings and ordered that "ecclesiastical and other religious symbols" were not to be "displayed in state, municipal, and parish buildings and those which are already in place must be removed."[36] Official Nazi propaganda was that displaying Hitler's image represented national agreement while the crucifix stood for old denominational fractures. Appealing to national Nazi unity, Pauly said that public buildings belonged to the German nation and not just to some segment of it.

Pauly, rather than Gaulieter Röver, became the public face of the new decree. Just as Hitler wished to put distance between himself and any antagonizing decrees, the Gauleiters also pushed responsibility downward. In characteristic form, Pauly also preferred to leave the actual conflict-causing removal of crucifixes to his subordinates while delivering a well-worn line of party propaganda. On November 10 a local official, August Münzebrock, pushed responsibility for the actual removal of crucifixes even *further* down the line by instructing the mayors in Cloppenburg County to give the school directors oral directives to remove crucifixes, adding that they were to do so in a way that drew as little attention as possible. This was asking the impossible, and that same day someone leaked a copy of the order to Vorwerk.[37]

The decree drew little attention at first since it was not published, but sent directly to a limited number of local officials who had been assigned to remove the crucifixes and report their progress the next month. Pauly's assessment was that the decree might cause some unrest but that "grass would soon grow over it again" and the people would return to their everyday business. But now Vicar Vorwerk was taking action. On November 14 he drafted a pastoral letter invoking the importance of the cross for the church: "Every attack on the crucifix, the symbol of our salvation, is an attack on Christianity." The church, he said, could never consent to removing the crucifix from the place where its children were educated. The Reich Concordat protected the crucifix, and the church, in sum, must meet the new decree with the "sharpest protest." The letter concluded with a request for everyone to "join us and stand up for the preservation of the crucifix in the schools."[38] The pastoral letter was read from pulpits on Sunday, November 15.

Bishop Galen wondered aloud whether the Catholic congregants would prove willing to stand up for the crucifix. Vorwerk responded that the letter had "struck like lightning, particularly among those who had not known about the matter." Now every Catholic knew about the ban and had been reminded of the importance of the crucifix, especially in the schools. Vorwerk stirred up a sense of righteous indignation, a commodity the regime wished to harness, and a milieu supporting Catholic protest developed. According to a report by Mayor Heinrich Prüllage of Essen (Cloppenburg), "In conversations on the street, at work and in restaurants and bars this decree is the only object of conversation." The talk "was almost only about the question, what will happen to the crucifixes in the schools?" Seeing this as an attack on Catholic identity itself, "almost everyone appeared ready to do something to guard against this attack." On November 16, conferences of priests in various locations, including Strücklingen, Friesoythe, Vechta, Emstek, and Lindern, met to determine what steps to take next.[39]

Now that the conflict was public and widespread in his region, Gauleiter Röver could no longer wait on the sidelines. He joined battle with the argument that in such momentous times, amid the grand masterpiece the Nazis were creating, the question of whether the crucifix hung in schools was a matter of no consequence. The magnificence of the new Nazi Germany would far overshadow such a paltry concern, which was a mere remnant of the old days. On November 17 Röver made his case at a mass rally the party had called in Löningen, an overwhelmingly Catholic village of 6,800. The rally, announced in the newspaper that day, featured Röver at the center of a propaganda extravaganza.

Mixing joviality with simplicity, his speech grew increasingly threatening. If he were to tell Hitler's deputy Rudolf Hess about Vorwerk, the Gauleiter commented, Vorwerk would be "thrown into a concentration camp." Liars were claiming that the state was against religion, he said, but the problem was merely that they did not know where the affairs of the church stopped and those of the state began. The following day the local newspapers spread the word about what they saw as Röver's brilliant and effective appearance.[40]

Röver enjoyed popularity as a man of power ready to mix with the people, but as his actions sparked bitter protests, he had reason to fear Hitler's wrath as the stakes mounted. Röver's presence was overshadowed by Chaplain Franz Uptmoor on November 10 at a war memorial service in the village of Bethen.

Commemorating those who had served in World War I, Uptmoor preached a dazzling sermon to an enthusiastic audience of some three thousand people from "Catholic Münsterland." With a rousing overview of Catholicism's thousand-year history in the region, he observed, "We are Christians because we are German and fought on the front!" He compared the battles of World War I with current battles for the crucifix and in conclusion said that "three thousand Catholic men have returned home in towns and villages of the land with the unbending will to retain the crucifix in the school!"[41]

Uptmoor's passionate appeal to Catholic heroes old and new earned him respect as the "preacher of the crucifix struggle," and the fervor of a united Catholic body began to sway local officials. Also showing an eagerness to find Nazism and their church compatible, a number of Catholics, who fully supported Nazism's claim to rule on behalf of the people, thought Minister Pauly might simply be acting in ignorance of how important the crucifix was to Catholics.[42] The common notion that Pauly would take their deeply heartfelt appeal into account also reveals how little at least some of these villagers and their leaders knew about the monstrosity of Nazi goals and the party's designs to shut down the influence of the churches altogether.

The popular response also revealed how far the Nazi Party had to go in its drive to move the people to an unreserved and total commitment to its beliefs—especially in the face of Catholic activism. In the village of Essen, the priest Wilhelm Niermann mobilized the people to seek the support of Nazi Party members who might protect them from punishment as "enemies of the state." Through personal contacts, Essen's Catholics organized a meeting of the city council the following evening. Hundreds crowded the meeting hall to demand action and found support from the mayor and local party leader. A commonly expressed sentiment was that "everyone had to come together" since "our ancestors would turn over in their graves—they and our fallen comrades [from World War I] resting under the sign of the cross—if we allow one to tear the crucifix from schools and thus from the hearts of our children." At this meeting so much clear, strong sentiment was expressed, without a voice of dissent, that the city council and the mayor—who, according to postwar reports, were unaware of Nazism's anti-church goals—resolved to warn the party that it was not in its best interest to remove or even reposition the crucifixes.[43]

In his letter to Minister Pauly of November 20, Essen's Mayor Prüllage reported that at the meeting he had assured the "excited crowd of folks" that he "would not enforce this decree." He followed this declaration of noncompliance with a reminder to Pauly of his loyalty and past value to the Nazi movement, stating that his leadership compared well with that of any other in the area and that indeed "through personal contact with individual comrades [Volksgenossen] the requirements and wishes of the party and state have been exhaustively fulfilled." He had been there for the party when it took power, and just that very morning he had again involved himself in hard work to build the movement. Now he felt "duty bound" to sound the warning: "Fingers away from the crucifix; don't disturb our religion!"[44]

Here was a party official who seemed to think that National Socialism really intended to be a fair representation of German sentiment. (Such an intention was just as Hitler had promised and led his followers to expect.) Also deploring the crucifix decree at the council meeting was the local Nazi Party leader, who had similarly come to the opinion that government officials simply did not realize the meaning of the crucifix for Catholics. So convinced were these Esseners of the revelatory importance of their town council meeting that they sent a messenger to fill in Minister Pauly on important omissions in the mayor's report about the meeting. They also decided to send a delegation of ordinary persons to meet with Pauly at his offices in Oldenburg on Saturday, November 21.

The mayor, exercising authority in Nazi Party style, also organized the party leaders in Essen to gather reports on popular opinion about the decree for Pauly's edification. To these reports the mayor added a variety of arguments, from ideological to practical, against removing the crucifixes—namely, that doing so could be associated with the atheism of Bolshevism, which Nazism fought, and that it would be detrimental to public collections by such Nazi organizations as the NSV (national welfare) and the WHW (Winter Relief Fund).[45]

Surrounded by sharpening protests, Pauly found an ally in the Cloppenburg Labor Front, which on November 19 had urged him to hold fast while repressing dissent. But this advice was hardly helpful given the scale of popular noncompliance. The following day the mayor of Lastrup reported to his superior in Cloppenburg that the decree had created a "completely untenable situation" and that if implemented, "all contact with the population would be lost." The trust in government was shaken, and he would not enforce the measure. Other mayors echoed this sentiment, with the mayor of Friesoythe explaining that enforcing the decree would "require a strong police escort" and would "inevitably lead to open rebellion."[46]

Amid an overwhelming sense of majority opposition, the propaganda branch chief raised the stakes, showing the extent of the fervor. It would be better for the people to "let themselves be beaten to death for their crucifix" if it came to that.[47] Like Bavaria's Protestants, who had been ready for martyrdom in 1934, these Catholics shared scriptures that warned about the costs of Christian faith and brimmed with stories of saints who would not be moved but chose to suffer and die for their faith, be it in a fiery furnace or a den of lions. The crucifix itself signified death for the greatest cause.

The dictatorship had struck a note that pitted Catholics against Nazism. Summing up the reasons why ruthless repression would not be a wise choice for the leaders of a mass movement, an official wrote on November 20 that "everybody is furious and this anger is by no means confined to opponents of the Party or particularly pious persons, but has also seized those who are normally cooperative and do not blindly follow the priests. With one blow a united front of the whole population has been created, which clearly is directed solely against National Socialism."[48]

But by the morning of November 21, it was clear that fear had been struck or rekindled in a few of those who had spoken so bravely at the city council meeting only a couple of days before. On this Saturday morning, the villagers who had agreed at the town meeting to drive to Oldenburg to represent their concerns to Minister Pauly did not show up; some called in only an hour in advance to renege. Those who did participate also felt fear but moved ahead anyway. Father Niermann, who had organized opposition from Essen's farming communities that included party and town council members, sensed that they were being watched.[49] Although some believed in their hearts that the party was a benevolent overlord on their side or that Pauly was acting in ignorance, these resisters now recognized the danger of what they were doing.

That morning seven men were sent to Minister Pauly, including replacements for the volunteers who did not show up. For the ride over, the delegation drove in two cars and took separate routes so that if one vehicle was apprehended, at least the other might make it. Back in Essen, fears for the delegation's arrest circulated, and the people convened at church to pray for its safety. Both cars arrived at Pauly's office without incident; the delegates delivered their carefully worded missive, which appealed to party values of quiescence and accord: "As reasonable and responsible men of the Essen community we raise a protest against the directive of the Ministry from the fourth of the month regarding crucifixes and other religious symbols in the Catholic Schools and urgently request the rescinding of said directive. An unbounded agitation has taken hold of the people that is gathering strength day by day, the result of which cannot be foreseen."[50]

From the seven-man delegation Pauly selected three for a forty-five-minute meeting, including Josef Holters, whose central argument for rescinding the decree was popular unrest and its negative effects on the Nazi movement. The minister, however, dismissed the men's concerns and was unwilling to rescind anything. A farmer, Louis Thole, alluded to the German hero Otto von Bismarck, suggesting that the great leader had, on occasion, changed his mind, and had even been forced to stand down from his struggle with German Catholics. The situation, Thole told the meeting, reminded him of "Bismarck, who even withdrew the *Kulturkampf* laws and nevertheless entered history books as a famous man."[51]

Although unsuccessful in changing Pauly's mind, the village delegation aroused interest around the region and led the way for further
delegations. People poured into Essen to learn what had happened, and
in the next days, delegations of ordinary Catholics visited Pauly to ask
him to rescind his decree. Outside his ministry, car horns rose in a
rhythmic beat of protest, reaching a peak on November 24 with about
seventy-five cars that brought deputations of two hundred people to Pauly's ministry.[52]

Among one of the delegations was the decorated, locally prominent
Josef Klinker, who had established Oldenburg's first Nazi Party local
group in his Cloppenburg village of Molbergen. He had been impressed
during the late 1920s with Nazi claims that Jesus Christ was a "total
ruler," wielding unlimited powers. Together with two Catholic farmers,
he had responded to the party's call by establishing the first local party
on Gauleiter Röver's birthday. For their accomplishments all three had
won the Nazi Golden Party Badge, and Klinker was named party leader
for southern Oldenburg.[53]

Klinker accompanied a five-person Molbergen delegation to Minister Pauly on November 23; it included Essen's Mayor Prüllage and a
farmer, Theodor Lake, who, once inside Pauly's office, refused the minister's offer of a seat. Instead, Lake invoked the delegation's loyalty to
Germany, saying that "we fought as five brothers in the world war, and
none of us returned home without the Iron Cross First Class. Would you
dare to tell these people, who have received this honor, to remove the
cross from it?" Pauly of course said he would not, and Lake continued,
"Thus you must know, Mr. Minister, that the crucifix that is in our
churches, that hangs in our homes and schools, means much more to
us than such medals of distinction and that is why we will not allow the
crucifix to be removed from the schools." Pauly's suggestion that they
build a beautiful little box for the crucifix, removing it each time it
was used, reflected the piecemeal Nazi approach of crab walking toward
its goals. But the townspeople flatly rejected it. "The entire population is
greatly infuriated," Mayor Prüllage reported, and "the ordinary person
simply doesn't understand."[54]

Next Mayor Prüllage, together with Herr Klinker, who wore the
Golden Party Badge, took their turns asking that the decree be rescinded.
Both threatened, in the event that the decree was not taken back, to turn

to Hitler personally! If need be, they were prepared to leave the party. Both expressed doubt that the decree would meet Hitler's approval. According to Prüllage, Catholic farmers wanted their children to grow up as Catholics and to "also follow Adolf Hitler." Under this pressure, Pauly offered to cancel the decree for Molbergen, illustrating the party's practice of breaking a problem into pieces to reduce the opposition. But the delegates refused this offer as well. They would be satisfied only when the decree was canceled in all communities, they said.[55]

It might seem odd that in 1936 the party leaders not only defended Catholic practices in the schools, but further claimed that Hitler was on their side. Their certainty about Hitler, however, signals that he was performing his job as the Leader very well by keeping his distance from the controversies so that Germans were free to interpret Hitler exactly as each one wished.

Thus Germans who violently disagreed with one another were all willing to believe that Hitler backed up their individual positions. Given the prevalence of claims in the Reich that Hitler would "put things right" if only he were adequately informed, Klinker's and Prüllage's invocation of Hitler's name was likely a sincere attempt, not just a tactic, to protect themselves from charges of rebellion. In contrast to the kaleidoscope of false notions about Hitler, there was no doubt as to National Socialism's populist claims; the Nazi theme of unity appealed to many individuals who could not agree on much else. For his part, Gauleiter Röver assured Alfred Rosenberg that Klinker was merely one bad apple and not indicative of others so highly honored by the party. "Even a wearer of the golden party badge participated in public against the decree and led one of the protest commissions that visited the Ministry," the Oldenburg Gestapo reported.[56]

Around the agricultural belt in southern Oldenburg in late November 1936 the protests were still gathering force and illustrating the dynamics of popular mobilization that the Nazi Party feared if it slipped from its control. On November 24, with church expressions of defiance escalating, Gauleiter Röver announced a meeting for the following day to take place at the largest Cloppenburg facility, Münsterlandhalle. An overflowing crowd of seven thousand (with five thousand more outside) assembled, with many expecting to hear swiftly that the crucifix decree had been rescinded. Instead, Röver began with a rambling primer on

Volksgemeinschaft, speaking of his travels in Africa. As he dallied, he was booed with shouts including, "You should have stayed there!" and "Get to the point." As soon as their Nazi leader announced the decree's repeal, the crowd hurried to leave.[57]

This was a defeat for the party leaders, and although they saw their compromise as provisional, they recognized that damage had been done. Meeting with Röver in late January 1937 to discuss what had happened in Oldenburg, Goebbels strove to get across to Röver that the crucifix action had been a "crazy mistake." The dictatorship also limited damages by limiting all press coverage of the decree and banning further protests, along with all press reports on any future crucifix struggles that might break out.[58] If the regime had failed to control the protests, at least it would limit publicity. Fearing that news of public collective protest would spread such protests further, the regime limited or destroyed reports about it, limiting the evidence that such dissent happened.

As for Röver, the degree of damage done to his reputation within the innermost circle of power was reflected in a meeting on January 13, 1937. Reich Church Minister Kerrl, together with Goebbels, sounded off against Röver's clumsiness. Goebbels assailed Röver as incompetent, in contrast to his "more clever" colleague, Gauleiter Bürckel, and thereafter referred to Röver as a "clumsy little oaf" [Tolpatsch]. Hitler, sounding somewhat less aggrieved and more loyal, thought that Röver had committed a "tactical error."[59]

Röver began his retaliation not with an arrest but with a public campaign of lies against Vorwerk, testing his own reputation against that of the vicar (though not against the more popular Bishop Galen). In January 1937 a new party campaign accused Vorwerk of lying and misinforming Galen. Röver fretted that "this accursed Black Münsterland" had kept him from reaching his goal and accused Vorwerk of being the pawn of Galen, the "traitor in Münster." To Vorwerk directly, he vowed, "I will subjugate you, you can be sure of that. I'll have you Münsterlanders feeding from my hand!"[60]

News of the struggle indicated that the pastoral letter and Catholic networks remained important forms of communication that the state did not fully control. Cardinal Joseph Schulte of Cologne and Bishop Konrad von Preysing of Berlin were especially active in spreading the word of protest via the Catholic networks, and in the Protestant churches word of the clash in Oldenburg spread through newsletters and sermons. The Münster-based *Diocesan Newsletter* reported on the conflict and published related documents, and Bishop Galen's pastoral letter of November 27, 1936, was read in various dioceses. Out of the desire to save the institutional church and its practices, Galen wanted a Catholic community capable of mobilizing at all levels. The police reports from Cloppenburg in 1936 reveal that the Catholics were remarking among themselves that the regime would back down again and again, if they responded to other incursions in a similarly united way.[61]

In Oldenburg, the crucifixes were restored. But illustrating the regime's commitment to gradual change while keeping its eye fixed especially on the future generation, the crucifixes were not to be hung in the new schools. Furthermore, the part of Pauly's decree banning religious consecrations of new schools remained in effect. When a priest in Peheim, Father Gottfried Engels, performed the usual ritual of sanctifying a new school, the Gestapo threw him in jail for six months. Engels had the liability of being a difficult personality—a loner not much liked by his parishioners who was easily severed from the protection of popular opinion.[62]

Oldenburg's Protestants had largely complied with the Oldenburg decree, which had required them to replace pictures of Luther with those of Hitler, and their protests came in the discreet form of writing. Given their relative inability to organize their laity, Protestant leaders had particular difficulty restoring the pictures of Luther in their schools following Gauleiter Röver's rescission order. Working alone, it took one pastor eighteen months of running around continuously from one office to another before Luther's image was restored. When Oldenburg's Protestant bishop, Johannes Volkers, complained to Röver on February 22, 1937, Röver shifted blame to village and school officials.[63]

In the spring of 1937, following some arrests and concessions in the dispute over school crucifixes in the Saarland village of Frankenholz, Oldenburg's Molbergen school received a new director who began to remove the replaced crucifixes—as his own personal directive. The party had brought in this new director from the outside, a man without intimate relations with the people or their customs.[64] By taking the time to divide the population and attack it piece by piece, the party could prevail against the local people.

Clearly the party, with the state's army of bureaucrats at its back, could easily wear down a population if that population's only effective response tactic was to mobilize hundreds in protest, day after day. The party had its own organizations, including the Hitler Youth and the SA, which it could easily deploy in huge demonstrations as well. Lines that the Hitler Youth were required to memorize were turned into a song and sung in public around Oldenburg.[65]

Despite the police suppression of the religious consecration of the new schools, Vorwerk continued his efforts. Illustrating the deepening capacity for resistance of someone who had started down that course, he continued to mobilize the Catholic laity in defense of its traditions. In late April 1938—an extremely disadvantageous moment for dissent given the roar of approval across the Reich for the German annexation of Catholic Austria—Vorwerk requested that his parishioners "demand restoration of denominational schools" since closing them was "worse than excluding the crucifix from schools." He concluded with the warning that "remaining silent today would be the greatest breach of our duty to conscience." In early May, parents—Protestant as well as Catholic—organized a strike in Oldenburg's Goldenstedt, protesting the new "community schools" by keeping their children home. This time, in keeping with Goebbels's maxim about how the authorities should handle mass mobilized opposition, the police struck quickly at the start, arresting more than a dozen people they perceived as the leaders and throwing some in prison, where they remained for several months. Five short days after it began, Minister Pauly broke the strike with an announcement that he would arrest all those who did not take their children back to school. Vorwerk asked that he be arrested and the parents released, but the Gestapo instead banished him from the district of Oldenburg. Five other Catholic officials, accused of being Vorwerk's "most submissive" accomplices, were also expelled from the district.[66]

Also during the wave of great acclaim for the Anschluss, Pauly ordered further suppression of Christian schools, beginning in April 1938 with smaller ones and later including larger ones as well.[67] Of course his order does not guarantee that a corresponding reality materialized. But the overall forward arc of developments showed that the party was inexorably, if slowly, moving ahead with its dispersal of church-based culture.

Victories in war, Nazis believed, could go a long way toward convincing everyone that Hitler was worth following, even if this required all to forsake some old customs or express religiosity in new ways. Pauly's need to resort to police measures in any case indicated that he had not suppressed the willingness for defiance among all Oldenburgers, a defiance that was likely expressed in some schools with the continuing presence of crucifixes, regardless of whether they had been declared secular. It is significant that protests in Oldenburg also had repercussions for further defiance, including in the East Prussian diocese of Ermland.

HEYDRICH COMPROMISES FOR BISHOP KALLER
AND ERMLAND CATHOLICS

One indication that the Oldenburg Catholics achieved more than a mere delay of crucifix removals in their own district was the clarion call from Bishop Maximilian Kaller that the courage of the Oldenburgers should serve to galvanize his own parishioners in their own struggle. In his East Prussian diocese of Ermland, Kaller and his followers together showed anew the concessions that a strong leader and a courageous community of the people could achieve.[68] Unlike the case in Oldenburg, where the most striking compromise came from Gauleiter Carl Röver, in East Prussia, the Gauleiter, Erich Koch, refused to make concessions.

Koch dreamed of uniting the different provincial Protestant churches and was known both for his extensive engagement with the Protestant Church and his concomitant hostility toward Catholics. Although he was forced to relinquish this notion of Protestant unity by late 1934, he continued to identify Protestantism with the Nazi cause while reviling Catholicism as an alien force. Protestantism, Koch thought, was the one true German Christianity since it owed itself to Luther, the "man who saved German cultural values." He himself was the elected president of his provincial Protestant synod, and he proposed that Hitler should become *summus episcopus*, head of the state church. Koch's links with the Protestants, up until he resigned his church membership in 1943, helped him govern his overwhelmingly Protestant region. His approach of winning the people by signaling acceptance of Christianity reflected Hitler's early tactics, although as the Gauleiter Koch's effectiveness depended on whether this solidarity with Protestants ultimately helped him lead them away from all aspects of their religion that contradicted National Socialism. In Berlin, Koch's Protestant policies were scorned by far more powerful men, including Heydrich and his boss, Heinrich Himmler.[69]

Gaulieter Koch was blatantly hostile to the enclave of East Prussian Catholics in his province, which comprised a mere 15 percent of his region. But in Bishop Kaller he faced a capable Catholic leader and motivator, just as Gauleiter Meyer had faced his superior, in Nazi-style mobilization of popular belief and practice, in Bishop Galen of Münster. In early 1933, Cardinal Adolf Bertram, with the agreement of the Fulda Bishops' Conference, published a pastoral letter encouraging Catholics to vote in the upcoming election without mentioning the Catholic parties; the Nazis promptly exploited this pastoral letter, thanking one Catholic bishop for urging the election of Catholic Nazis. Bishop Kaller, on the other hand, had forcefully and openly warned his parishioners not to vote for the Nazi Party, and after Hitler took power, he admonished them to vote for the Catholic Center Party in the election of March 5, 1933. His clout was reflected by a majority vote among East Prussian Catholics for the Catholic Center Party. This stood in stark contrast to the almost uniform pattern of support for the Nazis among the Ermlanders' Protestant neighbors, who had given their vote by an overwhelming majority to the NSDAP even before Hitler took power.[70]

Bishop Kaller, along with his clergy and laity, was well versed in ignoring official orders that infringed on Catholic practices. In October 1934, the nonconformist acted contrary to both church and Nazi authorities by leading a devotional procession of fifty thousand to the site of reported apparitions of the Virgin Mary in Dittrichswalde. Nazi leaders were indignant, and the Gestapo warned against "such collective movements of the faithful." Ecclesiastical authorities also feared that such "apparition mania" would continue to spur pilgrimages, rather than channeling devotion through proper, established venues. Both church and state hierarchies had a stake in maintaining centralized control, but Kaller, like Bishop Galen (and Bishop Meiser in 1934) founded his authority on the Catholics he mobilized. By 1935 Kaller had come to the attention of the dictatorship as an "enemy of the state," but the bishop responded to escalating pressures by calling on Ermland's Catholics to defend their church, including the disregarding of orders if necessary.[71]

In February 1937, pastoral letters from Bishop Kaller were banned from the pulpit, and a general ban on pastoral letters from German bishops followed six months later. Any business that copied these letters might be subject to closure. As the dictatorship sharpened its measures to eradicate church education that year, Kaller responded with acts of defiance. He first called from the pulpit for disciplined disobedience, praising the readiness of the parents in his diocese to resist state orders. "Do you not also have courage?" Kaller asked. "Are you not also Catholic? Defend your schools, defend the crucifix!" Later the same year, in September, the bishop responded in a forbidden pastoral letter read around his diocese that encouraged disobedience. Alluding to Gauleiter Adolf Wagner's observation that the churches were the only remaining impediment in public life to the undivided rule of National Socialism, Kaller agreed by observing that Wagner's "pronouncement proclaims where we stand."[72]

By the end of 1937 the East Prussian Catholics had stood up to the bans that forbade religious instruction in schools and orders banning crucifixes on school walls. Some of the teachers refused to attend a course designed to show them how to transmit the National Socialist worldview, indicating a degree of choice by teachers who were willing to face all the possible draconian consequences. In a display of unusual courage, 357 teachers out of over 22,000 in East Prussia had still refused to take this course by 1938.[73]

The Nazis compromised by exempting Kaller and his priests from punishment, even though by early 1938, the Gestapo detested Kaller more than any other bishop—even more than Galen. In spite of the ban, Kaller announced that a pastoral letter would once again be read simultaneously from pulpits around his Ermland diocese. Illustrating that a bishop with a record of defiance might still disregard the dictatorship in early 1938 with some impunity, on February 19, 1938, Heydrich issued a decision to suspend the ban on the reading of Bishop Kaller's letter. He explained that although the letter was certainly vile, he was not going to interfere "since experience shows that the reading would be ordered by the bishop without regard for the ban." Any copies of the letter distributed outside of the church were to be confiscated, however.[74]

Bishop Kaller was able to defy bans and compel Heydrich to compromise with him without regard to Gauleiter Koch's wishes or orders. Due to Kaller's established pattern of noncompliance, Heydrich's alternative was to issue an order only to have it flagrantly ignored in full view of the people. Kaller thus forced the security chief to compromise in order to preserve Nazi authority among the people. In doing so, Kaller sustained the motivation of his congregations, illustrating the style of Menschenführung leadership Hitler wanted to see from his Gauleiters. When Gauleiter Koch refused to make a temporary compromise, Heydrich stepped in to prevent a clash between Catholics and the party and protect the party's prestige.

Heydrich considered his compromise to be a stopgap measure until the regime gained greater control over the hearts and minds of the people relative to the churches. Had Kaller planned the reading of his letter for one month later, the enormous din of acclaim echoing around the Reich for Hitler's bloodless annexation of Austria might have drowned it out. A few weeks later, on March 12, as the German Army marched into Austria, Hitler proclaimed the Anschluss of Austria with the Great German Reich. Pointing to historical precedent, he observed that the raw repression of a people motivated by love of country tended to ignite a backlash that could spiral into increasing levels of repression and retaliation. His observation that repression could unleash spiraling cycles of violence was a self-serving accusation against Kurt von Schuschnigg's Austrian government but further evidence as well that Hitler recognized that terror could be counterproductive for certain aspects of ruling his own people.[75]

When he went to war, Hitler preferred working with the churches and their leaders, who could inspire the people. Bishops around Germany and across denominations called on the Christians to support the war, so it made no sense to suppress them. This is illustrated by Bishop Kaller himself. In early 1941, despite horrible German atrocities against fellow Catholics in Poland, Kaller sounded an unreserved endorsement of the Reich's war: "With admiration we regard our army, which through heroic struggles under superb leadership has obtained unprecedented success after success. We thank God for his assistance. Especially as Christians, we are determined to deploy our total strength so that the final victory for our Fatherland will be secured. Especially as the faithful, as Christians glowing with the love of God, we stand faithful to our Führer, who directs the fate of our people with a certain hand."[76]

Bishop Kaller's pastoral letter of January 1941 illustrates a claim that was sounded by other church leaders as well: Christians could bring special qualities to a war that the regime wanted (even in fighting fellow

Christians if they were not German). By taking Germany to war, Hitler added the force of patriotism to the winds pushing his sails. Beyond common patriotism was also the energy of self-interest, for even the Germans who did not like the regime might dislike the prospect of a German defeat still more. But Bishops Galen and Kaller did show that strong leadership could mobilize Catholics to take a daring public stance to protect religious interests. The defiance of a single bishop backed by his diocese caused the regime to move more circumspectly even without sympathy or protests from other Catholic bishops across the Reich.

With the Anschluss of Catholic Austria in March 1938 the number of Catholics in the Reich was nearing that of Protestants, and acclaim for the Anschluss among prelates was nearly universal. Although the bishops had agreed to ring church bells only for celebrations of national rather than political events, church bells rang across the country in favor of an official plebiscite that claimed more than 99 percent approval for the Anschluss. Church authorities forced priests who abstained from voting for this annexation to apologize publicly and then sign a declaration of loyalty to the Leader. The rationale for punishment in one of these cases reveals the church hierarchy's mentality: refusing to vote revealed a priest's "lack of understanding for the total situation." Surrendering church practices was not sought out or welcomed, but traditional practices were overshadowed by the primacy of the German nation.[77]

The Anschluss and the cause of war orchestrated a new level of German unity behind the Nazi leadership. The failed attempt on Hitler's life in late 1938 produced another resounding call from church authorities from both denominations to rally their congregants for Hitler and in some cases to further the worship of Hitler due to his apparent providential escape from death. It is all the more remarkable, then, that some Germans spoke out even during the height of German victories. In early 1941, when German jubilation for an army that appeared almost invincible appeased many dissenters, a handful of Ermland's priests showed that a faction still dared to express defiance. Four clergy from East Prussia were courageous enough to say outright that Germany must not win the war, lest Catholicism be obliterated. This time it was not on behalf of their church but against the pro-war nationalism of Bishop Kaller, the man who had nurtured their exercise of protest in prior years. Also in

1941, the judiciary in Königsberg reported that "the lively activities of political Catholicism continues as before" and concluded that in the region the "absolute majority of Catholic clergy have a position hostile to the state and the movement."[78]

As in the case of Protestant resistance in 1934 under Bishop Meiser, however, resistance was cut short without help from the top. It was too daunting for ordinary people to continue to mobilize opposition, especially during the war, while also earning their living and carrying on the duties of their daily lives. They were also not protected from being jailed as bishops were.

Nevertheless, although the dictatorship pushed the churches into positions of substantial compromise, the regime's suspension of provocations illustrates the compromises it made as well. Despite various regional suppressions of church schools, followed by Martin Bormann's directive of April 1939 terminating Catholic schools, religious influences persisted in German schools during the war, and church membership began to experience resurgence. Adolf Wagner's decree removing crucifixes from Bavarian schools in April 1941 revealed that decrees had not eliminated religious practices, including the hanging of crucifixes in schools. Hitler preferred to appease the people, even at Gauleiter Wagner's expense, by condemning the decree and reinstating the crucifixes. No matter how necessary the dictatorship thought it was to banish Christian morality so that the Germans fought with the reinforced strength of the Nazi worldview, and regardless of the fact that crucifixes hanging on school walls made a daily mockery of Bormann's authority in their disregard for his 1939 decree declaring all German schools secular, the Leader recognized that under the circumstances he could not use terror and intimidation to achieve this.[79]

Despite the Nazis, Christianity carried on, and churchgoing revived under the hardships of war. In August 1941 Hamburg's Gauleiter Karl Kaufmann expressed "astonishment" that priests were giving religious instruction to children who had been evacuated from Hamburg because of air warfare. But religious instruction in these evacuation sites would only increase under the pressure not just of parents, who were backed by some church leaders, but also of Germany's accumulating defeats as Germany's position in war crumbled. As German losses mounted, Hitler became less willing and less able to demonstrate that following him rewarded Germany and the Germans. By May 1943, the Gauleiters, no longer able to find much support from Berlin, were ignoring Berlin and competing with one another for resources to supply their own populations.[80]

No evidence that Hitler intervened in the Oldenburg struggle has been found. But it no doubt interested Hitler a great deal. The year 1936 was remarkably eventful, with Hitler's attention on the Olympics, the Rhineland remilitarization, the new relationship with Mussolini's Italy, and the Spanish Civil War. The new Four-Year Plan directed the German economy toward war, and given his belief in willpower and the importance of national unity for winning wars, Hitler would have been greatly interested in how his image was faring on the school-wall battlefield against the crucifix, the pope, and the German icon Martin Luther. His likeness was his direct proxy in matters like the crucifix struggle, where he could not be obviously present because of the paramount need to protect his public persona. Were the religious Catholics allowing him to stand in for their crucifix?

The Gauleiters in their regions conducted experiments in the expeditious but calm transition to a popular acceptance of Hitler as the Leader, and removing religious symbols from Catholic schools posed a very steep learning curve. The goal was to establish the Nazi conscience throughout all sectors of the Reich, with a resulting unity so strong that "community aliens" would be shunned and forced out by natural social processes. Beginning in April 1938, testing the progress of the drive to establish Nazi "law" in the customs of the people, Hitler enabled the use of street demonstrations intended to hound a bishop from his diocese. The popular mobilization of church crowds must have stung. Hitler was focused on maintaining the forward momentum of Nazism, and the dictatorship had rallied Germans to a remarkable extent around his image. But would the regime be able to turn the tables, driving a bishop from his home without calling in the Gestapo, already in 1938?

CHAPTER FOUR

Street Demonstrations

TOWARD USING THE LEADER'S TACTICS

IN EARLY 1933 Cardinal Michael von Faulhaber suspended the Benedictine monk Alban Schachleiter because of his unrestrained support
for National Socialism. In return the NSDAP staged a public demonstration of appreciation for the abbot's loyalty, amplified by propaganda.
For more than a decade Schachleiter had been rendering service to the
Nazis, highlighted at a mass to commemorate Nazi martyr Albert Leo
Schlageter, who had earned the party's exaltation by sabotaging French
troops who occupied the German Ruhr in May 1923. Schachleiter held
the Nazi-Catholic mass at Munich's St. Boniface Abbey, and it was attended by throngs of uniformed SA men, who marched in procession
past Schachleiter as he consecrated each SA flag with holy water. Burning with patriotic zeal, one SA man remembered being "transported" by
Schachleiter's sermon into almost "a holy rapture" that he could never
forget.[1]

By February 1931, when Cardinal Faulhaber banned Catholics from
membership in the Nazi Party, the grandfatherly Schachleiter had become a celebrated figure in the Nazi press, pictured in traditional Benedictine habit and glowing with frank enthusiasm as he gave the Hitler
salute or preached at Nazi rallies flanked by the SA or Hitler Youth. Faulhaber notwithstanding, Schachleiter rallied behind Hitler's 1932 campaign for Reich President, producing a leaflet exhorting Christian people

to back Hitler while also opposing the Catholic Center Party itself. Burdened by the vision of uniting Catholics and Protestants behind Hitler, Schachleiter entreated Hitler to "reassure Catholics" that they belonged in his movement.[2]

In response, Faulhaber banned Schachleiter from holding any further masses. In March 1933, the Nazi Party showed that it was the representative of the people by using crowds to rehabilitate the monk's reputation. On March 20, three thousand persons climbed the slopes of a mountain on foot to reach Schachleiter's monastery and show him their solidarity. Despite a terrible storm, the Nazi faithful persisted all the way to the top, carrying torches with them in honor of the monk's "loyalty." The demonstration was led by SA formations, Hitler Youth, the League of Nazi Women, and the League of German Girls and was trumpeted as exemplifying the new Germany, undergoing a long-awaited "resurrection" of spirit. Schachleiter, according to the press, had "finally dispelled all doubts . . . [proving] that glowing selfless love for people and Fatherland and struggle for homeland and soil under the swastika can be no sin! On the contrary it is blessed by the Almighty!" Soon afterward, on March 28, 1933, the German bishops publicly lifted the ban limiting Catholic involvement in the Nazi Party, and in May, Hitler himself paid the heroic abbot a visit.[3]

VOLKSGEMEINSCHAFT? NAZI DEMONSTRATIONS
AND GERMAN CATHOLICS

Regardless of how many levers of power he gained and created, Hitler remained engaged with the fundamental challenge of developing his people into a tightly knit collective, and he made decisions at hand in light of this long-term goal. In early 1934 Hitler said that by the time of his demise the people must be shaped into an entity so uniformly backing National Socialism that resistance would be as futile as fighting the entire people. "It will always be the first and foremost task of the government to bring about inner consensus," Hitler told the Reichstag the day it granted him dictatorial power. The Nazi national community would erase "rank, profession, class, and confession," Hitler told a rally of two million people in Berlin on May 1, 1934. National Socialism "will never lose sight of this [national community] goal and, even if only gradually, it is certain to reach it."[4]

Rather than resorting solely to dictatorial decree once in power, Hitler accumulated various ways of asserting influence over the people, camouflaging his aims that the people did not yet endorse. Hitler did not discard the Reichstag after it voted itself out of power but deployed it as an applause chamber for his speeches. It was assembled as a symbol of legitimacy when the dictator took particularly bold steps, such as the announcements of the Nuremberg Laws. He continued to assiduously script his appearances in public, playing his role as the Leader in order to continue to build the Nazi mass movement.

Previous groups in Germany had relied on street demonstrations to defend their interests and build their movement, but the Nazis set new standards in restricting and manipulating them for their movement. The dictatorship immediately set out to curtail the public mobilization of German Catholics, who had learned to assert their rights on the streets during the late nineteenth century. Catholic influence through public rallies had vexed the imperial German government, developed by the practice of public assemblies, which the state considered political. The Kaiser Reich saw Catholic Corpus Christi processions not only as a collective, open assertion of allegiance to the church, but also as a repudiation of modern society and the national liberal state. In 1874, during Chancellor Otto von Bismarck's Kulturkampf, the German state banned all church processions, other than those established before 1850, because it considered them a potential threat. Under Nazi rule, the German state of Prussia repeated this ban on December 7, 1934, with the same exceptions for long-established processions. Like the rulers of imperial Germany, the Gestapo considered the church's outdoor processions "political Catholicism"—a proclamation of Catholic identity and an advertisement campaign for others to join.[5]

The religious rallies engendered a sense of togetherness and of "we" under a banner outside of Nazism, and the dictatorship considered the church's outdoor processions an impediment to the growth of its national people's community. In Münster the city's police president noted that by mid-1934, despite the dictatorship's resolve to extinguish church influence, Catholic collective identity and the public rallies expressing it were on the rise. In October, officials noted an "astounding" increase in participation in traditional processions in the Münster diocese. While church publications portrayed these rallies as religious revival, the Gestapo feared they reflected a strengthened desire for independence that "could pose a challenge to the future development of the National Socialist idea." The Catholic laity had always shown respect for its bishop, the Münster police president wrote, but current public processions were no longer "harmless rallies." Instead they had become political demonstrations. Catholic crowds, for example, had broken out in public choruses of, "We want to see our bishop," or sang "church battle hymns" together in public. In November 1934, the Nazi leadership of the Münster region warned that if "appropriate means" were not found to decrease the public church demonstrations, the state would face "increased public disturbances." The Gestapo sounded an alarm that church rallies and processions had motivated inactive Catholics to renew their commitment and participation.[6]

DEMONSTRATIONS IN SIEGBURG

In some cases, local leaders attempted to mobilize Nazis on the streets as a way of eclipsing church assemblies. In Siegburg, a small city in the Cologne Gau, higher Nazi leaders were obliged to stop local Nazis whose attempts to use the streets in the church struggle were backfiring during the summer of 1935. Ideally, Nazi street actions represented national unity and stifled opposition. Above all, they were supposed to avoid evoking scenes of disunity, although some ambitious party members did not understand these Nazi fundamentals and turned too easily to police repression, which could magnify conflicts. The Siegburg Hitler Youth (Hitlerjugend or HJ), for example, intended to work toward the Leader's ideals but failed with its tactics. Suspecting that certain HJ members were attending a Catholic rather than a party function, the Siegburg HJ marched off one evening in July 1935 to confront what it called the "Catholic Youth Storm Troops." Arriving at an orphanage where the Catholic Youth were meeting, the HJ found the door locked and shouted to be let in. According to a police report, as a crowd of hundreds of townsfolk gathered and sided with the Catholic Youth against a group of one hundred HJ, a shouting match ensued.[7]

Within days, rumors of the events had spread throughout Siegburg and the surrounding area, in a display of social dynamics working against the Nazi movement. In response, however, the local HJ fanned the flames. It demanded that the Siegburg police intervene and then charged the force with negligence because "the entire Siegburg police force was denominationally contaminated." Such a division between a major party organization and the police quickly made its way to the attention of the party district leader, Gauleiter Josef Grohé, who immediately ordered that "under all circumstances" conflicts with the police were not to be managed "on the street" but "settled through official channels." Leaders were to display only unity when acting in public, according to Nazi principles. "Party members of all ranks must act hand in hand with the police in all instances—above all in public," Grohé added. "Anyone violating this order would reckon with expulsion from the Party!"[8]

During that same summer of 1935, other Gauleiters, including Julius Streicher of Nuremberg, spoke out against unauthorized acts of public violence because they violated Hitler's authority and achieved nothing but harm to Germany's reputation. Nevertheless, in Siegburg HJ leaders continued to demand the arrest of the Catholic leaders and planned a continuous series of "propaganda marches" until this happened. Grohé quickly intervened to stop them. Had the HJ leader of these demonstrations succeeded in intimidating the Catholics and enlisting their youth for the party, he would have been highly lauded. But instead a new order was issued, ensuring that in the future only the county leaders (Kreisleiters) or the Gauleiters, the highest party authorities in the region, were authorized to stage demonstrations.[9]

NAZI STREETS AND GERMAN JEWS

The Nazis murdered six million Jews, although Hitler viewed pogroms as "emotional" actions that disrupted the sense of security and order he wanted for the people. There was horrible violence on German streets aimed at humiliating and dehumanizing Jews and those who cohabited with them. Yet while the SS incited pogroms in eastern territories, public violence against the Jews was tempered by Hitler's overall obsession with removing Jews once and for all from Germany, with mass approval. "Anti-Semitism based in pure feeling will find its final expression in the form of pogroms, while anti-Semitism of reason must lead to systematic legal combat," Hitler had written already in September 1919, and finally to the "actual irreversible expulsion of the Jews." The following year he repeated in Munich and Salzburg to loud applause that "we don't want to be 'feeling-based anti-Semites.'" The "Jewish Problem" could be solved only by "removing Jews from our midst."[10]

Hitler preferred the professional channels of law and bureaucracy to remove every Jew from the German Reich. While indulging emotions was disorderly, professional or bureaucratic means of removing all the Jews from Germany also supported the regime's determination to control public perceptions. Bloody attacks against Jews on Berlin's fashion-conscious Kurfürstendamm Avenue prompted Hitler to speak out against such actions on March 10, 1933.[11] Illustrating the troublesome activities of the SA leading up to the Night of the Long Knives, the Breslau police in November 1933 reported that Storm Troopers had disturbed the public peace in their effort to compel the Germans to boycott Jewish stores. This put the police in the awkward position of having to reign in the SA without coming into conflict with the SA in public.

Police continued during the months of 1933 to carefully quell any public signs of unrest or conflict; local police offices monitored the boycotts of Jewish businesses, filing reports even when there were no incidents of unrest. Many people pitched in, voluntarily posting signs announcing that Jews were not welcome or not to be patronized. Well-meaning Nazis in the village of Jessnitz elicited public grumbling during September 1935 by marching Jews through the streets wearing signs that declared, "Whoever buys from Jews is a traitor of the people!" According to the police, some people even stood up for the Jews, so local police terminated this "unsophisticated" approach as soon as they heard about it. In Berlin, authorities preferred that local officials use the common charge of "sassy" (freches) behavior to arrest Jews. For example, in October 1935, Dr. Max Gumpel, a banker and owner of Gumpel and Samson in Bernburg, was taken into custody because his "sassy and provocative manner had recently led to considerable unrest among the people of Bernburg." Rather than divide the people over the issue of relationships with Jews, as happened in Jessnitz, the ideal approach brought masses of people together in unison against Jews, such as the gathering of thousands on the streets of Breslau on July 30, 1935, to greet the transportation to concentration camps of Jewish men accused of sexual relations with non-Jewish women.[12]

Only gradually did Hitler direct public violence against Jews into professional, legal channels, and he was careful not to alienate any wing of his support. During the early Nazi years, pogrom-like violence against Jews erupted on the streets from time to time. While it reached a peak under the SA in 1933, it continued off and on through the summer of 1936 and erupted again in the brutal Kristallnacht pogrom in November 1938. Initially even such powerful figures as Gestapo founder Hermann Göring spoke in contradiction to Hitler—perhaps intentionally, allowing Hitler to protect his public image while pleasing party members who wanted public violence. In early March 1933, this portly figure, known to some as the Third Reich's Falstaff, proclaimed that his orders would not be "emasculated by undue concerns for legality." On March 11 he refused to have Prussian police protect the Jewish businesses that came under isolated attacks.[13]

As the director of both the SS and party intelligence organ the *Sicherheitsdienst* and the Security Police (combined in 1939 under the auspices of the Reichssicherheitshauptamt, the Reich Security Main Office, or RSHA), Reinhard Heydrich played a prominent role in advocating a centralized regulation of Jewish persecution, making it easier to manipulate the image of persecution and facilitating the alignment of state agencies. As early as May 1934, a month before the purge of Röhm's SA, Heydrich was behind Hitler's "political anti-Semitism," which aimed to push all Jews out of Germany. At the same time street violence continued to erupt, especially in the spring and summer of 1934 and 1935. In 1935 spasms of public violence against Jews expelled them from public swimming pools, damaged their businesses, or caused such disruption at the weddings of Jews to non-Jews that the police sometimes took both the bride and the groom into "protective custody." Some actions were aimed at publicly humiliating or punishing those who did business with the Jews. Instigated by the Hitler Youth, more and more people joined in these attacks. When the police interfered, the "majority of the population" derided them as "Jewish lackeys."[14]

Consolidating support for the moment, Hitler tolerated this lawless rioting. In Berlin, authorities also found these outbreaks useful as public evidence that the Jews must be legally cordoned off. On July 30, 1935, following a bloody rally against the Jews on the streets of Berlin, the authorities met to identify ways to conduct the persecution of Berlin's Jews while precluding both public demonstrations and any *Einzelaktion* (unauthorized, individual) attacks on Jews. Berlin police president

Wolf-Heinrich Graf von Helldorf instructed marriage offices to reject petitions from Jews applying to marry non-Jews; Heydrich urged "in light of the unrest [that] arose from the racial defiling activities of German women," the Justice Ministry must "as soon as possible prohibit further legal intermarriages but also legally prohibit sexual relations between Aryans and Jews outside of marriage." In August 1935 the SD's Jewish Office declared that "a solution to the Jewish question was not attainable through acts of terrorism," adding that "individual outbursts against Jews must be stopped by 'clear legislation.'" A particular problem that had already drawn the attention of the SD was the "legal uncertainty regarding mixed [Jewish/non-Jewish] marriages."[15]

On August 20, 1935, Hitler issued another of his several orders banning unauthorized individual attacks on Jews, and again he found support from the SD. On September 9, Heydrich's deputy, Dr. Werner Best, explained that "the Jewish question cannot be solved by use of force, through harassment of individuals, destruction of personal property, or other individual actions." Rather, their dissolution should be brought about "step by step" in conjunction with a "more energetic enlightenment of the public through the press and the party." That September, the Reichstag (with membership transformed by the Nazis), unanimously approved the Nuremberg Laws to define and further exclude Jews from German society. Whereas just one grandparent had sufficed under the "Aryan Paragraph" of April 1933 to identify a German as Jewish, the Nuremberg Laws required three Jewish grandparents and only a fraction of persons with one Jewish parent were categorized as Jews by the Nuremberg Laws.

Hitler shared the overall aims of those pushing for a stricter definition, but he disciplined them to undertake persecution bit by bit, in stages. At a party ceremony two days after the approval of the Nuremberg Laws, Hitler again emphasized that following the new laws, "every individual action against Jews" was prohibited.[16] Several weeks later party radical Julius Streicher declared that any person participating in an *Einzelaktion* was an enemy of the state; the Germans would resolve the Jewish Question "by legal means!" Having portrayed the individual outbreaks of violence against the Jews that summer as the reason for the Nuremberg Laws, Hitler continued to present the laws as the new normative social behavior. As if handing over state enforcement to the people in trust, Hitler called for the laws to be "honored through the most rigorous discipline of the entire German people." The people, Hitler instructed, should ensure with their unbending will that the German race would be kept pure since this was the "basis for the prosperity of the people." Werner Best had been working for Hitler's bureaucratic approach. In December 1935, he expounded upon the importance of legally formulating and bureaucratizing the persecution of Jews in coordination with what was acceptable to popular opinion. He called for a "step by step" removal of the Jews as propaganda increasingly brought opinion in line. The Nazi leadership was bound to solve the "Jewish Problem," he said, but at the same time it must work toward the ultimate goal of aligning opinion and policies. Several years later, Heydrich said that this approach was working well since denunciations from the general public kept the Jews in the corner according to the regime's regulations.[17]

To restrain party zealots who thought that Gestapo methods were all the regime needed to exercise leadership, Hitler was tactful enough to repeat his orders against individual actions or have others repeat them. In February 1936 during the Winter Olympics hosted by Germany, it proved necessary for Hitler's deputy Rudolf Hess, collaborating with Interior Minister Frick, to once again issue a strict ban on any individual action against Jews. The assassination by a Jew on February 4 of Wilhelm Gustloff, the party's leading representative in Switzerland, might have resulted in wild reprisals. But at that moment, Hitler preferred a propagandistic response, changing the plan to christen a new cruise liner after himself and naming it instead the *Wilhelm Gustloff*.[18] Given its use by the Strength through Joy program to transport thousands of grateful Germans to vacations they had never before dared to dream of, the shrewdly named cruise liner served to alert many Germans to the murder of a Nazi leader by a Jew.

In February 1937, even as he contemplated throwing German Jews into ghettos, Heydrich advised the party headquarters in Munich that there were no reasons to prohibit Jews from constructing restaurants since this was no longer expected to spark individual actions. Allowing such construction was working in line with tactics toward the Leader's goals. SS Officer Adolf Eichmann, on the other hand, expressed a different opinion. The RSHA "Jewish specialist" who would soon be charged with expediting the emigration of Austrian Jews, Eichmann stated in early 1937 that "the anger of the people expressed in riots [was] the most effective means to rob the Jews of a sense of security." The rampages on Berlin's Kurfürstendamm, he thought, had demonstrated a real impact. Heydrich, by contrast, was so offended by the riots Austrian Nazis were staging against the Jews that he threatened to dispatch the Gestapo to stop them.[19]

For tactical reasons, the SD rejected violence against Jews during the spring of 1938 on the streets of Berlin, Magdeburg, and Frankfurt. The SD claimed that arrests were more effective for frightening Jews into leaving the Reich than street-brawling initiated by Goebbels. By late June 1938, worried that the street violence of radical party members might get out of hand, Hitler compelled Goebbels to rein them in. Goebbels fought back to protect his power, seizing the shooting of a German diplomat in Paris on November 7 by a young Jew, Herschel Grynszpan, as an opportunity for public rioting against the Jews. That same day, Goebbels's Propaganda Ministry had begun to shape German opinion by identifying Grynszpan's act as part of a Jewish conspiracy. During local pogroms that erupted—especially in Hesse—on November 7 and 8, Goebbels tested popular response.[20]

It seems that Hitler was not expecting to use the assassination by Grynszpan to initiate a nationwide pogrom since he considered different plans for a solution to the "Jewish Problem" with Goering, probably during the afternoon of November 9. Hitler supported the forced emigration of Jews, planning to use whatever police force and terror necessary, without resorting to riots. Although the Kristallnacht pogrom of November 9, 1938, went against Hitler's statements and orders questioning the effectiveness of pogroms, he nevertheless approved Goebbels's proposal, during the evening of November 9, to unleash the Reich-wide pogrom. As party elites assembled for the anniversary of the Beer Hall Putsch in Munich's Old Town Hall that evening, Hitler had an intense conversation with Goebbels and then left the hall. According to Goebbels's account and later statements from several Nazis present at the event, Hitler made a decision during his short conversation with Goebbels to allow demonstrations that had erupted against Jews to continue without police intervention. "Let the demonstrations continue," Goebbels reports Hitler telling him. "Withdraw the police. Allow the Jews to feel the people's wrath for once."[21]

With his power at this point so firmly established, Hitler's authorization of a pogrom cannot be explained as an appeasement of party members who agitated for street violence. Hitler did not, however, slight Goebbels's rivals who aimed to solve the "Jewish Question" with law and order. Himmler and Heydrich were brought into the implementation and execution of the pogrom on the evening of November 9, after Goebbels was already moving ahead with it, with Hitler authorizing them to arrest tens of thousands of Jews during the rioting.[22]

Attacks on Jews, including the burning of scores of synagogues across the Reich, began just before midnight. In hundreds of communities across the Reich, the Nazis initiated fifteen hours of improvised violence. The pogrom was carried out primarily by the SA, with the assistance of tens of thousands of Germans who joined in attacking and robbing the Jews. Since the Röhm Putsch the SA had not played such a prominent role, nor would there be any further such riots in pogrom style during the Third Reich. Scores of Jews were killed and tens of thousands sent to concentration camps in Buchenwald, Dachau, and Sachsenhausen. The pogrom pressured Jews to leave Germany after surrendering their property for cut-rate prices. Goebbels, raging and fantasizing, claimed that "the entire German people" had risen up against the Jews, with "popular anger" unleashed. Although many Germans did not support the disorderly destruction, their participation or silence allowed Goebbels to declare the pogrom a result of the righteous indignation in the collective German soul and the regime the direct agent of the people. His claim that popular opinion consistently governed public policy was a fantasy fitted to the regime's aspirations.[23]

Less than twenty-four hours after he had agreed to the pogrom, Hitler decided to stop the violence, while also telling Goebbels over lunch on November 10 that he was pleased with the pogrom. While such a large-scale event required Hitler's approval, he would not have wanted to be publicly associated with lawless destruction on the streets; indeed, according to the SD reports, the Kristallnacht pogrom had not been well received by the populace because of the disorder it caused. Once again, the German habit of giving Hitler the benefit of the doubt came into play, as the public did not blame Hitler. For his part that evening, Hitler expressed disappointment with the people for its aversion to another war: the people must learn that force was necessary for handling a problem if it could not be resolved by other means, and they should follow the party's belief that it would triumph in the end, regardless of setbacks, he said. Violence on German streets, on the other hand, could not be permitted to continue, and by November 12 Goebbels claimed that all had quieted down in the Reich, followed the next day by the assurance that "absolute quiet *(Ruhe)* rules the land."[24]

Maintaining the appearance of order was a very high priority for the Leader. In August 1941, when Goebbels pushed him to require German Jews to wear the Star of David, he took measures to minimize popular objections and public attacks on Jews. Hitler followed in the path of Graf von der Schulenburg, who in Prussia's weakened state following its defeat by Napoleon in 1806 famously declared that "Quiescence is the number-one civic duty." During World War I, the German people refuted this message by developing an independent public sphere critical of the faltering Wilhelmine regime (a development Hitler associated with a Stab in the Back). During their early months in power, the Nazis unleashed violence in public to repress their enemies. But Hitler quickly "restricted and formalized" the "threat of violence," wrote the historian Henry Friedlander, because it disrupted the social order and offended opinion at home and abroad. Kristallnacht was the last Nazi pogrom against the German Jews, and predictably the Germans clearly objected to the damage and disorderliness it caused. Wishing to preempt German unrest and protest because of the treatment of the Jews, the regime then resumed its persecution of Germans through professionals in the law and bureaucracy.[25]

STREET DEMONSTRATIONS AS NAZI POWER:
THE CASE OF BISHOP SPROLL

The practice of freezing out dissidents and outsiders was a familiar practice in Germany and not just in church circles. Bismarck's anti-Socialist laws, promulgated in the 1870s and 1880s to squeeze the life out of German socialism, were aided by "social boycotts." In the late nineteenth and early twentieth centuries the German Conservatives were also associated with this method, with General Josias von Heeringen telling the Reichstag in 1911 that anyone who spoke out against anti-Semitism in the military risked "the social boycott."[26] The Germans, including Nazis, who resisted the 1923 invasion of the Ruhr socially spurned French soldiers by collectively getting up to leave, emptying an entire locale the moment a French soldier entered a bar or restaurant.[27]

In the province of Württemberg, Catholics had a long acquaintance with the social exclusion of outsiders. Some fifty years before the Nazis a peasant girl from the village of Marpingen had reported seeing an apparition of the Virgin Mary. Great streams of people arrived in waves of religious enthusiasm to view the site of the vision. Alarmed, Prussian state authorities dispatched troops to quell the epidemic disquiet. Against the Catholic enclave, however, they proved inadequate: the pilgrimages continued despite heavy policing and fines. The community simply drove the police off by mocking and shadowing them; the locksmiths for conducting house searches had to be brought in from distant locations since none closer in wanted to break the village solidarity. Throngs of well-wishers greeted arrested villagers like heroes upon their release, as the widespread noncompliance muddled Prussian police control and proved Catholic solidarity "very hard to break."[28]

Decades later, Hitler envisioned a national society that would also act instinctively to defend its Nazi identity. Acting in solidarity, masses would discipline everyone to either fall in line or face social death. The general Nazi principle of upholding the image of public order shaped the party-initiated demonstrations against Bishop Johannes Baptista Sproll, in his Württemberg diocese seated on the Nekkar River, one hundred miles east of Marpingen. These demonstrations stretched from April to July 1938, four months before the explosion of violence against Germany's Jews during the Kristallnacht.

Bishop Sproll was an outspoken defender of the Catholic faith and its institutions although he, like other high-ranking clergy of both denominations, had openly thrown his support behind the new government. Together with his Protestant associate in Württemberg, Bishop Theophil Wurm, Sproll had pledged loyalty in 1933 to the Nazi "national renewal," and he supported the war at the outset. On September 8, 1939, as Hitler ordered a ban on state provocations of the churches, Sproll issued a pastoral letter read two days later, imploring God to be with those fighting for the Fatherland.[29]

Yet sooner and much more directly than others, Sproll expressed reservations and drew a line against state encroachments on church traditions. According to his biographer, his capacity to resist increased as he practiced speaking out. He stood out brilliantly, for example, in his objection to the mandatory sterilization of "incurables," required by law as of July 14, 1933. In an early and highly unusual exertion of his power as bishop, Sproll directed Stuttgart's Marien Hospital in February 1934 not to carry out these officially mandated sterilizations, a directive that went beyond the mere verbal objections from other Catholic leaders. Sproll's directive was sufficient to stop the sterilizations at the Marien, illustrating what one bishop with courage could accomplish, even against the tide of other bishops. Over the course of the next several years Sproll stepped up his dissent, holding a series of public meetings attended by thousands in which he decried the general Nazi threat to the Catholic Church. He openly questioned Hitler's decisions and wondered why Hitler trusted Alfred Rosenberg, an influential Nazi intellectual known for his unsparing denunciations of Christianity, "with oversight of the National Socialist worldview."[30]

On February 1, 1938, the senior prosecutor for Stuttgart officially charged Sproll for treason, filing an indictment with the Reich justice minister in Berlin. The prosecutor noted that "the head Gestapo office in Stuttgart" had backed his recommendation for prosecution "in the interest of the National Socialist state and the movement," finding it "absolutely necessary." All in all, the prosecutor warned, Sproll's admonitions were leading to "an increased hostility toward the party." The specific charges included the misuse of the pulpit during sermons from April to October 1937. Sproll transgressed the boundary separating politics from religion so flagrantly that his sermons reminded one incensed prosecutor of the political meetings of the Catholic Center Party.[31]

The dictatorship's determined efforts to undermine the loyalty of Catholic youth weighed heavily on Sproll. When he learned that religious instructions in the schools were to be given according to Nazi principles, he reversed his previous directives of obedience and ordered his subordinates not to take the oath of loyalty to Hitler. Again he acted against the pattern of his bishop colleagues. Sproll condemned the suppression of religious symbols and instruction in schools and criticized a law to facilitate divorce. From the pulpit he condemned a song popular in the Hitler Youth.[32]

Foreseeing an increased suppression of Christianity, Sproll appealed to his parishioners to be ready for a "great struggle." From his position of oversight, he was able to point out a pattern that individuals might miss: the Germans who had cast their vote to retain Catholic schools had ceased to receive state welfare assistance, in contrast to those who had voted for Nazi "community schools."[33] The bishop urged the faithful to take a stand against state incursions on church practices but warned that such a stand could cost them their share of public welfare assistance or even their jobs. The church, Sproll assured, would provide in place of the state.

The Stuttgart prosecutor admitted with regret that the bishop had made an impact and was regarded as a kind of "hero." As evidence, he reported that shortly after Sproll's recent speeches, the Catholic participation in the Harvest Festival had been very poor. The contributions in 1937 to the Winter Relief Fund also fell considerably, although the income of the rural population there had been up from the previous year. The prosecutor was sure that the blame for these changes could be laid on Bishop Sproll, a culpability he assigned by comparing the continuing high contributions of the region's Protestants. The regime understood the amount of contributions to its public welfare appeal as a plebiscite on its popular appeal, and the reductions in contributions represented a practice that impeded the party's forward momentum among the people, a bottom-line concern for Hitler. "The major part of the population of Württemberg-Oberlandes was stirred up by the bishop's speech on October 10," wrote the prosecutor, "and Catholics who were members of the party had now been drawn into conflicts of conscience by Sproll's declaration that the party was basically hostile to Christianity." One farmer was overheard saying to another, "I'm glad I did not join the party. I wanted to join the party too but now I'm glad, because only now is it known that the party is against belief. The bishop said it clearly today."[34]

It took courage, but by questioning the regime's line, the bishop had made an issue of matters where silence suggested that there was neither dissent nor reason for it. The prosecutor indicted Sproll in January, shortly before the Anschluss on March 13, 1938. Two days after the German Army marched into Austria, the archbishop of Vienna, Cardinal Theodor Innitzer, visited Hitler, following up with a proclamation throughout Austria that Catholics must vote "yes" on the upcoming plebiscite from Berlin. The church prized the accomplishments of National Socialism, he explained, domestically as well as internationally. In Germany the bishops, including Sproll, went along with Reich Church Minister Hans Kerrl's order that all the church bells throughout Austria and Germany be rung as "an overwhelming sign of the commitment of the entire nation to the Führer and his work." Propaganda officials then took the next step in aligning church and state by ordering church newsletters, published under the direction of the bishops, to print state press releases hyping the Anschluss by welcoming "returning brothers" home into the Reich and urging the faithful to approve of the Anschluss in the plebiscite. Only one bishop, Berlin's Konrad von Preysing, refused to print the state propaganda in his diocesan newsletter as if it were church literature (Sproll complied).[35]

The wall of nearly unanimous popular acclaim among German and Austrian people for the Anschluss seemed to present an opportunity for identifying Sproll as a lone, untrustworthy outsider in a national plebiscite of April 10, 1938, that asked, "Do you agree with the reunification of Austria with the German Reich that was enacted on March 13, 1938, and do you vote for the party of our leader Adolf Hitler?" Sproll stressed openly that he was fully in favor of the Anschluss; he "gladly greeted" the annexation of Austria and had celebrated it with a general ringing of the church bells.[36] But he had not voted because he disapproved of the Reichstag candidates associated with the same ballot.

German officials condemned Sproll's absence from the plebiscite as a "conscious demonstrative action against party and state, and some demanded that he be removed from his diocese." At the same time, the majority of the bishops continued to adhere to diplomatic tactics and some gestures of appeasement. In 1927, Eugenio Pacelli, the future pope, had characterized Sproll as "without fear of men" but lacking "the refinement in personal conduct and the sense of tact of his predecessor." He contrasted with the other bishops, who were tactful enough not to complain publicly. The German ambassador to the Vatican, Carl-Ludwig Diego von Bergen, reported to the Foreign Ministry on June 10, "In cler-

ical circles the bishop's behavior is considered abundantly unsophisticated," adding that it may have been "less honest but more effective had
[Sproll] participated in the vote but spoiled his ballot!"[37]

The case of Bishop Clemens August von Galen, however, shows that
Bergen was not necessarily correct. Galen successfully advocated the defense of church practices with sermons from the pulpit and mobilized
the laity in opposition to some Reich inroads on church practices. Hitler
acknowledged Galen's successes by identifying him as one of the "sly
foxes of the Catholic Church."[38] While Sproll did attract thousands to his
speeches and gained considerable public stature, the bishop did not increase the weight of his dissent by mobilizing the faithful for church
causes as Galen did. Nor did he coordinate his dissent clearly and openly
with his church public as Meiser had done, mobilizing obvious support
in his own defense. He did not push the Conference of Bishops to collectively mobilize the Catholic masses in protest, as Preysing and Galen did.

Nazi leaders were more confident about singling out Sproll for an
attack in 1938 because he was somewhat of a loner among the Catholic
bishops.[39] With popular support overwhelmingly on its side in the matter
of the Anschluss, the regime instigated demonstrations against Sproll,
saying that in the district surrounding Rottenburg the bishop was the
only person who had not participated in the vote on April 10, 1938. Beginning April 11, local Nazi organizations initiated an assembly of
crowds in front of his Rottenburg palace to angrily denounce Sproll,
while the judiciary could only look on.[40] These crowds were aimed at
convincing the bishop, who had already left town, to flee his diocese. The
Gestapo could have carted him off at any moment. But the dictatorship
aimed to test whether local residents could be mobilized to ostracize
Sproll, causing him to leave without creating a martyr of the bishop.
Authorities hoped the public would play the most visible role, acting like
a mature Volksgemeinschaft in line with National Socialist principles
on its own, by ostracizing a troublesome prelate through social bullying
and shunning.

The first official demonstration against Bishop Sproll mobilized
some five hundred persons the evening following the plebiscite and ran
according to the regime's plans as an orderly display of undivided popular opinion: Sproll had transgressed against the people, and now they
could no longer follow him as bishop. Members of the Hitler Youth and

the League of German Girls marched in disciplined rows to the bishop's palace, arriving at about 9:30 p.m., where the "large crowd" was already gathered. The crowd denounced Sproll in a chorus as a "Traitor." Other voices rose, sometimes alone and sometimes in unison, with some calling for Sproll's execution.[41] The hounding continued for some forty-five minutes, according to Vicar General Max Kottmann, Sproll's deputy.

This demonstration was the beginning of what Bishop Konrad von Preysing, the rare bishop who viewed the Nazi state as an outright enemy of the church, called a "showdown" *(Kraftprobe)*. Amid cries of "Bring that flag down," a storm of people broke into the bishop's house and confiscated the Swastika, which Sproll had on display under the eaves. While there were those who became eager for a riot and the intimidation of force, the Nazi leaders in Berlin demanded a more muted approach: they wanted the crowd to express a unanimous, insistent opinion without resorting to destruction. On April 13, Rottenburg's *Landrat* (district chairman) Alfred Chormann said that "population near and far" was so strongly agitated by Sproll's abstention from the plebiscite that he would be advised not to appear in public for at least several days.[42]

The following day, the chief of the German Security Service, Reinhard Heydrich, appeared in a coordinating role among national-level authorities with a report on the Sproll demonstrations that he sent to Göring, Bormann, Kerrl, Foreign Minister Joachim Ribbentrop, and various police agencies. Heydrich's first expressed concern was, not surprisingly, with legality. Sproll's flag had been rightly removed on the grounds that "traitors had no right to display the symbol of the Third Reich." The SS, he stated, was fully behind these new street "rallies" against Sproll on condition that they be conducted without violence, remaining strictly disciplined displays of people opinion. Should Sproll return, Heydrich warned, he would be met with further "rallies."

Sproll did return, on April 21, and Heydrich's "rallies" resumed that night and continued over the course of successive evenings. The following day, according to Kottmann, a "demonstration" with about one hundred persons in civilian clothing made an orderly march through the city, from the Rottenburg Rathaus to Sproll's palace, which they then surrounded. Again and again, for half an hour, the demands of the crowd rang out in a chorus: "Where is the traitor?" "The bishop must go!" and "We want a decent, German bishop!" Referencing Sproll's comparison of German and Soviet oppression, some yelled, "Off to Moscow!" Sproll claimed that basic Christian principles undermined the premise of the "racial" state. "All around one hears of a 'German God,'" Sproll said. "This is, however, not the God that Christ taught us. . . . One now makes meeting and school rooms out of church buildings, then calls it 'a national German Church.' . . . Christ did not want to create a national church, however, but a world church." The irony, according to Sproll, was that Germany was the only country other than "Russia" without a free Catholic press.[43]

Kottmann concluded that the April 21 demonstrators were locals since the bishop's household staff had recognized and recorded the names of "a considerable number" of them. Church leaders thought that in some cases the party paid the people to demonstrate.[44] For the regime it was a successful show of common opinion expressed in unison.

Under assault by the demonstrators, Bishop Sproll's staff had tried in vain to call on the police for protection on the evening of April 21. The following day the Gestapo office in Stuttgart informed the bishop's diocese in writing that the bishop would be receiving no protection from the police since he had earned his treatment at the hands of the people! Healthy people opinion, according to Nazi theory of the law, would act as prosecutor, judge, and jury. Sproll's behavior, the Gestapo charged, was contrary to that of "millions of faithful Catholics," as well as to that of "numerous other German bishops." Since the "entire population" saw his failure to vote as a provocation, "state officials have no reason to repress the justified exasperation of the people." Further demonstrations would not be hindered. Instead, Sproll was advised to leave the diocese and Württemberg.[45]

On April 23, four churchmen were attacked, arrested, and thrown in jail for eight days, raising the level of fear in the bishop's household. By the following morning, Sproll had left Rottenburg to avoid the pending rallies that had already been announced. He was leaving, he said, "to spare the entire people the sight of German comrades physically attacking a bishop." But according to Kottmann, the demonstrations continued through Holy Week and then during the following week of Easter as well.[46] Rather than dampening mobilization, his absence had been seen as a gathering force. Bishop Galen inquired of Kottmann on April 29 as to what the "clergy and the Catholic people had undertaken to protect and defend the bishop."[47]

In early May, the local Nazi leader in Rottenburg turned to petitions, another lawful tactic also used by Catholics to defend their practices. Showing how deeply the Nazi tactics had been able to pierce the armor of the Catholic milieu, Catholic Church members collected signatures for the petitions, which demanded the replacement of Sproll with a "Roman Catholic bishop in Rottenburg who is a good German." From various parts of Württemberg—the counties of Ehingen, Balubeuren Ellwangen, Mergentheim, and Spaichingen included—Catholics and some Protestants signed the petitions.[48]

Reich officials at very high levels weighed in about the possibilities of removing a bishop through the collective action of the people. Writing to the Foreign Ministry on May 5, Kerrl characterized the situation as the regime hoped it would be viewed: the "justified fury of the people" had forced the bishop to leave. Because Sproll had offended the people and its Führer, Kerrl said, the people "have justifiably turned against this man." Careful to separate Sproll from the other bishops and the church as a whole, Kerrl added, "It can also not be expected of the German bishops to enter into official business with a bishop who in such a way has closed himself out of the people's community."[49]

With almost no one publicly standing up for him and Catholics calling for him to leave, Sproll stayed away. On May 7, Kottmann reported that the demonstrations had been magnified by conversations: "throughout the entire province and beyond" the talk was about the demonstrations and related measures against Sproll.[50] The regime must have been eager to show that in the years since Bishops Meiser and Wurm had used these tactics to defend their church, the people had realigned themselves and had now turned against a neighboring bishop to side with the party and state.

For the most part, Sproll's fellow bishops did not come to his rescue. On May 5, Bishop Heinrich Wienken of Meissen expressed the opinion that the best response was to wait in "peace," neither speaking for or against the gathering petitions. And Bishop Albert Stohr from Mainz either had accepted the Nazi explanation for events or was propagating the party message: Sproll's action, he stated, had "brought the people's soul to a boil" (the phrase Goebbels used to explain the Kristallnacht attack on Jews). Stohr followed with a warning that the present disturbance was the result of confrontation, cautioning leading priests across

Germany that a pastoral letter questioning the regime, or any insistence on maintaining religious instructions in schools, might well lead to a similar scene. It was also possible, he said, that bishops other than Sproll would be put under state pressures. Perhaps hoping for safety in solidarity, he suggested that the bishops stand together in requesting Sproll's return.[51]

In fact, the Nazi effort to stir up a popular confrontation against Sproll had begun to encounter limitations without the leadership of a bishop. Some German Catholics pointed out that only the Vatican could select a bishop and that this process must not be compromised. On a more fundamental level, the struggle over Sproll had begun to cast light on the church struggle itself. Some Catholics were now coming to see for the first time what southern German Protestants had already learned in similar confrontations in 1934: church institutions and Nazi practices were not always compatible. A priest in Allmendingen now asked those who had signed the petitions for Sproll's replacement to rescind their signatures. But publicly he defended the church institutions rather than Sproll, as he led prayers "for the sins of the dishonor that our bishop Johannes Baptista himself has done against the Holy Father, the Church of Christ, and, yes, Christ himself!"[52]

For some, the issues were more complex. One Catholic priest said that the petitions against Sproll brought with them "unspeakable moral dilemmas." Sproll's case had brought to the fore a quandary that had been present since the Nazi assumption of power—that of two competing sources of authority: "No upright German, above all no official, would say that he is an enemy of the state," he said. "Just the same, no upright German Catholic, or German official, could take a position against his bishop and he may not do so."[53]

At the upper levels of the church, there were also some who were more courageous than Wienken or Stohr. Rather than allowing the party total control of the story, Bishop Galen of Münster displayed courage. Expressing a perspective that was being blacked out until he spoke, Galen took the pulpit on May 10 to say that Sproll was acting as a "free German man using his rights."[54] Sproll was "confronting the paganism of the state and we must back him up!" he declared. After all, Galen explained, Sproll was not opposed to the Anschluss but only to the list of Nazis attached to the vote, some of whom were enemies of the church;

this was a fact that the regime wished to bury. Appealing to the dictator-ship's concern for legality, Galen openly pointed out, "There is no law in Germany requiring one to vote. It is always claimed that full freedom reigns and that each can act according to his conscience. Thus whoever has pangs of conscience about participating in this so-called Reichstag vote has the right and the freedom to ignore the vote."

Bringing the discussion into the open from his position of author-ity, Galen aimed to challenge the official story of events in support of Sproll. His tactic depended on his pulpit, not on the support from other bishops. He also wrote to Archbishop Conrad Gröber of Freiburg to ex-plain and requested that clergy around the Reich set the story straight about Sproll by reading pastoral letters from the pulpit. He had already done so in a sermon in Hildesheim, Galen said, but that was hardly enough. "If everyone is silent and no one corrects the version of the story spread by officials, the result will be clear," he wrote to Wienken.[55]

Bishop Galen refocused the dispute on individual conscience rather than on Sproll's vote. In Berlin, Nuncio Cesare Orsenigo and the Ger-many episcopacy were most concerned with dispelling the unrest and the diplomatic difficulties the Sproll case caused. But tensions arose over the tactics they should use. Preysing, siding with his ally Galen, continued to favor a united public mobilization of church authorities and laypeople. Perceiving political influence to be grounded in Catholic solidarity, the two bishops' strategy for defending Sproll and the church included a role for ordinary churchgoers. The regime was responsive to political pres-sures of the crowd but not to diplomatic protests or arguments among in-siders, the bishops argued. Archbishop Adolf Bertram, chair of the Fulda Bishop's Conference and a strong ally of Hitler's popular stance of anti-Bolshevism, took exception. Throughout the Nazi period he and the majority of bishops continued to oppose popular mobilization and con-frontation.[56]

Having been ordered back to his diocese by the Vatican after it had refused his requests for a reassignment, Sproll reflected on his dilemma: "If I return, there will doubtless be further demonstrations," he wrote, "but if I stay away, I will be accused of cowardice and flight." A possible path around the horns of this dilemma was provided by a hope that the demonstrations would die down (a perspective oblivious to the party's role in instigating them). In Augsburg the Catholic bishop estimated it would be two or three weeks before "the wave of unrest calmed down somewhat."[57]

Party leaders now preferred a continuing demonstration of popular outrage—in contrast to the simultaneous 1934 arrests of two Protestant bishops. But the demonstrations were to remain limited to disciplined marches and catchphrases. In anticipation of Sproll's return to Rottenburg, the party district leader in Rottweil passed along commensurate instructions to all local group leaders on July 7, 1938, charging that "The Gau leadership will determine which measures to take in this matter. Other initiatives are forbidden. . . . The Gau leadership demands the most strict discipline at demonstrations, etc., for which I must make the local group leader [Ortsgruppenleiter] responsible."[58]

Meanwhile Württemberg's Reich Governor and Gauleiter Wilhelm Murr had invited further anger by publishing an article upbraiding and belittling Sproll in his region's newspapers. As one of the "few" who had not understood the great beneficence of the Leader in calling Germans together to greatness—and the call now included Austrians—Sproll had disobeyed the Concordat that bound him to loyalty to the German Reich and thus must be banned from his diocese. Murr concluded that the bishop wished for a glorious martyrdom but would be denied. On May 25 Murr had written to Ernst von Weizsäcker, the Foreign Ministry's point man for the anti-Sproll demonstrations, that Sproll was under orders from the Vatican to return to his diocese. Sproll had asked Murr for the promise of police protection, but Murr retreated behind popular opinion with the quip that people opinion would prevent the bishop from a "peaceful return."[59]

Forcing the bishop to leave had been a question of prestige for Murr. Like other Gauleiters, he fancied himself to be a man of the people, eager to prove himself the most effective of all. He had recently boasted, "There is no doubt that our political opposition in Württemberg has exhausted itself once and for all." Still, he proceeded cautiously lest Sproll be seen as a martyr and arouse anger against Murr's leadership.[60]

Sproll would not return until July 15. Upon arriving, the bishop threw down the gauntlet with an announcement that he would not be leaving again. The party acted quickly to avoid the appearance that the bishop was coming and going as he pleased. Planned "protest rallies" (as Ambassador Bergen called them) resumed in front of the bishop's residence, including a mass assembly on July 16 that Heydrich characterized as a "protest action by the party."

Emphasizing the importance of disciplined nonaggression in his report to Reich Chancellery director Hans Lammers, Heydrich wrote, "The responsible police department was informed that the necessary preparations had been met and no excesses were to be feared." Summarizing various official reports, he stated that 150–200 persons had gathered, of which 50 were Hitler Youth from Rottenburg and the rest were party members, including some SS men wearing civilian clothing. Up to 400 additional people had gathered out of curiosity, without taking part. The only protest slogan that Heydrich (like Murr) identified in the report was "We want a German bishop!" Ambassador Bergen, in contrast to Heydrich and Murr, wrote that the slogans had included "Traitor of the Fatherland!" and "Black Gypsy!"[61]

The diocese itself reported that the demonstration of July 16 consisted of only some one hundred people, mostly youth, but identified it as "by far the worst" yet. Rather than proceeding with the discipline that Nazi leaders had called for, "scoundrels" pushed their way inside and demanded to speak to the bishop, whom they found praying on an upper floor. Again, police refused to intervene. For more than an hour protesters shouted, some holding up posters.[62]

This demonstration proved to be a turning point, despite Minister Kerrl's explanation that "one cannot expect the German police to protect a man who has not observed his most basic duty to the people and Führer from the mass of the people." According to Bergen, this disgraceful treatment of a bishop made a considerable impression not just on the people of Rottenburg, but also on those in all of south and west Germany; several bishops also now spoke from the pulpit about the unworthy treatment of a fellow bishop. These church members and leaders were not talking about defying the state but only about order and the protection of a respected personage. Gauleiter Murr justified the regime's actions as the authentic displeasure of the people, which was registered "even in distant quarters," and four days later he added that the popular unrest was not likely to die down so long as Sproll remained bishop.[63]

But Murr's self-justifications hardly mattered since decisions on the demonstrations were handled well over his head. The aroused sympathy for the bishop drew concern from Berlin. Heydrich and Lammers were already following the Rottenburg events while Murr was sending his earnest Berlin reports to Kerrl, who had been allowed to express confidence, along with Murr, in people justice.

Various important offices were now tracking and reporting on the demonstrations. From Rome, Eugenio Pacelli (soon to be Pope Pius XII) reported that 2,000–2,500 demonstrators had gathered at the bishop's palace on July 19, where a party official rebuked the bishop for treason but also "repeatedly ordered the crowd to maintain discipline." Pacelli, who like the German bishops favored the methods of those of his aristocratic station over the street protests of the hoi polloi, now echoed Galen's sentiment that Sproll had only exercised his freedoms under the law not to vote, and thus the Vatican was not willing to remove him. Church leaders who favored diplomacy were willing to send appeals to Hitler. Although Hitler was the ultimate authority on the demonstrations, these appeals to him perhaps reflected the widespread notion that if only Hitler knew, justice would be done. In addition, the church sought legal action against speakers at the demonstration for vilifying Sproll.[64]

Like Bishop Meiser in 1934, the Catholic bishops separated Hitler from the demonstrators and their claims. "Our Führer Adolf Hitler has reached out his hand to every honest German," they said. They pointed out that a party spokesman who had addressed the demonstration on July 18 had repeatedly demanded that the demonstrators preserve order, stating, "We will reach our goals faster if we maintain discipline and don't allow ourselves to be drawn into physical attacks outside the law." At this point, Cardinal Bertram wrote to Hitler on July 21, requesting that the demonstrations against Sproll be curbed. Stopping demonstrations, he noted, was in the interest of reinforcing the appearance of Germany as a country ruled by law. Bishop Galen added that he would be very happy if he were soon able to report to his diocese that Bertram's appeal to Hitler had been successful.[65]

In Hitler's long-term vision, clamping down further on the church at this point was not important relative to having its full backing as war approached. The bishops on the whole had given him ample reason to believe they would support him as long as he was successful on behalf of Germany, although it was now clear that they would not back the state in its effort to remove one of their own. Furthermore, the Vatican and the German bishops now appeared united in questioning the regime's tactics. Even Germany's Vatican ambassador, Bergen, began to point out what he saw as counterproductive results of the dictatorship's methods, noting that they were not exactly optimal for creating an atmosphere of understanding and agreement.

But in response to complaints from the papal nuncio, Deputy State Secretary Ernst Woermann of the Foreign Ministry (Weizsäcker's successor) emphasized that the demonstrations were a popular response that Sproll had brought on himself. Thus, as if it were out of the state's hands, the only solution for the Vatican was to withdraw Sproll, Woermann advised. He took the position that Sproll's actions "should not be evaluated from a purely juristic perspective; politically the nonparticipation in the vote is to be seen as a demonstration."[66]

But opinion was changing, as Bergen now warned, and the demonstrations had aroused sympathies that might begin to make a martyr of Sproll after all. As the Foreign Ministry continued to express concerns about foreigners' impressions of Germany, Heydrich said that the state would continue to hound Sproll with further demonstrations and reiterated to other Reich officials that "excesses" (violence and destruction) would, as Cardinal Bertram had requested, definitely be curbed. The concern at the top with maintaining strict discipline reflected the apprehensions Hitler had shown all along about public riots if demonstrations spun out of control and the related fear that a display of controversy, rather than unity, would begin to stimulate open sympathy for Sproll.[67]

ONLY HITLER CAN DECIDE WHETHER TO TERMINATE THE DEMONSTRATIONS

On July 23 Kerrl acknowledged that the regime's intention was to achieve Sproll's ouster "with street demonstrations," if possible.[68] But that night a particularly violent demonstration led to a decisive break in the party's effort to drive the bishop out by the force of demonstrated united popular opinion. In its aftermath, Germans publicly questioned why the police had not protected the bishop, even though Archbishop Gröber had been at Sproll's palace that day. According to a report of the Stuttgart Gestapo to Berlin, the number of demonstrators was between 2,500 and 3,000. The party had stationed "watchmen" to prevent break-ins and other damage, but the "storm" of people beat them bloody, so "the action got completely out of the control of the party members responsible for it." Demonstrators pried and stormed their way into the palace, tossed "files out the windows and rummaged through the beds in the rooms of the palace. One bed was ignited. The Bishop was with Archbishop Groeber of Freiburg and the ladies and gentlemen of his ménage in the chapel at prayer. About 25 to 30 people pressed into this chapel and harassed those present. Archbishop Groeber was mistaken as Bishop Sproll, grabbed by the robe and dragged back and forth."[69]

As glass from the broken windows clattered to the ground, above the din, a party's county leader rebuked the marauders and then tried to reason with them: "Through your behavior you are providing the bishop the greatest service and hand[ing] him a weapon that he wishes to have. Such behavior is not consistent with our demonstrations." The crowd, however, would not be stopped. Ten minutes later another Kreisleiter spoke up, summing up the difference between a unified vocal representation of popular opinion and riots: "Such a powerful demonstration is destroyed and its meaning unfulfilled through such [aggressive] actions."[70] Naturally, no more prestigious party figure than the county leader addressed the crowd since that would have put his authority on the line and perhaps suggested to the public that the demonstrations were of more interest than just the locals. In written reports, Heydrich claimed that the violence was committed by party members coming from outside of Rottenburg. The Rottenburgers had not taken part but had rather "adopted a hostile attitude toward the demonstrators."[71] They also now questioned the police, and the Rottenburg party officials were accused of dereliction of duty. According to the Gestapo, commonly heard denunciations included "How can the police allow a building to be stormed and demolished?" and "The police merely stick their paychecks in their pocket and then take a walk."

After the demonstrators had departed, two to three hundred Rottenburgers gathered in front of the bishop's palace and cleaned up. By 1:30 in the early morning of July 24 public order had been restored. Now the disaffection was changing the minds of the officials: an anonymous SA man confessed to Sproll that the violence of the demonstrations had turned his stomach; the "shameful deeds" had caused him and other SA men, he said, to question their loyalty to the party and suspect that the church in this case was in the right. In Tübingen, the senior prosecutor observed that "the residents of Rottenburg who following the vote were

positioned totally against the bishop now take a stand openly for him. . . .
Cries of 'Hail to the Bishop' reportedly rang out late into the night," and
some declared that if state authorities did not protect the bishop at future
rallies, the people themselves would.[72]

Now a conflict between the party and the church had opened and
was beginning to work against the party. For pragmatic party leaders it
made sense to look for a quick way to back out, rather than stoking the
conflict and drawing more attention to it. "Long-standing party comrades" had begun to speak "of the scandalous conditions" and questioned
whether they should obey orders, the Tübingen prosecutor reported.
"In various circles of the [Nazi] movement, the acts of violence in Rottenburg are often condemned."[73] Had parishioners engaged in comparable
acts of violence and destruction during their demonstrations on behalf
of Meiser in 1934, it seems very probable that the public in Nuremberg
and Munich would have been in favor of the restoration of order by the
police.

In Rottenburg the warning of District Chairman Alfred Chormann
that an undisciplined crowd of disorderly demonstrators would arm
those on Sproll's side soon proved correct. For the first time, the people
gathered in an open expression of support for "their" bishop. Chormann
reported that a crowd of about 150–200 well-wishers gathered around
the bishop after he concluded the morning service in Rottenburg. The
bishop's supporters "broke into a rousing demonstration, waving their
hats vigorously amid cries hailing the bishop." The crowd accompanied
the bishop to his palace while filling the air with hymns. By this point,
according to the careful and detailed report from the Stuttgart Gestapo
to Berlin headquarters, there were "300 to 500 churchgoers gathered
in front of the bishop's palace to render homage to the bishop." Following
the singing of several church songs, the crowd broke into a chorus to
make its wishes publicly known, chanting, "We want to see our bishop!"
and "Bishop give us your blessing!" Sproll came to the window in ac-
knowledgment; the crowd left, promising, "We'll be back again!" It was
a scene to make Murr envious. The mannered behavior of those demonstrating loyalty to Sproll contrasted sharply with the crowd of the previous evening, which had made such a "bad impression," in the words of
Chormann.[74]

For the regime and its propaganda, the critical development was the public rift in opinion that had opened up publicly; people were siding with the church and against the Nazi leadership. The party was no longer the lord of the demonstrations. Unsurprisingly the authorities, including the Stuttgart Gestapo, now wished to stop them entirely. This move, however, was up to Hitler, said Friedrich Wilhelm Kritzinger, Hans Lammers's top deputy at the Reich Chancellery. According to his information from Heydrich, the demonstrations had "far overstepped the bounds of the permissible." Continued public protests against the bishop would almost certainly lead to further violations, but "presumably further demonstrations can be prevented only by an order issued from the Leader on the matter."[75]

A few days later the Reich Chancellor's personal assistant made it clear that Lammers would not be taking any measures in regard to the "situation at Rottenburg" because this was the prerogative of only Hitler himself, and Lammers wished to be informed at once of "the Leader's decisions regarding the case." The correspondence of July 23 from Heydrich's office to Hitler's personal adjutant indicates that Hitler was being kept informed and behind the scenes would signal the dictatorship's response.[76]

Hours before the violent demonstrations on July 23, Church Minister Kerrl (who corresponded with Murr but was not close to Hitler) had said that Sproll's expulsion was to be achieved by demonstrations "in the interest of preserving the State's authority," a matter of maintaining "quiet and order." If the goal of procuring Sproll's resignation should somehow not be reached, "the Bishop would have to be exiled from the land or there would have to be a complete boycott of the Bishop by the authorities." The following evening a small group from Stuttgart arrived on Rottenburg's streets as the evening prayer meeting was dismissed, intending to create another demonstration, but they were stopped by the regular street police and returned to Stuttgart.[77] Apparently Hitler had made a decision.

Now Rottenburg officials turned to pre–National Socialist legal means, not as a propaganda ploy but as a genuine effort to communicate. In the presence of a great number of "well-regarded comrades of the people" and the unanimous agreement of the assembled city aldermen,

Rottenburg's mayor, Wilhelm Seeger, issued a resolution: "We protest against the return of Bishop Dr. Sproll and stand behind the measures of the party and mayor demanding the departure of the bishop," he said. "Only in this way can peace and order return to Rottenburg and its surroundings."[78]

Now that the tide had turned, however, the leaders of Rottenburg "anticipated that the bishop's departure from church next Sunday will once again cause ovations," noting that "this, however, must most definitely be hindered." Rather than using the police, district officials sought the collaboration of Kottmann to restrain interactions between the bishop and his flock and reached an agreement with him that the diocese itself would make sure there "was no sharpening of the situation." On August 8 the Foreign Ministry instructed Ambassador Bergen to inform the Vatican that the German government regretted the riots against the bishop and that arrangements had been taken to prohibit excesses from recurring.[79]

That Monday, Bishop Sproll stood at the pulpit to express gratitude for the "ovations" on the previous day but kindly requested that people "refrain from further ovations and return home quietly." The church and the state were both seeking a pragmatic way forward, as happened on other occasions when the struggle between the two started to go against the state. The Gestapo asked the diocese to immediately repair all the damage done by the demonstrations, and the church responded, quickly, by fixing the broken windows and busted doors that might have served to remind the people that the police had stood by as the damage was done.[80]

Once again, Hitler was able to maintain his power by backing away as soon as it was clear that his vision had been thrown into question in public. Quiescence returned to the streets, and Sproll attended the bishops' conference in Fulda from August 17 to 19. A few days later the Gestapo took him without objections, as if prearranged, to the Catholic archdiocese quarters in Freiburg, banishing him as a "menace to public peace," under provisions of the Protection of People and State Decree enacted following the Reichstag Fire in February 1933. He would not return to Rottenburg until after the war. In Berlin, the Propaganda Ministry together with the Church Ministry carefully prepared a notice for publication in the regional press justifying Sproll's ouster from his diocese.[81]

From exile, Bishop Sproll, like the other bishops, rallied the people around the cause of nationalism behind Hitler, in a pastoral letter:

> Following the call of the Leader, the men of weapon-bearing age from all our communities have already left home and hearth to hurry to the border. We know that they, true to their oath, will fulfill their duty even to the point of sacrificing their lives. Gladly I assume that, just as 25 years ago, all those called to the service of weapons have cleansed their conscience in holy penance in German or garrison churches and have strengthened themselves with the bread of life. God be with them all who have taken upon themselves the difficult work of war and grant them courage and strength, to fight or die courageously for the beloved Fatherland.[82]

Bishop Sproll's exile stands out in the dictatorship's treatment of bishops and has been used to indicate that the regime did not shrink back from using force even against such a high-ranking church official. But Sproll's treatment under Hitler's orders was remarkably lenient in comparison to the sentences routinely given for the offenses the Stuttgart senior prosecutor laid out. Lower-ranking officials, especially priests, were sent to jail or met worse fates for "misusing the pulpit" in less "treasonous ways." In 1940 Sproll's loyal friend, Father Franz Weiss, was tried for crossing the line of religion to talk about politics from the pulpit and went to prison for a year and was further punished with a denial of his petition to fight for the Fatherland.[83]

Of course the dictatorship could have punished Sproll in any way it wished. But it seems likely that on balance church leaders were doing more to help the regime than to oppose it. Two priests from the Passau diocese who, like Sproll, did not vote in the April 10, 1938, plebiscite on the Anschluss were required by church authorities to issue a public statement, making it unmistakably clear that they supported Hitler. "We affirm explicitly that our conduct did by no means aim at opposing the state existing today or the Leader," they were made to confess on April 13, 1938. In Augsburg, a priest who was also absent from the polls for the plebiscite was chided by the diocesan chancery for a "lack of understanding of the *total* situation" (national triumphs trumped church practices).[84] Then higher *church* authorities transferred him to another parish, consequences similar to those the state imposed on Sproll.

Yet consensus for driving out a Catholic bishop did not exist, nor, despite concentrated efforts, could the appearance of it be manufactured. After his exile, the bishop's parishioners were assured that he was not in a camp, and Sproll continued to be honored by his diocesans and in correspondence with the pope. He did face challenges through a contingent of his fellow bishops, led by Faulhaber, Wienken, and Nuncio Orsenigo, who sought his resignation in March 1939 and again in the spring of 1941. In both instances Sproll refused.[85] Had Germany won the war, it probably would have been hard to find any bishop still willing to speak out; any bishop who still refused to throw his support to the regime, instead of bending his skills in leading the people in line with Hitler, would have suffered the harm the Nazis thought it best to avoid in 1938.[86]

As the regime prepared for war during late 1937 and 1938, Hitler's bellicose actions also caused uneasiness among some of his military officers. Two months before Hitler launched an attack on Bishop Sproll, he had signaled a major new consolidation of his power by easing the war minister and his commander in chief of the army out of power, along with his foreign and economic ministers. He did this not with the blunt force used when he consolidated power by crippling the SA threat during the Night of the Long Knives, but through claims that the top army officials had engaged in behaviors the public considered scandalous. Compared with the churches and families, which sometimes defended their traditional "private sphere" stubbornly, the army had given up its tradition of independence quickly when Hitler came to power. The displacement of two men at the top of the army hierarchy, through accusations of scandals, also proved to be easy, unlike the removal of a Catholic bishop.

CHAPTER FIVE

Führer Power and the 1938 Military Conspiracy against Hitler

"THE REICHSTAG [WAS] MORE tense than I have ever felt it," wrote the American journalist William Shirer on March 7, 1936, as German troops reoccupied the Rhineland in violation of the Treaty of Versailles and the Locarno Treaties.

> General von Blomberg, the War Minister, sitting with the Cabinet on the left side of the stage, was as white as a sheet and fumbled the top of the bench nervously. . . . Hitler began with a long harangue which he has often given before but never tires of repeating, about the injustices of the Versailles Treaty and the peacefulness of Germans. Then his voice, which had been low and hoarse at the beginning, rose to a shrill, hysterical scream as he raged against Bolshevism. . . . Then in a more nuanced voice . . . [he said] Germany no longer feels bound by the Locarno Treaty. In the interest of the primitive rights of its people to the security of their frontier and the safeguarding of their defense, the German Government has re-established, as from today, the absolute and unrestricted sovereignty of the Reich in the demilitarized zone! Now the six hundred deputies . . . leap to their feet like automatons, their right arms upstretched in the Nazi salute, and scream "Heils," the first two or three wildly, the next twenty-five in unison. . . .

It is news to this hysterical "parliamentary" mob that German
soldiers are already on the move into the Rhineland. . . . A few
generals made their way out. Behind their smiles, however,
you could not help detecting nervousness.[1]

The army leadership of Werner von Blomberg and his deputy, Walther Reichenau, was pleased with Hitler's new dictatorship. From their
narrow focus on army privileges, they seemed to be doing well: Hitler
had given the army the resources it requested—and more. Like so many,
they were prone to a romantic rather than critical relationship with the
new Leader, as Hitler expressed it. "The miracle of our age [is] that you
have found me," Hitler told the 1936 Party Congress to lengthy applause,
"and that I have found you; that is Germany's good fortune!"[2]

But performing his role as Leader, or "god," of the people could also
bring Hitler into conflict with the military elite, spurring him toward
what military leaders saw as grave and unnecessary risks, like an imminent remilitarization of the Rhineland. Hitler's growing base of power
in popular adoration required him to take risks that would inspire the
awe of his people, but it also allowed him to discount the will of military
leaders. Hitler's acclaim allowed him to assume formal control of Germany's armed forces without much struggle on February 4, 1938, as he
appointed himself chief of the armed forces in place of the disgraced
commander in chief of the army, General Werner von Fritsch. With his
massive prestige among Germans further boosted by the annexation
of Austria the following month, he was able to humble the military elite
once again, much as he had done by remilitarizing the Rhineland on
March 7, 1936, despite the military's cautions.

Hitler's assumption of personal command of the armed forces in
early 1938 represented a consolidation of power comparable to that of the
1934 Röhm Purge but without the ruthless bloodshed. In 1938, however,
there would be no need to repeat the hasty retroactive declaration following
the Night of the Long Knives that all had proceeded legally. In 1938,
Fritsch left his prestigious post quietly even though he was backed by
the army elite, who knew that the charges of homosexuality that Hitler
used to snub him were patently false. Hitler's prestige allowed him to
adjudicate such matters of morality. When he warned his henchmen in
1937 against punishing church officials before consulting him, he did

not have to raise the specter of concentration camps; he threatened only that he would publicly disavow them.

Fritsch's meek departure suggests a sense that Hitler could sway public perceptions almost at will, except when it came to church leaders with their well-established popular followings. The dictatorship's carefully orchestrated efforts to shame Bishop Johannes Sproll into leaving his diocese would fail a few months later because he had a following, a faithful constituency willing to risk demonstrating its loyalty publicly, while in the background, the bishop had the pope's backing for his bid to stay in office. Fritsch had a considerable cadre of army colleagues backing him, but this did not comprise a comparable force with Sproll's backing. Counterdemonstrations on behalf of Sproll formed publicity that circumvented the media the regime controlled; official publications carried only the dictatorship's perspective, but the demonstrations of support for Sproll comprised a separate form of communication.

After Hitler gave himself formal control of the military, even the elite officers who conspired against Hitler under the leadership of army chief of staff General Ludwig Beck, later in 1938, wondered whether they could kill Hitler without either disguising it as an accident or pretending that their coup was working on behalf of Hitler, rather than against him. As long as the people esteemed their Leader so highly, these military men calculated, an open attack on Hitler could not secure them a position of authority to govern. On the contrary, it would bring down massive outraged indignation against them.

FÜHRER POWER AND PERSPECTIVE:
THE RHINELAND REMILITARIZATION

The Versailles Treaty had demilitarized the Rhineland, a status that was entrenched by the 1925 Locarno Treaties signed by Germany. Hitler nevertheless envisioned occupying the Rhineland by 1937, although his time frame shifted in October 1935, when Mussolini's Italy invaded Abyssinia (Ethiopia). Following World War I, Italy, together with Britain and France, had formed the "Stresa Front" against German territorial expansion. All three had rejected Berlin's petition to remilitarize the Rhineland under the pretext that the new Franco-Soviet Pact required the area for German self-defense. With Italy's invasion in Africa, this alliance crumbled. Britain and France fumed about it, and the League of Nations applied mild sanctions. Estranged from the Western powers, Mussolini shifted toward an alliance with his fellow dictator in Germany. Hitler was quick to take advantage of this new foreign alliance to burnish his image at home. Watching the French Olympic team parade by his stand at the winter games in Bavaria on February 5, 1936, Hitler observed to Blomberg that he might strike soon to remilitarize the Rhineland. Blomberg was shocked, and at the games as well, Hitler was careful to assure French leaders that he was dedicated to European peace, as the French ambassador enthused about how well Germany had presented the Olympics.[3]

As the army's commanders waited on his decision about whether to march German troops into the Rhineland, Hitler feared a military response from Britain and France. He did not, however, fear resistance from the reluctant German generals. For centuries Prussian-German military leadership had customarily calculated the risks of potential military actions, taking account of international politics and the balance of power in Europe. This tradition had survived into the Weimar Republic following the substitute monarchy of Generals Hindenburg and Ludendorff during the war. When Hitler became chancellor, the German conservatives thought they were fully in control of him, in part because Hindenburg had selected one of them, General and Field Marshal Werner von Blomberg, to lead the War Ministry. Blomberg had held the German Army's conventional view of its special relationship to the state, but he quickly proved tractable under Hitler. The field marshal soon became known for championing Hitler's ability to plan everything correctly, and as a consequence some colleagues came to view Blomberg as too quick to leave political calculations to Hitler while restricting the officer corps to a technical military role.[4]

Officially, the army was alone in Germany in maintaining its independence from central government control, following the Law for the Reorganization of the Reich in early 1934. However, Hitler's next step in consolidating his power would not be an effort to dominate the military formally but to win its allegiance. In late June 1934, the army leadership readily assisted in the Night of the Long Knives purge and did not complain that two of their own, General Kurt von Schleicher and his collaborator, Major-General Kurt von Bredow, had also been slaughtered. Rather,

it expressed gratitude to Hitler for his discipline in cutting down an organization of his own party that they saw as a threat. Top officials, including
men who would later resist the regime—Dr. Carl Goerdeler and General
Ludwig Beck, for example—signaled acceptance of the grotesque murders. Two days after the Night of the Long Knives President Hindenburg
congratulated Hitler for having "nipped all treasonous doings in the bud
by your own determined action and your brave personal intervention!"
After Hindenburg died four weeks later, Blomberg volunteered to have the
army take an oath of allegiance to Hitler personally. But for Hitler it was
not the army's oath of allegiance that assured him of his power over the
military. Rather it was his military conscription decree in March 1935,
which filled out the ranks of the army with Hitler's true base of power, the
"masses of the people," as he told his fawning confidants years later.[5]

Toward the end of 1935, Hitler's prestige and his ability to lure the
Germans toward his goals showed signs of faltering. Across the population that winter the heavy cost of rearmament took a toll, challenging
Hitler's basic resolve that his movement's momentum must always be
sustained. In January 1936, morale sank into what official reports called
"uncontrollable territory." Discord, especially between the party and the
Catholics, was becoming dangerously public, and even Hitler's personal
popularity, while still largely intact, had begun to suffer. Almost half of
the German workers were earning wages below the poverty line while
food prices were on the rise. In cities, standing in line for food had become a daily experience. Berliners blamed the government and the Nazi
movement itself for falling standards of living. Hitler had been monitor-
ing the souring mood since the autumn of 1934 and had promised the
workers that he would not allow an increase in prices. In early 1936, fearing that a revolutionary mood might break out unless resources were
redirected to bolster food supplies, Hitler channeled an additional 12.4
million Reich marks for the import of food. This forced Blomberg's War
Ministry to forgo its budget allocation for rearmament until the spring. To
rally opinion on the tough economic choices it faced, the regime launched
a propaganda campaign, as Propaganda Minister Joseph Goebbels in
January 1936 supplemented an old Nazi slogan of "Freedom and Bread"
with "Guns or Butter."[6]

While the army generals as well as Hitler's closest party advisers
couldn't understand his haste, Hitler schemed about a way out of the

"Guns or Butter" trap. In lieu of pay raises, the November 1933 Strength through Joy program had substituted the psychological incentives for some workers of middle-class pleasures previously out of their reach.[7] Since, as he thought, the people esteemed a strong leader and loved military victories, he might ignite passion for his leadership by remilitarizing the Rhineland in lieu of greatly improved material conditions across the Reich. Germans shared Hitler's passionate rejection of the Versailles Treaty, which prohibited the stationing of German military forces along the Rhine River, stretching west to the neighboring countries on Germany's western border. Remilitarizing the Rhineland would throw off those shackles, with the Germans reasserting their rights at the expense of the Allied oppressors—a feat certain to boost morale without diverting further funds from rearmament.

The aristocratic German military elites lacked Hitler's breathtaking fantasies, as well as a comprehension of the way he based power on mass adulation. Army commanders had been conditioned to fear that the next war would repeat the results of 1918. Hitler was also haunted by the possibility of another Stab in the Back, but he envisioned Germans remaining united, during the next war, in fanatical dedication to their national cause under his leadership, and maintaining his romance with the people was key to this challenge. Army opinion of course did not take this into account; Generals Ludwig Beck and Werner von Fritsch concurred that the exercise of full sovereignty over German territory along the Rhine was a military necessity for national defense but advised waiting. Beck did not oppose reoccupation so long as war was avoided but thought that to hold a French attack at bay, at least thirty to forty field divisions would be required. In November 1935, Germany could muster only eight, backed by three police brigades.[8]

While sycophants like future foreign minister Joachim von Ribbentrop clamored to support Hitler in any case, in early 1936 core diplomats and other military advisers also counseled postponing a reoccupation. Predicting that repercussions to German foreign relations would be minimal, Foreign Minister Konstantin von Neurath saw no reason to take the risk. Even Hitler's propagandist sided with caution. Hitler was isolated, but he apparently continued to seek advice as if he were really taking it into account. On February 28, 1936, according to his diaries, Goebbels repeated his advice to Hitler to wait until the French Senate had actually ratified the new Franco-Russian Pact, which Germany claimed as a reason for remilitarizing at once. On February 29, as Goebbels and Hitler met for lunch, Hitler had still not declared a decision. But on the following day, Hitler appeared in a bright mood at Goebbels's hotel in Munich to say that it was now time to take action! Goebbels fell in line, cheering that "Fortune favors the brave! He who dares nothing wins nothing."[9]

Hitler was willing to take greater risks than his advisers since he was striving to achieve so much and because his role as the people's Leader required great feats. Neither Germany's civilian leaders nor its generals stood to gain as much as Hitler's acclaim, should his decisions pay off (nor did they stand to lose as much). Foreign Minister Neurath preferred diplomacy but observed that Hitler chose to move into the Rhineland militarily in March 1936 because he needed to rekindle support for the dictatorship. The "timing and character" of the remilitarization were emblematic of Hitler.[10]

On March 2, Hitler met with a handful of military and foreign policy experts to inform them of his decision. Hitler customarily mixed aggressive moves with declarations that he was intent on maintaining peace, and he now proposed measures to soften any sense that advancing German troops represented a threat. Although Germany attempted to placate its neighbors with promises of nonaggression agreements, Hitler was "nervous, jumpy and confused" according to the French ambassador, who saw him that day. Still Hitler moved ahead, setting March 7 as the date for reoccupation. The military plans called for small units to occupy the Rhineland, joining German police in fighting, while withdrawing should they meet military resistance.[11]

While Hitler's defiance of international treaties was daring and allowed him to appear indomitable, German forces reoccupying the Rhineland were careful not to provoke France. The German press was instructed, in the event of remilitarization, to abstain from any nationalistic displays while emphasizing the "happy sentiment in the Rhineland" that the Rhinelanders were "finally liberated from a nightmare" of French occupation. On March 7, as German troops moved into the forbidden territory, the German people responded at first with anxiety, fearing a French counteroffensive. Most of the German troops that marched into the Rhineland, a single infantry division of about thirty thousand men, remained on the right bank of the Rhine River. Fewer than three thousand German troops moved across the Rhine River and forward toward French-German border posts close to Aachen, Trier, and Saarbrücken. Although backed by units of police, several thousand troops represented little more than a gesture; just one of France's thirty army divisions would have been sufficient to repel Hitler's foray into the Rhineland.[12]

When French troops in fact did not meet the German advance with their superior army, the German generals withdrew to their stations, "humbled and puzzled." The "objections raised by the generals" to the Rhineland occupation "had turned out to be without substance," General Erich von Manstein testified after the war. "Hitler had carried his point." Although possessing the weapons to overthrow Hitler, the general staff was now probably psychologically incapable of using them against him.[13]

France had overestimated Germany's military strength and did not even have a plan to rebuff German troops. Nor did it wish to act alone or with the assistance of no more than a few East European governments. It sought counsel from Britain, which was dedicated to avoiding war and refused to take countermeasures other than denouncing Germany for breaching the Versailles Treaty. British opinion further held that the treaty had dealt Germany an unfair hand, and furthermore, strong popular views in both France and Britain opposed war for reasons other than the defense of borders.[14]

The sense of crisis about the Rhineland remilitarization blew over as quickly as it had appeared. Hitler's stature was the big winner, although he admitted privately that he could have lost as much as he had gained. Although the risk of a French attack was rather small, the prestige he had been carefully building up in the minds of the people was on the line. Hitler's translator, Hans Frank, recalled Hitler saying, "If the French had really been serious, it would have become the greatest political defeat for me." More than once Frank heard Hitler remark, "The 48 hours following the entry into the Rhineland were the most agitating, unsettling hours of my life."[15] Had the French "charged into the Rhineland, we would have had to pull back, in dishonor and shame, because the military strength we possessed could have in no way mounted even a moderate resistance," he elaborated. "In order to set the minds of the people at rest,

I went personally to the Rhineland. But the German people . . . proved conclusively that they both understood and approved my policy."[16]

Especially along the French border, Hitler's gamble boosted his stature yet further. It also encouraged the Leader to take further risks, even as it trained the German people to trust their Führer as he pushed ahead into unknown terrain. More convinced than ever that he was destiny's agent, Hitler boasted on March 14 that "I go with the certainty of a sleepwalker along the path laid out for me by Providence." Hitler's press chief and confidant, Otto Dietrich, also noticed that the success buttressed Hitler's growing confidence in his own infallibility.[17]

In Catholic areas, the recent hub of disaffection, Germany's Catholic leaders led the way in lauding Hitler. A common theme of their individual messages about the remilitarization was that the German nation was finally exercising its rights and regaining its honor. On the day of the reoccupation, Cardinal Joseph Schulte of Cologne sent a telegram to Blomberg hailing the German Army as the "protectors of peace and order." Bishop Clemens August von Galen followed the next day with a telegram to Commander in Chief Fritsch declaring, "In the name of the loyal German Catholics from the Münster diocese and in particular from the lower Rhineland, I congratulate the German Army, which from today forward again shields the German Rhineland as protector and symbol of German honor and German rights." And Bishop Ludwig Sebastian, whose diocese lay partially in the Rhineland, was quoted in the *Frankfurter Zeitung*, thanking God for the "fortune and honor of the remilitarization of our homeland."[18]

In the glow of this heralded victory, Germans began to hang out the flag. Showing the extent to which Hitler had consolidated support, the flag they displayed this time was "without exception the swastika flag," rather than the old pre-Nazi German flag, according to police reports. Popular opinion held that the "crafty statesmanship of Hitler would succeed in delivering Germany from foreign policy difficulties," the police said, adding that "the events of March 7 have further heightened the repute of the Leader, and those who until now still criticized the Leader himself or his foreign policy have shrunken together into an insignificant clump." Within the party too, acclaim for Hitler had swelled. The party leaders "moved around Hitler" and "strained to catch a glimpse of him," efforts that "exhilarated Hitler as wine would other men."[19]

With Goebbels exulting that the Rhineland was a "sea of joy" and that the "masses are wild with happiness," the time was ripe for a national plebiscite. In order to demonstrate and boost his support, Hitler held such votes on matters the people already completely supported. For several weeks in advance of the referendum, Luftwaffe Commander Hermann Göring, as well as Goebbels and Hitler himself, made speeches almost every day, calling on Germans to vote their approval of Hitler's great stroke of genius. There was a new basis for closeness with the old foe, Hitler said, generously offering that France and Germany should embrace each other as friends.[20]

The Catholic bishops individually and collectively put themselves at the service of the Nazi message, calling on the people to vote in conscience for Hitler's plebiscite, which included the election to the Reichstag of known enemies of the churches. Parishioners were enjoined to support the plebiscite by keeping the big picture in mind without endorsing the infringements on church practices. Even Bishop Preysing, a longtime vocal critic of the regime, joined the unison as the Catholic bishops prepared an endorsement carrying Hitler's message for him from pulpits across the Reich: "In order to assist you in the choice of voting "yes" [on the Rhineland remilitarization] we the German Bishops declare in the name of all faithful German Catholics that we give our voice to the Fatherland. This does not signify approval of those things, which our conscience does not allow."[21] The larger picture of grand national advancement pulled church leaders along despite the repression of church practices.

On March 28, a monumental demonstration of popular approval for the plebiscite stretched from Berlin to Eisenach. "Leipzig, Weimar, Eisleben, Eisenach, and Halle" were "shouting approval of the whole campaign," American ambassador William Dodd noted. The plebiscite of March 29 garnered an almost 99 percent approval rate, according to the dictatorship.[22] Ambassador Dodd estimated that while some 40 percent of Germans were "Nazi in faith," fully 90 percent of the German population enthusiastically cheered Hitler's restoration of "German honor and the right to violate a treaty in order to militarize the area demilitarized in 1919." Although some may have been punished for refusing to support the regime, Victor Klemperer, a German Jew in Dresden, voted "no" and also wrote "no" on the plebiscite ballot. Also with impunity, his non-Jewish wife left hers blank.[23]

Having completed the feat and the propaganda follow-through, Hitler set his work aside and went on vacation. He was not known for careful calculations, but according to his standards of political leadership, he had just made enormous strides forward. What need was there for briefing and policy papers if he could draw the people forward with successes like his Rhineland gamble? He had already led the people through an "inner transition," he said, and it was this attitude change that had wrought "external success" for Germany far greater than what might have been achieved by "day-to-day work!"[24]

FASCIST POPULISM: HITLER FORMALIZES
HIS MASTERY OVER THE ARMY

When Hitler assumed personal command of the armed forces on February 4, 1938, he did not imagine burdening his leadership style with a greater day-to-day workload. Although it is not clear how much "inner transition" among the Germans Hitler achieved, his swelling popular acclaim, including his prestige among Germany's power elite, drew trust from the people and enabled him to dominate the military. It also protected him against an army conspiracy in 1938, although he had angered a powerful group of senior officers by refusing to replace Blomberg with Fritsch. The scandal that led to Blomberg's resignation as armaments minister precipitated what Joseph Goebbels identified in his diary on January 27 as "the worst crisis for the regime since the Röhm affair."[25] The result of this crisis of similar proportions would be a consolidation of Nazi power to a similar degree. With the scheming Goebbels at his side, Hitler turned the crisis to his massive advantage within a week, much as his forces had during the Night of the Long Knives, only this time the SS was not needed. Instead, the Leader exercised authority without the force of arms, just as he had when he held the Storm Troopers, pulling at their leash, from mounting another putsch.

The secret "Hössbach Conference" of November 5, 1937, had already revealed a hint of tension between Hitler and a handful of foreign policy and military leaders in attendance. Hitler himself had arranged for the meeting, and it was immediately clear that the Leader did not intend the conference to become a forum for consultation. He expected the military leadership to play the role of functionaries, fighting the wars he planned and commanded. At this conference he presented his aims for aggressive war as the plans of the Reich, and he represented the Reich. At the conference, Hitler abandoned defensive justifications for war, saying instead that Germany would fight for *Lebensraum*—living space or territorial expansion—due to the rightful "self-determination" of ethnic Germans.

Hitler's projections at the Hössbach Conference derived from National Socialism rather than conventional military reasoning. In *Mein Kampf* Hitler had rejected a return to Germany's 1914 borders as absurd. Just about all Germans could agree that Germany deserved the return of the territories taken by the 1919 settlement. But Hitler's aims were breathtaking. Germany, he asserted, must gain vast tracts of agricultural land in the east in order to allow for the rightful expansion of the German "race" so that it no longer depended on trade with other countries. "The industrious labor of the German plow" would be "given land by the sword." In the short term, Hitler explained at the conference, Germany would advance its military-political position by taking control of Austria and Czechoslovakia, which would serve as steppingstones for conquests of territory after territory in countries farther east. It was clear that Hitler now included Britain and France on the list of potential war enemies, and this caused anxiety among army leaders.[26]

Blomberg and Fritsch, along with Foreign Minister Neurath, questioned aspects of Hitler's plans on the spot. They asked Hitler about his timetable and his prediction of how events would develop. After all, German armed forces offices had just concluded that Germany did not need to fear military aggression because opposition to war was strong throughout Europe, and the Soviet Union and other countries were ill prepared for an attack. To convey their concern that Germany might not be equipped to fight the wars Hitler identified, Neurath coordinated with Generals Beck and Fritsch to make an appointment with Hitler. When Hitler finally met with them in mid-January 1938, he reassured the anxious foreign minister that his war plans would not interfere with the vacation Neurath planned to take in two months.[27]

From the beginning, objections to Hitler's plans were hesitant and scattered. No one disputed his claim that Germany needed more "living space," although some questioned Hitler's proposed timing and tactics. Reich Marshal Hermann Göring favored reaching an agreement with Britain, while General Beck also questioned whether war was necessary. Two years before, in 1935, Beck had refused to develop the outline of an armed forces plan for a surprise attack on Czechoslovakia, although in the same year he had also written a memorandum on Germany's need for further "living space" as a matter of military defense.[28] The military leadership had also aligned with Nazi anti-Semitism. None of the Wehr-macht commanders objected to a ban on Jews in the military, although then colonel Erich von Manstein quipped that a soldier was a soldier, and Beck expressed a personal opinion that decisions about whether Jews might remain in regiment associations should be made on the basis of "local and personal conditions." Nazi persecution of Jews during the 1930s also seems to have met with the approval of General Fritsch's sense of propriety, considering his pronouncement that it "goes without saying that an officer [should seek] a wife only within 'Aryan' [German-blooded] circles." Also in 1934, Blomberg had expedited the new practice of determining whether army men were of "Aryan heritage," in line with Nazi ideology and the requirements established for civil servants the previous year.[29]

Blomberg thought that ministers should follow instructions set down by Hitler, and following the Hössbach Conference, he rallied to back Hitler's Rhineland plan. The pliant chief of defense staff, Colonel Alfred Jodl, followed by altering previous plans for the mobilization against Czechoslovakia, to take account of the possibility of a war against France. Fritsch also proved willing to carry out Hitler's orders, notwith-standing his questions about timing.[30]

Despite their loyalty, Hitler convinced Blomberg and Fritsch to slip away quietly in early 1938, while the accommodating Neurath resigned. The role of the principal actors and decision makers in the "Blomberg-Fritsch Affair" remains somewhat clouded, although there is general agreement on skeletal facts. By the end of 1937, the career military man and widower Werner von Blomberg had become infatuated with a woman some thirty years younger, who in the eyes of his professional peers had an unseemly past. Margarethe Gruhn, in 1931 at the age of eighteen, had posed for pornographic photographs. The following year the Berlin police registered her as a prostitute, one of more than one hundred thousand in the city, many of whom, like Gruhn, were from lower-class backgrounds and in need of income.[31] Blomberg was well aware of military propriety and the code of the general staff, but Göring had reassured Blomberg in private conversations that National Socialism erased old differences between the aristocracy and the people! Nazism welcomed matrimonial unions between "racially pure" Germans of all classes.

With Hitler and Göring as wedding witnesses, Blomberg married Gruhn on January 12, 1938. Although the event was shielded from publicity, rumors soon flew across the city. Prostitutes were reportedly in stunned awe that one of their own had made such a distinguished marriage. Then the police file on the new Mrs. Blomberg began to surface. It was said to include nude photographs taken by a Czech Jew, and condemnation within the military was harsh.[32] General Fritsch was scandalized. General Beck declared that "one cannot permit the highest-ranking soldier to marry a whore. Such a person should be forced to divorce the woman or else be taken off the list of officers; he could no longer be the commander of even a regiment." While the murders of fellow officers during the Night of the Long Knives four years prior had hardly raised an eyebrow, Field Marshals Wilhelm von Leeb and Siegmund von List were self-righteously indignant. Even after the war, they still spoke of the disgrace the general had dealt the army by marrying such a woman.[33]

A resolution of the crisis was awaiting Hitler upon his return on January 24 from his mountain retreat in Bavaria. He might have humiliated the military leaders by keeping Blomberg despite their objections. A slavish follower of ideology would have stood by Göring's assurances that in the new Reich only race and not class mattered, but Hitler did not. Instead, showing that he was probably not yet thinking of snubbing the army elite, he told Blomberg he could stay at his post on the condition—demanded by General Beck—that he annul his marriage. But Blomberg preferred to leave his job, and Hitler accepted Blomberg's decision, allotting him his full pension along with a handsome payoff on the condition that he leave Germany immediately and stay away for a year.[34]

Soon, if not already at this point, Hitler was thinking of formally subsuming Blomberg's position for himself, under the title of the Leader.

Blomberg's abrupt departure raised the question of succession, and many thought that Werner von Fritsch should take charge. Unlike Blomberg, Fritsch was respected, even revered, among his peers and viewed by many of them as Blomberg's rightful successor. However, he had a powerful enemy in the head of the SS and chief of police, Heinrich Himmler, who had spread fatuous rumors in 1936 following the Rhineland remilitarization that Fritsch and his generals were plotting against Hitler.[35]

Hitler, with Goebbels at his side, seized the occasion to test whether he might be able to control the top military leaders through the assertion of his will.[36] Several days after Blomberg's resignation, a police dossier was unearthed that accused Fritsch of homosexuality. The case rested on the testimony of a convicted criminal, Otto Schmidt, who claimed to have seen a retired captain, Achim von Frisch, in liaison with a known homosexual behind a Berlin train station in 1933. Two years earlier, when Himmler wanted to take action against Fritsch, Hitler had dismissed the same file as evidence against Fritsch because he needed his professional expertise and reputation to rebuild the army. Now Fritsch was no longer needed, and the name of the accused was changed in the dossier from "Frisch" to "Fritsch" and then to "General von Fritsch."

Many did not believe the charges and the evidence. Unlike Blomberg, Fritsch had many allies who were expected to unleash a string of protests. General Beck, voicing the objections of some of his peers, told Hitler that the allegations against Fritsch "demanded an exhaustive investigation by the military judicial authorities."[37] Perhaps the story would have taken a different turn had Fritsch dug in to fight the charge. But although innocent, he did little to defend himself during a meeting with Hitler when confronted by his accuser.

Fritsch's lack of protest is sometimes said to have convinced Hitler of his guilt. Yet Hitler was not interested in the question of guilt so much as in the presence of opportunity. Perhaps he thought that Fritsch's paltry self-defense showed a lack of fortitude. According to Fritsch, Hitler had opposed his promotion in 1934, and Fritsch (like the others) did lack Hitler's vision.[38]

On February 3, 1938, Fritsch—as if also recognizing Hitler's authority as total despite his innocence—complied quietly with Hitler's request that he resign. On the following day, during the last cabinet meeting of the dictatorship, Hitler announced major changes and restructuring in the upper echelons of the army. Sixteen officers were retired and forty-four were transferred to lesser positions. He announced that he would personally assume control over all military forces; Wilhelm Keitel, as Hitler's deputy, took charge of the Armed Forces Office, now called the Supreme Command of the Armed Forces (OKW); and General Walther von Brauchitsch replaced Fritsch as army commander. Goering coveted Blomberg's job as leader of the War Ministry and as consolation was promoted to field marshal.[39]

At the time, Hitler wanted to divert attention from the changes he was making at the top of the Wehrmacht. In his diary Goebbels was blunt: "The real background must be obscured behind a smokescreen," he wrote. "The real motives will be drowned in the great reshuffle" of generals.[40] On February 5, immediately following the cabinet meeting, Hitler released letters in the press that he had ostensibly written to the two generals, rewriting the recent events for public view. Appearing under the headline "Blomberg and Fritsch Step Down," the story began:

> The Leader and Reich Chancellor has written the following letter to General Field Marshal von Blomberg: Since the complete restoration of full German sovereignty, concerning its military and territory, in the year 1936 you have occasionally asked to be relieved from a service that takes a heavy toll on your health. Now after the completion of the fifth year of the reconstruction of our people and its Wehrmacht I will comply with your newly repeated request. May you find recuperation in the time of safety lying before you.

A more curt if still courteous "letter" to Fritsch followed in the press:

> In consideration of your weakened health you have urgently asked me to relieve you from the duties of your office. Since the recent stay in the south did not have the hoped-for effect, I have now decided to grant your request.[41]

No doubt there was gossip within Germany about Blomberg's marriage, and the foreign media were informed, with the American weekly *Life* magazine reporting in its back pages on February 14 that "Germany's No. 1 Soldier Quits His Job for a Wife."[42] Fritsch was still covered in scandal, and considering Hitler's public stature, his letters may well have been sufficient to cast doubt on any contrary claims.

Still the regime cautiously spread additional camouflage. To deflect attention from the additional resignation of Foreign Minister Neurath and to allow for the appointment of the approbatory Ribbentrop in his place, Hitler established a "Secret Cabinet Council," with Neurath as its president, and propaganda to make it look as though Neurath had been promoted. This council, however, was "pure fiction" and "never met at all, not even for a minute," Göring testified. Even the departure of Economics Minister Hjalmar Schacht was covered for the sake of appearances with a cabinet assignment for Schacht as "Minister without Portfolio."[43]

General Fritsch's allies knew better, of course, and persuaded Fritsch to put his case before a military tribunal. Hitler preferred a Gestapo court and agreed only reluctantly to the tribunal, a situation that would presumably create a further news story that, if not carefully managed, would show that Fritsch had been unfairly pressured.[44] Yet by the time the military tribunal acquitted Fritsch of charges of homosexuality on March 18, no one could use the acquittal to restore Fritsch to his position because the news and indeed the popular mood was blanketed with exaltations about Hitler's Anschluss of Austria.

ANSCHLUSS ACCLAIM FOR HITLER CRIPPLES ARMY PROTEST

Hitler had not achieved total dominance of the army with force or threat of force. Rather he had relied upon another continuous backdrop of the Third Reich—the Leader's prestige and his widely accepted role as the rightful judge (even on matters of decency). Now, he achieved a much-awaited union with Austria to stoke his popular appeal.

Although he steered foreign policy, Hitler had no fixed timetables for his major foreign policy initiatives, preferring to improvise like an opportunist par excellence. But he did keep his goals firmly fixed in mind, and he could instantly recognize and exploit circumstances that permitted him to move forward in his trajectory toward his goals.[45] Beyond exploiting all opportunities, Hitler saw himself as shaping circumstances to develop the Volksgemeinschaft and to achieve German hegemony.

Hitler was able to strategize beyond striking when he perceived an opportunity. The Anschluss illustrates an instance in which Hitler influenced the timing of circumstances in order to promote his image while inhibiting opposition and establishing a setting for German military aggression. Austria's annexation was an aspiration of many from both Germany and Austria, and its achievement by Hitler, finally, was magnified by a drumroll of propaganda that culminated in another plebiscite, which would drown out opportunities for protest by generals angry about Hitler's high-handed emasculation of the professional army leadership.

During the Hössbach Conference of November 1937, Hitler had laid out his aim of occupying Austria, and at some point during the following two months he stated his intention to stage a coup in Austria sometime in June or July of 1938. With the Blomberg-Fritsch crisis still likely to draw attention, Hitler moved up his negotiations with Austrian chancellor Kurt von Schuschnigg, directing attention away from the internal crisis in Germany to the Austrian question. There was a real possibility that the regime's treatment of Fritsch might lead to protests from high military officials, and Schuschnigg's announcement that he would hold a plebiscite on Austrian independence triggered Hitler's advance into Austria, the success of which would stymie the voices of opposition.[46]

Hitler credited Schuschnigg for creating a "favorable situation," for Anschluss, but it was a shift by Mussolini that had set the stage for Hitler to achieve this annexation earlier than previously anticipated.[47] This shift occurred during Mussolini's five-day state visit to Germany beginning September 25, 1937. Crossing the Alps into the Reich, Mussolini was greeted by a brilliant display of the Nazi dictatorship's capacity to shape opinion and thus influence circumstances. The goal of top German diplomatic officials for Mussolini's visit was to procure the Duce's consent for the Nazis to initiate a replacement of Schuschnigg, along with Rome's permission for Germany to develop closer economic and political ties with Austria.

But Hitler was more ambitious and more cunning. Rather than scoring a one-time victory of Mussolini's agreement to an Anschluss, he aimed to achieve a fundamental change in the Italian dictator's attitude toward Germany itself. He aspired to build a foundation for Italian trust and goodwill toward Germany that would serve as the basis for a long-term alliance that would have Italy working with the Reich to help achieve its aims. With these prospects of more substantial gains over the long run in mind, Hitler proceeded by appearing more conciliatory than many of his advisers countenanced.[48] At the same time, he made a show of the industrial strength of Germany, as well as the "unified enthusiasm of the German people"—the basic foundation of Fascist power.

Mussolini was impressed by his celebrity treatment while racing through a flurry of visits to armament manufacturers and inspections of vast military maneuvers and parades. He was enthused by Hitler's flashy displays of strength and gracious indications of compromise. The Duce expressed gratitude that Germany had not joined in sanctions against Italy for its attack on Ethiopia, as Britain and France had. The Nazi treatment created a "most profound impression" on Mussolini. He had watched Hitler's spectacular advances and now saw Hitler as a "man of destiny."[49]

The Leader had sought an "inner transition" for Mussolini like the one he sought within his people, and he had achieved it. Mussolini began to see Hitler as a fast ally whose cooperation he could depend upon. Mussolini left the impression in Berlin that Germany could expect to proceed toward foreign policy goals in Austria without Italian opposition. Specifically, Italy abdicated its role as the guarantor of Austrian independence. Beyond this, Mussolini soon expressed clear sympathy for a close fundamental cooperation between Germany and Austria. Hitler was ecstatic about the alliance, although he realized that having cut its ties with the Western alliance, Italy had few alternatives.[50]

During the months following Mussolini's German visit, an international climate was created in which the question was not whether but when Germany would exert some form of control over Austria. The principle of self-determination, a key tenet of U.S. president Woodrow Wilson's position at the Paris Peace Conference, played a role; Western powers stated that they would not want to go to war for Austria if German-speaking Austria wished to unite with Germany. In a conversation with Ribbentrop on November 6, 1937, Mussolini allowed that Austria was a German country, and no one could interfere with its natural course. The Italian minister of foreign affairs, Galeazzeo Ciano, concurred. With Mussolini siding with Hitler, Britain as well as France refused in effect to guarantee Austrian sovereignty, stating a preference for a peaceful resolution of Austrian-German relations.[51]

On December 14, 1937, Hitler expressed to Göring a desire to annex Austria without force, although the dictatorship was keeping options open. A little later, at the end of the year, Hitler told Gauleiter Albert Forster that he would be assigned as ambassador to Vienna, where he would "stage a coup in June or July" of 1938.[52] Why did Hitler move into Austria five months earlier?

Hitler had originally planned a meeting with Schuschnigg at the Berchtesgaden mountain retreat for the end of January 1938, in advance of his annual speech celebrating the Nazis' 1933 ascent to power. At that point, however, Hitler was caught up in turning the sex scandals in the military to his advantage, and his meeting with Schuschnigg was pushed to February 12. Hitler dominated the meeting with Schuschnigg through various forms of bullying, refusing to allow the chain-smoking Austrian a single cigarette. Threatened with a German military invasion of Austria, Schuschnigg agreed to meet all German demands while in return Hitler agreed to declare Germany's respect for Austrian independence and to promise to refrain from interfering in its internal affairs in his upcoming speech to the Reichstag. Hitler of course made no such promise during his speech, which he delivered on February 20. He did, however, praise the agreement they had arrived at together, which was now empty as far as Schuschnigg was concerned. Claiming a degree of power his fellow Fascist Benito Mussolini never reached, Hitler also proclaimed that "there is not a single institution in this state which is not National Socialist."[53]

On March 10, the same day as Fritsch's military trial opened, Schuschnigg announced a plebiscite on Austrian independence for March 13. But Hitler wanted his own plebiscite on annexation instead, and now that he no longer feared foreign intervention, he ordered the military to prepare for an immediate occupation of Austria. General Beck set to work to improvise plans quickly for the annexation.[54]

On March 12, as the German Eighth Army marched into Austria, it was greeted by the enthusiastic cheers of tens of thousands. Jews and Socialist leaders were plunged into massive suffering, but no one seemed to notice. Hitler had delivered a long hoped-for unification that previous leaders had only dreamed of achieving; great majorities of Germans as well as Austrians thought the Anschluss fulfilled "an age-old" vision that had eluded even Bismarck and the liberals at the Frankfurt Conference of 1848. Upon his arrival in Austria, Hitler immediately announced a plebiscite on the Anschluss. Catholic leaders now came to his assistance, as they had in the Saarland plebiscite. Cardinal Innitzer of Vienna, reflecting sentiments about Hitler previously expressed by the archbishop of Salzburg and the bishop of Linz, ordered that "both priests and faithful . . . stand unconditionally behind the Great German State and its Führer."[55]

Hitler found loyal and pliant adjutants easily enough. But he also knew how to shape the behavior of those under him without Stalin-like purges, and he prepared in advance to exploit various circumstances. According to Schacht, he took pragmatic steps toward his ideologically determined policies and showed more interest in results than in being punitive or gratuitously violent. For example, Hitler kept a tally of offenses by subordinates not so much in order to punish the offenders as to use such information to "force each one of them into a position of absolute submission." Hitler's bloodless consolidation of power in early 1938 displays what he considered to be the essential basis for his authority, the seemingly unshakeable faith that German elites, and not just the masses, vested in Hitler as a "knight without stain and without reproach," whose aims were undefiled and would put everything right if only he were not disgracefully misled by henchmen. Fritsch, for example, like various other army commanders, was sorely humiliated by Hitler's dismissal and yet still clung "to the delusion that his real persecutors were the SS leaders" and that Hitler was acting only on their behalf.[56] Blomberg and Fritsch complied loyally, and there is little evidence that either man feared a fate similar to that of Röhm. Blomberg later wished to return to military service under Hitler. According to a statement apparently written by Fritsch dated December 11, 1938, one month after the Kristallnacht pogrom and less than a year after Hitler had removed him from office, the general was deeply supportive of Hitler's three-pronged domestic repression aimed against the "working class," "Catholics," and "Jews." Neurath too, despite leaving during the same period, faithfully served Hitler on occasion and when his successor, von Ribbentrop, was absent.[57]

HITLER'S POPULARITY BESETS THE MILITARY CONSPIRACY OF 1938

Hitler's high-handed mistreatment of Fritsch, followed by the formal appointment of himself as commander in chief of the armed forces, was an emasculating snub of the military elite, and following the resignation of Fritsch and his acquittal on the false charges by the military tribunal, thoughts of rebellion took root among some military leaders. By late July 1938, it seemed to Beck that resentment about Fritsch had "torn a rift, also regarding trust, that can never be bridged." According to one report, Hitler was apprehensive that Beck in fact might lead a revolt.[58] Among military commanders, only Beck aroused Hitler's anxieties, which may have arisen owing to the general's clear awareness of the Nazi methods for mobilizing opinion. Hitler probably did not truly fear a coup, but given the mystique surrounding his power, his apprehensions began with public displays of dissent far short of a successful putsch.

Hitler had reached an apex of glory, and within weeks of the Anschluss he was already targeting Czechoslovakia as the next country for the expansion of German "living space." On May 28 Hitler proclaimed before the assembled leaders of the army and party that Germany would eliminate Czechoslovakia from the map by the following October. The confrontation, he now said, was "unavoidable" and awaited only certain groundwork, including the "psychological preparation of the German people." Hitler's confidence had increased since the Rhineland remilitarization. Under the code word "Operation Green" the conquest was set to proceed without contingency plans for retreat should the Western powers respond militarily. Britain, Hitler claimed that summer, would not mount a counterattack, France would follow Britain's lead, and Germany would thus be free to smash Czechoslovakia in one to three weeks. "The Leader wants war," military intelligence official Helmuth Groscurth concluded in late August 1938, as other diplomats and national leaders recognized this as well.[59]

But German generals questioned whether France and Britain would respond militarily, plunging Germany into an unwinnable war. After all, the 1925 Locarno Treaties provided that Czechoslovakia and France would come to the aid of one another if Germany attacked either country, and Russia was also committed to assist Czechoslovakia in case of a German attack if France took up arms against Germany. General Beck had been developing plans for German expansion on the condition that it did not provoke war with Britain, but now Hitler was no longer ruling out such provocation. Beck was also convinced that "Germany needed more 'living space,' both within Europe as well as in colonial territories" but added that "the strength of Germany currently" was not greater than it had been at the start of World War I, and "the fate of Germany in a future war can be seen only in the blackest of colors."[60]

Although others in the army, also for strategic reasons, began to question Operation Green, the newly minted army commander in chief, General Brauchitsch, turned a deaf ear to all objections. Lieutenant Colonel Rudolf Schmundt voiced the new belief in Hitler, criticizing Beck not for thinking Hitler would take Germany to war but for failing to "understand the dynamism of the new regime." War, in fact, was a positive good in National Socialist thought that would assist the Germans in developing mastery over the "races."[61]

At this point Beck, along with some fellow military leaders, began conspiring to stop Hitler's aggression before he destroyed Germany. The conspirators focused on military plans, but once these were worked out—including the assurance of Berlin police chief Wolf Heinrich Graf von Helldorf that his force would remain neutral—the conspirators stumbled over the problem of the Leader's popular acclaim, which limited the options of anyone seeking to challenge him and complicated the conspirators' efforts to agree on a common course. Since efforts to prevail against Hitler with only military force might well ignite a civil war, which Hitler loyalists could dominate, some proposed controlling or perhaps gagging Hitler while they spread word that the putsch had been undertaken on behalf of Hitler himself. Others, like Franz Halder, wished to kill Hitler but feared this would unleash a sea of hostility from the masses, which trusted the Leader with Germany's destiny. Another idea was to assassinate Hitler while making it appear like an accident. Halder agreed but preferred to bomb Hitler's train and represent it as a foreign attack, fearing that an attack on Hitler from within would give rise to another myth of Hitler's greatness.[62] On the other hand, if the conspirators took the high road of arresting and trying Hitler in a court of law, the people would demand his release and view them as villains rather than liberators. Captain Friedrich Wilhelm Heinz argued persuasively against imprisoning and trying Hitler since "even from a prisoner's dock, Hitler would prove more powerful than all of them, including [General] Witzleben and his army corps." Just as unlikely to pass muster in the court of popular opinion was the proposal of the lawyer Hans von Dohnanyi to have a panel of doctors declare Hitler insane.[63]

Of all the conspirators, Beck dealt most directly with the challenge of Hitler's popularity. He wanted to align popular opinion with the plotters by portraying the SS as the real conspirators. It was abundantly evident in 1938 that most Germans were eager to settle into peacetime prosperity. Hitler had reckoned that the battle against Czechoslovakia alone would be short, low-cost, and glorious, enticing Germans further into a united front favoring war, but Beck hoped that antiwar opinion might provision his conspiracy with leverage. The German people saw the prospect of war with "terror because they sense[d] that [it] would not remain limited to Czechoslovakia," Beck thought. Beck placed further hope in the assessment that "here and there in the Army similar thoughts are establishing themselves." The general's efforts were directed first of all toward a "collective strike" of senior commanders that would force Hitler to back away from war. A collective refusal within Germany would prevent the country from starting a war, but could Beck convince others to go along with him? To avoid civil war some plotters considered influencing opinion so the public would see the coup as an act to save rather than topple the German government. Hans Bernd Gisevius, a former Gestapo and Interior Ministry official who worked for German military intelligence during the war, concluded that an assassination would have to be accompanied by a takeover of power, in any case, to avoid civil war.[64]

Beck sketched out a four-sided program to mobilize support beginning with the army. He imagined that a united delegation of military leaders would meet with Hitler to persuade him that Germany was not yet prepared, militarily and economically, for a long war, underscoring the fact that the people (as Hitler agreed) were not prepared to withstand the hardships of a long conflict. Because he understood how firmly and widely rooted the belief in Hitler was, Beck acknowledged that the Nuremberg Nazi Party Rally was an exercise in Führer adulation and recommended that the delegation to persuade Hitler would have to wait until after the "the noise of the day" had died down following the rally's conclusion on September 12.[65]

Beck recognized the importance of opinion for dealing with Hitler, but opinion was not on his side. By mid-1938 the dictator was surrounded not only by a seemingly untouchable aura, but also by military men with little or no appetite for noncompliance, and the desire to believe in Hitler outweighed any inkling to question him. General Brauchitsch felt reassured that Hitler had opinion solidly behind him. "The German people had elected" Hitler, Brauchitsch said, and "the workers, like all other Germans, were perfectly satisfied with his successful policy."[66]

Some military men thought that political calculations, such as the ones Beck was making, belonged only to civilian and not military leaders. But Beck continued to plan as if a rebellion might succeed. In notes dated July 16, 1938, he observed that Hitler's decision for a "solution of force" against Czechoslovakia was "unalterable" and reinforced by voices around him. This course was in opposition to "technical as well as state-political knowledge and conscience," he cautioned. Beck advocated an appeal for non-collaboration by top military leaders in case Hitler ordered war or preparations for it and issued a statement, addressing soldiers of all levels, on the basis for the violation of a soldier's oath:

> Your soldierly obedience has a boundary where your knowledge, your conscience, and your responsibility forbid following an order. If your advice and warnings in such a situation fall on deaf ears, then you have the right and the duty before the people and before history to abdicate your duties. *If you act collectively, with a united will,* you make any action by the army impossible. . . . You have thus protected your Fatherland from the worst—from destruction. . . . Duty cannot be viewed within the limited perspective of military instructions without awareness of the highest responsibility toward the entire people. Unusual times require unusual actions. Other upright men in positions of official responsibility outside of the army will join you on your way.[67]

Beck's scheme looked beyond military leadership to the people, with proposals that the conspirators appeal to the "true sentiments of the people, which has been very much influenced through the emerging big shots of the Third Reich." During the summer of 1938 others, including the chief of the naval staff, Vice Admiral Günther Guse, proposed a similar platform based on influencing popular opinion and representing the conspiracy as a battle "for and about" the Leader. In successive memos on July 15 and 16 to Brauchitsch, Beck suggested that the popular fear of war was finding its way into the military. The "people and the army—which today is again a people's army—will make the military leaders responsible for seeing that nothing military is undertaken." To combat counter-propaganda from the dictatorship, Beck dashed off a list of slogans aimed to appeal to the working and middle classes and to all "upright and decent men of the party." His "short, clear catchphrases" included the following: *For the Leader! Against war! Against big boss bureaucrats! Peace with the churches! Freedom of expression! End Cheka methods! Restore justice in the Reich! Reduce all fees by one-half! No building of palaces! Housing for the people! Prussian simplicity and decency!* Goebbels surely would have been bemused to hear that the generals imagined themselves as his and Hitler's competitors in shaping opinion. Hoping to build on rather than directly negate Hitler's appeal, Beck advocated associating the conspiracy with support for Hitler with the following slogan: "There can and there must be no doubt about it that this great effort is conducted *for* the Leader."[68]

By embracing Hitler and attributing any violence to "radical" big shots and the SS, Beck hoped the conspiracy could take advantage of the people's readiness to separate Hitler from less popular Nazi agencies. The army, at least, was uncomfortable with the SS, and the conspirators thought they might be able to stage a putsch against the SS, much as Hitler had done against the SA in 1934. Did Beck really believe that Hitler's war plans were the responsibility of the radicals around him, a charge he repeated up until he resigned in August 1938? In any case, he would not shrink from claims of "free[ing] the German people and the Leader himself" from "big shots who . . . resurrect communism!" It was simply a fact that "the German people are proud of the achievements given to them by their Führer of regained international standing and liberation from the yolk of Versailles."[69]

Beck surrendered the hope of restraining Hitler in August, when he resigned his office and handed his duties over to his deputy, General Franz Halder. Hitler was happy to accommodate Beck's resignation but once again carefully controlled the story. He requested that Beck refrain from publicizing his resignation, and Beck agreed. Then, against Beck's expressed wishes, the regime awarded Beck an honorary promotion to colonel general upon leaving office. It was an exercise, as the general said, meant "to decently bury the corpse. . . . I have to come to terms with it because the corpse now lies in a nice coffin." The rude honor made it publicly clear that Beck's chapter in German history, at least concerning political advice on military action, was over.[70]

After Beck resigned, the conspirators' effort to take opinion into account so as to avoid a civil war divided the plotters along the lines of disparate opinions. Lieutenant Fabian von Schlabrendorff and others were certain that successful resistance required winning only the support of top military leaders. But Schlabrendorff's statement that "nothing could be accomplished by democratic means" in a dictatorship overlooked the fact that while Hitler hated democracy, he excelled at mobilizing the public, which legitimated and maximized his authority. Halder and Gisevius, in contrast, came to the conclusion at the end of August that Hitler had "such strong support among the common people that there was little prospect of overthrowing him."[71] Speculation at that moment, in fact, was coursing among generals that the uncanny Hitler had somehow arranged with the Western powers to give Germany a free hand in the east to fight Bolshevism.

Gisevius thought it might be possible to turn the all-pervasive belief in Hitler to the conspirators' advantage, if necessary, by claiming Hitler was unaware of an SS treachery against which the conspirators were protecting him. "People believed that Himmler was capable of any crime including an attack upon Hitler or the army," and many soldiers were eager to "settle scores" with the "black rabble of the SS." "A vast number believed in Hitler as a . . . knight without reproach" and were "unwilling to believe that Hitler himself wanted war" (a comment that also points to the tendency of Germans to project their own perspectives onto Hitler). Gisevius noted the eagerness of the people to protect their image of Hitler as a magnificent and just leader, revealed by the common exclamation, "If the Leader only knew!" Such eagerness to believe in Hitler, Gisevius observed, was so attractive because it offered "great assistance in avoiding the consequences of serious and independent thought." Equally maddening was the British leadership's "incomprehensible and unforgiveable patience with Hitler."[72]

Gisevius held out hope that rank-and-file soldiers would support the conspiracy because they had the "closest contact with the bulk of the soldiery and therefore with the broad masses of the people." Here, however, Halder disagreed with him, arguing that the soldiers were as "unreliable for our purposes as any other group in this population" since "they owed everything to the dictator; they constantly cheered him as their hero." For Halder, then, there was only one possibility—a succession of bad experiences, which would enlighten the army. What was needed, Halder said, was a setback for Hitler of such proportions that no counter-propaganda could disguise it, to "induce the army to cooperate with an uprising against Hitler."[73] Halder eventually withdrew from the conspiracy because he thought plotting was useless until Hitler and his men had suffered a diplomatic or military defeat sufficiently serious to "destroy their prestige with the people and with the troops. This, in effect, could only come about when these two powerful factors of public opinion had been disabused of their now confident belief that Hitler could achieve all his designs by miraculous and peaceful methods."[74]

General Erwin von Witzleben also thought Hitler would consolidate support if he won. Popular morale was still "vitally important" despite Gestapo terror. This only indicated that if Hitler won a bloodless victory in Czechoslovakia, as he had in Austria, any attempt to overthrow him would become foolhardy and impossible.[75] In the end, the conspirators hoped that Hitler's plunge into war would bring down foreign military forces against Germany on two fronts, in which case the conspirators were prepared to stage a coup without being certain they had swung opinion.

But the appeasement at Munich followed instead, and it came as somewhat of a relief for those like Beck, who had since May been focusing on preventing a war Germany would lose. A year later the retired general was gratified by the prompt conclusion of Germany's attack on Poland. He regretted that his friend of many years, General Fritsch, had been killed in that battle but explained to his son that due to the humiliation of his dismissal on February 4, 1938, "I knew he [Fritsch] was seeking a decent opportunity to fall [in battle]. As a man of 'high feelings of honor,' he was never able to 'overcome' the stigma of his dismissal." Schlabrendorff agreed that Fritsch, unable to control the accusations, was "embittered and broken" and sought death during the attack on Poland.[76]

The 1938 conspirators faced the problem of establishing their own legitimacy in the eyes of a critical mass of Germans if they were to avoid civil war and lead the country after deposing Hitler. But by the time of the more famous conspiracy of July 20, 1944, they were concerned not only with success, but also with making a statement of honor for the record. This is illustrated in the statements of Major General Hermann Karl Robert "Henning" von Tresckow. In 1940, Tresckow thought that an attack on Hitler's dictatorship would be "possible only if the offensive operations in France failed." The following year he thought the offensive against the Soviet Union would have to fail for the resistance to succeed, for if Germany were to succeed, "neither the generals nor the nation could be convinced of the necessity to resist the regime." In 1944, Hitler had certainly had his military debacles, but there was no groundswell of resistance, and Tresckow identified "the reason for conspiracy" as "prov[ing] to the world and to future generations that the men of the German Resistance movement dared to take the decisive step and to hazard their lives upon it. Compared with this objective, nothing else matters."[77] Conscience demanded it regardless of the cost.

APPEASEMENT AND GERMAN MOBILIZATION FOR WAR

When on August 22, President Edvard Beneš of Czechoslovakia announced a mobilization of his military, Hitler responded by giving him until September 28 to back away from the Sudetenland territory on the western boundaries of his country or face a "terrible" German strike. The western rim of Czechoslovakia, known as the Sudetenland, was home to almost 3.5 million ethnic Germans, and Hitler demanded that they be allowed to return home to Germany, on the principle of self-determination, just as the Austrians had been absorbed into Germany. Hitler was ready to go to war for the Sudetenland. But at home, in August 1938, questions of war were discussed around the country and "weigh[ed] heavily" on everyone. Goebbels worried about a growing "war psychosis." In early September William Shirer doubted that there would be war since the Germans "are dead against war." Reports on popular opinion by secret agents of the SD, which served perhaps as one source of Beck's knowledge on the matter, showed that the people were comfortably enjoying Germany's growing status and prosperity, and concerned that a war could spoil it all.[78]

With Hitler making bellicose threats, the Germans welcomed British prime minister Neville Chamberlain to Munich as a peacemaker. On September 15, German crowds thrilled to the sight of the amiable Chamberlain riding in an open car on his way to meet Hitler, at the outset of negotiations that would conclude in two weeks with the appeasement of the Munich Agreement. At Berlin's Sportpalast on September 26, the assembled masses also shouted approval as Hitler demanded that Czech president Beneš hand over the Sudetenland by October 1. "For the first time in all the years I've observed him," Shirer wrote, Hitler seemed "to have completely lost control of himself . . . shouting and shrieking in the worst state of excitement . . . full of venom." After Hitler concluded his speech, Goebbels sprang to his feet and, in Shirer's account, began to shout, "One thing is sure, 1918 will never be repeated!" Hitler turned toward Goebbels with a "wild, eager expression in his eyes, as if those were the words which he had been searching for all evening and hadn't quite found." It was a demonstration of Hitler's belief that the next war would be won by maintaining German unity and will to fight.[79]

But the following evening, as Hitler stood gazing from his balcony facing Wilhelmstrasse, he saw a German public that seemed to shy away from war and gave him pause. As a German mechanized division rumbled through the Berlin streets and up the Wilhelmstrasse, Hitler observed that rather than cheering, Berliners shrank away as they caught sight of the passing military show of force. The division was supposed to impress foreign journalists and diplomats, but instead it was the German dismay at seeing signs of another war that impressed Hitler and other observers that evening. British diplomat Neville Henderson, viewing the same scene from the British Embassy, thought "the picture which it represented was almost that of a hostile army passing through a conquered city." Shirer, who observed the Germans recoil at the sight of the army division called it "the most striking demonstration against war I have ever seen." People "ducked into the subways, refused to look" at the parade, wrote Shirer, "and the handful that did stood at the curb in utter silence." The deputy of the Reich Press Chief described the crowd of two hundred gathered below Hitler's balcony as "silent and grave." The dour German response to the military parade caused Hitler to look grim and furious and to turn away.[80]

Hitler, who had been confidently demanding that European powers meet his demands or face the German military, now drew back. Evoking the spirit of National Socialism, he had often identified willpower as the essential backbone of a people at war. In *Mein Kampf* he identified the key to "regaining Germany's power" as "produc[ing] that spirit which enables a people to bear arms" because "once this spirit dominates a people, the will finds a thousand ways, each of which ends with arms." A coward with "ten guns" on the other hand "will be unable to fire a single shot." Goebbels too was certain about the foundational importance of the people's will: "It may be good to have power based on weapons," he told the assembled masses at the 1934 Nuremberg Party Rally. "It is better and longer lasting, however, to win and hold the heart of a people."[81]

Sobered after seeing the Berliners respond to the symbols of war, Hitler sent Chamberlain a note that same evening of September 27, withdrawing his threat of a military intervention by 2:00 p.m. the following day. On the morning of the following day, September 28, as the expiration of his ultimatum to Beneš bore down, Hitler compromised "fundamentally," as Groscurth described it, to the terms of a negotiated settlement. He now agreed that German troops would not move beyond the Sudetenland boundaries the Czechs had already agreed to cede. Standing down in the face of confrontation was obviously not an image the Leader favored, but Mussolini stepped in to help him save face with a proposal for a twenty-four-hour suspension of military mobilization and an invitation to Chamberlain and France's prime minister Édouard Daladier to attend a conference on the matter in Munich. The pact that followed, which became known as the Munich Agreement, endorsed an occupation by the German military of the Sudetenland by October 10, legitimizing the new German expansion and removing obstacles to further eastward expansion.[82]

Following the German occupation of the Sudetenland in October 1938, Carl Goerdeler, the former Reich Price Commissioner and mayor of Leipzig, watched Germans rejoicing at the expanding national "living space" and tried to convince the British and the French that under Hitler "the world's future" would be determined by "naked force"—naked force directed *by Germans* against Germany's enemies. Halder went back to the service of Hitler because Hitler "succeeds in everything he does." General Heinz Guderian agreed but was pleased that Hitler "was a very great man" whose achievement of "such a victory without a stroke of the sword is perhaps unprecedented in history." Alfred Jodl enthused about the "genius of the Leader" and hoped that Hitler's "doubters have been converted and will remain so." Most Germans thought Hitler was merely righting a wrong done by the Versailles Treaty.[83]

Still, Hitler was concerned about how to keep the mood buoyed. A month after the Munich Agreement, as the smoke rose from the ruins of synagogues set ablaze during the Kristallnacht pogrom and tens of thousands of newly arrested Jews suffered in camps, Hitler expressed his disappointment with the lack of German enthusiasm for war to the German press: "Circumstances have forced me decade after decade to speak almost only of peace," he declared, but his first goal for the coming year was the gradual preparation of the people for war:

> Only under the continued emphasis on a German will for peace and the intention of peace was it possible for me to gain liberty, piece by piece, for the German people, and to give it arms, which was again and again the necessary presupposition for the next step. . . . It would above all also lead to the point that the German nation instead of facing events well armed, would in the long run be filled with a spirit of defeatism. It has now become necessary to henceforth gradually transform the German people psychologically and to slowly make it clear that there are things that, if they cannot be achieved with peaceful means, must be attained by means of force. For this purpose it was necessary not to propagandize violence itself, but it was necessary to show certain international events in such a light, for the German people, so that the inner voice of the people itself slowly begins to cry for force.[84]

Hitler thought of war as the ultimate stage for displaying his magnificent feats and forging the Germans into the conquering race. His judgment that winning wars united the people was not incorrect, considering the rapid movement of the people from reluctance for war to the faith they displayed in Hitler following the victories in Poland and France. There would always be camps and plenty of terror in National Socialism, but in Hitler's plans there would also be the growing core of the people following the Leader.

The story of the rise of the German people behind their Leader would now face the test of war. Hitler wanted to fight war with the people united, and the church struggle was supposed to remove the denominational basis for differences from the people. But clearly the regime had not yet aligned all of the church leaders with National Socialism. Catholics, with their tighter communities, familiarity with the nonconformity of a minority, and an international hierarchy headed in Rome, were more oppositional than Protestants. But it was evident from the Catholic bishops' resounding support for Hitler's foreign policy that the siren song of nationalism was in fact a common denominator that would draw the leaders of both denominations together under the Leader. When he launched war in September 1939, Hitler was careful to prohibit unnecessary provocations against the churches, whose leaders were throwing their influence behind him. Indeed, even though Hitler's dictatorship had undercut the church as viciously as it dared, when Germans went to war, the overwhelming injunction to the faithful from Catholic as well as Protestant bishops would be to gird themselves for willing sacrifice, a Christian tradition.[85]

Challenges on the Home Front

NAZI LEADERSHIP AND "EUTHANASIA"

> Patients scheduled for transfer and transport as "unproductive
> national comrades" . . . will soon be put to death . . . because,
> in the opinion of some department, on the testimony of
> some commission, they have become "unworthy of living." . . .
> If one is allowed to forcibly remove "unproductive" fellow
> human beings, then woe betide all the courageous soldiers
> who return to the homeland seriously disabled, as cripples, as
> invalids. As soon as we accept the notion that people have the
> right to kill "unproductive" fellow humans . . . then there will
> be no guarantee for any of our lives.[1]

THESE WORDS WERE FROM Catholic bishop Clemens August von Galen, denouncing the Nazi "euthanasia" program from his pulpit at the
Münster Cathedral on August 3, 1941. The regime itself had used arguments heavily relying on material cost to promote the idea that even some
"racial" Germans had to be pushed out of society. It had introduced compulsory sterilization openly. But it denied the rumors that some Germans
were taken to asylums where they were killed rather than cared for. Now
the popular bishop used his authority to legitimate the people's anger
and anxiety.

The evolution of Nazi "euthanasia" from ideology to policy illustrates how the dictatorship sculpted popular opinion while also allowing

opinion to influence its timing and methods. Even as they drilled the people on the importance of "purifying the race" and eliminating unproductive persons, Nazi leaders shaped their eugenics policies against these "useless eaters" with an eye on popular opinion. While wartime conditions undercut resistance in some ways, they also increased the regime's resolve to maintain popular morale and will to fight the war.

NAZI "EUTHANASIA": A SEARCH TO RETAIN POPULAR LEGITIMACY

Hitler wished to begin the so-called euthanasia as quickly as possible, but opinion during the first Nazi years was deemed not yet "ripe" enough to support it. He reportedly feared that the two churches would close ranks against it but found that the church authorities were easily divided and that most could be nudged into quiet acceptance if not full support, considering their underlying enthusiasm for Hitler's rule. Germans were asked to compromise gradually, as Nazi eugenics grew harsher in a pattern of advancements followed by periods of compromise and consolidation. The regime began its attacks on the mentally ill and handicapped in July 1933 with compulsory sterilization, pointing out that this was also the lawful practice in northern Europe and the United States. Many Protestant officials opposed forced sterilization in principle but did not totally reject it, and once it was law, they supported it. On the Catholic side, the Vatican and German bishops also compromised their opposition to sterilization for political reasons, with rare exceptions like Bishop Johannes Sproll.[2]

The churches did draw a line that rejected euthanasia but proved to be exceedingly reluctant to speak out against it in public. In an early test of opinion, Prussian justice minister Hanns Kerrl published a memorandum on "criminal law in National Socialism" suggesting that murders that the regime identified as mercy killings should not constitute a criminal act when carried out according to specified legal procedures. But the German Catholic bishops objected in principle to killing the "incurably insane," as they told Reich Justice Minister Franz Gürtner in 1934. Gürtner then rejected Kerrl's proposition, reasoning in Nazi terms that an attack on just one person was an attack on the entire Volksgemeinschaft, the nationalized community of "racial" people.[3]

In 1935, when euthanasia policy was still taking shape in their minds, officials gave speeches promoting the funds Germany would save by reducing the number of persons with inherited diseases. Nazi Propaganda also promoted their deaths as an act of mercy. A letter published in an SS newspaper suggested it would be better to "let the [sick persons] go to heaven." Common slogans, such as "Common Good before Individual Good" and "Law Is What Serves the People," were also purveyed through films released as of late 1936. Neither Hitler nor Goebbels, however, thought propaganda would be sufficient to quickly close the gap between Nazi eugenics and the people, so the regime proceeded by using various tactics, including secrecy. In a characteristic pattern, the regime supported its propaganda with a stealthy implementation of euthanasia so that people might begin to become accustomed to it. Steps toward euthanasia were introduced in asylums, achieved through the cooperation of ordinary Germans, without compulsion. Hitler said in September 1934 that he was the "highest judge," above any in the judiciary, and he guaranteed that no physician would be punished for assisting in deaths carried out "for the well-being of the people," and this license to kill began to penetrate practices at some asylums.[4] A psychiatrist who was also the director of an asylum was convinced that by the mid-1930s the regime was definitely headed toward full-scale "euthanasia." "There was a progressive deterioration in the care of the mentally ill," he said, "governed by the motto: we must save [resources]. . . . The meat rations were cut. The ratio of doctors to patients was reduced. . . . Serious cases of neglect of patients went unpunished because the view was 'Oh well, they're mental patients.' As a result there was a decline in the sense of duty."[5]

In the drive to strangle church influence, the dictatorship worked in a pattern of advance and consolidation, sometimes retreating tactically if social unrest flared to proportions that could not be ignored. Fighting for power, Hitler had avoided alienating the churches, but after wooing them with promises and treaties in 1933, the dictatorship began suppressing church influence. Then in mid-August 1935, Hitler decided to let up since (as Goebbels wrote) "the Leader sees matters in the question of Catholicism as very serious." The following month, according to postwar testimony, Hitler talked to the director of Reich physicians, Dr. Gerhard Wagner, about the churches and euthanasia. War would provide cover for the instigation of euthanasia, even if propaganda had not yet changed opinion, he said, since the open resistance he expected from the churches would be muted. "When the eyes of the world are glued on the battle lines of war and the value of human life in any case weighs less heavily" the state could expect less resistance to "euthanasia," Hitler told the physician Karl Brandt, who, along with Phillip Bouhler, would play the prominent role in directing that mass murder.[6]

In March 1937 the dictatorship reacted fiercely to what it saw as a challenge to its authority, the pulpit-to-pulpit reading of the papal encyclical *Mit brennender Sorge*. The encyclical expressed dismay about the violation of specific Catholic interests guaranteed by the Concordat of July 1933, without mentioning the plight of German Jews. Distributors of the encyclical were arrested (but not the church bishops who had organized it). Organized resistance was stymied by the appeal of the regime, together with its terror, and only a small minority of the German Catholic bishops cooperated with the Vatican on the encyclical. A dozen publishing houses were closed, and the currency-exchange and morality trials were recontinued, in an effort to sculpt opinion. The Austrian ambassador in Berlin observed that Hitler had his eye on "long-term goals. The attack on the churches . . . is a war of attrition which begins with the soul of the child and aims slowly and by degrees to do away with Catholic schools, and to drive the faithful away from the churches, religious houses, and other church institutions, so that these become, over decades, redundant."[7]

Catholic leaders lacked a united front on tactics as well as on agenda, and church dissent was sporadic. The majority of Germany's Catholic bishops favored a diplomatic style of protest conducted privately and discreetly. Bishop Galen, on the other hand, favored defending church practices publicly, from the pulpit (this did not extend to protecting the Jews). In April 1937, Galen attempted to promote the reading of pastoral letters from the pulpit, as the most effective tactic for resisting attacks on church practices, to his fellow bishops. He referenced the 1936 Oldenburg crucifix struggle, and had the bishops presented a united front from the beginning, using their authority to mobilize parishes in defense of church traditions, they could have impeded the implementation of Nazi policies. But Cardinal Bertram, chairman of the Fulda Catholic Bishops' Conference, which spoke with the authority of all the German bishops, responded with a sharp admonition that Galen had no "feel" for politics. The bishops were somewhat divided, but Bertram scolded

Galen for acting as though he might "command the German episcopacy as if they were Westphalia farmers."[8]

The perception that the church's strength was grounded in the Catholic laity, rather than in their office, was key to the difference between Galen and Preysing and the others. Six months later, in October 1937, Bishop Preysing followed up by arguing a strong case for Galen's suggestion. Preysing thought that the sole consideration that had caused the regime to make concessions to date was its assessment that it could not yet wipe out the church entirely since some of the people remained loyal to the churches.

Preysing pointed out that the bishops' history of negotiations with the regime showed that they moved the church inexorably, step by step, toward total defeat. "Public and mass reaction are the factors [the regime] fears most," he pointed out, "because they symbolize most effectively a still existing limitation on its claim to universal power." Thus, Preysing argued, it was completely senseless to hope that the church could win this or that concession only through negotiations. Rather, "only proven power could cause regime leaders to perhaps relinquish their battle against the churches." Government negotiators, Preysing continued, moved closer and closer to total domination of the churches, backing off from time to time "because circumstances do not yet allow [the state] to take everything." To stand up for itself properly, the church had to recognize the regime as the "enemy" because the regime perceived the church as its enemy, due to its capacity to mobilize the people.[9] Bertram and the German bishops rejected Galen's and Preysing's appeals to mobilize their faithful, and the regime could be sure that any public church protests would remain local and easily isolated, without support from a united church leadership.

Munificently, Hitler offered control in the next world as a comfort to church leaders who complained. It was another way of saying that his regime was merely recognizing the proper purview of the churches in contrast to the state. "The Churches may determine the fate of the German being in the next world, but in this world the German nation, by way of its leaders, is determining the fate of the German being," he told party leaders on November 23, 1937, sweeping across the history of hundreds of years to the conclusion that "only if there is such a clear and clear-cut division can life be made bearable *in a time of transition.*"[10] Thus the regime enticed and bullied the churches into a shrinking sphere.

The transition in the German eugenics program from involuntary sterilization to systematic mass murder occurred sometime during the winter of 1938–1939. The fateful step was taken when Hitler authorized the secret euthanasia of a child. During the following summer, Hitler expressed his intention to secretly kill adults, in addition to children, who were insane, "inferior," and otherwise "useless eaters." In October 1939, when Hitler authorized euthanasia, he continued to associate euthanasia with war, backdating his order to the start of the war. The decision to conduct euthanasia in secrecy was an unmistakable sign that the regime was still very concerned about popular opinion, even during war. Matching Hitler's expectations, the war did curb dissent by heightening patriotism, focusing attention on an outside enemy, softening society's norms against death and destruction, and focusing the total reallocation of energy and resources for war. The removal of asylum patients to places that proved to be mass killing centers, for example, was justified as military necessity.[11]

The regime was driven to war by economic necessity. Hitler also had other reasons for war, relating to his far-fetched schemes for Germany and the fatuous notion that he had to work quickly to lay an unshakeable foundation for permanent Nazism. "Essentially all depends on me, on my existence," he remarked while addressing his military leaders on August 22, 1939. "Probably no one will ever again have the confidence of the whole German people as I have. There will probably never again in the future be a man with more authority than I have. . . . But I can be eliminated at any time by a criminal or a lunatic."[12]

With a string of increasingly improbable foreign victories bolstering his acclaim to ever-greater heights, Hitler wanted to follow up with war. Again Hitler took steps at war's onset that some eager satraps did not understand. On September 8, 1939, shortly after the first shots were fired in Poland, Hitler banned "every action against the Catholic or Protestant Churches for the duration of the war."[13] With the regime's usurpation of the churches' influence far from complete, the reason for this truce, spelled out in the order, was to preempt social unrest. Bormann's decree declaring all German schools secular "community schools" did not stop Germans from hanging crucifixes in them, and during war, Hitler did not want to coerce his people into obeying it or burden morale with further struggles over church practices.

In contrast to Hitler, several prominent members of the Reich leadership, including Heydrich, Bormann, and Rosenberg, thought the war offered unique opportunities to crack down on opponents. During the early war phase, in light of German successes as the Wehrmacht smashed across Poland, they persuaded Hitler to continue attacks on the churches. Hitler remained cautious, however, and again on January 19, 1940, he declared that "tough political" attacks on the churches before "Germany's position was completely secure" were counterproductive. Otherwise, he said, the "domestic strife which would break out would ruin us." Decrees that had eliminated paid holidays and overtime pay rates were also rescinded because they had resulted in "so much bitter discontent and absenteeism in industry during the Polish campaign." Hitler, in fact, went beyond calling off attacks on the churches to restoring the salaries of various priests. He also quashed some seven thousand indictments of Catholic clergymen. During March 1940, while in Rome, Foreign Minister Joachim von Ribbentrop told the pope that Hitler wanted "to maintain the existing truce [with the Catholic Church] and, if possible, to expand it." Four months later the interior minister relayed Hitler's attitude to the Reich governors as well: "The Leader wishes to avoid all measures that could worsen the relationship between the church and the state and party which are not absolutely necessary."[14] Of course the dictatorship could have pushed aside all objections with terror, but another Stab in the Back had to be avoided.

THE POLITICS OF PARDON: HITLER'S "MERCY EDICT"
FOR JUDGE KREYSSIG

Dissent by the church hierarchy was also tempered by the belief in a biblical call for submission to state authority. Protestant bishops had not joined in a common petition against euthanasia during the early Nazi years, and some local pastors were quicker to take action. But church leaders often protested after personally affected parishioners did. Knowledge of the murders itself came from the parishioners, with information "filtered from the laity via the priesthood to the Roman Catholic episcopate," according to some reports. Catholics and in some cases their local leaders had been petitioning their bishops to speak out in an "open declaration" but were met with silence for many months.[15]

The Confessing Church, which had branched off from mainstream Protestantism, produced a clear exception: Judge Lothar Kreyssig. He is identified as one of the few who survived while also voicing dissent as his conscience demanded, and his fate raises the question of why he survived—unpunished save for the temporary suspension of his pension. In October 1935, with the Confessing Church emerging as the main obstacle to Hitler's desired Reich Church, the Saxony district court director complained to the Reich justice minister that Kreyssig was appearing in the role of keynote speaker at numerous meetings, where he publicly criticized the state despite knowing "that the church struggle with the state created difficulties, in particular with regard to its endeavors to continue creating the Nazi national community [Volksgemeinschaft]." The following month the district court director filed a list of offenses Kreyssig had committed with the Justice Ministry. But Roland Freisler, the deputy minister of the Prussian Justice Ministry who would become the notorious judge of the Nazi People's Court, reasoned that punishing Kreyssig could lead to popular unrest in Saxony, the province where the judge was active in the Confessing Church. In 1938, Kreyssig participated in the writing of a resolution by the Confessing Church condemning the arrest of the church's pastors. The following year, he publicly refused to join the Nazi Party because of its church policies. Unintimidated by Gestapo interrogations, Kreyssig, in May 1939, stated that he had graver qualms of conscience now about joining the NSDAP than he had held in 1933.[16]

Kreyssig began objecting to euthanasia at the highest levels during the summer of 1940, an awkward moment for anyone in Germany to express doubts. In May and June, Germany's swift defeat of France evoked jubilation and dispelled German fears of war. Britain had not been able to stop the German subjugation of Denmark and Norway, and Western powers were shocked by the Wehrmacht's speedy dispatch of the French forces. Protestant and Catholic leaders wished Hitler well. In his birthday greetings to Hitler in April that year, Catholic cardinal Bertram assured the Leader of his support.

Expressing a Nazi principle about the use of terror domestically, Goebbels instructed the Gauleiters on August 13, 1940, that Germany's quick conquest of France permitted the party leadership to dispense with certain restraints that it had observed up until then. At the time, the generous level of popular contributions to the wartime Winter Relief Fund had convinced Goebbels that the people would not "shirk its duties" during war, with the life of the Reich itself at stake. Goebbels pointedly added that the extent to which the people were willing to make sacrifices depended on a swift and victorious end to the war, rather than terror.[17]

On July 6, two days after Hitler returned to Berlin from France in triumph, Kreyssig condemned euthanasia in a letter that reached the desk of Justice Minister Gürtner. Acting as soon as he became certain that the state was conducting murder, Kreyssig explained that he was only doing his duty. Taking a clear stand on principle rather than politics, the judge did not argue from the perspective of the regime that euthanasia was sending shock waves through the people, but instead staked his judgment on the positions that these killings were morally wrong, that they were criminal according to German law, and that they caused heart-rending pain. Kreyssig also blazed a trail that Galen would tread a year later, by pointing out that no one could be sure of safety, since "the conditions for the death decisions" were unknown. Relatives of the victims never knew why their family members had been selected. This hardly met the standards of the claim that Nazi law serves the people, he concluded.

Judge Kreyssig followed up with actions that stood in the way of euthanasia in his district. In August 1940, he informed hospitals that wards under his jurisdiction would not be transferred to them without his prior consent. Then he informed the Justice Ministry of his action. Although he repeatedly and publicly attributed the euthanasia murders to a misunderstanding of a statement from Hitler, Kreyssig also took the daring step of formally filing charges of murder against Bouhler.[18]

When Justice Minister Gürtner asked Kreyssig to rescind the allegations against Bouhler since Hitler was the one who had ordered the murders, the judge refused. Gürtner then disclosed a photocopy of Hitler's handwritten note of October 1939 to Bouhler and Brandt, predated to September 1, authorizing the "mercy death" of the "incurably ill." The note demonstrated Hitler's unlimited power to create agencies—*so long as* there were persons ready to do his will. Kreyssig replied to Gürtner that a wrong could not be made legal in such a way. This response represented a new level of subversion, and Gürtner warned Kreyssig that he would not be permitted to continue as a judge if he refused to "recognize the will of the Leader as the origin of rights and justice."[19]

On November 27 and 30, 1940, stating that he could not continue to serve in good conscience under the oath of his office, Kreyssig requested retirement. Then on December 2, he asked to be granted a leave of absence "as soon as possible," and he was sent into early retirement. Fifteen months later, Hitler overruled efforts from party officials and the Gestapo to punish Kreyssig. Instead, as the chief arbiter of particularly delicate issues related to popular sentiment, the Leader granted Kreyssig a "mercy edict." The case against him was closed; he was awarded his pension without penalty and lived quietly through the war.[20]

Similar to other despots, Hitler undoubtedly "cherished the death sentence," but he perceived the importance of "maintaining bonds of obedience and deference" and realized that "terror alone could never have accomplished these ends." Terror suppressed opposition, but the open executions of "racial" Germans on a large scale would have scandalized the people.[21] The reasons for Hitler's "mercy" here were consonant with those behind his orders banning unnecessary provocations of the churches during the war.

While open dissent about euthanasia remained infrequent, popular discontent was mounting during 1940. Popular agitation had begun in January 1940 with killings at Grafeneck, the first of six euthanasia centers outfitted with gas chambers. The mass-gassing center was a former castle high in the Swabian Alps of Württemberg that had previously served the handicapped. Although some of the asylum personnel refused to cooperate, there was sufficient collaboration for the program to proceed at "great speed." As early as the beginning of February 1940, a local Protestant minister, who had been informed by the relatives of victims, wrote that in Grafeneck the sick were "killed and burned." The workers at the Grafeneck facility were reported to have reverentially doffed their hats upon the arrival of new victims, and within months the apprehension and fear spreading among Württembergers alarmed some of the officials. According to the Stuttgart prosecutor, there was much

"talk about such conspicuous mass death," and some were even referring to it as "mass murder." The news spread "like wildfire."[22]

Some members of the German judiciary were also uneasy because
there was no law authorizing "euthanasia." But the sense of the dictatorship was expressed in early July 1940 by the director of the killing center
located in Brandenburg an der Havel, who wrote to the headquarters in
Berlin of the T-4 program (a code name for Nazi euthanasia) that legalizing euthanasia would unleash popular unrest, especially among the
victims' relatives, and make it "much more difficult" to persuade the victims to come to the killing centers. Hitler agreed. Several months later
he stated that any law on the matter should remain in the "drawer" until
after the war since a law could also be used in enemy propaganda, inside
or outside of the Reich.[23]

PASTOR BRAUNE DEMONSTRATES OPPOSITION

Like Kreyssig, Bishop Galen became convinced first in July 1940 that
the state was conducting killings. Galen sent a letter to Bertram asking
whether the bishops should not protest, and Bertram responded on
August 5 that a protest was not yet merited. In Rome, the pope opposed
public expressions intended to mobilize opinion against Nazism. The
bishops were loath to ask questions lest it ruin their negotiating position. On the whole they were determined to be true Germans, as much
as the Protestants. At the annual bishops' conference in Fulda in August
1940, Preysing tried again, with the cause of euthanasia at stake, to suggest transforming "the previous silent protest into a public one," but his
proposal was met by a dramatic departure from the room by Bertram.
The meeting later reconvened, again under Bertram's leadership, and a
strict rejection of the tactics Preysing advocated soon followed.[24]

Although they rejected mobilizing the laity to protest openly with
one voice against euthanasia, the bishops were keenly aware that the
dictatorship responded to this kind of "unrest" more readily than to their
own written protests. Thus in their correspondence with officials, they
sought to make an impression by accentuating the domestic liabilities of
the current unrest. On August 1, 1940, Conrad Gröber, the archbishop
of Freiburg, wrote to Hans Lammers, chief of the Reich Chancellery.
Gröber boldly identified conscience as well as patriotism as his motiva-

tions for speaking out and directing the Reich Chancellor's attention to the fact that a "war with the sacrifices it demanded is not the appropriate time to burden the soul of the people with euthanasia matters." Several months later, on November 6, Cardinal Faulhaber of Munich wrote to Justice Minister Gürtner, drawing attention to the treacherous unrest that euthanasia had awakened in various circles of the people, and warned that it was spreading. Growing anxiety could not possibly be good for the people of the National Community, and mistrust was also spreading. The bishops also stressed that such taking of life conflicted with not only principles holding life sacred but also article 16 of the Reich Concordat, which required the bishops to attend to the "welfare and interest of the German state" by protecting the people from "every damage that could threaten it."[25]

While voicing reservations about the state's inroads on church conventions, the bishops had continued to urge the faithful to support Hitler and the war as they would defend the faith, and Faulhaber now reiterated that "we understand that in wartime extraordinary measures must be taken and we tell the people that it is certainly necessary during wartime to make great sacrifices, also sacrifices of blood, and to take up the spirit of Christian sacrifice." Fauhaber cautiously assured the Justice Minister that he was not rejecting the Nazi principle that "Law is what serves the people," but continued killings would corrode the shaken belief of the people in the state: "It can do our people no good and cannot be right." His letter builds to a conclusion by repeating in various ways the theme that the killings were causing mistrust and anxiety. "No one with open eyes and open ears can deny that today among our people a great unrest has set in due to the mass dying." The morale of the people was shaken to the core in the face of this "naked materialism."[26]

The Protestant leadership also remained adverse to mobilizing dissent or speaking out publicly, although in October 1940, the Stuttgart prosecutor wrote to Justice Minister Gürtner that he was surprised to find the Protestants voicing dissent as much as the Catholics about euthanasia. The Protestants in Württemberg, home of the majority of the victims killed at Grafeneck, were especially active because they were most affected. Bishop Wurm wrote repeatedly to government offices and raised alarm in July 1940 that the trust of the people in official authority had been "shattered." In September the bishop asked Reich Interior Minister Frick whether the Leader himself knew about the killings and had actually approved a plan for them.[27]

A more troublesome opposition for the regime came from Protestant pastor Paul Braune, also in July 1940. Braune, the vice president of the Central Committee for Home Missions and director of an asylum just north of Berlin, encouraged a mass protest. He suggested that all those who "carry fury and horror in their hearts about these things should very clearly . . . send their protest to the Reich Chancellery in Berlin or to Mr. Reich Minister Dr. Lammers, as Director of the Reich Chancellery." At the same time, a memorandum by the Württemberg Church Council sent out similar suggestions to pastors and deacons. The Stuttgart senior church officer, Reinhold Sautter, collected information he thought would be especially potent in catching the eye of authorities in Berlin because it showed that the program was destroying trust in the "Führer and the Reich."[28]

Also leading the Protestant dissent at the lower levels was Friedrich von Bodelschwingh, a prominent pastor and representative of the Protestant Church, as well as the head of Bethel asylums. The case against euthanasia on grounds that it alienated the people could hardly have been been presented more clearly than in Bodelschwingh's letter to the interior minister on September 28, 1940. He was writing, he said, because of his "duties to Führer and Fatherland." He opened by reporting that unrest throughout the country "is growing from week to week. What happens to the sick in Grafeneck, Brandenburg, etc. is commonly the topic of daily conversations in greater proportions than what the men of the Health Leadership in Berlin apparently are aware of. . . . Every aspect of our work . . . is burdened by this unrest and concern [and has created] a serious crisis for the entire service of comrades who are psychologically ill." He stated that the killings were "commonly known within the army and the same thing will happen within the civilian population of the entire country," and he concluded by asking, "Is it really worth inciting this unrest throughout the entire land?"[29]

In May and June Braune and Bodelschwingh sought out meetings with German officials in high places, including Justice Minister Gürtner, who made the impression that he was greatly surprised to hear about euthanasia killings. When they met with the Interior Ministry's Herbert

Linden and Viktor Brack, from Hitler's chancellery, Brack and Linden assured their two visitors that the government would never authorize such killings. It was unfortunate, they acknowledged, but the war did require that some of the patients be "transferred" from one location to another. Affably, Brack and Linden referred to the rumors of the killings as "horror stories." They hoped to win the prelates over, or at least reassure them that nothing could be done, telling Braune that his efforts to intervene would have the same effect as to "lie down in front of a steamroller." When Braune and Bodelschwingh persisted, Brack and Linden threatened to denounce them to the Gestapo. Braune's account emphasized the considerable anxiety about domestic sentiment among top officials in Berlin. "They were clearly concerned about the mood of the people," Braune recalled.[30]

On July 9, 1940, Braune finished a memorandum on euthanasia that he would send to Hitler, carefully identifying the details he knew about the program. The memo went to Lammers and perhaps reached Hitler. In response, Heydrich ordered the Gestapo to arrest Braune, who was taken into custody on August 12, 1941, but released from prison on October 21, after promising not to commit further acts of sabotage. To maintain secrecy, officials were constrained to deny that Braune's arrest had anything to do with euthanasia. Braune's penalty was strikingly light for charges of having "sabotaged measures of the state in an irresponsible way."[31]

Nazi authorities, in fact, were not having their way entirely. In July 1940, the chief prosecutor in Stuttgart, Wilhelm Holzhäuer, warned Freisler about the extensive unrest in his Protestant region, particularly in church circles but above all in victimized families. According to the official story, the killings had not happened, and prosecutors were instructed to forward complaints to Reich offices in Berlin without writing an indictment. Acting Minister of Justice Franz Schlegelberger (who succeeded Gürtner) explained the attempted secrecy, writing that it would not be wise to prosecute rumormongers because the process would spread new reports, whereas the regime wanted silence on euthanasia, lest discussions draw the official denial of the killings into question. One attorney general thought it a pity that the judiciary had become notorious and was now no more welcome than the hangman had once been. In Berlin the justice minister himself was helpless to achieve the hoped-for regulations on euthanasia.[32]

The regime's concern for the opinion of a single group of professionals, even one as important as the judiciary, was not of importance
relative to its preoccupation with popular opinion. In September 1940
the Brandenburg euthanasia operation, which Kreyssig and his allies
had complained about, was closed—only to be replaced by Bernburg.
Discussions among officials, including Reinhard Heydrich, about legalizing euthanasia to match the will of National Socialism continued into
the late fall of 1940, when Hitler finally expressly forbade any further
pursuits of legalizing euthanasia.[33] Hitler preferred the legitimacy of
legalities—but only for practices done openly of course.

FORESHADOWING HITLER'S "HALT" OF EUTHANASIA,
HIMMLER CLOSES GRAFENECK DUE TO "GREAT AGITATION"

In November 1940, a state prosecutor wrote that the regime's attempted
secrecy was not working. "Secret deaths did not remain secret and could
not remain secret." What was said in the official press—whether the killings were denied or misrepresented—was not decisive since "large segments of the population" were already convinced about the truth.[34] The
dictatorship could not afford to lose credibility, but the growing number
of reports on the bitter mood revealed that continued faith in Hitler
could operate as an alternative to stopping the program; social cohesion
might still be obtained as long as the people continued to believe that
Hitler would put things right, once informed. The prevalent insistence,
from various stratums of society, that Hitler was a figure of rectitude as
well as a super-politician is illustrated in a letter of November 25, 1940,
from Else von Löwis. As the leader of the local Nazi Women's Organization, Löwis wrote to the wife of Walter Buch, the presiding judge of the
Nazi Party court. Löwis was an old family friend of the Buchs, and her
dispatch begins with a confession that she had "kept unwavering faith
in the Leader through all the thickets" and had full trust in German victory, adding the following:

> You may not fully realize . . . the terrible impression [the Grafe-
> neck killings] have on the population. Here in Württemberg . . .
> this place has taken on a very eerie reputation. . . . This affects
> not only the helplessly stupid and benighted, but it now
> appears as though gradually all the incurable mentally ill—in

addition to the epileptics, who are not at all mentally disturbed—will be taken. . . . Now the people are still clinging to the hope that the Leader does not know about these things, can't know about these things, otherwise he would intervene against them; in any case he does not know in what ways and to what extent they happen. I have, however, the feeling as if this too cannot go on much longer, or else this trust will also be shaken. It is always so moving to meet this trust, especially in simple people, this natural "the Leader knows nothing of it." And we need to preserve this weapon untarnished, like no other![35]

Here was a woman convinced of National Socialism who also knew its secrets. The belief that Hitler only did everything right as soon as he knew was a weapon like no other, a structure of social control in the Reich. Walter Buch transmitted her letter to Himmler on December 7, calling Löwis "one of my oldest acquaintances" and an "ardent" Nazi. Of course there were "certainly things" that men could handle that one should never allow a woman to do, he said. On the other hand, if there really was so much unrest, one should find different methods for achieving the goal, he thought.

On December 19 Himmler replied to Buch. He acknowledged that Hitler knew about the murders and that he would stop the killing at Grafeneck because, as he wrote, "in one point I agree with you. If the matter is so public, there must be errors in the process. . . . I will get in contact with the appropriate offices and let them know about the mistake and advise them to allow Grafeneck to close." That same day Himmler wrote to Viktor Brack, staff leader of Bouhler's office in Berlin. "The population," he noted, "recognizes the gray automobile of the SS and thinks it knows what is going on at the continuously smoking crematorium. What happens there is a secret and yet is no longer one. Thus the worst feeling has arisen there, and in my opinion there remains only one thing—to discontinue the use of the institution in this place and in any event disseminate information in a clever and sensible way by showing motion pictures on the subject of inherited and mental diseases in just that locality."[36]

The Grafeneck facility, after claiming some 10,654 lives, was now restored to a home for the physically disabled. Some of the staff of 80–100 were transferred to the killing center in nearby Hadamar to continue their work. Around Grafeneck, the closure was immediately obvious to locals because the buses stopped running, victims stopped dying, and the crematoria stopped smoking. The unrest in the region quickly faded. Himmler called for further propaganda, and the Führer had been advised that popular faith in him was not indestructible.[37]

The closing of Grafeneck for reasons of popular sentiment foreshadowed Hitler's decree to halt euthanasia eight months later. The other five killing centers, however, remained open. The regime played something of a shell game, closing one killing center and ending one locus of unrest while ramping up operations at another. After Grafeneck closed, the focal point of popular anger and dismay moved to Westphalia, where the Hadamar killing operation was located some fifteen miles from the provincial capital of Münster. News that a "murder commission" had arrived pulsed around the region. The death certificates for those sent to Hadamar spread from hand to hand, with an effect "worse than enemy agitation flyers." The people were aghast that such "obvious lies" could be found in official documents. During 1941 "in the face of mounting protests and growing agitation about the murders among the population," the number officially targeted for euthanasia murder was lowered from a range of 130,000–150,000 down to 100,000.[38]

OFFICIALS' EFFORTS TO LIMIT REPORTS OF UNREST

The regime was constrained to keep all signs of social dissent hidden, particularly if it threatened the secrecy of a program. Why did the regime handle secrecy so poorly? It is plausible that the regime hoped that the people would grow accustomed to euthanasia as the new norm, as word slowly leaked out. But if so, this was risky, as a gathering of townspeople in the Franconia village of Absberg on February 21, 1941, showed. A crowd was attracted as unfamiliar buses pulled up in the market square and parked conspicuously in front of the Ottillienheim Convent. Fifty-seven of the convent's "feeble minded and stupid" residents had been identified to be transferred as a matter of military necessity ("removed in the course of defending the Reich"). One by one they were pushed onto the buses as "the entire population" of this largely Catholic Franconian village watched. The local priest from the convent, with the help of nuns, held an informal communion service, and several onlookers began weeping. Nazi Party members were also reportedly present and lamenting. According to a local party leader, some of the comments made were "irresponsible." The party Gau office in Nuremberg reported to Hans Hefelmann of Hitler's Chancellery that the event had "caused much unpleasantness." Hefelmann, more annoyed by the scene than the murder, responded in his own defense that the removals from Ottillienheim had happened not on orders from Berlin but on the initiative of the Bavarian State Ministry in Munich.[39]

In Weissenburg, the Nazi district leader blamed the Absberg "demonstration" on Catholic groups and held the local priest particularly responsible. "It goes without saying," he grumbled, "that certain circles will exploit this event psychologically . . . causing unnecessary difficulties and delivering water to the mill of our opponents." An official at the Gau office in Nuremberg advised the Chancellery of Hitler that a state authority must be informed the next time similar actions were taken so that disquieting scenes like those at Absberg could be prevented.[40]

In Berlin Martin Bormann, who would soon take the place of Rudolf Hess as head of Hitler's Chancellery, stated that church members were forming a "confessional front" in order to "carry out resistance under a religious cover." Thus they were able to "operate with some effect in a particularly villainous manner against the state." Four months later, in June 1941, Bormann issued his infamous memorandum proclaiming Nazism and Christianity irreconcilable. In his thinking, and despite Hitler's orders, it was important for the party to continue repressing all church influence. Reich Minister Albert Rosenberg also took a hard line: "War is a struggle for the soul and character of the people," and "The party dare not let this opportunity [wartime] for leadership slip out of its hands." Hitler must have questioned Rosenberg's view that the churches inevitably "aided only the enemy."[41]

In any case, awareness of social dissent had to be suppressed. In general, the dictatorship preferred to limit reports on opposition, particularly in public since these reports could carry the suggestion of public protest to potentially wayward comrades who still "did not understand." A letter from the Weissenburg district leader's office asked that the report on the Absberg event not be given to Police Sergeant Pfitzner since as a Catholic the sergeant might be prone to side more with the villagers

than the regime. This revealed the degree to which the regime was constrained to regulate social relations. Like Pfitzner, anyone might be
introduced to a new social group of dissenters by learning about the dissent. In fact, on March 6, 1941, a report from the Ansbach district leader
reached the Nazi Gau office in Nuremberg about another conspicuous
action of solidarity between individuals destined for a killing center and
their neighbors, an event possibly encouraged by the Absberg episode.
News of the imminent removal of patients in the village of Bruckberg
"caused the greatest unrest among the population." The disturbance
was compounded by the realization that some of these persons were perfectly healthy and were going door to door, "into nearly every house," to
bid their farewells. Suspicions that someone had put the patients up to
going door to door were thought less likely than that "one [patient had]
probably imitated the other." The party leader's advice illustrated the
course, in dealing with such matters, that Hitler and his associates often
preferred. "A certain amount of unrest will continue to arise which will
be fostered especially by the churches," he wrote. *The more reserve the
party shows towards such attacks, the sooner calm will be restored.*[42] The
regime feared news of agitation like the agitation itself.

The solidarity with victims that was found in German villages was
inimical to the development of the Nazi movement. Villagers did not
need to mobilize openly to worry authorities but needed only to follow
normative behavior—crying or complaining as friends and acquaintances were being carted away to their deaths, bidding farewell—to raise
suspicions that some sort of organized nonconformity was afoot. While a
single person was easy for the Gestapo to strike down (such as Pastor
Braune), villagers acting in unison with traditions were hard to suppress.

Perhaps a swift rout of the Red Army, as Hitler vainly anticipated early
that summer, would have stirred a belief in the overall Nazi achievements strong enough to overwhelm the questioning that the systematic
euthanasia stimulated. But the course of events during 1941 forced Hitler to reinstate his ban on actions alienating the churches and also halt
and then restructure the regime's programs. By late summer, as the
Wehrmacht was put to unanticipated tests, the dictatorship went so far
as to disavow a program for a non-Christian Reich Church that was
being rumored about. In September 1941 Gestapo church specialists

convening in Berlin decided that all comprehensive measures against the church must stop. The following month, Reinhard Heydrich went further by definitively banning measures that might in any way weaken the people's capacity to resist.[43]

The year 1941 had begun auspiciously for German military forces, and there was as of yet no general decline in German confidence, although Britain had resisted a German invasion. Assurance was bolstered in the spring, as the Wehrmacht smashed through the Balkans and Greece, which had routed Mussolini's armies several months earlier. The costs had been low relative to the grandness of the conquest, and on April 23, 1941, the day Greece signed an armistice in defeat, Bavarian cultural minister Adolf Wagner ordered the removal of crucifixes and other religious symbols from Bavarian schools, along with the discontinuation of daily religious instructions. The Bavarian minister, who was known as "Hitler's Double" because of their close relationship and physical resemblances, required the school walls to be hung with items more "suitable to the present." This might have seemed like a superfluous initiative since Bormann had directed in June 1939 that by the end of the year "no more denominational schools or monastic or convent schools should exist. . . . No educational institutions should exist which are under denominational influence. . . . Take all other possible steps to remove denominational influences from the German educational system." These directives from Bormann to the Gauleiters had allowed for an exception in locations where Christian establishments were so thickly settled that the party could not expect to compete with them well.[44]

Wagner's resumption of the struggle against crucifixes in April 1941, particularly his clampdown to enforce the decree in mid-August, precipitated a flare of disturbances, followed by the retraction of the decree. Throughout the Catholic milieu in villages, hamlets, and cities across Bavaria, the rebellion continued into September, expressed in various forms of disobedience. Crowds convened outside schools and collectively insisted that the crucifixes be restored; some took matters into their own hands and replaced the crucifixes directly. With the population behind the church, even officials and professionals from the district offices joined in. Soldiers home on leave became local heroes for their stand against Wagner's order. Petitions accompanied talk of boycotting Nazi welfare collections. Mothers threatened to remove their children from the schools. And churchgoing women threatened to write to their husbands on the front to tell them "what was going on." Fear that "the struggle against the church [would] really begin after the war," as one official noted, exacerbated the public outrage about Wagner's decree. The scenes of unrest continued through the first months of Germany's attack on the Soviet Union, beginning June 22, 1941. They ran contrary to Goebbels's instruction to the press that day, in which he stated the "decisive duty at this time [is] to direct the hearts and emotions at home *[Heimat]* so that the [war] front can again depend upon those at home."[45]

Wagner's assault had been joined by Martin Bormann, who was confiscating church properties, mostly in the Catholic areas of western central Germany. Like euthanasia and the Bavarian crucifix decree, the seizure of church properties generated some popular unrest, and as he initiated an intensive wave of church confiscations in 1941, Bormann looked for rationalizations that would dampen objections, such as presenting confiscations as a means to improve the people's material welfare. He promised that confiscated property would be used, for example, for hospitals or holiday camps. Bormann continued to express concern about the people's reaction, although the bishops' criticisms were ignored unless they were made from the pulpit in a way that legitimated and expanded popular complaints. For example, when Archbishop Bertram, who led the Fulda Bishops' Conference, penned a complaint about the SS seizure of the Grüssau Benedictine Monastery, he had to wait five months just for a response, only to be curtly informed that unfortunately the war had necessitated the confiscation.[46]

GALEN'S PULPIT PROTEST RIDING ON POPULAR AGITATION

Stressed by attacks on churches, popular faith in Hitler continued. Dissatisfied opinion "invariably" faulted the government but not Hitler, according to official reports. In Lower Franconia, for example, the people blamed their Gauleiter, Dr. Otto Hellmuth, for Bormann's confiscations from the Catholic Church. Rumors circulating across the region about the closing of the Münsterschwarzach monastery showed how much the people were willing to make things up in order to protect their image of the Leader. One rumor held that Bishop Mathias Ehrenfried of Würzburg had given a report to the pope, who in turn had passed along the news to Mussolini in Rome, who finally, from his lofty position, had been able to get news to Hitler of the confiscations. Once Hitler knew, it was rumored, Hellmuth had quickly turned heels and fled for safety.[47] This tale also indicates the rare access to power the people thought that the bishops held.

As the regime closed the Münsterschwarzach monastery on May 8, 1941, Criminal Inspector Michael Volkl appeared leading a police formation of almost sixty persons. Although Volkl cautiously instructed local leaders that they must avoid stirring up curiosity or protest, crowds of hundreds gathered in the open square by the monastery. When the monks refused to leave, they were detained. In response "all kinds of shouting broke out" from the onlookers. A farmer who had with him medals of honor from World War I made a display of throwing them away. The incensed wife of a party member on the front declared she would instruct her husband to "turn his rifle around and fight against his own comrades." For "reasons of expediency," neither these two nor anyone else at the demonstration was punished, according to the Würzburg Gestapo. Officials were denied even the weapon of propaganda since it would only lead to further declarations "from the clergy or their sympathizers so that the discussion over Münsterschwarzach would never end." Two days later about one hundred people arrived at the monastery for what the presiding Landrat official identified as a "demonstration carried out according to plan ... to compel the government ... to make the abbey church available to church-goers." He reported further that a decision was taken *"not to use force* against the demonstrators *because direct resistance was not offered* and we were supposed to avoid too drastic measures" so that the unrest would die down.[48]

The official formula here was that resistance by force must be met with force, but opposition expressed without it must be played down so that the opposition and news about it would also die down. While the regime did its best to maintain silence and keep word of the Münsterschwarzach confiscation and unrest from spreading, members of the Catholic Church bravely circulated the news. For his part in organizing the distribution of flyers, rather than for protesting, Father Sales Hess paid dearly with four years in Dachau. In contrast, Bishop Ehrenfried's pastoral letter denouncing the closure of the monastery was read from pulpits around his diocese without incurring punishments, even though Church Affairs Minister Hans Kerrl considered the reading of this letter important enough to alert Himmler. The president of the Würzburg Court reported that "even in circles with a thoroughly positive attitude to National Socialism, the measures . . . were condemned because they were likely to cause unnecessary unrest amongst the population at a time when everything had to be done to preserve unity." Bishop Ehrenfried was interrogated at the Bamberg Special Court for having his pastoral letter read but was not tried.[49]

As Germany launched the drive to Moscow on June 22, 1941, the dictatorship was pursuing three separate programs that angered the faithful, each generating continuing or mounting unrest. At this point, early in the summer, officials were fully confident that they would very soon have a victory to outstrip even the previous year's conquest of Paris. Just six months earlier, Hitler had said the Red Army was likely to crumple faster than the French Army. By June 1941, Hitler thought this conquest would take up to four months. Goebbels thought that the Wehrmacht would overtake Moscow within eight weeks.[50] At that point the people would be flooded with pillaged goods as well. Victories like the Anschluss or the defeat of France boosted morale, and the war also yielded booty for individuals and communities, including of course the property of Jews sent to their deaths. The victory over the Red Army was to be a convincing demonstration that Hitler's way was well worth the cost of removing crucifixes and refitting monasteries, as well as accepting the deaths of those who would otherwise be hindering Hitler and the great German march forward.

While Wagner refused to back down in Bavaria, the protests at Münsterschwarzach and the reading of a joint pastoral letter from the German Catholic bishops, read on July 6, 1941, were met with an increase in the confiscation of Catholic property in the heavily Catholic areas of Cologne and Münster. The bishops' public statement, referring to the confiscations as well as euthanasia, was vague and laced with protestations of patriotism. Catholic soldiers, the bishops said, could rest assured that they were serving the Fatherland and God's sacred will.[51] This underscored the regime's bottom line.

As the summer weeks passed, it became clear that officials had underestimated the time it would take for the army to reach Moscow. Across vast stretches of foreign terrain, often with sketchy maps, pockets of fierce fighting disrupted the Wehrmacht's course. At the same time, serious unrest erupted at home, which Lammers documented for Hitler. Concerned about growing distrust in government, Hitler once again ordered that all discussions about euthanasia, the focal point of unrest, were to be avoided.[52] But there was more bad news for the regime on the home front: the decline in church membership that the regime had achieved was reversing. In the teeth of war's anxieties, people were turning back to the churches and religious faith, as if years of Nazi indoctrination had blown away like leaves in a gust of wind. An official reported in early 1943, "With the increasing toughness of the war the churches have a following like never before. . . . The newly awakened interest in the churches has penetrated so deeply into the circles of our supporters that we cannot disregard it."[53] At the same time, any hopes that discussions about euthanasia would be upstaged by victories began to fade.

Over the summer of 1941, Bishop Galen preached his sermons condemning first the confiscations and then euthanasia. No longer willing to wait for the support of other bishops, Galen mobilized his people with sermons on July 13 and 20 at Münster's Lambert Church, denouncing the confiscation of church properties. These sermons came just days after the British RAF had concluded a series of major air raids on Münster. From July 6 to 10, RAF bombings brought home to the German populace the fact that the Reich had increasingly potent enemies whom it could not stop. The leadership worried about the strains and fears this added to the German psyche. From this point onward, the Allied bombing of Germany became more and more intensive, while the Nazi regime could do little except to promise that the day of reckoning in response to these "terror attacks" was on the way.[54]

The day after his sermon on July 13, Galen sent a telegram to Reich Chancellor Lammers, petitioning Hitler, "in the interest of justice and the solidarity of the home front, to protect the freedom and property of honorable German people against the arbitrary measures of the Gestapo and against this theft for the benefit of the Gau leadership." The following Sunday he raised the stakes when he read his telegram from the pulpit. As had Bishop Meiser before him, rather than condemning Hitler or the state, Galen made sure to declare his own loyalty and that of the Catholics to Germany and their government, and against the communism that the regime associated with the Jews ("We Christians, to be sure, are not aiming at revolution"). The bishop's act of reading aloud the telegram he had sent to Hitler could well be seen as an appeal to Hitler's justice, a long-needed call to get the attention of Hitler that the people thought was missing. Galen also concluded with a clear signal that he intended to limit his resistance, at a cost to his integrity, by identifying Jews as outsiders who had earned their own misfortune. The debate about Galen's integrity and resistance is set aside here in favor of identifying whether his sermons, as a catalyst for the force of popular unrest, had an impact on the regime.[55] But by reading his telegram publicly and appealing to Hitler, Galen demonstrated that Hitler must know about the confiscations.

On July 31, just days after Galen's objections, Hitler ordered Bormann to stop the confiscation of all church property unless he had first obtained Hitler's permission. Hitler was said to be angry about the "nonsense" of party hotheads assaulting the church. Bormann instructed the Gauleiters that the seizures of church and monastic property are to stop immediately until further notice. The confiscations stopped with the exception of some of the properties that Bormann claimed Hitler had designated for confiscation before his ban. In Poland, however, where the regime was not concerned about popular opinion, the onslaught was unfettered. Under Alfred Rosenberg, Reich Minister for Occupied Eastern Territories, almost all Polish religious houses, including monasteries, were closed, and virtually all Jesuits imprisoned.[56]

BISHOP GALEN LEGITIMATES QUESTIONS
ABOUT THE OFFICIAL STORY

Rather than resting after this ban, the popular, fiery bishop turned his condemnations on Nazi "mercy killings." On August 3, the third sermon of his triptych began with reiterations against confiscations from the churches but moved to a powerful attack on so-called euthanasia. In his sermon Bishop Galen wisely appealed to the public beyond the group whose family or close friends had been killed, pointing out that a program of extermination existed without a clearly defined category of victims. A growing range of categories of persons had been drawn into the killing centers, and considering the logic of destroying persons who could not earn their keep, one could expect that wounded soldiers would be killed as well. In fact, Galen added, no one at all could feel safe from the arbitrary grasp of the Gestapo—not even the Reich's most conscientious constituent.[57]

Galen spoke explicitly so that he was clearly condemning the euthanasia killings that were deeply upsetting the public across Germany. His sermons are viewed as a public protest because popular unrest legitimated his condemnations, especially on euthanasia. In turn he lent authority to the voice of the anxious masses, strengthening popular opposition, lending legitimacy to people's doubts about the official story. The bishop's sermons were also finely timed. As he spoke, uncertainty loomed in the East and air raids horrified increasing numbers of Germans in cities across north and western Germany, exposing cracks in Hitler's claims. A single bishop as clever as Galen was able to compete with Nazi authorities in shaping opinion but nevertheless served as a catalyst more than a cause.[58] The power of his influence rested on eighteen months of popular agitation. His sermon dealt a blow to the already faltering myth of secrecy, stiffening the backbones of those who had doubts, and in his shadow a few Catholic bishops also spoke out against the killing centers or the taking of life.

One week after Galen's final sermon the court president for Westphalia reported that the population had already "been very disturbed by rumors and whisper propaganda about euthanasia for many months." It was a conversation many were having across the Reich, as Galen's sermons were copied at once and circulated through informal channels among Protestants as well as Catholics. The permeation of the issue throughout the Reich reveals the partial public space that the Catholic Church, in these specific and all too unique circumstances, still maintained. The British Air Force assisted, air-dropping copies of the bishop's words from the sky over Germany, aiming in particular at the national loyalties of German Catholics. The soldiers on the front who read the sermons were anxious about whether they too really could be "euthanized." More than three months later, as reported by the senior attorney general for Düsseldorf, Galen's sermons were still much discussed in Catholic circles, assuring that "euthanasia measures . . . are known throughout all of Germany."[59] The regime would have longed for a polite exchange of mail instead. A missive in the diplomatic style of the highest clergy would be resting in a file cabinet, probably unanswered and perhaps hardly read. Perhaps it soothed a conscience but was nothing to dispatch the Royal Air Force into a special leafleting mission.

In Berlin, discussions at the highest levels on how to respond to Galen's treason illustrate the compromises the regime was willing to make for such treachery at this point. Gauleiter Alfred Meyer of Galen's West-phalia region had called for Galen's head already after his second sermon on July 20. He accused Galen of the high treason of having led the people astray. Meyer advised that propaganda could rectify the situation but warned that further discussions of euthanasia were certain to disrupt the peace. The Gauleiter recognized that executing Galen would stir up ill will but recommended that the punishment would be possible if the regime waited until a resounding victory had been won at the front. Reflecting the Nazi stratagem at the highest levels, he suggested that such a moment of victory would renew patriotic fervor and overshadow the removal of Galen.[60]

Meyer's advice about the right moment for the punishment of a bishop does reflect a sense that the people must be kept satisfied one way or another. Goebbels agreed, based on his statements the summer before about the additional latitude the Gauleiters enjoyed for cracking down, following victories like those over France. Rapid promotions to national-level positions placed Gauleiter Meyer among the Nazi elite attending the notorious Wannsee Conference of January 20, 1942.

Galen's fate was no mere regional concern over which Meyer as Gauleiter could exercise authority. Nor did Galen's sermons cause local troubles only. Rather his case raised questions touching on how the people perceived the dictatorship that only Hitler could make.[61] From his Propaganda Ministry's division chief in Westphalia, Reichsminister Goebbels received a memorandum classifying Galen's words from the pulpit as high treason. These charges were quickly counterbalanced with cautionary advice, however. "It is to be feared," the division chief wrote, "that this sermon and the utterances of the bishop will get around by propaganda of mouth and will be believed in wide circles of the Reich, especially among the Catholic population" and "will find their way to the Protestant population, especially among families who have relatives at the front." Furthermore, "measures taken by the state police against the

Bishop can hardly be successful" because by his "arrest and judgment the bishop would be made a martyr by the Church. . . . I beg the Reich Minister [Goebbels] to decide whether or not the Leader should be asked by group leader Bormann whether the camouflage of Euthanasia thus far in practice ought to be modified so that defense against the treasonable claims of the Bishop of Muenster can be inaugurated by launching a campaign of popular enlightenment."[62]

The highest Nazi authorities linked the question of how to punish Galen directly to how the people throughout the Reich would perceive it, a perception that in turn was coupled with the popular perception of euthanasia. The punishment of Galen would represent a verdict against the masses angry about the killings. Galen's suggestion that wounded soldiers faced execution had the potential to mobilize anyone who had a relative at the front—in addition to anyone who had a relative in an asylum—and to damage the willingness of soldiers to fight. Goebbels recognized the merits of prosecuting Galen, writing that such a course of action would "set an example and show the high church dignitaries that everyone is equal before the law." Still, an execution was not possible because, as Goebbels regretted to say, the regime was not in a good position at that moment to carry it through. Goebbels's advice, to "preserve appearances" rather than make a "counterattack on the church during the war," reflected a common response to public scenes of unrest. It would be "nearly impossible" for the regime to sustain popularity if Galen were punished, he said, cautioning against an "open breach" with the church. As the master of propaganda, Goebbels recognized its limits in this case better than his subordinate, Walter Tiessler, who thought Galen could be executed after a barrage of propaganda pointing out his "vulgar lie." Goebbels countered with a position that Hitler shared. "It would have been wiser, in my opinion, not to challenge the Church during the war but to try only to steer it according to our interests as far as possible," Goebbels conceded.[63]

Although both Bormann and Gauleiter Meyer, as well as Tiessler, had recommended execution, the dictatorship proceeded more cautiously. The Justice Ministry recommended sending Galen to a concentration camp, but Hitler ruled that out too. The crisis of confidence for the regime was only deepening, and people were returning to the churches. As Bormann indicated, the question that Hitler now faced was not just how to handle Galen but "whether enlightenment concerning euthanasia matters should be launched." Hitler was "quite sure" that "Galen knows full well that after the war I shall extract retribution." He would have perhaps preferred to strategize with Galen rather than with Rosenberg, who, as he complained, had "let himself be drawn into a battle of words with the Church."[64]

Given the remarkably wide distribution of Galen's sermons, it became untenable for the regime to continue as if Hitler was unaware. Lammers, taking account of the accumulating reports of unrest throughout the population, had reported to Hitler that distrust of the government was growing. Goebbels, following another meeting with Gauleiter Meyer on August 23, also tied popular outrage regarding euthanasia to the actions of Galen and the church, taking the position that euthanasia could not be continued without serious consequences. "After the war the church question can be solved with the stroke of a pen," he wrote; "during the war it is better to be hands off. . . . The people are now encumbered with such serious worry that one must strive for reasons of justice not to expand this worry." Though he maintained that the euthanasia program "was necessary," he did not believe that the time was right, stating, "One should avoid open conflict whenever possible. We do not have enough time and energy now in order to push it to its ultimate consequences. We would rather save this for better times." The next day, August 24, 1941, Hitler issued a decree to halt the euthanasia of adults. Victor Brack, who had supervised the T-4 euthanasia program within Hitler's Chancellery, said that he "received an oral order to discontinue the euthanasia program." There were plans for a "new euthanasia program after the war."[65]

According to one postwar testimony, Hitler's decree responded to the breach of trust, resulting primarily in a rumor spread by the Propaganda Ministry that Hitler had just discovered the truth of what was happening and had just as quickly ordered a cessation of "euthanasia." If so, the regime had found an opportunity to shore up an important delusion, the Hitler Myth, turning the loss to some advantage by maintaining the people's belief in Hitler. The order from Hitler banning further attacks on monasteries and nunneries was followed on September 3 by another directive declaring it "absolutely essential" that there be no further measures "which might adversely affect the feeling of unity among the populace."[66]

Hitler's order on euthanasia soon ushered in a compromise solution with the people, initiating a new, decentralized phase of "mercy killings" among Jews, Poles, orphans, forced laborers, and others with fewer ties to the Reich that killed fewer people. These murders, known as "wild euthanasia" in official documents, comprised an "initially virtually uncontrolled" program that relied more on the willing efforts of local doctors and nurses.[67] The victims were killed in ways that would more easily be portrayed as "natural causes," such as starvation, overdoses, or poisons. Murder by medication rather than gas permitted the killers to "space the deaths of their victims over weeks or months" in order to hide them. For the regime, the trade-off with the people was fewer murders.[68] The number of deaths under this "wild euthanasia" was thirty thousand during the forty-four final months of the war, compared with seventy thousand during the first nineteen months. At the euthanasia killing centers, gas chambers and crematoria streaming oddly scented smoke were moved to the killing centers in the East to victimize the Jews.

Officials also sharpened their deceptions to soothe morale. A goal of the new "wild euthanasia" program was "to make death by euthanasia and natural death indistinguishable." One perpetrator later testified that "to calm the people at the nursing homes," the sick were now removed under cover of the excuse that it was for their own protection. Typical of the new deception was the instruction that they lived in an area especially vulnerable to air raids. The doctors behaved so unusually kindly to the patients that "the deception worked completely." Some of the patients now begged to be included in the "transportations."[69]

In Berlin, officials initiated new propaganda to eventually enlighten the people about euthanasia. A film that opened in Berlin on August 29, 1941, titled *Ich Klage An* (I accuse), urged Germans to accept euthanasia. The film was clever propaganda, and its arguments found some general if qualified reception, indicating that the regime was moving the people gradually toward Nazi norms. The film also generated protests according to the SD. More daunting, the SD found cracks developing in the regime's credibility. Indicating the already developed capacity of the people to decipher camouflage, the SD reported the striking conclusion that the majority now saw through the regime's machination for what it was, understanding the film as the regime's propaganda response to Galen's third sermon.[70]

HITLER'S HALT DECREE AS A STEP TO OPTIMIZE THE PARTY'S ADVANCE

Within the space of a few weeks in 1941, three attacks on the churches were terminated or dramatically altered by decrees on July 31, August 24, and August 28. The regime compromised in order to quiet social agitation and preempt further provocations. Hitler's halt of euthanasia on August 24, like his disruption of property confiscation on July 31 and a retraction of the Bavarian crucifix decree on August 28, had the effect of stemming the popular dissent and protests on these matters.[71]

The Bishops' Committee for the Religious Orders let it be known that "the Leader's stop decree [of confiscations] on 31 July 1941" was "produced by sermons of His Grace the Bishop of Münster" and "has for the most part been observed."[72] Then, on September 20, 1941, Pope Pius XII conceded in a letter to Bishop Preysing that the bishop's advice on tactics of speaking out publicly had merit: "The bishops who with such courage and at the same time in such irreproachable form stand up for the causes of God and the Holy Church, as did Bishop von Galen, will always find our support."[73]

Hitler's August 24 halt order fits into this pattern of compromise made in response to the pressures of domestic opinion. From the beginning, Hitler had shaped the conduct of the euthanasia program in ways that reflected sensitivity to popular opinion, beginning with the postponement of euthanasia until wartime. Then, the regime had attempted to conduct euthanasia secretly because the people were not yet "ripe" enough to stand the news. To maintain the official story, the regime compromised yet further by suspending the normal punishments for those who spread rumors about it. Popular opinion also closed off the possibility of legalizing euthanasia to quiet the unsettled judiciary, and the regime was moved by domestic opinion as well to close the Grafeneck murder center in December 1940.

On August 28, 1941, an incensed Hitler made sure that Gauleiter Wagner's decree removing crucifixes from Bavaria was rescinded.

Still, the faithful continued to mobilize in protest, so Hitler issued another decree in September reinstalling the crucifixes in schools. In Wagner's Bavaria, Nazi Party Bavarian governor Franz Epp accused the Catholics of taking the offensive against the crucifix decree with Nazi methods, comparing the Catholic mobilization of opinion and public assemblies with the methods the party used to extend its support. Wagner, he accused, "has provoked demonstrations, school strikes, and unrest in the entire province." Epp thought that Wagner's real role as a responsible domestic leader during wartime was to preserve morale on the home front "during the hardships of war and [to avoid] unnecessary strains on that morale since, as every participant in the First World War was aware, morale at home could lift or depress morale at the Front."[74]

There was no doubt in Goebbels's mind that popular opinion was a powerful force that Hitler could not reckon with during war merely through terror. Wagner's decree, he wrote in September 1941, had "been really devastating. Seldom in this war had a decree been so short-sighted and led to so many nasty consequences as this. . . . If one has so little clarity about what the people want and desire, then he really ought to be deprived of the possibility of issuing edicts from the safety of a provincial office."[75]

Goebbels was still revisiting the debacle with Bishop Galen in the spring of the following year, worrying it like a scab that wouldn't go away. In the bitterness of the German failure to reach Moscow in December, Göring had written to Bishop Galen and his colleague from Osnabrück Berning, rebuking them in the most severe terms for their "treasonous behavior." With the bishops' response in his hand, Goebbels resolved to force the hard truth home to Galen, recommending that Göring pen a new letter, "above all to Galen, in which he very clearly makes the accusation that his claims about the liquidation of the severely wounded of the Reich have caused the most severe disarray and that it is precisely his remarks that the English propaganda service has used against the National Socialist regime." Goebbels was hoping to force the bishop into unqualified support for the regime, but he was no doubt aware that this was much more difficult now that the turn in the war would cast doubt over the popular belief in Hitler.[76]

Hitler and Goebbels apparently agreed that the urgent demands of the war compelled the Nazi leadership to not antagonize the people.

Following the protests against the Oldenburg crucifix decree, Goebbels had sought out Gauleiter Röver of Oldenburg, earnestly imparting to him the senselessness of provoking the people. In March 1942 he began to formulate in his diary his belief that the crucifix struggles had developed into a wedge of protest that worked against, but also in conjunction with, what he saw as the mistakes of Nazi leaders. Placing some of the blame for the people's receptivity to Galen's criticism of euthanasia on the actions of the Reich leadership itself, Goebbels modulated his attack on the bishop. "Certain actions of the party, above all the crucifix decree, have made the propaganda of the bishops all too easy," he added. Although other bishops had protested, the galvanizing effect of Galen's protest was singular for the regime, as Goebbels points out. There was an enormous difference between the impact of Galen's public declarations and the private "protests" of other bishops, including Wurm, whose letter Goebbels tossed into "the waste paper bin."[77]

Enemy air raids would soon lead to civil defense measures that generated further compromises between people and regime. The degree to which the people disregarded the regime's will was often met with a similar degree of concession. Just as he had intervened against Gauleiter Wagner's crucifix decrees, on behalf of his image and popular morale, Hitler himself intervened in 1944 to prevent his Gauleiters from deploying even soft forms of coercion to bring the people in line. This move was prompted by another protest by hundreds of women in Witten in October 1943. Goebbels thought that public dissent had to be dealt with at once so that it did not become a lesson in dissent and spread. Following the women's Witten protest in October 1943, he expressed his fears that the people were exploiting the concessions Hitler made to collected public displays of opinion.[78]

CHAPTER SEVEN

"The People Know Where to Find the Leadership's Soft Spot"

AIR RAID EVACUATIONS, POPULAR PROTEST, AND HITLER'S SOFT STRATEGIES

FEW PROGRAMS TESTED the Nazi dictatorship's capacity to manage popular attitudes more than the massive relocations of civilians, ongoing throughout the war and culminating in late 1943 as Allied bombing raids forced the Germans from their homes. The programs to evacuate children and other endangered civilians sent millions fleeing their homes to unfamiliar yet safer rural regions, which often proved unwilling hosts. When many Germans defied the dictatorship and returned home in spite of the air raids, the regime had to decide whether to use coercion to keep the evacuees away from their homes and families.

The peril, as Hitler saw it, was that forcing unwilling Germans to relocate might cost more than it would yield, alienating some who otherwise were still loyal. The dictatorship responded with measures forged by interactions between its will and the will of the people. Success or failure in the war could also influence its calculations about how effective raw coercion of its people could be. During the early phase of German success, as it increased pressures on Catholic institutions, the regime began a pattern of tolerating ordinary people who rejected directives for the evacuations of civilians.

From the earliest mass civilian relocations as war threatened in 1938 through the large-scale evacuations due to intensifying enemy bombings raids, the Nazi leadership struggled to manage the people by controlling the volume, pace, and public perceptions of the evacuations. While the party claimed to represent the unified masses, the people had yet to fully internalize its ideology and ultimate goals. Hitler wanted the war to deal a decisive blow in the Nazi struggle for the unreserved loyalty of the people. But by the time the enemy bombings were unleashing one firestorm after another on cities along Germany's western border, Nazism's exalted claims came into conflict more and more with the re-alities of everyday German life.

Yet as the hardships of the evacuations became commonplace, Hitler continued to balance coercion with compromise even late in the war, as if he could never abandon his faith in his formula for taking power and governing at home as the crisis deepened. He continued to insist that evacuees must be able to retain the sense that they were relo-cating voluntarily, without coercion. Hitler continued to stick to his ideal of "educating" rather than coercing civilians into cooperating with the regime's plans for evacuations. Gaps between popular opinion and Nazi policies were treated as problems of perception and managed with pro-paganda until perceptions and Nazi ideals matched. This was a hard sell as the bombings intensified.

Air raids did not crush the German will to fight as some Allied lead-ers had projected, although they did burden the regime's capacity for totalitarian control by drawing its credibility into question. Air raids also disrupted home and family life, sharpening the conflict between private sphere values and Nazi demands. The ensuing grumbling challenged the regime's control over information and its propaganda claims that the overwhelming majority of Germans were united under Hitler's lead-ership. Ironically, the air raids did draw the Germans together in a "community of fate," in the solidarity of fear, and when this happened, the regime turned to ingratiating itself with the besieged people by play-ing the role of their best ally.[1]

Waning confidence in the German military along with the increas-ingly desperate conditions of war forced the authorities to live with some forms of dissent and disobedience. Germany's debacle at the Battle of Stalingrad in early 1943 depressed respect for the Leader and his claims. By July 1943, "the telling of spiteful jokes and jokes damaging to the state—even about the Leader—[had] increased enormously," reported the SD, whose secret agents were charged with accurately codifying pop-

ular opinion. Because such complaints were so common, a state prosecutor was forced to set aside the trial of a woman who had said that the
"brown [Nazi] big wigs" sat at home rather than fighting on the front—
in contrast to the "red [Soviet] commissars." Antagonistic expressions
were so widely prevalent, the SD reported, that singling out just this one
woman for punishment would be "untenable."[2] Throughout the war,
compromise with long-standing customs continued to form part of
Hitler's strategy for securing the mass cooperation he needed to win the
war. The dictatorship's investment in the image of the Leader, and its
claim that a consensus supported his dictatorship rendered it vulnerable
when realities betrayed this mystique.

HITLER INDULGES THE PEOPLE RATHER THAN THE ARMY ELITE

Following World War I, during the rapid evolution of aircraft, Germany,
like other military powers, had developed plans for air warfare. But
where other countries planned for shelters to protect civilians, the Nazi
government placed hope in the transformation of civilian attitudes. The
German officials did plan for anti-aircraft guns and bomb shelters as
well, but the basic component in their strategy was to develop a tough-
ened people united behind national goals, a superior people who would
stand and fight rather than run for the shelters.[3] Nevertheless, Reich
Minister Hermann Göring's Air Defense League drills revealed that as
war approached, Germans had not yet evolved beyond "fear, doubt, and
unwillingness." In June 1938, when a German plane loaded with bombs
crashed into a Hessen village, only some of the party and government
officials remained calm while the rest fled in panic.[4]

Not until September 1940 did British air raids force the dictatorship
to begin civilian evacuations. But during the Sudeten crisis in 1938, sectors of the population along the French border also demonstrated a sense
of freedom to move regardless of official measures, as they grew nervous about possible troop movements and enemy fire.[5] Fearful of a
French invasion if Germany went to war in Czechoslovakia, Germans
along the French border moved away from the borders *en masse*, without
waiting for official directives. By late September 1938 so many Germans
were in flight that General Alfred Jodl described it as a "refugee movement" that was steadily "increasing."[6] The evacuees clogged the roads,
and the complications of discovering where individual persons had

resettled also hampered centralized authority and military planning for combat.

Nevertheless, Hitler refused to issue regulations. Nazi propaganda had raised the stakes with proclamations that the German people would prove their superiority by orderly adherence to official plans. The claim that Germans worked together under their Leader because they were the superior race fit a propaganda pattern that portrayed Nazi ideals as reality. Orderly communal action, according to Nazi claims, "bolstered the self-image of the German nation and reinforced the idea that Germany was born to rule."[7]

Hitler's unwillingness to act caused disputes within the army general staff about how to respond to the flood of refugees.[8] Similar tensions between the general staff and Hitler arose a year later, as Germany prepared to launch its war against Poland. In March 1939, France, together with Britain, had guaranteed the defense of Germany's neighbors, and in August 1939, as they planned an attack on Poland, German Army leaders anticipated another eruption of German masses fleeing border zones. They wanted to issue regulations for the orderly evacuation of civilians but agreed that such regulations would not be possible without an order from the Leader.

In this 1939 confrontation with Wehrmacht leaders Hitler chose to represent his main constituency, the people. At a meeting with Hitler on August 25, 1939, the army chief of staff, backed by other army leaders, broached the urgent necessity of evacuating more than five hundred thousand Germans along the French border. On the spot, Hitler agreed to issue regulations, but the following day he retracted this agreement.[9]

Hitler voiced apprehensions that an evacuation would have upset Germans by separating them from their belongings. A governing concern for him was to "avoid everything in the civilian area that would lead to continuing disturbances to the life of the public." The Wehrmacht leaders countered not with arguments about traditional military strategy but with an appeal to the Leader's concern for morale: a hurried evacuation of civilians—without sufficient advance warning and perhaps under panic-ridden conditions—would have a negative psychological impact on the German soldiers. No doubt Hitler wanted to limit awareness that Germans were not acting according to propaganda. Also, perhaps the Leader was reluctant to test his authority in the face of crowds moved by fear, even though he was always deeply interested in testing whether the people were willing to fight a war. On August 29 the army high command alone issued orders for the evacuation along Germany's western border, but as the SD reported during the coming days and months, German civilians did not fall in line.[10]

To preempt unrest and uncertainty until the evacuations were absolutely necessary, all open discussions of any evacuation plans were strictly prohibited. The military was joined by the SD in criticizing this stipulation because it afforded less time for the population along the border to prepare for an evacuation. When rumors erupted that the regime was planning evacuations, the dictatorship chose to deny such plans.[11]

Matching propaganda and policy on related matters regarding German Jews, however, was not as challenging. In all evacuation measures, according to the regime's information, the Germans wanted a complete separation of Jews from other Germans, preferring that Jews be sent to camps rather than sharing their evacuation quarters. Germans in Stuttgart and Mannheim who gave accommodations to evacuees refused to provide housing for Jews. In this way, Germans were not just passive, but also encouraged the regime's persecution, just as the people themselves, along with local leaders, made sure that German Jews did not share the safety of their air raid shelters to which bombings drove them night after night.[12]

While Hitler waited, masses of ordinary people began to take actions on their own. Between August 30 and September 2, 1939, almost four hundred thousand Germans living along the French border took the initiative to pack up and leave home, lest they get caught between invading French troops and the Wehrmacht. The official, orderly evacuation of hundreds of thousands of French on their side of the same border is ironic in light of Nazi claims comparing French disorderliness with German discipline for collective action. Only after most of the German civilians whom the Wehrmacht had wanted to evacuate had already fled did Hitler issue directives, on September 2, for evacuations along the Palatinate and Saarland borders, and these were not strictly enforced.[13]

By early October the number of Germans who had left their homes was 573,234.[14] Some of them began to wander aimlessly, ignoring official relocation areas. Exiled Social Democratic Party observers reported that officials had no record of where they had resettled. Separated friends and family members were compelled to request the whereabouts of their loved ones over radio broadcasts or in newspapers. Free-flowing masses disrupted the army's plans, forcing the military authorities to abandon their arrangements for keeping civilians out of certain areas. Arriving in the official reception areas, some of the evacuees became very indignant about the official orders limiting their movement. In addition, another problem arose that was to plague the regime throughout the war: the evacuees were not received with open arms in the manner of a people's community or official propaganda. The local populations ridiculed those from the western border with France as "typical French," "Saar French," and even "Gypsies"—a slur perhaps referring to their itinerant condition. Even some of the party and state leaders turned a cold shoulder.[15]

The evacuees themselves also did not always live up to Nazi ideals. In the coal-mining village of Dudweiler something resembling a demonstration developed, and local authorities were compelled to call upon neighboring district officials for help to restore order. "Impassioned refugees gathered in front of the town hall" and "quieted down only after someone from the party's district leadership in Saarbrücken delivered an explanation" for the regulations to the aggrieved protesters, the police reported.[16] These refugees showed few signs of awareness of the terror and intimidation commonly identified as the backbone of Nazi domestic control, moving about as they wished and assembling together in protest in front of a symbol of government. Like the masses of disorderly evacuees around them, they were not punished. Rather than registering the troublemakers by name, the SD recommended that the dictatorship establish an agency with unlimited power for the prevention of future disorders. Various official reports that autumn of 1939 identified additional gatherings of disorderly and protesting persons.[17]

A further sign of feelings of autonomy followed as hundreds of thousands of evacuees returned home in contradiction to explicit official orders. Within two months, in some cases up to 80 percent of those who had left home because of the war had returned home or "embarked on 'wild wandering.'" Bringing order at least to its files, the SD identified "wild wanderers" in three ways: those who left home contrary to the regime's plans; those who left according to plan but then sought out their own destinations rather than following directives; and those who returned home before or without official permission.[18] Civilians roaming about disrupted army planning considerably. Returnees reported the bad conditions they were fleeing, depressing the morale of their relatives in the military. Many proceeded to enter the houses of others while their owners were still away, looting and destroying property. Further illustrating the unrealized quality of the Nazi "national community," civilians crowded onto trains and insisted on taking up so much space for their own goods that it became very difficult for the army to transport its own necessities.[19]

Characteristically, the regime preferred to bully and badger wayward Germans with peer pressure. The party faithful mocked the "wild wanderers" as "suitcase patriots."[20] Good Volksgenossen (comrades of the people), they asserted, waited for the government to organize them and to tell them when and where to move. The Gestapo was effective at eliminating anyone who was organizing opposition, but in this case each family was motivated by self-interest, while all the families acting together added up to what General Jodl had identified as a "movement."[21]

In early December 1939, after most evacuees had already returned, the army chief of staff released a directive granting permission to the evacuees on the western border to return home, once again surrounding circumstances the people had created independently with regulations to make it appear as though it had total control.[22] A week after this army directive, the Reich Interior Minister representing the regime also recognized existing reality by releasing additional regulations permitting civilians to return home. Each order urged the people to return with as little fanfare as possible. Their journeys were to be made without the assistance of added train cars, and celebrations welcoming the wanderers back home were banned.[23]

The freedom these ordinary Germans exercised clashes with general images of a dictatorship that drew up plans according to ideology and proceeded accordingly, having had its way by force wherever opposition arose. Of course, Hitler had nothing to fear at the time; there were no serious domestic threats to his authority as the great Führer—and such threats were his bottom line—and he was handily winning the war. From the projected perspective of the regime's having taken over the continent, its tolerance of the evacuees' disregard does not portray a "weak dictator" so much as one calculating the quickest way toward its goals *within* the constraints it allowed popular opinion to place on it.[24]

Hitler continued to be apprehensive that opinion might sour if the war demanded too much from the people, even as war victories paved the way forward for him. Germans, including some of those who would later try to assassinate him, were jubilant as the Wehrmacht destroyed Poland at little cost to their nation and their army. Hitler's ascent in popular estimation continued. His survival of a single-handed assassination attempt by the carpenter Johann Georg Elser on the evening of November 8, 1939, provided another occasion for Germans to fulfill what seems to have been a monumental need to believe in his power and justice. His escape became a common topic of conversation and "strengthened the people's sense of solidarity. . . . Love of the Leader has grown yet stronger," the SD reported, and as a result "the attitude toward the war has become more positive in many circles." Church leaders, Protestant and Catholic, led a festival of belief in the Leader. In various regions around the Reich, congregations held services of thanksgiving and condemned the diabolical Elser. Hitler's survival from yet another grave danger proved that God had again "held his protective hand" over their Führer.[25]

While the adulation following the mighty Leader's providential escape from the lone worker was extravagant, Hitler waited for a yet more optimal moment to identify his authority with the story of the German evacuees. Several days after Germany defeated France in June 1940, Hitler announced that evacuees had returned to the French border (most had been back home six or more months earlier). The evacuees were *now* permitted to return, he said, adding that the evacuations due to war had been carried out according to "well-prepared" plans. The behavior of those involved, as well as those concerned, had been "exemplary!"[26] In the glow of such a great victory he could expect his propaganda to be perceived as beneficence, a recast image of reality that might guide behavior in the future.

Still, few evacuees seemed interested in the Nazi dream of more than 60 million "racial comrades" working in harmony like a hive of bees. Some evacuees turned their backs on their homes and struck out for something new. Other "wild evacuees" overlooked regulations, and the movement of hundreds of thousands did present new opportunities for moving around. On the other hand, masses of evacuees returned home without receiving the required authorization. Nevertheless, authorities bragged that the evacuation of German civilians had been carefully organized and was carried out as planned. They had proven the German superiority over the incompetent and bungling French.[27] Rather than applying police force, the SD recommended simplifying the process for returnees, a suggestion consistent with other changes that officials made to remain in step with the people when the people lagged behind.[28] In future propaganda, the dictatorship would represent the evacuation of civilians in harm's way as benevolent state-paid opportunities for recreation and recovery.

POPULAR OPINION WEIGHS ON POLICIES
FOR EVACUATING CHILDREN

Hitler was counting on the recurrence of glorious moments like those following the conquest of France to continue exerting the magnetism of his leadership. Yet a few months later, the Luftwaffe's failure to win the war against England rendered German cities open to enemy raids from the skies. Up until Churchill succeeded Chamberlain as prime minister in May 1940, the British RAF raids had not raised serious concerns for Germans. The situation changed during June, when a single air attack killed ten and wounded twenty-four. By July the increasingly destructive raids had caused an increasing nervousness.[29] Beginning in August, the bombing of Berlin dealt a profound shock to city residents and caused "a considerable sensation" throughout the rest of the Reich. One casualty was Reich Minister and Air Force Director Hermann Göring, following his pompous claim that enemy aircraft could not penetrate air space over the Reich capital.[30]

Still a readiness to believe Hitler counteracted much of the populace's anxiety. "Of course I will prepare everything cleverly, carefully, and conscientiously," Hitler declared in an address to the people on September 4, 1940. "You understand that. And when one in England today is very curious and asks: fine why hasn't it happened yet? Be calm, it will happen."[31] All over Germany, the words, "Be calm, it will happen," began to course through public conversations as a reassurance from the Leader that the British would now be brought to their knees. In conversations people gushed that "only a man who has already crossed the greatest obstacle and already has the final victory almost in hand can speak like that!"[32]

Such magical thinking was not unfamiliar to Germans at the time, as the mystique underlying German belief in Hitler infested everyday perceptions. Following Germany's defeat of Poland, a rumor that England had signed an armistice spread by telephone, telegram, and mail into "all regions of the Reich." Upon hearing this "news," workers in various factories went on break, and business leaders rejoiced that wartime measures would no longer be necessary. Stockbrokers immediately took special interest in Reich bonds, and at the University of Berlin students erupted into a celebration of the supposed armistice. At the Heinersdorf train station civilians eagerly greeted the troops with, "You can go home, the war is over!"[33]

Propaganda pushed wishful claims that the German military was invincible, and the SD fretted in September as the Reich failed to invade England that the people no longer closely followed the military situation. A day after Hitler's speech, a note of caution had also crept into Goebbels's diary. "Everyone hopes that it will come to an end this fall," he wrote. "May it be God's will. Another winter would not be as pleasant."[34] As victory over Britain slipped from Germany's hands, Goebbels worried that the coming air war over Germany might cause "very extensive and massive terror." Rumored among the people was the claim, perhaps planted by the Propaganda Ministry, that the British were "in their final despair" and might even turn to using gas against innocent German civilians.[35]

As the Germans realized that the RAF would continue to bomb their cities, a "flood of letters from anxious parents" poured into the offices of the Gauleiters and Reich Chancellor, complaining that the raids were preventing their children from a good night's sleep.[36] In response, the dictatorship devised a program to evacuate endangered schoolchildren that would also serve to indoctrinate them. Based on the recent experiences with civilian evacuations, the judgment was made that the moment (following Germany's failure to defeat Britain) was not right for using coercion to gain public compliance with the new plans.[37] Orders required children's evacuations from cities targeted by enemy aircraft to be carried out voluntarily. Reports from September 27, 1940, stated, however, that this was an initial order: "To avoid the impression of a co-erced evacuation it is recommended that the children initially be sent away on a voluntary basis."[38]

Concurrently, Hitler's private secretary, Martin Bormann, issued a secret mandate for the "extended evacuation of children to the country-side" from Berlin and Hamburg; it was billed as an extension of the so-called Kinderlandverschickung (KLV), a program the Nazis had used in 1934 to provide urban children with vacations in the countryside.[39] Bor-mann directed officials to justify the relocation of children as a way of protecting them from the disease that might spread during the cold months (suggesting it was only a wintertime measure). Jews were not to be included, and the term "evacuation" was not to be used at all. German authorities preferred the term "re-accommodated."[40]

Abstention from coercion was also the wish of Hitler's minister of propaganda; Goebbels approved of the evacuation of children but in agree-ment with Hitler—"not with force." The use of coercion, he explained, would be "unbearable at this stage [gegenwärtigen Stadium]" since "above all this would drive the mood down quite hard." Using force to evacuate children, the propagandist calculated, would "without doubt" cause "ex-ceptional ill will," particularly among mothers. The preferred method for encouraging these relocations while maintaining popular morale, Goebbels said, was "encouragement," exercised by representing the re-locations of schoolchildren as a service the party was willing to under-take on the people's behalf.[41] The evacuations were to appear "from the outside not as an evacuation but as a strengthened welfare program for recovery during the war."[42] The official promotion crediting Hitler with this largesse was articulated in a memo by Bormann on September 30: "The Leader imagines how uncomfortable it must be for parents to get their children from bed at night during the cold and take them to a more or less distant, partly unheated air raid shelter, so the purpose of the Leader's order was to dispel the worries of mothers for their children. . . . The Leader rather conceptualized the evacuations as a shining example of social welfare precisely for the poor."[43]

This image of caring concern for children might seem misplaced in conceptions of Hitler and Nazism as the enemy of Christian values of charity. But the people needed to strengthen each other against their enemies. Nazi propaganda for women was "from the beginning filled with appeals to love, love of leader, love of heroes, love of children, even Christian love" and "touched the hearts of" German women "least identified with German Feminism." Hitler was continuously portrayed as "kind to women and children." Notably, however, at least some saw the KLV evacuations not as welfare but as a sign that the leadership was anticipating further trouble, showing that the Germans were capable of parsing propaganda.[44]

Although Bormann's order for civilian evacuations had been confidential, rumors about an official evacuation of children soon ricocheted around Berlin. The SD characterized the rumors as "wild"—unauthorized from Berlin—but Bormann was not so sure. He suspected the source of the hearsay might have been Goebbels, who was eager to test opinion. Goebbels had in fact built a massive "mouth radio" system that was well practiced by 1940 in spreading rumors to test popular response and that reported to Berlin from numerous locations around the Reich on what the people were saying. As Reich Minister, Goebbels was the nationwide expert on mood and presided over manipulations to control popular sentiment. He paid particular attention to the feeling in Berlin, where, as the Gauleiter, Goebbels was responsible for the evacuation of children.[45]

The rumors gripping the capital revealed fears that the state would be taking children from their parents. The SD recommended that the officials hasten to correct this impression with "calming official statements" in newspapers and on the radio, and on September 30 Goebbels hastily called the press together. "Regarding the evacuation of children, "mothers are free to go to safer areas with their children as the party stands to the side and provides the trip free of charge. . . . There is no coercion," he said, acknowledging social pressures by adding that "mothers [must] not be afflicted with the stigma of cowardice." Goebbels informed the editors of the *Frankfurter Zeitung* that evacuation plans were the source of considerable complaints that must be counteracted. "Great value" was assigned to making sure that "the sentiment of the people in no case suffers" because of evacuations. "Regarding the evacuations from Berlin, one wants to advise as many parents as possible to send their children away," Goebbels confided. "One hopes that to begin with we can send at least 50,000 Berlin children away."[46]

Goebbels identified the Berliners' initial response as a "crisis in the people's mood."[47] Like Hitler, Goebbels understood the significance of domestic unity and the crucial role of compromise with the people for achieving it, and he increasingly became an important confidant of Hitler during the war. Not surprisingly, as the enemy air raids escalated, so did Goebbels's authority on matters of domestic governance, and he intervened in every aspect of the air war.[48] To evacuate all children while procuring the voluntary consent of their parents the regime invoked charitable German church and state programs, which had existed since the end of the nineteenth century. Under the Kaiser, before World War I, the transfer of children from the big cities to the countryside for a break from city routines became part of a respected German custom.[49] Beginning in 1914, the Landaufenthalt für Stadtkinder continued to send children to rural areas to enjoy the fresh air, food, and exercise; during the Weimar Republic, political parties had had their own competing programs.[50] Now it was the Nazi Party rather than the state or churches that directed the activities and education of the German children and youth.

During the ensuing years, as some of the parents held back, officials would return again and again to discussions of what forms of force they could use in persuading parents to comply. Bormann and the SD, as well as Goebbels, issued repeated assurances that the parents could choose whether to participate, so there was no need for unrest. In early October, Goebbels publicly offered the assurance that parents who had already sent their children away could retract their permission and retrieve their children at any time. Many parents, particularly Catholics warned by their church leaders that religious instructions were lacking in the KLV sites, did bring their children back.[51] Within the context of so many parents sending their children away, doubtless some of the parents did not perceive that they had any choice but to comply. But those who could imagine making a decision that went against official will had the possibility of exercising choice—in the face of social pressures, of course, and at the risk of alienating themselves and their children in the eyes of Nazi officials who would privilege those who complied. Some exercised this choice.[52]

Hitler, as well as Goebbels and other Gauleiters, was beset not only with clashes between reality and party propaganda, but also with the lower officials who erred on the side of fulfilling the regime's desire to remove all children, regardless of the cost to support for the regime. The SS and police leader for western Germany, for example, thought that "the consent of the parents for the relocation of their children [was] to be induced." Leaders like him continued to create conflicts.[53] Even in parts of his own Gau of Berlin, Goebbels complained, some parents had been put under pressure to send their children away at once. Far from Hitler's being aloof from domestic matters, "the problem of the evacuation of children also occupies [Hitler] very severely," according to Goebbels, who wrote on October 1, 1940, that Hitler agreed with him that the evacuations must not be coerced.[54]

By that point, air raids had begun to challenge public confidence in official promises of protection. In Berlin as of October 23, 1940, bombs had killed thirty-two persons in the streets and thirty-three in shelters. The SD reported an "extraordinarily large number" of complaints about the "uniformity" of daily press reports on the air raids, as attacks were obviously growing ever stronger and more damaging.[55] As of early 1941, the public had encountered so many contradictions between the official descriptions and what they were experiencing that many had ceased to believe government claims. From time to time SD agents noted that the public thought that propaganda "does not relay or only partly relays the truth."[56]

ENEMY "TERROR" AND THE PARTY AS THE PEOPLE'S LOYAL ALLY

Under the leadership of Baldur von Schirach, a young but experienced Nazi, the evacuation of German schoolchildren soon grew in purpose and scope. Whatever humanitarian goal the program had, it also planned to use the conditions of evacuation as a hotbed for rearing loyal Nazis under the supervision of the Hitler Youth.[57] Schirach also understood Nazi politics of mass mobilization. After joining the party in 1925, he had led demonstrations across Germany to attract people into party organizations. Beginning in 1931 Schirach was director of the Hitler Youth organization. As one of Hitler's trusted inner circle, he was named Gauleiter of Vienna in the summer of 1940.[58] In late September 1940, just days before entrusting him with the position of plenipotentiary for youth education, Hitler approved Schirach's suggestions that the party take on the education of German youth at the evacuation sites, and the state began to surrender its established role as administrator of education across Germany to the NSLB.[59]

Following the initial evacuations from Berlin and Hamburg, the evacuations were extended in October 1940 to regions along Germany's western border, particularly in the industrial Ruhr area, where the danger of air strikes was greatest. Since the regime initially turned over the removal of evacuees from their homes to the Gauleiters, removing civilians in danger demanded increasing attention from Gauleiters in areas under attack from the air.[60] Although regional officials wished for uniform national guidelines from Berlin, Reich authorities refrained from specifying even so much as how long the evacuated children should remain away from home. Responding to their own regional constituents, some of the Gauleiters resisted Berlin's call for complete evacuations.

In July 1941, as the air raids multiplied as fast as the questions about Germany's fate in the war, Schirach asked the Gau officials how he could increase voluntary cooperation with the evacuations and was told, Schirach said, "that new evacuations are not considered necessary despite the attacks." He added, "I hold myself responsible to advise that the evacuation of children from the Gaus under the threat of air raids is the express, oft-repeated wish of the Leader." To resolve tensions between the will of the parents and the regime, Schirach suggested that regional officials use "appropriate propaganda," stressing that "evacuations are what the Leader wants."[61] Reich officials speaking on behalf of Hitler, however, continued to avoid issuing instructions beyond a broad sketch of the desired results, to be achieved with parental consent.[62]

Despite propaganda (and contrary to some postwar assessments), the number of parents complying with the evacuation plans of the Nazi regime sank along with the growing realization that the war would not be concluded quickly. The ability of the German people to make sacrifices that the war demanded, and to fight on despite the severe deprivations, did not correspond evenly with their belief in the regime or even in Hitler. The war generated its own dynamics, and society held together at a national level due to organizations of mass volunteers and efforts of the churches and party organizations. But the sacrifice of sending children away was leveraged from parents in part by promises that this was a stopgap measure due to a war that would end soon. Parental compliance corresponded roughly with the credibility of Nazi propaganda characterizing KLV relocations as a short-term program to safeguard children until the final German victory. The high point of KLV success, reached in October 1941, also corresponds approximately with the cresting of German success in the early, Blitzkrieg, phase of war.

Hitler continued to reject police force compulsion of parents to hand their children over to the party through the KLV transports. Rather than sending their children to the official evacuation sites, many parents opted to keep their children at home without formal school training or to have them live with friends and relatives in safer areas. The regime saw little choice but to welcome this independence because the air attacks had made it clear that the regime was woefully unprepared to lend its citizens the assistance they needed, and the parents who made private arrangements demanded less from the regime coffers.[63]

Nazi authorities compromised somewhat to meet the demands of parents regarding the education of their children at evacuation sites, but they refused to change certain characteristics of the KLV program, preferring instead to have parents opt out if they could tolerate the risks that came with this.[64] Life within the more than five thousand KLV camps established by 1943 was regimented seven days a week, with children and youth attired in uniforms, participating in drills and marches, and otherwise learning their place in the German national community. The lack of religious instruction constituted a basic stumbling block for millions of parents, and church officials spoke out. Regulations forbade the distribution of anything in writing, whether religious or not, that the party did not produce. Under pressure to encourage parental cooperation, Schirach in December 1940 had authorized religious education in KLV camps but only on condition that a religious instructor was available.[65]

Bishop Clemens August von Galen of Münster was a prominent critic of religious training at KLV evacuation sites. On October 26, 1941, soon after his public sermons against euthanasia and the confiscation of church properties, as well as his unrestrained injunction for Christians to sacrifice themselves fully in Germany's war, Galen penned a pastoral letter complaining that these evacuations did not further religious training for Germany's children. Galen also complained that some of the

parents had been unduly pressured to send away their children and concluded that only the parents who were certain about the maturity of
their children should entrust them to the program. The bishop advised
parents instead to send their sons and daughters to live with relatives
who lived in safer areas, rather than to camps run by the Hitler Youth.
Upon hearing the bishop's remarks, many parents rescinded their permission and retrieved their children, an indication that prelates could
make a real difference at home, at least while Germany's military offensive was failing. The SD noted that "in Catholic circles the word is spread
that the KLV consciously sabotages religious instruction," and under the
duress of the last several years of the war, the Nazi Party saw the Catholic Church as becoming a competitor.[66]

Reflecting the regime's dilemma, the SD in turn warned against
increasing church influence on the youth in KLV camps, complaining
in particular that religious tracts or letters were undermining KLV ped-
agogy. Still, in the face of continuing parental and prelate complaints,
Education Minister Bernhard Rust issued a guarantee in 1943 that KLV
children would receive religious instruction. The SD regarded this directive as "a major setback for National Socialism in its ideological confrontation with the church."[67] The dictatorship loathed the separate loyalty the
churches claimed on the people, but its position of compromise, taken
under duress of war and articulated by Heydrich's order of October 1941,
was that the regime must safeguard all institutions (i.e., the churches)
that strengthened Germany's capacity to fight.[68]

Efforts to evacuate schoolchildren and youth continued the trajectory of
give and take between the people and the dictatorship initiated in the
early stage of the evacuations and illustrated by the matter of religious
instruction. The party's training stressed the principles of the Nazi national community, replacing the usual subjects with the experience of
belonging within a community and the importance of being ruled by
the common good over individual interests. Activities were planned on
Sundays as well, with three per month devoted to Hitler Youth activities
for those over age ten. Many parents feared that under the KLV curriculum their children would be left with such great gaps in their knowledge
that they would not be promoted to the next grade. In response, Schirach
issued adjustments in April 1941 to meet this concern without addressing

the real concerns: any pupil who had missed at least three months in the regular system due to KLV evacuations would automatically be passed into the next grade. In addition, the Education Ministry devised measures in theory that were supposed to help the students returning from KLV camps to catch up. The results, however, were so poor that the party leadership itself later acknowledged that those students who had been trained away from home were falling short when they returned.[69]

During 1942 the decline in parental willingness to send children away from home persisted despite official warnings that this was what Hitler wanted and that such nonparticipation threatened the success of the German national community as a whole. In September 1942, for example, the Gau officials for the city of Hamburg informed parents that although sending their children away was voluntary, the possibility of "success" would be greatest if every child went along. Reluctant parents were now asked to submit in writing their "important reasons" for "withholding" their children. This procedure of ostracism presented a further chance for the authorities to separate those considered trustworthy from those who were not; at the same time the noncompliance by some sent a signal to other parents that they did have a choice.[70]

Although the regime preferred to compromise by deferring to parental discretion while also holding the line at evacuation sites, there were illustrations of the regime's compromising on the sites as well in order to mollify parents. An order of July 1941, for example, read: "Visits from parents in the sites must fundamentally be excluded. . . . Parents who travel to the reception area without explicit permission of the department are to be denied entry to the site and a meeting with their children." Facing a flood of complaints from the parents, however, the authorities allowed this ban to erode. By the time the formal order came from Berlin in 1943, many regional KLV departments had already begun to allow parents to visit. In time, the regime even financed regular rail trips known as "Visiting Parent Trains," carrying parents to visit their children on "Parents' Visiting Day," with the NSV footing the bill.[71]

As the Reich failed to secure any crucial victories in late 1942, Hitler began showing signs of being disconcerted if not embarrassed. On November 7, 1942, according to Albert Speer, who was traveling by train to Munich with him, Hitler's train idled to a halt as he and his guests sat dining at a table sumptuously set with silver, cut glass, expensive china, and floral arrangements. Hitler and his entourage had just received news that Allied troops had broken Germany's positions at El Alamein by a "mighty armada" of enemy ships that had entered the Mediterranean through the Strait of Gibraltar, turning the tide in the battle in North Africa against the Wehrmacht. The mood in Hitler's car was somber, and without drawing Hitler's attention, a freight train eased to a stop on an adjacent track.

> Bedraggled, starved, and in some cases wounded German soldiers, just returning from the east, stared at the diners. With a start, Hitler noticed the somber scene two yards from his window. Without as much as a gesture of greeting in their direction, [Hitler] peremptorily ordered his servant to draw the shades. This, then, in the second half of the war, was how Hitler handled a meeting with ordinary front-line soldiers such as he himself had once been.[72]

THE CHALLENGE OF PERCEIVING OPTIONS TO EXERCISE CHOICE

During 1943, as bombing damages worsened, the regime was able to achieve a brief, if minor, upturn in the numbers of children evacuated through a new practice of "complete school transfers." The success of this new approach was grounded in pressures of conformity created by the simultaneous evacuations of all students in a school class along with their schoolteachers.[73] The regime used parental visiting privileges at the KLV camps to prove its generous patronage: "It should be made clear to parents repeatedly that they must be grateful to still have an expense-free possibility for visiting their children evacuated to the countryside, despite the difficulties of the fifth year of war," Nazi authorities said in November 1943. "It is to be pointed out to parents again and again upon request that the KLV sites are at the moment the only really appropriate locations for an orderly and effective training and educational care for our young boys and girls."[74]

But once they perceived that they had a choice, some parents mustered the capacity to say no. In Hamburg, the parents who refused to take part in these uniform student evacuations faced a sense of social ostracism and isolation, an exposure especially uncomfortable and risky in a police state. In Berlin, according to an SD report of August 30, 1943, of some 260,000 Berlin schoolchildren only about 32,000 were in KLV camps. The parents of 132,000 children had made their own arrangements to place their children with relatives who lived in safer places. Among the parents of the nearly 100,000 children who remained in Berlin, 62,000 had refused to allow their children to be evacuated in the KLV evacuations.[75] In Arnsberg, a town forty miles west of Witten, rather than continuing to insist that they evacuate, the officials decided to recruit the students for work, a tactic disregarding the national mandate for children to be enrolled in school, but aligned with defiant parents.[76]

Complaining that the Berliners were making evacuations particularly difficult for him as the Berlin Gauleiter, Goebbels in December 1943 procured Hitler's permission that in the cities where entire schools were evacuated, "no classes should take place . . . because otherwise mothers will return with their children," and depending on where the Allies were bombing, "we would end up repeating the evacuation process a dozen times per year, something the Reichsbahn is not in a position to do." The national rail was already overstretched by the demands of war, Goebbels said. He planned to close Berlin schools entirely beginning early in 1944 so that evacuated mothers would no longer return to see their children who were in school.[77]

The regime was unable to relocate all the children merely by closing all the schools. In the Ruhr city of Bochum, after the schools were closed, the local paper reported on October 8, 1943, that "it has unfortunately become known that some irresponsible parents did not send their children along with the [students and teachers from closed] schools but instead have kept them at home." At the same time, in the nearby city of Dortmund, the "massive resistance of a considerable portion of parents finally forced the authorities to surrender, at least in part."[78] In Aachen, the Catholics revived youth organizations, which the dictatorship had repressed during its early years. A Gestapo agent noted that the young Germans apparently preferred the Catholic meetings to the Hitler Youth's "often boring ceremonies."[79]

To solicit cooperation, authorities gave parents the benefit of the doubt. In December 1943, Gauleiter Alfred Meyer of Westphalia-North wrote that many parents refused to evacuate their schoolchildren because they "simply lacked understanding." Similarly, the SD wrote that the Germans consorting with the Poles "show no understanding. . . . The Church does not seem to grasp the enormity of Polish crimes against Germans."[80] The number who lacked understanding probably rose as Germany's fortunes fell during the final phase of the war. By early 1944 the SD reported regretfully that "even still a considerable portion of parents have not found themselves ready to evacuate their children."[81] In September 1944, months away from Germany's unconditional surrender, the authorities in the city of Hamburg were still striving to persuade reluctant parents to part with their children; in the city of Trier that year, the women "jeered and hooted" at the Nazi Kreisleiter leading the effort to evacuate children; only 50 percent of those eligible had registered.[82] The Nazi response in the autumn of 1944 was to relax regulations further so that some parents were allowed to make their own arrangements for visiting their children. Especially during the end phase of the KLV program the churches, in particular the Catholic Church, sent priests and chaplains to serve in camps for evacuees.[83]

Nazi officials blamed church propaganda for convincing large numbers of Germans to *openly* reject the KLV program by 1944. But they could do nothing about the renewed popular interest in the churches.[84] The regime did not see itself in a position to rely on brute force to evacuate children any more than it could coerce millions of Germans to abandon the churches. Furthermore, as we shall now see, the regime's efforts to evacuate adults who were endangered by the bombings also resulted in such massive noncooperation that by late 1943 it had become clear that stricter regulations and attempts to enforce them simply weren't worth the trouble they caused. In the city of Witten on October 11, 1943, women met increased official pressures with an escalated display of defiance and public protest.[85]

THE RELOCATION OF ADULTS NOT ESSENTIAL TO WAR INDUSTRIES

The British aimed to cripple the German civilians' will to fight by bombing cities; these efforts became known as "area bombings."[86] A directive of February 14, 1942, instructed the British Bomber Command to focus on "the morale of the enemy civil population and in particular of the industrial workers." Churchill also thought that "an absolutely devastating, exterminating attack by very heavy bombers" might bring down Germany. Arthur Harris, the Bomber Command's new head, told Churchill on February 23 that leveling "Berlin from end to end" would cost the

Allies 400–500 aircraft but would "cost Germany the war." Although Harris was proved incorrect, Allied attacks grew exponentially almost month by month. The first "thousand-bomber" raid, carried out against Cologne in late May 1942, did more damage to the Rhineland city than the RAF's previous seventy bombings combined.[87]

By 1943 the growing intensity and destruction of the assaults on German cities by Allied air forces had reached such dimensions that official efforts to help the victims proved almost farcical. Any civilians who were not essential to production in the war industries were pressured to leave targeted cities. The regime also relocated entire factories and evacuated nearly a half million employees as well.[88] As of February 1943, it encouraged cooperation with material incentives and rewarded the individuals who left targeted cities voluntarily with the transportation of their furniture, as well as allowances.[89] Once relocated in evacuation sites, they had to be convinced not to return home, not only because of the bombings, but also because the travel between the relocation sites and their homes weighed heavily on railroad transportation already overburdened with the demands of war and genocide.

The frontline Nazi organization charged with presenting the face of the Nazi Party as a charitable caretaker was the NSV, or National Socialist People's Welfare. While on the war front the Germans were trained to exterminate, on the home front the NSV tried to impart another critical element of National Socialism: the belief that racial Germans must support one another in the effort to subordinate the others. Before the war the most visible function of the NSV had been organizing the Winter Relief, Child Care, and Mother and Child Relief aid campaigns, but with the arrival of air warfare it grew to be the second largest party organization, smaller only than the German Labor Front, and according to some accounts it did have a relatively high regard among the population.[90] As it provided food and shelter in the wake of bombings, it exhorted Germans to lend a hand to the injured and to the survivors of the deceased until they were once again psychologically strong enough to manage life's duties on their own. By the beginning of 1945, the NSV had coordinated the evacuation of 8,944,976 persons.[91]

The NSV placed emphasis on Germans cooperating with Germans.[92] But in the regions where people were being relocated, the locals complained bitterly that the NSV was wasting German money on the evacuees. The countryfolk resented the lazy urbanites and saw the mothers as looking for a good time, willing to leave their children in the care of others. Some thought that the NSV was "too generously emptying its coffers on the so-called bomb women!"[93] Even the "leading men of the party and state," who were supposed to set good examples, were reluctant to take in adult evacuees, Bormann reported in late 1943. In mid-1944, one evacuee, a twenty-eight-year-old widow who had fled the bombings of Berlin with her child, felt so aggrieved by her reception in the village of Lechbrüch (Bavaria) that she reached out by letter to Minister of Propaganda Joseph Goebbels, "in my hour of need and my despair." In a six-page letter she asked Goebbels to take her side against the "underhandedness" of her hosts, urging him to weigh in for her because she was determined not to move back to Berlin, despite frequent insults from her neighbors for being a big-snout Berliner. "I have spent enough time at the school of the terror-bombers," she told the Reich Minister.[94]

The regime hoped that the trauma of the air raids followed by the party's assistance through the NSV would knit the people and National Socialism together in solidarity—and to some extent it did. But on balance, rather than strengthening the ties between the people and the party-governed state, the air raids probably weakened those links, as attacks pressed the state to allow ordinary Germans some latitude in coping with the war. The SD noted that civilians saw little sense in staying away from home once the raids on their home cities had stopped. Local officials retorted that bombed housing was still not safe and would take time to rebuild. But the number of "wild evacuees" returning home increased sharply during 1943 so that by October there were more returning to their homes than there were being evacuated.[95]

GAULEITER EXPERIMENTATION WITH TACTICS OF SOFT COERCION
The need for evacuations on a truly massive scale followed the Allies' five-month bombing of the Ruhr beginning in March 1943. This Battle of the Ruhr followed new agreements between the United States and Britain for carrying out a combined bombing offensive and represented a new marker in bombing devastation. In London, Arthur Harris was pleased with the first Ruhr attack on Essen on March 5, 1943, for it

indicated that the previously invulnerable region was now at the mercy of Allied bombers.[96] The Reich authorities in Berlin finally issued regulations for uniform evacuations of civilians across regions. Germans would no longer be permitted to relocate wherever they wished even if they moved on their own recognizance.

Nevertheless, the Reich leadership continued to rely on the Gauleiters for enforcement of these regulations. Typical of his style, Hitler in mid-1943 charged the Gauleiters together with the Propaganda Ministry with "causing all parts of the population not directly tied to production to voluntarily leave particularly endangered areas." Hitler suggested to Goebbels that the people be instructed that evacuating their homes was an honorable duty! Goebbels, assuming a role as the coordinator of the Gauleiters on matters of civilian air defense and as their de facto representative to Hitler, sent a memo on June 14, 1943, to all Gauleiters stating that Hitler considered these evacuations to be "an urgent imperative." Yet authorities were still enjoined to "continue to refrain from coercive deportations *due to psychological reasons.*"[97]

The directive to "cause" civilians to relocate while also avoiding compulsion led the Gauleiters to try "soft" coercion methods—pressures short of police intimidation and physical force. Civilians had to be compelled to evacuate but without causing what Hitler and Goebbels referred to as "psychological problems"—popular dissent. In June 1943, party officials attempted to tighten control over the evacuees from the Ruhr area, including Witten, by ordering people to remain in their existing evacuee accommodations in Baden. SD agents warned that such an order might prove challenging because the population was not only increasingly disaffected, but also increasingly unafraid to show it openly. Describing the horrors of air raids from which their government was not able to protect them, evacuees carried the "terror of air attacks into remote villages."[98]

Respect for the regime suffered. The "German Greeting" ("Heil Hitler") "was rarely used in the affected cities after the attacks"; instead the civilians pointedly used "other" greetings. Germans complained that they had sat in air raid shelters night after night and also day after day and had the feeling that they were living as if on the war front, abandoned to their fate by Berlin. At his "Total War" speech in Berlin's Sports Palace on the night of February 18, 1943, Goebbels had promised the

German victims of the Allied raids a horrible revenge. By that summer the people began to complain that the revenge was too long in coming. But according to secret police reports, when Hitler addressed the people in early September 1943, exuding confidence that Germany would prevail, Germans took hope.[99]

The SD concluded that Germans no longer sensed danger in hearing and retelling political jokes, even among circles of "decent" Germans and National Socialists. In the chaos and misery of the bombings in the Ruhr, dissent sharpened into a spontaneous crowd rebellion on April 12, 1943, when an army captain in Dortmund-Hörde reproved a soldier for bad behavior. The soldier's identification revealed that he was a military deserter, so the captain began further investigation. But by now a crowd had gathered and began taking the side of the detained soldier. According to the SD, a crowd of three or four hundred persons, mostly women, became incited "terribly quickly and took on such a threatening posture that the officer had to flee outright in the street car." From the crowd erupted excited shouts of "Give us our youth!" and "Give us our menfolk back!" *(Gebt uns unsere Männer wieder)*—the same chorus that had been repeated just one month before by the German-blooded wives of Berlin Jews on Berlin's Rosenstrasse. The SD report concludes that "the excitement was such that a press release was needed to clarify the incident, and at a meeting of the National Socialist Women in Hörde the facts were also corrected."[100] The Nazis also thought it was dangerous to allow ordinary persons to think that they could get away with public protests.

Instructions on civil defense from Goebbels and his ministry show that the leadership redoubled its efforts to meet the people on their terms in mid-1943 to achieve more orderly evacuations. In April, Deputy Interior Minister Wilhelm Stuckart informed Goebbels that government officials at various levels were treating civilians too harshly. Arguing against the manipulation of ration cards to pressure the people into leaving their home cities, Josef Grohé, Gauleiter of Cologne-Aachen since 1931, emphasized how unwilling the people had been to leave despite the bombing. Goebbels suggested to the Gauleiters in a mid-July 1943 memo that evacuees who relocated to areas other than those assigned to them should find no accommodations at all. But he immediately cautioned that the "deployment of measures of force" must be avoided "under all circumstances." As an example of what could go wrong, Goebbels sin-gled out one particular district administrator who had gotten the idea that the new regulations finally allowed him to resolve conflicts with co-ercion. But as Goebbels warned, such a course was not possible because it would "discredit the entire re-accommodation." From the perspective of the Nazi leadership at the highest levels, putting too much pressure on inhabitants of even just one Gau could discredit the program across the Reich because opinion spread within the populace from region to re-gion. The solution the Propaganda Ministry offered once again lay in *convincing* the people to join hands with the party. One week after Goeb-bels sent out this mid-July memo, Grohé stressed that "one does not pressure anyone to leave his home area if it is at all possible to provide him with even the most humble shelter [at home]."[101]

Writing again to the Gauleiters on July 27, Goebbels continued to sound solicitous of the people, basing his instructions on ideas, as he wrote, that had arisen "from the people" themselves. Goebbels went so far as to echo Christian values over the Nazi principles he had voiced earlier: the Gauleiters were to provide safe haven first of all not to the strongest and most productive but "to small children, to pregnant women, the old and the frail." Furthermore, Goebbels now expressed less inter-est in harshly punishing the offenders than in subtly undermining the Germans who complained loudly while standing in line to receive food ration cards. Ration card lines afforded a rare opportunity, given the bans on public assembly, for Germans to complain publicly in a legal way. Opinion voiced in public and backed or at least not refuted in a public assembly of the people might begin to shape collective opinion, and to combat such a possibility, Goebbels planned to infiltrate the crowds with party members who could gradually turn the conversation away from grumbling.[102] Rather than identifying and punishing offenders as the war entered its end phase, the highest leaders were reinforcing efforts to "educate" people's opinions.

Meanwhile, the increasing destruction borne by the German civil-ians due to the air raids that the regime could not stop was causing offi-cials to take a greater account of the civilian plight. Instructions from Berlin in the late summer of 1943, as Germany lost its massive Panzer offensive in the battle at Kursk, suggest that the more authority a Nazi

Party leader had, the more responsibility he also bore for convincing the people to freely give whatever the party asked. The test of leadership at the highest levels was not so much coercion as cajoling.[103]

Over the summer of 1943, Goebbels continued to focus the attention of the Gauleiters on the morale of the people in the attempt to maintain their spirits at previous levels. On August 15, in an effort to bring the people together in viewing the evacuees empathetically, Goebbels telexed the Gauleiters a summary of the evacuation measures: Gauleiters in areas receiving the evacuees were extremely hard pressed by "flooding streams of humanity," many injured, pouring into their regions. The challenge was to care for the evacuees in a way that diminished public "discontentment." This was work, Goebbels entreated, "which for the outcome of the war can be of great importance." Officials could only succeed by demonstrating the concern of the party for the people, a concern that in turn would yield "the total willingness" of the people to fight the war. Goebbels elaborated that a "front" had to be erected to stymie the efforts of certain "unschooled persons who due to their own demands for comfort refuse to share their quarters," even when refusal was contrary to the directives from the NSV. Although many evacuees were prompted to return to their homes because their "hosts" did not welcome them, Goebbels portrayed those who did not share what they had as a fringe minority.[104]

Contrary to counseling increased coercion as Germany witnessed a reversal of fortunes at war, Goebbels enjoined regional officials to convince the people that the party was their partner by trying to meet their needs. A problem for Berlin was that it could not offer many resources so much as onerous work to the Gauleiters, who were expected to make ends meet with their own resourcefulness. In lieu of material assistance, rewards of public recognition were used to increase willingness among the people to fight on. For example, following the "Operation Gomorrah" bombing of Hamburg it was determined that in some cases the persons who died during air raids could be decorated with the same honors as those who were associated with heroic service in the military.[105]

Despite the party's efforts to win the people by helping them, the number of "wild evacuees" continued to mount. In mid-September 1944, the *Westfälische Landeszeitung*, a daily Nazi Party newspaper for the region that included Witten, branded these returnees as "*Schädlinge*," or pests, a classification for people whose behavior subverted the Reich and its war, a form of treason. Public sympathy for these "wild evacuees" was evident but misplaced, the paper warned, since they were endangering the "most precious possession of our people" by "sabotaging the measures to protect children."[106]

Faced with Hitler's orders to remove civilians from the dangers of air raids but to do so voluntarily, SS Gruppenführer Albert Hoffmann, who was the newly appointed Gauleiter of Westphalia-South, tried a new method of soft coercion, short of police force, during the late summer of 1943. Local authorities in his Gau would be authorized to withhold food rations from the evacuees who had returned without permission, Hoffmann announced, although he was careful to allow the local authorities to decide whether they wished to adopt this measure. Not many municipalities accepted the initiative, perhaps preferring to escape popular outrage. This outrage was demonstrated in several cities, including Witten, when those arriving home found that the ration cards they had received in their Baden evacuation site were not valid in their hometowns. The women became even more indignant once they learned that the evacuees returning to neighboring areas, where administrators had decided against adopting Hoffmann's measure, were able to buy food.[107]

On September 22, 1943, Witten city authorities closed schools and evacuated entire classes along with their teachers, which stirred up "strong unrest," according to party agents.[108] With education for schoolchildren no longer provided in Witten, parents who refused to relocate their children received a stern demand in writing from the mayor, asking that they comply; they were warned that this was the last opportunity for them to fulfill their legal obligation to put their children in schools. But the threats apparently met with little response since another order followed three weeks later, this time threatening the parents with "coercive measures" if they did not put their children on the next KLV train. On October 9, 1943, Gauleiter Hoffmann complained that his method of withholding ration cards "is not only not sufficiently observed by individual citizens, but also not carried out everywhere with the necessary energy by the responsible government offices."[109]

PROTEST AND PUNISHMENT: HITLER BLOCKS RADICALIZATION

Two days after Hoffmann's complaint, on the ninth anniversary of Bishop Hans Meiser's arrest in Munich, three hundred women of Witten mobilized in protest. On October 11, 1943, in front of City Hall, the central symbol of government, on the city's central square, Adolf Hitler Platz, they rebelled against Hoffmann's ban. "Indeed, the women in question tried to *force*" the regime to do their will, the SD reported, "in order to take a public stand against the measures that led to this prohibition of the delivery of food ration cards. Shameful scenes developed so that the city administration of Witten found itself forced to call on the police to restore order. [The police] refused to get involved, however, since the demands of the women were fair and there was no legal basis for not handing out food ration cards to German people who had returned [home]." In April of the previous year, Goebbels was certain that Germans would simply laugh off the Allied propaganda, which claimed that German women protesting food shortages had been cut down by machine guns. This propaganda was "too idiotic to make any impression on a German," he wrote in his diary.[110]

When the women in Witten rebelled, it was clear that Hoffmann had moved toward failure and away from the model of exemplary leadership. It did not matter that the protests were not against the regime itself or that popular opinion continued to exempt Hitler from criticism. SD agents on location attested that "most women took a position remaining behind the person of the Leader." Many of them, however, could not square the desire of the regime for evacuations with their need to keep their families together. The SD identified the Witten demonstration as just one example of public protests by women. The day after the Witten demonstration, and perhaps spurred on by it, the "wild evacuees" in the nearby cities of Hamm, Bochum, and Lünen protested on October 13 in what the SD account identified as "wild scenes." In these three cities a notice from October 12 about the new restriction of food rations "led to *a first-hand rebellion among the women.* Agitated crowds of people waited in line for the distribution [of rations] . . . [and] those waiting began to exchange accounts of their experiences in the evacuation sites. Miners [from the Ruhr coal pits] declared that they would not return to the mines before they had received the necessary food ration cards for their families. Women announced that they would rather suffer bombs here than to once again return to the quarters for evacuees assigned to them.[111]

The same SD report described the protesting crowd as "capable of everything, without the least restraint or attention to the consequences." Authorities reported that "friendly cajoling" was said to have had the opposite effect of calming them down. Demonstrating a hardness wrought by the circumstances of war, according to the SD report, one woman said that "they should just rather send us right away to Russia, point machine guns at us, and have it over with." Another said: "My children will not leave, and if I have nothing to eat, then I can drop dead together with them." Others came closer to an attack on the regime by attacking Nazi officials. "Insults against official and foremost persons were the order of the day," the SD police reported.

Perhaps the Witten women had organized their "demonstration" as the SD called it. "Affected women" wanting to "take an open position" gathered with the intention of "forcing" the government to yield. The SD's description of the protests in Witten's neighboring cities of Hamm, Lünen, and Bochum, on the other hand, tends to indicate spontaneous eruptions of anger and frustration of "agitated crowds of people waiting in line" for rations, rather than intentional gatherings to make a statement. The rebellions, however, may have been spurred on by reports of the demonstration that had occurred the previous day in Witten. In these three cities some of the protesting women applied for work in essential industries, a position that entitled them to receive rations in their home cities. The freedom they felt to manipulate the dictatorship to suit their purposes was displayed by their claims that they had arranged for child care while they worked, even if this was not the case.[112]

These workers in the Ruhr area also gained the support of their employers—industry officials who used the regime's obsession with public mood to argue that it was in the "interest of the morale as well as the productivity of the workers to arrange for the workers to have their wives and children" return home as soon as possible. Authorities discovered that for husbands, the arrival after a hard day's work to a cold and lonely apartment, without a wife's care and in the absence of children's laughter, "robs them of the desire and the strength to work. One often hears the remark in workers' circles that if it is important to maintain their work morale and their strength then one should let their wives stay put. . . . Above all, the married men say that family is the only compensation they have for their heavy workload."[113]

The Ruhr protests in October 1943 represent the high point in the conflicts between the dictatorship and the people over civilian evacuations. It was clear that these families from bombed cities supported one another and that their rebellion was bolstered by the traditions of the private sphere. In its reaction to the Witten protest, the dictatorship again made efforts to assuage the people. The day after the unrest Goebbels's staff telephoned the region's housing evacuation camps, inquiring about how "to direct [but not stop] the 'wild' returns of mothers from the reception areas." Three days later, Gauleiter Hoffmann embarked on a several-day trip to Baden to meet with evacuees and discuss their difficulties in an "open conversation."[114] During the weeks and months following the Witten-area protests, further discussion ensued at high government levels about what forms of coercion were appropriate for achieving orderly evacuations. Goebbels proposed noncoercive ways— for example, evacuating families intact together with their neighbors to the countryside—that would increase the chances that they would stay there.

With the wave of "wild" returnees growing, the question of how to deal with them continued to divide the Gauleiters, and the need for a definitive, Reich-wide response became increasingly urgent. Some favored harsher measures, and Bormann and Himmler also leaned toward using coercion. In early November 1943, reflecting on the Witten-area protests, Goebbels mulled the question of whether to resolve the matter with force since the people had apparently discovered how to manipulate the regime: "One dare not bend to the will of the people at this point," he wrote. If "friendly cajoling" would not stop the wild evacuees,

> then one must use force. It is not true that force does not lead to results. Of course it leads to results as long as it is explained to the public with the necessary specificity and then is actually deployed. Up until now, this has not been observed, and consequently the people know just exactly where the soft spot of the leadership is, and will always exploit it. . . . The state may never, against its better insight, give in to the pressure of the street.[115]

"Giving in" to the people on the streets was increasingly dangerous, wrote Goebbels, since each time it happened, the state lost some of its authority—and in the end could lose all power.

Meanwhile, officials wrestled with the impact of the "wild evacuees" on the Reich's war effort as "the most difficult domestic policy matter we face."[116] In his Westphalia-South Gau, Albert Hoffmann also experimented with banning the sale of train tickets to persons trying to return from the evacuation sites. The party officials succeeded in convincing the Reichsbahn officials to ban ticket sales to "wild evacuees" wanting to return. The local agents, however, were not always so cooperative, perhaps because of local, personal relationships. Thus a party officer in the Westphalia-South Gau who complained about the "mania of our women" to return to their homes had to admit defeat. He wished "to block the train tickets of women who are leaving without permission," but since some ticket agents had not cooperated, "it [was] unfortunately not realizable in all districts." Due to this partial noncompliance, he concluded, other means of prohibiting women from returning home would have to be found.[117]

In his Berlin Gau, a month after the Witten protest, Goebbels was gratified that the heavy attacks on Berlin had stemmed the rush of "wild returnees" in his Gau. Still, he continued to consider a crackdown, working together with Himmler to devise a plan that would exert "significant pressure on the evacuees after all," perhaps through further regulations of transportation and ration cards that the police would enforce.[118] Goebbels found an unlikely ally in Bormann, whom he had battled at various points previously—for example, in 1941, when Bormann had called for the public hanging of Bishop Galen and Goebbels had taken the stance that the bishop's hanging would seriously repress morale and enthusiasm for the war in Galen's diocese. Now that Goebbels was considering force, Bormann was a ready ally, and in mid-December 1943, he sent Goebbels a letter suggesting the introduction of evacuations of women and children from dense urban areas by means of *force*. "Suddenly [Bormann] is taking the position here that I had proposed months ago already," Goebbels wrote. The problem with using coercion, for Goebbels, was that he associated its success with the phase of grand victories that would afford expanded opportunities for controlling the people. But this phase was failing to materialize. The impact of the bombings on the people was escalating: air raids had killed 2,650 in December alone, by his estimation, while the total since 1939 was an "extremely alarming" 102,000.[119] "Domestically, we are concerned almost exclusively with air war," he wrote on December 14, 1943.

Goebbels complained that each Gauleiter was acting selfishly, serving his own ego by seeking the exclusive welfare of his regional population. But competition was an inherent part of the Nazi system. In his region, Gauleiter Hoffmann continued to use the distribution of ration cards to control civilians through 1943, while dutifully assailing the people with information about the benefits of wartime evacuations in keeping with Hitler's call for "education." In December 1943, Hoffmann reiterated his unyielding stance on using ration cards to control the movements of evacuees, and Alfred Meyer of the adjoining Westphalia region to the north joined Hoffmann in support of this method.[120]

Following the introduction of Meyer's measure, great unrest rippled through the affected populations. Soon thereafter Goebbels—whom Hitler had just granted greater authority over domestic matters by naming him Reich Inspector for Civil Air War Measures—removed Hoffmann from his position as Goebbels's adviser on matters of the air war, on the grounds that he was seriously ill. In his place he installed Josef Grohé, a longtime loyal Nazi who had avoided direct confrontations with the people as Gauleiter of his mostly Catholic region around Cologne. Unlike Hoffmann and Meyer, Gróhe based his evacuation policies on their projected impact on civilian morale and believed that using coercion to achieve evacuations and keep evacuees in place would injure morale.[121]

Goebbels decided to seek a "Führer decision" on the manipulation of ration cards to control evacuees. The Leader was the only one who could make a decision of such great significance for the popular sentiment and bring all the Gauleiters in line with it immediately, and his attention was given to it regardless of how deeply he was absorbed in military strategy. Just as the Leader had to adjudicate the conflict among Nazi Party officials over how to deal with the Protestants who had been led in protest by Bishops Wurm and Meiser, his judgment was needed now in the delicate matter of managing morale while evacuating the people. Just as it had been procured in the question of whether to allow the party-initiated demonstrations in 1938 against Bishop Sproll to continue, Hitler's judgment was needed now. Only the Leader was able to decide whether to punish Bishop Galen for his treasonous sermons in August 1941 because the way Galen was treated would greatly affect the way the people perceived Hitler's dictatorship. Ten months earlier, Goebbels had also sought out the Leader's sanction for his decision not to deport some two thousand intermarried Berlin Jews whose non-Jewish partners had protested on their behalf, due to the "psychological" problem that refusing to release them would have. All of these decisions depended on calculations at the heart of how to best manage Hitler's mass movement, and all of them required the Leader to determine the place of using force in the delicate balance of providing maximum incentives for the people to do his will under the prevailing circumstances.

In mid-January 1944 Goebbels visited Hitler in his East Prussian headquarters and over lunch received a quick verdict on the use of even just soft forms of coercion to achieve the regime's will in the evacuations. Hitler specifically banned using Hoffmann's ration card method to coerce civilian behavior.[122] He also rejected proposals from the Gauleiters calling for legal regulations to assert official control over the evacuees. In the interest of the general public mood, Hitler ordered the Gauleiters not to levy fines. Instead he wiped from the table both the legal obligation and the "soft force" measure it had provided.[123]

The next day Goebbels informed the Gauleiters that "The Leader has ordered that [you] should refrain from blocking ration cards." Hitler thought "other ways and means" would have to be applied. "The Leader believes that the goal we aim for can be reached particularly through propaganda activities that once again bring before parents' eyes quite graphically the dangers their children face."[124] Although circumstances had changed dramatically, Hitler's recommendation for keeping the people in line with the leadership had not changed since the day he issued the orders to begin the "expanded" evacuation of children in September 1940. Hitler in fact would not change his position. In late July 1944 Bormann and Himmler issued a joint statement declaring that "the use of coercive measures" to prevent evacuees from returning "continues to be seen as inappropriate." Only in some urgent situations might it be possible to forcibly evacuate the people. In October Martin Bormann confirmed yet again that coercion was not to be used against "wild returnees" or evacuees who chose to return home without permission.[125]

MASS NONCONFORMITY: HITLER FAILS TO ENFORCE
HIS DECREE ON WOMEN

In early 1943, the dictatorship's "Total War" conscription of women into the wartime workforce resulted in noncompliance on a massive scale, revealing the limits of terror to achieve domestic control even as the Reich hurried toward its end in one defeat after another. Other countries at war, including Germany's democratic enemies, had conscripted women earlier. But Hitler had opposed compulsorily enlisting women; he wished instead, through the spread of propaganda, to encourage the millions of German women who did not work to take up "war-important" jobs. The people, however, proved once again that they were capable of disregarding the regime's request when it did not serve their perceived interest. The propaganda campaigns became abysmal failures. In Dresden, of the 1,250 women invited to enlist, only 120 voiced a willingness to begin work at once. In the neighboring city of Leipzig the Labor Bureau registered just one additional woman for work.[126]

During war, Hitler's aversion to female conscription stemmed from his wish to provide as great a sense of normalcy as possible on the home front, although it also underscored a principle of his ideology— that the woman's place was in the home as a mother and provider of stable shelter and a shelter for the recovery for her husband.[127] Only Germany's epic military debacle at Stalingrad finally enabled Goebbels, after trying for more than a year, to convince Hitler to conscript women aged 17–45, with the exception of those who had one child under the age of five or two under the age of eight. Signed on January 13, 1943, Hitler's decree was calculated to induct up to 5.5 million women into "war-important" work, approximately the difference between the number of German men conscripted into the army and the number of slave laborers whom the regime had forced into the service of Germany's war economy. The decree helped to minimize dissent by relying on the economic pressures felt primarily by working-class women, who had long been resigned to working because of their need for income. The German middle-class women, however, saw the work as more of a disruption brought on by the regime, while many middle-class men thought that having a wife who worked insulted their identity as the family breadwinners.[128]

Notably, Hitler avoided signing the January 13 decree in public. As he might have suspected, relatively few women complied. As of May 1944, the number of German women employed had increased only 1.2 percent above the number working before the war. So many able-bodied women remained unemployed that Armaments Minister Albert Speer, who recalled Hitler's general anxiety about "an insurrectionary mood," called the decree to conscript women a "total failure."[129] Few if any women directly refused to comply as a conscious act of civil disobedience, although the SD reported increasing signs of defeatism and even opposition to war among women. The SD reported women saying that "if all women got together, then this madness would soon be over!" Rather than openly opposing Hitler's order, women evaded it with a variety of methods. For example, some women used their married or maiden names or moved without leaving a forwarding address.[130] Others gave excuses for not showing up for work that the Gestapo knew to be fabricated: according to official reports from Karlsruhe, "There are not even as many ailments as those registered [by women seeking an exemption] here in the Labor Office."[131]

Facing rampant noncompliance, Nazi leaders adjusted to stay in step with the people; prosecution of women for disobedience "was rare." Hitler did not interfere, although again mass noncompliance opened up divisions among leaders or exacerbated existing tensions. Historians have written that the dispute over whether to conscript women for wartime work divided the Reich leaders into pragmatists and idealists. In this schema, Hitler is cast as an "idealist" because he held to his ideals about the place of women even after his controversial "Total War" decree.[132] Yet his decision not to enforce his conscription decree likely resulted from holding to a more immediately urgent imperative of maintaining social support, an elementary form of Nazism.

The last two years of the war are frequently characterized as a period when the regime ratcheted up the use of terror to work its will: the ever-expanding losses in the war radicalized the regime to rely more and more on coercion, as cooperation disappeared along with the memories of early victories. This increase in terror is illustrated best by the execution of some twenty thousand German soldiers for disobedience.[133] But the radicalization in the use of force for domestic control during the final years of the war did not extend everywhere. For tactical reasons the regime did not use force even against the hundreds who intentionally created a very disagreeable scene in public settings.

Was it possible that the dictatorship would also defer to stubborn patterns of popular behavior if they interfered with the expulsion of German Jews? In his sermon condemning "euthanasia" Bishop Galen and the many Germans he represented had shown that open protest was possible and that it could be done with impunity. Protest had reshaped "euthanasia" so that it did not stir further protests. But Galen also condemned the Jews, offering a rationale to the Catholics for turning Jews over to their suffering at the hands of the regime by picturing them as forces of betrayal, anarchy, and Bolshevism.[134] What would happen when the traditions of family collided publicly with National Socialism's overriding obsession with annihilating the Jews? Germany's intermarried couples, those in unions between one German that the regime considered to be an Aryan and one German that the regime considered to be a Jew, did in fact pose this test, culminating in a street protest of early 1943. These German-blooded wives had a unique motivation to stand fast against the new state and its society relative to Germans generally because the Nazi dictatorship saw their personal lives as an act of treason.

CHAPTER EIGHT

Germany's Rosenstrasse
and the Fate of Mixed Marriages

I have set for myself a goal to make Berlin entirely free of Jews by the middle or end of March at the latest. [February 18, 1943]

The people gathered together in large throngs and even sided with the Jews to some extent. I will commission the security police not to continue the Jewish evacuations during such a critical time. Rather we want to put that off for a few weeks; then we can carry it out all the more thoroughly. [March 6, 1943]

I discuss the news about Berlin with Gutterer [Goebbels's deputy]. . . . I describe my actions to the Führer as generous toward the people, hard toward the wrong doers. The Führer also considers this completely correct. [March 9, 1943]

The Jewish question in Berlin is still not yet completely solved. A whole collection of so-called "Geltungsjuden" [half-Jews counted as Jews who wore the Star], Jews from privileged intermarriages ["full Jews" according to the Nuremberg Laws who were exempted from wearing the Star], and also Jews from intermarriages ["full Jews" required to wear the Star of David like all other German Jews] are still to be found in Berlin. . . . I do not want Jews with the Jewish star running around the Reich capital. Either one must take the Jewish star away and privilege them, or on the other hand once and for all evacuate them from the Reich capital. [April 18, 1943]

—*Joseph Goebbels, diary entries*

DURING THE EARLY decades of the twentieth century, as Jewish assimilation in Germany increased, the proportion of Jews marrying out to Gentiles reached nearly 50 percent by the time the Nazis came to power. From its earliest days, the dictatorship relied on a range of pres-

sures, from economic disadvantage and propaganda to social ostracism, to dissolve these marriages of Jews and "German-blooded" or
"Aryan" persons. Considering the bandwagon rush of support for the
Nazi dictatorship, German leaders might well have expected intermarried couples to divorce voluntarily. Businesses were eager to boycott
Jews, professional and sporting associations expelled them, and Germans everywhere began to drop any social engagements with Jewish
colleagues and neighbors. In 1935, the Nuremberg Laws defined German Jews in a way that made no exception for those married to Jews:
anyone with three or four Jewish grandparents was a "full Jew" regardless of marriage. For the Nazis, in fact, Jews in mixed marriages were
particularly odious and presented a greater threat to Nazi goals than
other "full" Jews. Authorities feared that Jewish-Gentile liaisons would
cause high degrees of *public dissension—the opposite of the unity Hitler
sought.* Their children were the subjects of extreme inconvenience for a
regime determined to separate Jews and Gentiles. Goebbels thought
that intermarriage alone could destroy national character, as he wrote in
March 1942, shortly before seeking Hitler's agreement for deporting all
of Berlin's Jews. Himmler complained that it was through intermarriage that the people had developed feelings for the Jews. On August 20,
1942, Himmler received the following alarm from Gottlob Berger, head
of the central SS office, expressing his opinion and that of Walter Dick-
wach of the German Labor Front: Gentiles married to Jews were "traitors"
who, due to their obviously hostile worldview, could not possibly orient
their business "according to basic National Socialist principles in the
struggle for securing German rights of life. . . . We don't want anything to
do with people who don't know the meaning of racial defilement."[1]

It seems unlikely that such despised Aryans could protect their Jewish partners, and on more than one occasion Goebbels drew the logical
conclusion that they should be thrown into the maw of death along with
the Jews they refused to leave. But in the interest of maintaining an un-
darkened line between German Jews who were railroaded off, never to
be seen again, and German "Aryans," who must never need to fear ac-
companying the Jewish "sub-humans," the regime did not deport intermarried Aryans.[2] The regime did its best to remove intermarried Jews
at every opportunity without drawing attention to them. The Aryans
most likely to protest were of course those who refused to divorce Jews,

and the clear indication that the deportation of intermarried Jews hung by a silk thread on the consent of their Aryan partners was the permanent Nazi policy of deporting intermarried Jews as soon as these partners died or agreed to a divorce. Beginning in 1938, the Gestapo applied a gamut of increasingly draconian threats to force these couples into divorce, from icy Gestapo visits to the arrest of intermarried Jews in an unusually brutal "Final Roundup" conducted in Berlin by elite SS men in early 1943.

To make it easier for intermarried Germans to accommodate the new Nazi order, the bureaucracy rewrote German law in July 1938 so that any intermarried German could be granted divorce merely by requesting it. In December 1938, Hitler issued a decree that divided the intermarriages into two categories, privileging the majority while identifying the remaining one-quarter as "simple" or "non-privileged." Unlike the widely heralded Nuremberg Laws, this decree was secret, allowing greater flexibility and opportunism in the persecution of intermarried Jews. Mixed marriages with children baptized as Christians, as well as mixed marriages in which the wife rather than the husband was Jewish were now defined as "privileged." This bisection followed a similar division in the 1935 Nuremberg Laws that had exempted the majority of German "half Jews," or "Mischlinge," from treatment as Jews, allowing the regime to proceed by stages in the persecution and eventual eradication of those persons with "mixed blood."

With the division of intermarried Jews into two categories, the persecution of the "full" Jews in intermarriages could also proceed in phases, beginning with the non-privileged intermarried Jews with fewer ties to the German-blooded Reich, whether through church membership or other associations their children had developed as Christians rather than Jews or through Christian men in these marriages with greater contacts in the political world. In April 1939 the regime ordered Jews from "non-privileged" intermarriages to move into so-called "Jewish houses." The social stigma alone, not to mention the increased threat of official persecution, that pursued an Aryan who moved with a Jewish partner into a Jewish house was extreme. But relatively few divorces followed, as illustrated by the decision of Victor Klemperer's wife Eva to move with him into a Jewish house in Dresden. Remarkably, fewer than 10 percent of Germany's intermarried couples chose to divorce over the entire course of the Nazi years.[3]

The decree to mark German Jews publicly with the Jewish Star of David, on August 20, 1941, created a yet greater divide between "privileged" Jews in mixed marriages versus those who were not: only Jews from non-privileged mixed marriages were required to wear the Star. Thus the dictatorship indicated its resolve to remove at least the minority of intermarried Jews from Germany who wore the Star—like all other persons marked by the Star as Jews. Goebbels wrote in November 1941 that persons wearing the Star were marked as criminals—enemies of the people—and would have to be removed from Germany. There were to be no Jews in the Nazi Reich, and anyone siding with them should be treated like a Jew: "Whoever wears a Jewish Star is marked as an 'enemy of the people.' Whoever still goes around with [a Jew] privately in everyday life belongs to him and must be valued and treated as a Jew. He earns the contempt of the entire people, whom he abandons in base cowardice at the hardest moment, by putting himself at the side of his despiser." Germans often disdained or ostracized German Gentiles married to Jews, with some suggesting that they should also be "marked" by the Jewish Star.[4]

Nevertheless, when the regime began the systematic deportation of German Jews wearing the Star in October 1941, it compromised once again, although only "temporarily," in its calculations. Aryans married to Jews were not required to wear the Star, but even the intermarried Jews who were not privileged (and thus wore the Star) were exempted— "temporarily"—from the deportations. Although loath to compromise its "racial" ideals, the regime was even more reluctant to draw attention to the existence of intermarried couples and the scandals that could arise by forcing them apart, and it was certainly not about to send a chill up and down the Reich by requiring some Aryans to wear the Jewish Star. The regime's solution was to wait for an opportune moment to deport these non-privileged intermarried Jews who wore the Star, whether it followed a great war victory or was fabricated through increased terror and intimidation. As it waited, its policy of deporting intermarried Jews whose partners had died or divorced demonstrated that the reason it waited "temporarily" at all was due to Aryans who would not consent to let go of their Jewish partners.[5]

The fate of Joachim Gottschalk, one of Berlin's most popular actors, illustrates the challenges that intermarried couples caused a regime that attempted to control all popular perceptions. Goebbels was "deeply impressed" by Gottschalk, "Germany's Clark Gable," and pressured him to divorce his Jewish wife by precluding him from all roles in film and on stage. But on November 6, 1941, Gottschalk responded not by divorce but by committing suicide, together with his Jewish wife and their young son. This was a mistake like those of Gauleiters whose measures caused public disruptions, and Goebbels allowed that applying coercive pressure to the point that it backfired was "somewhat embarrassing." Gottschalk, he reasoned, "could no longer find any way to escape the conflict between state and family. I will thus immediately see to it that this case . . . is not used to construct alarming rumors." As always when the regime had made such miscalculations, it began a process of covering over the evidence and denying that anything "embarrassing" had happened. To limit popular awareness of his miscalculation, Goebbels forbade obituaries and banned anyone from attending Gottschalk's funeral. Nevertheless, a number of Gottschalk's professional associates attended the funeral in a demonstration of sorrow and loyalty.[6]

Two weeks later, on November 22, 1941, Hitler urged caution in dealing with mixed-marriage Jews, giving his instructions directly to Goebbels, as the Gauleiter of Berlin: "The Leader . . . wants a forceful policy against the Jews, though one that does not cause us unnecessary difficulties. . . . Concerning the Jewish mixed marriages, especially those in artists' circles, the Leader recommends that I follow a somewhat reserved course of action since he is of the opinion that these marriages in any case will die out bit by bit, and one shouldn't get any gray hair over this."[7]

Characteristically, Hitler's instruction is vague and leaves room for different interpretations. Hitler was indicating that intermarried Jews in artists' circles formed another category that needed special attention (considering the Gottschalk suicide). He elaborated on his tactic of dividing mixed marriage Jews into categories in order to temporarily defer those most likely to cause problems, by adding a note on a new category demanding special attention. He reiterated his desire to drain as much "Jewish blood" as possible from the Reich and may have been speaking only of intermarried Jews in artists' circles when he said that these Jews would die out bit by bit. A dominant interpretation of the evolution of the persecution of Jews into genocide perceives Hitler's subordinates competing to please him in a way that led to a spiral of increasingly radical measures, without any intervention from the Leader, in which case this instruction to Goebbels would have been of little comfort to intermarried Jews. Was Hitler making an exception for intermarried Jews that formed an exception to this radicalizing process as well, as he had done when he had intervened to prevent Gauleiters from escalating the use of coercion to keep civilian evacuees in line? If so, how did he expect to have this applied across the Reich by telling only Goebbels?

Hitler encouraged Gauleiters to pursue a plan of action suited for their respective territories, and his mandate for the deportation of German Jews threw the doors open to a range of initiatives, from officials at the local level on up.[8] And like his temper, Hitler's instructions could change quickly. Despite his note of caution to Goebbels, in December 1941 Hitler told the assembled Gauleiters—the party officials responsible for clearing their respective regions of Jews—that if any European Jews survived, the war would have proved only partially successful. According to Goebbels, Hitler had decided at this point to make a clean sweep, although no new orders were given, so that each Gauleiter faced the challenge of clearing the table but without causing "unnecessary difficulties," probably such as the Gottschalk suicide and funeral.[9]

The enormous amount of nail-biting that intermarried persons caused Nazi leaders is illustrated by the Wannsee Conference, held in a villa in the Berlin suburb of Wannsee by the banks of Lake Wannsee on January 20, 1942. During this conference, Reinhard Heydrich announced plans for the murder of eleven million European Jews. Yet he expended almost one-half of his considerations on strategies for handling the thirty thousand German Jews married to non-Jews.

All hesitations to deport the especially troublesome Jews from mixed marriages trace back to the dictatorship's anxiety that doing this would further provoke and unmask dissent or discussion of the "Final Solution." At Wannsee, Heydrich showed impatience with the policy of waiting to deport intermarried Jews until the Gentile partners died or took the initiative to ask for a divorce. In the interest of "the complete settlement of the [Jewish] problem," Jews from mixed marriages must also be murdered (in line with their designation by the 1935 Nuremberg Laws as "full" Jews). Heydrich allowed, however, that the treatment of intermarried Jews "must be decided from case to case whether the Jewish spouse should be evacuated or sent to an old-people's ghetto in consideration of the effect which such a measure might have on the German relatives of the mixed-marriage partners." The head of Reich security never considered the possibility that these Jews would remain in the Reich but only whether they would be sent directly to Auschwitz or Theresienstadt. (Jews arriving in Theresienstadt were almost always shipped on to Auschwitz, once those concerned could no longer trace the process.)

Interior Ministry deputy secretary Wilhelm Stuckart noted that currently a Jewish partner was exempted until the couple was legally divorced, and thus he made the conclusion that a law must be issued to declare all mixed marriages annulled. But at a follow-up meeting on March 6, 1942, Goebbels's Propaganda Ministry objected to the law Stuckart proposed due to "political reasons, especially in view of the stand which the Vatican could be expected to take." The regime decided to wait for the non-Jewish partner to request divorce "in order to avoid the outward [public] impression of a divorce under compulsion." Divorce through "compulsion" was never undertaken. Acting Justice Minister Franz Schlegelberger agreed, in early April 1941, that "even if [compulsory divorce] would break the legal tie, it could certainly not break the inner ties. . . . Persons married for a long time, who have withstood long years together, are expected to hold fast to their Jewish partners." Himmler, who on June 9, 1942, had announced his determination to exterminate all of Europe's Jews within the coming year, impatiently proscribed such laws the following month because they might limit his possibilities for acting with surprise at an opportune moment.[10]

Goebbels also looked to deport anyone identified by the Jewish Star at the earliest opportunity so that he could satiate his passionate anti-Semitism while achieving the Nazi goal of "racial purification" and pleasing Hitler. In May 1942 Goebbels voiced a new reason for deporting all those who were publicly criminalized by the Star in public as Jews. He believed that Jews were responsible for the assassination of Reinhard Heydrich earlier that month and apparently feared for his own safety, commenting that he wanted to clear Berlin of Jews because "I have no desire to have a 22-year-old eastern Jew . . . putting a bullet in my guts."[11]

But Goebbels as well as Himmler and their men were compelled to circumscribe their actions in order to maintain the appearance that all was well. When "unrest broke out in Berlin" during the summer of 1942 about the brutal treatment of Jews being deported, authorities held the news in "strict secrecy." In Darmstadt, when a Gentile came to the train station to see his Jewish wife one last time before her deportation to Auschwitz, a Gestapo agent hissed at him to leave as quickly as possible and to do so without drawing any attention.[12]

By late 1942, with the population of German Jews rapidly dwindling, the Reich Security Main Office (RSHA) was planning to deport at least some German Jews in mixed marriages. In Vienna at the time, Gauleiter Baldur von Schirach and his accomplices "clearly intended" to clear Vienna of non-privileged Jews—those who wore the Jewish Star. Armaments producers had protected thousands of Jewish workers, many of whom by this point were intermarried, by designating them as irreplaceable. But during a meeting in late September 1942, Hitler ruled that such protections must now end. He ordered Plenipotentiary-General for Labor Mobilization Fritz Sauckel "to transport all Jews working in the Reich's armaments factories to the Eastern concentration camps." By this order, Hitler "mainly referred to the Berlin Jews," according to Armaments Minister Albert Speer. Goebbels concurred, writing on September 30, 1942, that Hitler had voiced "firm determination to remove the Jews at least from Berlin."[13] Authorities in Berlin began double-checking their lists of Jews—already the Reich's most painstakingly registered population.

Also in late 1942, Berlin's push to expel the last Jews from German soil was reinforced by a separate and urgent pull from Auschwitz for laborers. Anticipating a massive movement of slave labor from factories in the Reich to the camps in the East, Himmler had begun to relocate armaments production factories within the concentration camp structure. The German armaments producer IG Farben was persuaded to build a prisoner camp at Auschwitz known as Monowitz, following promises from Himmler that he would supply the camp with thousands of skilled slave laborers. In early 1943, however, the labor supply at Monowitz remained well below what Farben wanted. This led to a further promise on February 10 by Obersturmführer Gerhard Maurer, of the SS Economic and Administrative Department (WVHA), "to make sure" the labor force would soon increase severalfold. In Berlin, the RSHA agreed to Maurer's request to take laborers directly from the freight cars packed with German Jews as they arrived at Auschwitz.[14]

In Berlin, the RSHA scheduled what it called the "Entjudung des Reichsgebietes" (Elimination of Jews from the Reich) arrests for early 1943, in conjunction with the tenth anniversary of Nazi rule.[15] In Berlin the code name for the upcoming arrests was the Schlussaktion, or Final Roundup, of Berlin Jews.[16] Sometime after the war these arrests in Berlin were dubbed the "Factory Action."

THE ROSENSTRASSE PROTEST INTERRUPTS PLANS
FOR INTERMARRIED JEWS

Up until February 1943, Jews in mixed marriages had generally been exempted from the deportations, as the regime looked for the moment to end their "temporary" exemption. In the case of hundreds of intermarried Jews, in fact, the exemption had already been lifted. Some had been crammed onto trains along with other Jews, while others were sent to their deaths on false charges of criminal activity. During its massive arrests of February 1943—that is, the arrests for the "Elimination of Jews from the Reich"—the regime decided to deport as many intermarried Jews as it could without causing a scene. On February 18 Goebbels wrote down his intention to make his city free of Jews, a goal that, according to his diaries, must include all Berliners wearing the Star.[17] "The Jews in Berlin will now once and for all be pushed out. With the final deadline of February 28 they are supposed to be first brought to collection centers and deported, up to 2,000, batch-by-batch, day-by-day. I have set for myself a goal to make Berlin entirely free of Jews by the middle or end of March at the latest."[18]

Well-informed Germans now suspected that intermarried Jews would be deported. Gertrud Luckner, who worked for Bishop Gröber of Freiburg, warned an associate on February 24, 1943, that a *"Schluss,"* or "final" arrest, "was about to take place in Berlin," according to the Gestapo's report on its interrogation of Luckner, who was sent to the Ravensbrück camp in late February on charges of being friendly to Jews. The

Gestapo's report emphasized that Luckner had many "points of contact" throughout "the entire Reich" and had been particularly active in warning intermarried Jews and Mischlinge of "impending actions" (arrests). Luckner's information was that the "intermarriage law" that had previously protected Jews "has been postponed as of now" so that "measures against intermarriages and Mischlinge" were now impending. Her warnings that the persons affected must avoid all unlawful actions shows that she had good sources of information, in light of Nazi efforts to murder intermarried Jews one by one after first criminalizing them.[19]

A Gestapo order from Frankfurt/Oder dated February 24 underscores the regime's desire to avoid drawing attention to the intermarried Jews problem while also deporting some on criminal charges. The decree instructed officers to assemble Jews inconspicuously, even in this region, where Jews were relatively sparse:

> The assembly of the Jews working in factories is to take place without attracting attention, possibly with the involvement of factory security personnel. However, attention must be given so that disturbances by Jews and attempts to escape are avoided. Indeed, under no circumstances may there be any overstepping boundaries of authority on the side of officials or the men assigned to keep guard, especially not in public or within the business area itself. Impudent behavior by Jews who still live in existing mixed marriages is to be punished by taking the Jews into protective custody and filing an order to bring them to a concentration camp. These actions can be carried out very generously, although the impression must be avoided that this action is a means to fundamentally solve the mixed marriage problem once and for all. If there are no reasons to justify the arrest of Jewish marriage partners, they are to be dismissed to their homes.[20]

This order gave the arresting officers wide discretion to do as they pleased. "Impudence" was a common charge against Jews, and local officers now had wide latitude for using it. Encouraging arrests was the fact that the administrator of the Frankfurt/Oder district of Calau, upon forwarding this decree to the police administrators of his district, underscored the point that officers could arrest intermarried Jews "generously."[21]

The encouragement for officers to press charges "generously" while avoiding the appearance that *all* intermarried Jews were being deported at that moment indicates that the RSHA wished to deport some intermarried Jews even in this backwater region well removed from Berlin. Arresting intermarried Jews after charging them with crimes was a tactic the RSHA was already employing elsewhere in the Reich. In cities around the Frankfurt am Main region, Gauleiter Joseph Sprenger imprisoned Jews after falsely indicting them, and it is doubtful that more than a few, if any, survived. The Gestapo intended the incarceration of numerous intermarried Jews in and around Vienna to lead to their deaths as well. By early 1943 some two hundred intermarried Jews had been criminalized in this way and sent to camps to die or be killed. It was an effort to draw intermarried Jews from the Frankfurt am Main area into the genocide while reducing the risk that such actions would draw widespread attention.[22]

Struggling to meet Hitler's divergent imperatives of removing intermarried Jews during the war without drawing public attention, whether because these marriages still existed or were being forcibly dissolved, the RSHA issued contrasting orders, perhaps for the sake of deception, so that while anxieties were lowered they could be shipped off, although "without authorization." Even as it authorized the removal of intermarried Jews on criminal charges, the RSHA also, on February 20, 1943, issued an order that "temporarily" deferred intermarried Jews from deportations. This method of gradually deporting intermarried Jews by criminalizing them could work in regions with smaller Jewish populations like Frankfurt/Oder but not in Berlin, with more than eight thousand intermarried Jews. The deportation of Jews from the Reich capital necessarily created a different pattern than that in Frankfurt/Oder, fitted to a dramatically different situation. As Hitler had ordered, ousting Jews from Berlin took precedence over all other locations in the Reich (next in priority were Vienna and Prague).

Given the singularity of Berlin, it is not surprising that the arrests there during the "Elimination of Jews from the Reich" did not resemble those in Frankfurt/Oder or other cities where on February 27, 1943, the

Gestapo launched a massive arrest of the last Jews. The Frankfurt/Oder order authorized what could be described as a "Factory Action"—the arrest of Jews only from factories—but the order did not hold sway in Berlin. The sheer numbers of persons arrested in Berlin, not to mention the participation in the arrests of the most elite SS division on February 27 and 28, made circumspection difficult.[23] During the first two days of the arrests in Berlin, the SS Leibstandarte Hitler was prominently visible, as a phalanx of covered furniture trucks stormed through traffic. Some ten thousand Berlin Jews were taken from their jobs and homes, including about two thousand in non-privileged intermarriages wearing the Jewish Star. Persons wearing the Jewish Star were chased down in public and sent to the collection centers. Even out-of-town Jews who were visiting Berlin were arrested and carted off. Based on identifications that those arrested carried with them, and that did not have to be verified further, some intermarried Jews and Mischlinge were released on the first day of their arrest.[24]

Most of these Berlin Jews ended up in Auschwitz during the following days, while the two thousand from intermarriages were imprisoned at a Jewish Community office at Rosenstrasse 2–4. The overwhelming majority were men whose wives arrived at the building to investigate the fate of their partners. Some arrived as early as the evening of February 27, and by the following morning voices of the wives could be heard calling in unison for the release of their husbands.[25] From time to time, as they held their demonstration over the course of the week, the police scattered them briefly with threats that they would be shot if they did not leave.

On March 2, Dr. Margarete Sommer, the director of Bishop Preysing's Catholic Relief Office, wrote that this was an "evacuation of a magnitude and severity never before seen." Also different was that this time no special consideration was given to those persons living in an intermarriage; "this time partners were separated." A week earlier, Sommer had been told that "the mixed marriages would not be affected by the planned raid," but now she realized that "the opposite is the case." Contrary to earlier practices at the collection camps for the Jews who were awaiting deportation, no one was allowed to bring "useful or comforting items," and "those who tried were refused harshly and chased away." This restriction, Sommer reported, had the effect of changing a fear that the imprisoned intermarried Jews had no future into a "certainty" that they would perish. At the Foreign Ministry, officials were also expecting the imminent deportation of intermarried Jews. The Gestapo took this opportunity to arrest at least three intermarried Jews who were detested as intellectuals. They were supposedly "temporarily" exempted according to the RSHA directives but died in Auschwitz.[26]

In Auschwitz, on March 2, the SS received a telegram from the WVHA Berlin headquarters stating that "On March 1, 1943, the transports of Jews from Berlin will begin . . . [including] about 15,000 healthy Jews fit for work." Further revealing the plan to deport some of Berlin's intermarried Jews is the fact that this many Jews fit for work could not be supplied from Berlin without including Jews married to Aryans. As of February 27, 1943, there were just eleven thousand Berlin Jews in armaments work, and of these, seven thousand were from intermarriages.[27] Two-thirds of Berlin's Jews most suitable for work in Auschwitz were intermarried; to send the number of laborers Auschwitz was expecting from Berlin, the temporary ban on deporting intermarried Jews would have to be lifted, at least for the moment, in Berlin.

Yet on March 4, the sixth day of street protests, Bishop Heinrich Wienken heard from Adolf Eichmann that "the non-Aryan Catholics in racially mixed marriages who were arrested in Berlin . . . will be *released,* and also put to work again in the armaments industry."[28] Nevertheless, arrests of Jews continued, and on March 6, 1943, twenty-five intermarried men, selected because they had no children, were sent from the collection center at Rosenstrasse to Auschwitz.

The contradictory directions taken by different segments of the Gestapo and RSHA might have originated in the divisions that were developing on how to respond to the street protests. Erwin Sartorius, who drove a Gestapo truck that transported Jews, told the postwar German judiciary that he had heard rumors that rival factions had arisen within the RSHA about how to handle the situation, resulting in "conflicting orders." This statement also coincides with the recollection of Goebbels's Propaganda Ministry deputy Leopold Gutterer after the war.[29]

With conditions now causing some Germans to seriously question whether Germany could prevail in the war, the Rosenstrasse protests brought Hitler's and Goebbels's plans to make Berlin "free of Jews" into conflict with the regime's will to repress public dissent and avoid drawing attention to Germany's mixed marriages. The protests on Rosenstrasse, which were noted in the diaries of at least two Berlin women, drew the attention of many Germans, as well as foreign journalists and diplomats, to thousands of mixed marriage couples in the Reich capital.[30]

On March 6, when most of the Jews imprisoned at Rosenstrasse were released, Reich Minister and Berlin Gauleiter Goebbels recorded his decision to release the Jews:

> The people gathered together in large throngs and even sided with the Jews to some extent. I will commission the security police not to continue the Jewish evacuations during such a critical time. Rather we want to put that off for a few weeks; then we can carry it out all the more thoroughly. One has to intervene all over the place to ward off damages. The efforts of certain offices are so lacking in savvy that one cannot leave them on their own for ten minutes. The basic malady of our leadership and above all of our administration consists in operating according to Schema F [rote attention to orders without adapting appropriately to circumstances].

In his report of mid-March 1943, Dr. Gerhard Lehfeldt also identified Goebbels as the authority who made the decision to release the Jews and claimed public protest as his motivation.[31] Lehfeldt was a Jewish-born Protestant whose superior contacts at high levels of the Nazi leadership are readily apparent in this well-informed report to the Vatican. In fact, given the flexibility of the RSHA's directives, which encouraged Gestapo agents to arrest intermarried Jews at this time—so long as they could do so inconspicuously—the RSHA itself could have decided that the arrested intermarried Jews had to be released due to the protests, except in Berlin, where Goebbels presided.

On March 9, the second workday after he ordered the Jews released, Goebbels visited Hitler, who agreed that Goebbels had responded correctly to the "psychological" challenges of clearing Berlin of Jews, but he reiterated that Goebbels would nevertheless still have to make Berlin *"judenfrei,"* according to Gutterer's recollection, with the help of Goebbels's diary. Two days later, Goebbels regretted that Jews from "privileged" intermarriages (not those from non-privileged marriages) had been among the first Berlin Jews arrested in an effort that "proved to be a fiasco." The arrest of some intermarried Jews from privileged inter-marriages who did not wear the Star of David, Goebbels feared, had made it look as though the regime was going to deport all Jews in mixed marriages at this time.

Goebbels was clear about the differences in the status of privileged intermarried Jews in contrast to those who were non-privileged and how this affected his plans to make Berlin "free of Jews." "A whole col-lection of . . . Jews from privileged intermarriages and also Jews from [non-privileged] intermarriages are still to be found in Berlin," he wrote on April 18. "I do not want Jews with the Jewish star running around the Reich capital. Either one must take the Jewish star away and privi-lege them, or on the other hand once and for all evacuate them from the Reich capital."[32] From his comments we can infer that the definition of "clearing Berlin of Jews"—which Goebbels had vowed to achieve by mid-March 1943—would have at a minimum removed intermarried "non-privileged" Jews because they wore the Star. The alternative he was considering because of the Rosenstrasse Project was exempting them from wearing the Star, but there was no general order for Berlin's Jews to remove the Jewish Star.

Well-informed government ministers, as well as church bishops, also could not believe that intermarried Jews had been released because the RSHA did not want it at this moment. On March 8, RSHA head Ernst Kaltenbrunner informed Interior Minister Wilhelm Frick that the deportations had been limited to Jews who did not live in mixed mar-riages, indicating that for at least some in government, their fate had been in question. High church officials also shared this perception: Bishop Theophil Wurm of Württemberg stated in a complaint of March 12 to the Reich Ministry of Churches that "the Jews who live in intermar-riages with Christian Germans—some of whom are themselves mem-bers of the Christian Church—were taken from their home and workplace to be deported to the East." Those same Jews, he continued, were "re-leased." On April 6, 1943, Catholic bishop Wilhelm Berning of Os-nabrück also used the word "released" to describe his sense that another fate had been planned for the intermarried Jews.[33]

In fact, during the course of the Berlin arrests, 120 intermarried Jews had been deported to Auschwitz, including the 25 imprisoned at

Rosenstrasse. Upon arriving in Auschwitz, these intermarried Jews from Rosenstrasse were sent to work at Auschwitz-Monowitz. On the morning of their twelfth day an SS man informed them that on the order of "high authorities," they were to prepare to return to Berlin. Upon their return to Berlin they were charged with crimes and sent to nearby hard-labor camps. When a surprised Gestapo secretary wondered why Jews had been released from Auschwitz, she was told that overzealous underlings had transgressed their orders in sending them off in the first place. This makes little sense, except as propaganda, considering the Nazi drive to annihilate all Jews and also the fact that the large majority of Berlin's intermarried Jews sent to Auschwitz at the same time were not returned. On April 1, an American OSS dispatch from Leland Harrison in Bern, Switzerland, stated that "a source which is considered trustworthy has reported that actions against Jewish wives and husbands on the part of the Gestapo, reported in my telegram no. 1597 dated March tenth, had to be discontinued some time ago because of the protest which such action aroused."[34] Lehfeldt's information corroborates that of the OSS.

Four months later Dr. Sommer was still certain that the protests had retrieved the Jews imprisoned at Rosenstrasse from deportation. In August 1943 she reiterated her conclusion that five months earlier in Berlin there had been a causal connection between "unusually heated protests" and the "release" of those imprisoned at Rosenstrasse. In the same report she backed up her judgment about the Rosenstrasse events by reporting the results of another protest: "In Innsbruck and other cities of Tyrol," she wrote, "non-Aryan spouses were apprehended without any stated reason and brought to a concentration camp. Following extensive protests from the Catholics in Vienna, these spouses from intermarriages were reunited with their families."[35] Gestapo and other official records of these protests in Innsbruck have vanished, as they also have for those on Rosenstrasse, and even the best-informed experts on Austria and intermarriages have not heard of them. Given its reasons for anxiety about popular protests, the regime was also eager to destroy records about them. In January 1944, preferring to ignore the problem than risk more publicity, Hitler ordered that further discussions of intermarried Jews "should be avoided." Clearly his directive was "ignored or taken lightly."[36]

Had Germany's intermarried couples complied, the regime would have eagerly murdered the Jewish partner in each union. As it was, those intermarried couples who refused to separate caused the regime to make a series of compromises that delineated a pattern of "temporarily" deferring an increasing number of German Jews, although still relatively few, from the genocide. Like other genocide perpetrators throughout world history, the Nazis compromised the purity of their ideology and spared certain members of the targeted group to help them consolidate their forces, defuse dissent, and move toward a complete genocide.[37] Nothing demonstrates the stubborn power of the private sphere in the face of Nazi terror better than Jewish-Gentile marriages. A dictatorship committed to the complete biological extinction of the Jewish people was compelled to stop short of a boundary drawn by the traditional regard for marriage.

Conclusion

THERE ARE VARIOUS explanations of Hitler's march to power and why the Germans attended him to the gates of hell. How did such a drifter at the edge of society make his way to the levers of destruction on such a cyclopean scale? Why did so many choose to believe in Hitler as Germany's nearly infallible Leader, insisting that he was never to blame but always made things right as soon as he knew about a problem? Why did the very people slain by his power work long and vigorously to support him? The incomprehensible scale of crime and suffering during the Third Reich has led to a spectrum of answers to such questions, from those who see Hitler as a demonic force outside of history, like a miracle in reverse, to the more commonplace view that Hitler was always a Goliath, a malevolent giant who used the Gestapo to take whatever he wanted. Many point to Hitler's ability to enthrall an audience, or to Germany's desperate circumstances and the peace settlement following World War I, or to his savage anti-Semitism. In the national humiliation that followed World War I, Hitler did make himself out to be Germany's savior. But the vast majority of those who voted for Hitler had never seen him speak, and the animosity he voiced against the Jews found lots of echoes in and around Germany. Why did Hitler prevail in the field of so many contenders? There were others who also offered a land of promise if only the Germans followed them, and many were just as opportunistic. Why was Hitler so deft at perceiving and creating opportunities?

This book traces a different side of arguments that Hitler always prevailed with overwhelming force whenever he encountered opposition. It argues that he persuaded Germans through listening and compromising and placating and that he became a much greater force because he used a range of tactics within a broad spectrum of compromise and coercion. The dictatorship was not just determined to murder tens of millions, but also to have the Germans welcome its goals and carry them out. This vision compelled Hitler to lead with substitutes and incentives in an effort to reshape the attitudes of a society accustomed to thinking that mass extermination was wrong. The radical dimensions of the Nazi mission actually caused the dictatorship to try harder to ingratiate itself to the German masses in every way possible.

Although the goal of social revolution was out of his reach, Hitler did not think he could take a shortcut by only using force to change behavior on the surface. With Teutonic thoroughness, Hitler set out to align individual and social attitudes with his own. Of course what mattered most in the short run was taking power and using it, however brutally, and then winning wars. Mere adjustments in behavior were always welcomed, although Hitler hoped for a deeper change of values because he did not seek power merely to become the next chancellor. He wanted to become the Leader who convinced his clan that he could show it a more effective way to achieve the wealth and power of a modern nation. By dint of the softer side of influence, persuasion, and compromise, Hitler was convinced that old habits and customs that clashed with the new myths and norms of National Socialism would fade away.

The purposes for reshaping social attitudes within and among his own "race" reached beyond Hitler's shorter-term goals of winning wars for the continent. This new German-blooded national community would also serve as the foundation for permanent, total Nazism. The one-thousand-year Reich was not an empty phrase for Hitler but his ultimate objective, which set his overall course. It determined the Nazi direction, while the Nazi style was to improvise by using a range of tactics suited for the circumstances of the moment to optimize the party's overall advance. Steps taken, however, must not interrupt what Hitler saw as the ever-growing popular conviction that his leadership deserved unquestioning loyalty. He wanted a total state, but he did not think that this was possible without establishing a total society, shaped by Nazi ideology. A goal of the national community the Nazis aspired to create was a communal conscience that required all Germans to sacrifice their energies and lives for the Reich. Invoking examples like the French Revolution, Hitler concluded in prison that "the forces of the will" are decisive in the struggle for domination.[1]

The compromises that characterized Hitler's popularity, group loyalty, and exercise of power also marked his rule of the Third Reich. When it came to ruling his people, Hitler was not eager to grasp the brutal powers of dictatorship and then discard his incentives of compromise. Instead, he carefully accrued separate bases for his authority, one by one, such as cultivating the appearance that all he did was legal. Camouflage was critical, but when this failed, so was compromise rather than an immediate turn to brute force. This tactic is illustrated by Hitler's strategic choice to take power the "legal way." Conquering the energy of the masses was not all that mattered. The Nazis also had to earn trust and cooperation from the military, as well as from economic and government elites in order to take power and then to rule a dictatorship. Hitler achieved his position to negotiate with the elites for the office of chancellor because he commanded so much popular support. From this position, his choice of the legal way opened up the possibilities for negotiation and compromise, in contrast, for example, with the less flexible and less successful tactics of the German Communists. The tactics of the underdog the Nazis used are represented in Goebbels's declaration that Bernhard Weiss, with the force of the Berlin police at his disposal, had power because people saw him as worthy of power, and his power could be undermined by changing this perception. It is also exposed in Hitler's instructions on the SA in November 1926, which emphasized the importance of persuading Germans to join the party. Hitler's rejection of another coup after his failed Beer Hall Putsch of 1923 was based on a calculation that the party could lose the gamble of another putsch. More important, Hitler had his eye on his ultimate goal of changing the Germans into a national community with perpetual mastery over everyone else.

In power, the Nazis wooed the workers themselves, although they cut down the leadership of the workers' parties—the Communists and the Socialists. Would Hitler have crushed the leadership of opposing political parties with such brutality if such a move threatened the tremendous surge in the popularity of his leadership? Such a choice between terror and popularity was not necessary in this case, because Nazi terror against the Left worked in Hitler's favor; Marxism was not only opposed by the majority, but also opposed with a great passion. Hitler's ascent in popular esteem pressured groups and organizations from garden clubs to professional associations to align themselves with the new party and eliminate Jews from their membership. The alignment of the elites progressed smoothly since there were no significant gaps between their immediate goals and those of the Nazis: rearmament, reemployment, a new sense of order and coming prosperity, along with the exclusion of the Jews. But the mass movement with its popular allegiance to Hitler's rule was not just put on hold while the new regime moved the pieces into place so that the people could fight its wars. The dictatorship could not have won over the Germans so well if its brass knuckles had not been paired with the solicitous hand of national welfare and compromise.

It did not create a National Community, but the dictatorship set out to forge this by attracting the people with incentives so irresistible they were willing to give up values long entrenched in German traditions. Christian charity, in Nazi thought, sapped energy and resources that should go toward strengthening the forces of German aggression, which would be turned outward so that the Reich would dominate all others. Hitler was eager to start killing hundreds of thousands of German-blooded "incurables" who burdened the new social order. But he estimated that it would take more than a few years of reshaping German values before these murders could be conducted openly without offending large numbers of people and that this goal could not be accomplished with anything like the terror and savagery the regime unleashed against its enemies. In contrast to the evil of charity applied indiscriminately, Nazi propaganda for women taught love for fellow Germans; during the air raids, while Nazi torture and savage annihilation of millions hastened forward with all possible speed, the party strove to feed, clothe, and comfort the bombed-out Germans.

Like the elites, a majority of the German people soon thought that by serving National Socialism, they were also serving themselves and their own because the party began by veiling its real aims to the extent

that they clashed with traditional German appetites. Unbridled nationalism that excluded the Jews afforded substantial common ground to
begin with. But realigning patterns of social behavior elsewhere, like
shifting the tectonic plates of society without triggering seismic trem-
ors, was more challenging than convincing professionals to serve a new
power. The Nazis aimed to avoid all appearances of dissent because it
could stymie the momentum of deepening popular support, and when
the preemption of unrest failed, compromise was used. The masks hiding the most alien Nazi goals had to be pulled away discreetly, in a series
of phases that kept step with a growing Nazification of collective and
private thought patterns, until the full Nazi perspective was accepted as a
substitute for traditional viewpoints. Or to use a different image, the old
carpet had to be slipped out from under the people with such cunning
that they had barely noticed before they also observed that they were
resting comfortably indeed on the new Nazi tapestry.

The most demanding trick on the Nazi program was wheedling the
private and communal acceptance of the obliteration of the private sphere,
and friction was met with compromise. The needs of the Nazi national
community must always take precedence over those of any individual or
group, including the churches. Thus, for example, a German should
gladly consign a congenitally ill child or mother to a "mercy death," or
revile sexual intercourse with Jewish persons as a defilement of the race,
or produce a flood of biologically superior offspring, abandoning them to
state "care." Here church traditions and the providentially assigned allegiances they represented also stood in the way of the destruction of some
private rights. The Catholic Church, with a pervasive network of social
welfare institutions and a vast store of resources enfolded within a world-
wide structure led from Rome, posed an especially important potential
obstacle for the Nazis.

For Nazi leaders, the churches also represented a tantalizing opportunity, if only their structures and values could be turned to serve them.
As church bishops of both denominations demonstrated frequently
enough, ecclesiastical authority could be enlisted, even for summoning
the strength of the Christian values of sacrifice and martyrdom for the
regime's war in the East. But to achieve this cooperation, the regime had
to balance its demands with compromises as well as deceptions. Tests of
Nazi leadership were woven into the fabric of the goal of bringing popular

and religious behavior totally in line. Hero worship loomed large in Nazi notions of leadership, but the regional governors and Gauleiters were also responsible for engineering a shift in German commitments without provoking public signals of dissent that would be backed by large segments of the masses.

We have witnessed several cases. The first major popular challenge to the surging momentum of Hitler's mass movement took the form of autonomous protests feared by the dictatorship, although they were organized not by Catholics but Protestants. Led by their bishops, two provincial churches refused to merge with the twenty-six other provincial Protestant churches under the leadership of a Reich Bishop reporting directly to Hitler. Efforts to suppress these churchgoers with police force and the arrest of their bishops only inflamed the swarms of Protestants who congregated to defend their structural independence. In a battle for popular allegiance on this issue against the most popular regional Nazi officials, the Bavarian bishop, Hans Meiser, demonstrated particularly well what a bishop, hailed as a hero, could achieve by leading his congregations in the defense of a church tradition. Given the considerable degree of conflict between church practices and Nazi practices, the defense of church customs was deeply significant, and this opposition of 1934 was especially noteworthy since Hitler had just shown how ruthless he could be during the Night of the Long Knives murders, even while the Protestant protests were gathering strength. To be sure, it was not at all likely that someone who wielded church authority to express opposition like Meiser did needed to fear the fate of SA leader Ernst Röhm. Hitler had consolidated his popular support with that first and only purge of its kind in June 1934, but he relented to these Protestant demands for the same reason: to consolidate power through releasing the bishops and restoring them to their offices in October 1934. Although the other twenty-six Protestant bishops agreed to Hitler's plan for a national church, the continuing protests of two provinces derailed Hitler's rapid progress, depriving him and the Reich of achieving an important goal.

Hitler showed that he could compromise even when it thwarted his political effort, even when he was very close to succeeding. Had he succeeded, he would have centralized his power by directly subordinating the convenient hierarchy of the traditionally autonomous Protestant Church. It was a setback Hitler considered temporary. As if a deal had been struck, Bishop Meiser never again mobilized public opposition but became a reliable voice of authority for the regime. Indeed, following the bishop-led Protestant opposition in 1934, the bishops working with their congregations in mobilized public opposition to regime policies were Catholics. Illustrating the disarming authority he would use to take formal control of the military in February 1938, Hitler threatened his powerful subordinates in late June 1937 not with Nazi terror but with a public repudiation by the Leader himself, should they ignore his order by disciplining church authorities without first consulting him. The decision about whether to punish prelates was balanced so delicately between the Nazi goal of unquestioning obedience and the possibility that the use of police force might impede the forward momentum of the party that only the grand master of such calculations, the author of National Socialism itself, could make such judgments.

As Hitler's ability to keep his powerful accomplices in line with the threat of public disgrace grew, it became more difficult for Catholic bishops to oppose him, not least because he gained in stature with the people and also among the bishops, who did not stand together to mobilize the laity in defense of cherished customs. Hitler's compromises with the few who did rebel helped keep them in check. Not wishing to give them cause for cooperative dissent, the dictatorship typically struck at Catholic customs region by region rather than attacking church customs from Berlin with national decrees. The dictatorship struck at the heart of Catholic tradition and independence with regional directives for Catholic schools to replace crucifixes with portraits of Hitler. While Protestants complied with orders to substitute Hitler's picture for that of the German hero Martin Luther, local and regional Catholics defended their crucifixes alone, without assistance from the bishops collectively. Illustrative of Catholic protests, the bishops in Oldenburg and East Prussia led their faithful in protesting the replacement of such a sacred symbol in 1936 and 1937. They won concessions, forcing the regime to rescind its replacement of crucifixes. Subsequent decrees at both the regional and the national level reasserted the order for the removal of crucifixes by declaring that all schools were secular "German community schools," but these decrees also depended upon compliance. The replacement of sacred symbols with Hitler's image could have been a mighty step toward breaking down the confessional (Catholic-Protestant) divide in

Germany, but crucifixes remained in some schools, and under the pressures of war, Germans began to turn to their churches in increasing numbers despite Nazi indoctrination and terror.

In 1938, the dictatorship evaluated whether allegiance to the party was now sufficiently strong for it to deploy public rallies against a Catholic bishop, like those the churches assembled to demonstrate the depth of opinion against regime policies. Popular approval of the purge of the SA in June 1934 showed that the people could be convinced to reject the old system of law in exchange for the new Nazi code based on the "healthy" sentiments of the people. But were the people of Bishop Sproll's diocese mature enough by Nazi standards to drive a bishop away with a solid wall of publicly expressed opinion? Instead of prosecuting the bishop for treason, the party initiated a series of street rallies against the bishop outside of his residence from April 11 to late July 1938. Authorities repeatedly entreated these crowds of thousands not to grow destructive, as the crowds repeated together, with one voice, slogans that Sproll was not fit to be part of the Nazi national community and had to leave his diocese. These were the essential characteristics of potentially convincing displays of social dissent, in contrast with the undisciplined protests of Catholic Youth during the "rosary festival" at Vienna's St. Stephen's Cathedral, which brought down a spree of violent anti-church rioting in September 1938 that punished the church for a week.[2] A Nazi demonstration against Sproll in July turned so destructive and threatening to the bishop himself that it finally brought out crowds on the street, in counterdemonstrations for the bishop who was being treated so shamefully. With this new display of opinion, pitting loyalty to the church against allegiance to the party, regional leaders wanted to stop all the demonstrations. But as they discovered from the Reich Chancellery, only the Leader himself could make this decision, as in the case of Protestant protests against joining the Reich Church. The demonstrations stopped, and in late August, a month after the attempt to substitute street demonstrations for judicial processes failed, Gestapo agents arranged for the bishop to be driven to the residence of Archbishop Conrad Gröber in Freiberg, and he returned to his diocese only after the war.

In contrast with Bishop Sproll, the most elite officers of the army had no popular backing and were easily displaced. The weaponless authority Hitler exercised to subordinate the party's armed (paramilitary)

Storm Troopers before 1933 was also displayed in a series of actions that first robbed the German military of its will to resist and then enabled him to take formal control of the army in February 1938. Army leaders quietly complied with his request for them to depart. Unlike the crowds backing Sproll, the array of elites backing General Werner von Fritsch did not help him either save his position or compel Hitler to promote him to war minister, as they wanted. Because there were no crowds in public, the story of the generals was much easier to control with the regime-dominated press. Although he maintained ultimate oversight of the delicate matters of street demonstrations behind the curtains, Hitler avoided public associations with controversies. A cornerstone of Hitler's popularity was the belief across the Reich that Hitler made things right as soon as someone brought an injustice to his attention. He remained aloof as long as he could, but he compromised in 1934 to restore the bishops because, as his immediate assistant Rudolf Hess said, there was no one else who could resolve the matter. When he stepped in to compromise, he calmed the folks who were most in doubt about whether Hitler the Leader really was on their side, protecting his image, and reaffirming for the moment, for those who had begun to wonder, that faithfulness to church and Hitler were absolutely compatible.

To keep this pillar of consent in place Hitler was compelled to compromise with the people, even during the war, and even on policies implementing the most basic ideological mandate to "purify the race." Thus in December 1940, the chief of Nazi terror, Heinrich Himmler, closed the euthanasia killing center at Grafeneck because, as he said in black and white, it was upsetting too many people and the killing would have to be done in a different way to stem the agitation while popular attitudes were adjusted. Himmler's decision followed the warning from a trusted Nazi that Germans across different social sectors were held together by a belief that Hitler would stop the murders if only he knew about them—but this insider also warned that this belief was not indestructible and had to be protected before it was stretched too far. Finding opportunity even in dissent, the dictatorship treated mass unrest and protest as a sign that it was moving too quickly or using the wrong methods, allowing Hitler's compromises to underscore the belief that he made things right as soon as he was informed of an injustice. In any case, Himmler as well as Hitler held to a belief that Germany would win the war in a blaze of glory that would demolish virtually all remaining will to disagree with such a triumphant leader, and compromises would be redressed.

For Hitler the war was another stage for a still greater feat in his succession of triumphs that proved to the people his unmatched prowess, and his management of euthanasia illustrates how carefully he avoided weighing on that prestige with execrated policies, by compromising. Hitler allowed domestic opinion to influence his timing and methods in these killings, at the heart of the Nazi campaign to strengthen the German biological stock. Because the people would not accept mass murder, Hitler put euthanasia off until war, when, as he said, eyes were fixed on battle lines and human life was cheapened. But even during war, when resistance was undercut by the unity required to defeat the enemy, the dictatorship bowed further to opinion by conducting the euthanasia of "useless eaters" in secret. For fear of drawing attention to euthanasia the regime did not punish those who spread news about it. In August 1941, Hitler revised the euthanasia program yet again to appease the popular foment that had very occasionally burst into open gatherings of protest and was legitimated by a powerful sermon by Bishop Galen. The methods for the euthanasia killings of adults were altered dramatically, de-centralized, and moved eastward to decrease public awareness and unrest. Despite the call by powerful regional leaders for the bishop's execution, the decision was up to Hitler, and he did not punish him. The Leader knew the bishops strongly supported his war in the East, and several weeks later, Hitler's decision was requited when Galen urged German soldiers onward in a spirit of Christian duty and the promise of eternal paradise, as he called upon Germany's youth to give everything in the war.

To maintain his prestige, the Leader was willing to step back for the moment and then continue toward his goal on a different, less direct course that the people would follow. The war did help Hitler square up with popular opinion, especially when the Reich was winning, but it also brought an increased dependence on the people, and Hitler's deep anxiety about another Stab in the Back on the home front bolstered his reasons for compromising with the people. Hitler did not suppose that he could prevent the feared Stab in the Back by force without crippling the popular will to fight war, just as there was never a question for him about whether he could conduct euthanasia openly under any circumstances, thumbing his nose at popular traditions. During the first week of war, Hitler moved to preempt incentives for an unhappy home front by ordering an immediate stop to all unnecessary provocations of the churches. Although he allowed top satraps in Berlin to crack down on the churches during Germany's spectacular Blitzkrieg victories, in 1941 he redoubled his order against attacks on institutions from which the German people took strength, demanding the end to the confiscation of church property and reintroducing crucifixes that had been banned from Bavarian schools.

There is further evidence that the dictatorship at the highest level was pressured to compromise in the last years of the war because it felt that it had less freedom to use terror to control the Germans when they were acting to protect their private sphere when the war, going against the Reich, was already terrorizing them in a whole spectrum of ways. Goebbels commented to the Gauleiters in August 1940 that in the wake of victories like Germany's rout of France that spring, they could use force more freely, compared with the earlier, more compromising approach. Although some agencies, especially the army, did crack down with terror to control Germans, Hitler continued up until the final weeks to ingratiate himself with the people by ordering his Gauleiters not to use even soft forms of coercion against Germans who rebelled against the regime's wartime evacuation of civilians, although normally these Gauleiters had the freedom to choose their methods. If anti-Jewish policies escalated due to the radicalizing competition among Hitler's subordinates wishing to please him, in the area of domestic management Hitler intervened to prevent escalation of the use of terror.

The attempt to control civilian relocations during wartime illustrates Hitler's willingness to move the boundaries of admissible behavior on the home front in order to avoid a Stab in the Back and public unrest that might escalate toward it. Some German prosecutors decided by the summer of 1943 that there were so many complaints and jokes about the highest German leaders that they could not judiciously bring charges against a single person because so many were committing similar offenses. Still, Hitler continued to urge "education" rather than force as the appropriate means to bring the people into line. A street demonstration by three hundred women in the Ruhr city of Witten during

October 1943 influenced Hitler to rule against the Gauleiters who wanted to compel them with soft methods of coercion, manipulating the distribution of food rations, and to reiterate this ruling through at least October 1944. These women protested effectively only to defend the traditionally private liberties of family, and in fact the bonds of family also protected even German Jews if they were married to German-blooded non-Jews. The overwhelming majority of German Jews who survived did so only because their Gentile partners refused to separate from them, even though their remaining together ultimately demanded of them the most courageous and sustained street protest by ordinary Germans during the Third Reich. Like Bishop Sproll, and contrary to the path of the overwhelming majority who moved in the opposite direction, the protesting women grew into their capacity for opposing the regime when it affected their private lives, until they were able to assemble and reassemble in protest on the street for their Jewish family members, despite repeated threats that they would be shot if they did not leave.[3] Following this climactic showdown between the private forces of family and the regime, the Jewish family members were released, and very few intermarried German Jews were sent to the camps during the remaining years of the war. This was another example of compromise exacted by an unyielding street demonstration, which Joseph Goebbels deplored as a force that corroded Nazi authority.

Hitler used force instrumentally so effectively because he recognized its limits in some cases. The image of Hitler as a raging carpet biter must also accommodate his considerable capacities as an instrumentalist, as demonstrated not just by his advances within the Reich, but also by the costly misjudgments on the part of Western powers. Some made the mistake of supposing that Hitler operated within a set of assumptions and objectives similar to their own. But they were wrong. His goal of establishing permanent National Socialism was breathtakingly unrealistic, and as he advanced and became firmly convinced that he was the instrument of providence, his timetable for reaching this goal became even more compressed, even as he continued to urge his men to align old German customs with Nazism by using propaganda rather than sheer force. He read the SD secret reports on opinion regularly, even when he had other pressing work, because he wanted to know the facts.[4] The disconnect between his goals and his abilities initially took him far in accruing power, encouraging him to make highly risky gambles to lead the people toward his goals at all possible speed. Finally it also led to a destruction of Europe on a scale comparable to the power he had accumulated—and his downfall.

Hitler was only defeated by forces capable of greater destruction on the war's battlegrounds. But he did not strive toward every goal with the same means he used in war and occupation. In ruling his own people, he was a very capable tactician. According to credible descriptions, like those of his valet, Heinz Linge, Hitler could be brutally cruel and yet was calm and self-possessed, repulsed by drunkenness, and able to throw a fit for effect. Yet in today's world, where Hitler is the embodiment of archetypal evil, he is commonly associated with simplistic images of such evil. A three-dimensional image of a man who led such barbaric forces and yet could use soft tactics if it suited his purposes could humanize Hitler, and it poses moral questions. But such an image helps us avoid misleading impressions that rob history of its challenges, nuance, and subtleties. This book likens Hitler, in his direct relationship to the German people as their Leader, to a leader and his partner on the dance floor, intent on teaching the dance and thus willing to make accommodations for missteps. Because Hitler depended on the people to fulfill his savage purposes, and because he hoped the Reich would form the foundation for permanent National Socialism, he cultivated the German people not just by preventing certain behaviors with force, but also with incentives and camouflage. In the Third Reich we see that compromises followed when preemption failed.

Afterword on Historical Research:
Back to the "Top Down"?

We are misled by the narrowness of our assumptions about what
constitutes an advantage in any given situation.

—*Malcolm Gladwell*

HITLER VIEWED SOCIAL DISSENT in opposition to particular policies
as a sign that the dictatorship was pushing too fast or using the wrong
combination of tactics. Crushing dissent that was grounded in habits
could alienate the people, and he wanted to demonstrate that he knew
what was best for them. He did not think that he could prevent another
fateful Stab in the Back on the home front with brute force but feared
that too much coercion would sap the will of the people to fight. These
conclusions, from this book, are impossible within the totalitarian "top
down" models that predominated for fifteen or twenty years after the
war. In that paradigm, all power was held by Hitler and his henchmen,
who stood apart from the people and subjected them to their will by irresistible propaganda, if not by the Gestapo's brute force.

During the 1960s, German historians began to argue that this totalitarian paradigm, by holding only a few at the top responsible, exculpated
many who were morally and criminally guilty. During that decade as
well, a new social history of ordinary people and their institutions was
foreshadowed by church history. Sustained, focused research on "history
from below" began during the 1970s, a point at which some totalitarian
interpretations, made by important historians, were already well established and hard to dislodge. The new "bottom up" perspectives argued
that the dictatorship thrived because so many Germans shared its goals
and infused it with their own energy; society itself had acted as an agent

274

of repression on behalf of National Socialism. A zenith of this perspective was expressed in 1976 by Hans Mommsen, who wrote, "Hitler drew back whenever he met public resistance such as on euthanasia [in August 1941] and the Church question."[1] This compromise on euthanasia shows that Hitler was willing to make concessions on "racial hygiene" matters, which comprised the foundation of Nazi ideology, and not only on lesser matters. It illustrates as well that the dictator was willing to make these compromises on a national rather than merely local level.

In 1977, Martin Broszat led the publication of what would be a six-volume study of Bavarian everyday life as it related to Nazi rule. Broszat questioned whether the already firmly established definition of "resistance," derived from the July 20, 1944, military-led conspiracy to kill Hitler, might be expanded.[2] This concept limited "resistance" to politically motivated and centrally organized efforts to overthrow the regime itself. Broszat examined a variety of often partially veiled acts that ignored or opposed the regime's efforts to forge a total state; scattered throughout everyday history were various examples of noncompliance or nonconformity to a regime that tried to erase private rights, although such examples did not seem to rise to the standard of resistance. This opposition, regardless of how the dictatorship responded, was only "partial" since it singled out policies to oppose while supporting the regime in general.

During the 1960s and 1970s, some historians also viewed resistance through the history of a particular social sector, specifically the churches and Marxist theory and the working class. Hitler's concessions to the laborers prevented a larger revolt by that class, argued Timothy Mason, since the dictatorship's fear of alienating workers limited its willingness to coerce their cooperation with force. Mason and others concluded that worker dissent "was of an entirely different order of importance" for the regime because it "potentially endangered the stability of the regime and the accomplishment of its aims." In this view, which saw Hitler's apprehension about unrest as focused almost exclusively on the workers, the regime evaluated opposition by the working class as political dissent, even when it was not politically motivated. Further, "the sensitivity shown [by the regime] towards the working class was not matched by similar regard for opinion in other social groups."[3]

Following the 1970s, there was not much study of heightened social unrest that was public, cooperative, and caused a public scene sufficient to prod the regime into responding. Detlev Peukert was unusual in drawing attention to "protest" as a distinct form of popular behavior, and he located it on a scale of acts of opposition more challenging than nonconformity but below resistance to the state itself. Otherwise, scholars of Nazi Germany have used the term "protest" in a range of ways so broad that the term has encompassed, for example, both a private letter and crowds of ordinary persons risking their lives in defiance of the Gestapo on the street. This lack of precision regarding public protest is a remarkable oversight in the assessment of a regime so sensitive to the political meaning of crowds in public spaces.[4]

There were some investigations of popular protest during the 1970s, albeit without a search for the important context of other acts of opposition that had taken a similar form. Already in 1965, the German weekly *Der Spiegel* published part of the SD report on the October 1943 protest by three hundred women in Witten, and in 1976 Richard J. Evans was probably the first historian to interpret its meaning within a broader interpretation of Third Reich history. Evans placed this event in the context of women's history, and women did in fact engage in street protests more than men, as Jill Stephenson has recently shown. Some have explained the fact that women were not punished for protesting, and even got their way, with arguments that the dictatorship responded to crimes by women leniently, although the evidence for this argument, based in crime statistics kept by the regime, does not take account of open mass dissent. A pioneering regional study of 1978 by Jeremy Noakes, on a church struggle over crucifixes in Catholic schools, is still the best work on this part of the church struggle.[5]

Remarkably, one example of defiance that protected some two thousand German Jews from death in the Holocaust—the Rosenstrasse protest—remained largely unexamined until the 1980s and 1990s. This is an especially important example of popular, collected protest that stands alone in significance because it was on behalf of Jews. Its distinction is evident in its variance with the incisive, generally accurate observation that Germans who opposed a single policy of the regime generally supported the regime itself. Certainly the Rosenstrasse protesters objected to the Nazi racial policy only as it affected their families, but because that policy put their families at stake, they could never support the regime even partially. Their personal lives were fundamentally political in the eyes of the Nazis, whose core ideology required the removal of all Jews from Germany.

Intermarriages and their defiance have eluded attention for various reasons, not least of which was the Nazi reluctance to leave any record of open defiance such as that by intermarried couples. Intermarriage itself was an uncomfortable matter, as was the question of whether assimilation helped even a small fraction of Jews in very specific circumstances to survive. Sometimes popular dissent was removed from discussion entirely, with arguments that it was not really resistance. The focus on the motivation of persons who had acted in opposition to the will of the regime served the important purpose of limiting the commemoration of such courageous behavior, a focus that was important because there had not been much resistance inside the Reich. The July 20 conspiracy became the German Resistance, filling the national need for a clear symbol of resistance, despite studies that questioned the motivations and objectives of the conspirators. The conspiracy was an important symbol because it had finally been acknowledged as an act of resistance rather than treason, in the face of the popular disdain and legal setbacks that prevailed during the years immediately following the war.[6]

During the 1990s, some historians began to reverse the conclusions about the significance of social protest from the 1970s by arguing that social dissent could never have caused Hitler to draw back. Recently, distinguished historians have written that the long trend of "bottom up" interpretations of the Third Reich has come to a close and has in fact reversed, tracing its way back toward the "top down" perspectives that had initially held so much sway up into the 1960s.[7] This could be the case. But the history of protest during the Third Reich is still incomplete, perhaps because the ongoing negotiations between the people and their Leader, which are most evident in popular protests, do not fall easily within the paradigms of Hitler's power as projected either from the "top down" or from the "bottom up." The dictatorship did not use force whenever it encountered resistance, nor did the will of the people always contribute to Nazi power, but it sometimes stood in its way. In a process of continuing interaction between the "top" and the "bottom," Hitler made compromises by shaping and then reshaping policies. The regime moved continuously between the two fundamental principles of building support on the one hand while also maintaining the Leader's image, avoiding unrest, and reforming social norms.

Hitler thought he was leading a development that would shape the Germans into a race that would perpetually dominate everyone else. Eugenics policies inside the Reich illustrate the ways that efforts from "the top" to change perspectives at "the bottom" forced the policymaking process into a series of compromises, starting with the position that the regime could not even begin "euthanasia" until war provided cover. Similarly, the regime's policies for evacuating civilians during the war illustrate this process of interaction, as "the top" sought to reposition "the bottom" on a different set of principles, while accommodating its dissent meanwhile.

Not only did the people support the regime "from below," they also demonstrated a capacity to slow the regime's progress toward its atrocious goals, particularly when the Nazi drive for a total society impinged on the private sphere and its traditions of family and religion.[8] Protests occurred when Germans felt they were entitled to dissent; sometimes the protesters had faith in Hitler and thought they must raise their voices so that the Leader could hear them over the impediments raised by local leaders. Hitler appeased church protests because he never dared to demand that the people choose between loyalties to their church and loyalties to the Nazis. Other protests occurred, as at Witten, because some women had faced enough hardship to free themselves from caring about the worst Nazi threats or perhaps because they had arranged to protest with the complicity of others in the community, including the police. They were sure that euthanasia's murders were wrong or were sorely offended when they affected their own families. In the case of Rosenstrasse, women protested out of a desire to stand in the way of the death of family members and also to show those in danger that they cared enough about them to put their own lives on the line. It was keeping faith, demanded by what Václav Havel would later describe as an attempt to live in the truth, despite the certain opposition of Hitler and society generally.[9]

In the official histories of German memorials of Nazi history—those supported by state funds—open protests have been overlooked. The following contextualized sketch of the attention historians and German memorials have given a few events of popular protest suggests that historians might be moving away from the interpretation of the 1970s that Hitler accommodated public protest. In contrast, this book argues that the regime's response to those Germans who did speak out together in public with one disciplined voice was governed by its efforts to construct and govern its national community while maintaining public images that matched its propaganda claims of total popular support. This history merits further study as a way of investigating the ways that the dictatorship governed within the Reich. For all of his savagery, Hitler was also able to moderate his methods shrewdly, through a set of compromises that placated but also ensured the support of his constituents.

HISTORIES OF HITLER'S DECREE TO HALT "EUTHANASIA" AND THE CRUCIFIX STRUGGLES

Over the decades, a range of mainstream historians have found that when he ordered adult "euthanasia" to stop in August 1941, Hitler bowed to German popular opinion brought to a head by Bishop Galen's sermon of August 3. In the view of these historians, Hitler's way of governing included the capacity to compromise to keep the people on his side. Most historians did not, however, identify the elements and circumstances of the opposition that caused Hitler to concede, as a first step toward identifying other events that caused concessions for similar reasons. Were Hitler and his circle likely to respond in a specific way to collected, orderly protests in public? Were the events of popular street protest sufficient to comprise a separate category of popular response to Nazism?

Rather than an investigation of this history, there has been something of a trend since the 1990s that runs against earlier conclusions, maintaining that the dictatorship did not change its policies because of popular sentiment. This is illustrated by a change in the interpretation of the protests against euthanasia.[10] In 1989, after editing an exhaustive seven-volume series researched by a number of German historians, Götz Aly concluded along with many historians who had preceded him that "the vehemence and publicity signified by Galen's protest delivered a decisive impulse for Hitler to end [euthanasia] at least temporarily." He qualified that opinion by adding that Galen's protest was not the only reason.[11] During the following decade, some historians for the first time mounted sustained arguments against this standard position by excluding popular opinion as a possible cause of Hitler's decree to halt euthanasia.

Scholarly disagreement is healthy and invites an investigation of how this transformation in perceptions of how Hitler ruled occurred. Michael Burleigh was the prominent voice of the new interpretation during the 1990s. He attributed Hitler's "halt" order to quotas established beforehand and the need to transfer the killing technology used in euthanasia to the death camps for murdering Jews. He dismisses earlier interpretations as "wishful thinking" because "The 'euthanasia' program was not halted because of some local difficulties with a handful of bishops."[12] He questions Galen's ethics because he did not speak out as soon as he knew about "euthanasia" but instead waited a year to give his famous sermon; Burleigh added that a Catholic theologian had even justified the "euthanasia" program in writing.[13] He is concerned that the church is receiving credit for resistance by making Galen into a hero, when in actuality Galen served the regime more than he hindered it, as did the churches in general.

It is important that the churches receive only the acclaim for resistance that they have earned, just as it is important to acknowledge that resistance to Hitler was overwhelmed by the eager reception of Hitler as Germany's Leader. But the question at stake concerns Hitler's motives, not those of Galen. Nor are the bishop's motives a key to determining the impact of Hitler's actions in this case. Rather, the question is why Hitler acted as he did, in response to the way that Galen acted. Galen's motives here did not matter, although his willingness to assist the regime in bringing his people into the service of the regime certainly did make a difference.

Burleigh conflates the pressure exerted by a "handful of bishops" with the pressures they represented, questioning the argument that "Galen's sermon had some direct effect upon Hitler's decision to order a 'halt' to the mass gassing of mental patients." But a focus on Galen's sermon misses the point of concern for the dictatorship. Popular opinion lent Galen's sermon force, as shown by the discussions by the highest Nazi officials as they considered how to punish the bishop. It is no doubt true that "euthanasia" was not halted due to "local difficulties with a handful of bishops," because the opinion that concerned the dictatorship had spread throughout the Reich. Far above local officials, Hitler himself had to make the decisions about Galen. The regional party leader in charge of Bishop Galen's diocese wanted to hang the bishop but was brushed off, as was Bormann. Hitler had to decide Galen's fate because popular unrest made the matter a pressing national concern.

It is also important to recognize the distinction that this image-sensitive dictatorship made between public objections and those in writing. Even Cardinal Adolf Bertram, leader of the Catholic bishops, had to wait five months before receiving a curt reply to his letter objecting to the confiscation of church property. His protest was beside the point since Germany was at war, he was told in 1941. On the other hand, Galen realized that to be effective he not only had to speak publicly, but also at the right moment. He could not, by simply preaching a sermon, reverse the direction in which the regime was heading at full pace. But with Moscow further from the Wehrmacht's grasp than anticipated, the dictatorship was confronted with popular unrest about euthanasia, which by August 1941 had been building for well over a year. Galen's sermon at this point had a greater impact because of these circumstances. Perhaps the bishop had heard that Himmler had closed the Grafeneck "euthanasia" center in December 1940—not because the regime had killed its quota of human beings, but, as Himmler wrote, because of popular agitation. Hitler considered Galen "a sly fox" among the bishops, not only because he mobilized opinion by speaking out, but also because he knew when to do so.[14]

A plausible challenge to the view that opinion pressured Hitler on "euthanasia" contends that Hitler issued the stop decree because the program's "teams of practiced murderers" were needed for the more urgent task of the genocide of the Jews. In July and August 1941, in fact, there were significant changes in the deployment of mobile killing squads, as they began slaughtering Jewish women and children regularly, rather than only Jewish men. Himmler was reportedly upset while witnessing a mass shooting in Minsk and decided to experiment with gas vans after his adjutant, Erich von dem Bach-Zelewski, worried that the deeply shaken shooters were being turned into "neurotics or savages."[15]

Himmler wanted to find other ways of killing large numbers of people at once, but his position doesn't mean that Galen's sermon, backed by popular sentiment, did not precipitate Hitler's halt order. Indeed, given the new, more widespread killings in 1941, the regime would have been less eager at this point to have the people talking about official mass murders. Further, it is not clear why the genocide of Jews would not have proceeded without the practiced murderers from euthanasia. The euthanasia program showed that ordinary men and women were quite willing to become killers and to learn how to do so at once. The technical skills of killing Jews in the new method for killing Jews in the East—Jews packed into vans and exposed to the vehicles' exhaust— were not hard to learn. Many of those carrying out euthanasia within the Reich did end up in Poland, playing a key role in the genocide of Jews with gas chambers by 1942. The period between then and Hitler's halt order was considerably longer than that needed to train new personnel. After all, the regime's first gas chamber had been conceived and invented, as well as built and demonstrated at the Brandenburg "euthanasia" killing center, within a period of several months.[16]

Key to the argument that the "euthanasia" murders were not stopped because of popular unrest is the argument that the regime had filled its quota, according to the notes taken as the head of the euthanasia program, Viktor Brack, spoke on October 9, 1939. These notes show Brack's calculations: one out of every one thousand Germans was sufficiently mentally ill to merit the "euthanasia" death sentence. Thus, he figured, "If one applies this to the population of the Greater German Reich, then one must reckon with 65,000–70,000 cases [of euthanasia]." This figure is used to explain Hitler's halt order, since "euthanasia" had claimed 70,273 victims by August 1941, when Hitler issued his halt.[17]

In this logic, Hitler had merely been waiting to pull the plug until Brack's rough-hewn estimate was reached. But such initial target figures (whether regarding victims of "euthanasia" or the Holocaust) were quickly adjusted and then readjusted. Brack's figure itself had been adjusted quickly upward, as later "expansion" was planned. By the autumn of 1940, the number of deaths expected due to euthanasia had been raised to between 130,000 and 150,000, according to Werner Blankenberg, Brack's chief associate. Blankenberg wrote on October 1, 1940: "30,000 finished. Further 100,000 to 120,000 are waiting. . . . The Führer gave the order. The law is ready. At present only clear cases, that is 100 percent ones, are being settled. Later an extension will take place." Target figures moved up and down, as they did for the genocide of Jews, reflecting the way the regime improvised to match what it perceived to be possible within the current context. Due to the challenges of social unrest the regime subsequently changed this target figure once again, lowering it in the face of friction to 100,000.[18]

Further, the laxity of Brack's instructions to the "assessors" for selecting the victims of "euthanasia" indicates why his initial target figure soon had to be adjusted. Brack's "65,000–70,000" figure could hardly represent a ceiling since it was calculated separately from the loose process he set down for selecting victims, which he also set down in October 1939. Brack instructed "assessors," whose job it was to select victims for "euthanasia" by viewing their files, that "assessments were to be drawn up so that in cases of doubt, or in marginal cases, the person should be included in the program." Brack's instructions, according to one assessor, were so inclusive that they "went beyond the bounds of medically justifiable criteria" that he mentioned. No assessor needed to fear sanctions for having identified too many to kill rather than too few.[19]

This free-wheeling selection process by assessors led to deaths in numbers that had little to do with Brack's initial target figure, tied as they were to calculations about the number of Germans who were mentally ill. In his October 1939 instructions to assessors, Brack stressed the importance of weeding out "useless eaters" (a subjective category much broader than the mentally ill). They had to be "removed from the food sector" so that the productive would eat first. The first patients killed at Grafeneck in early 1940 were schizophrenics, chosen alphabetically rather than by condition. In the summer of 1940 Bishop Wurm said "euthanasia" victims had been identified as "lunatics, feeble-minded, epileptics" and "inmates of old-age homes." A number of persons killed—taken from productive work on farms—were beyond even Brack's "useless eaters" category.[20]

Moreover, Hitler was not about to be restricted to Brack's notes or those of anyone else. He made decisions strategically as well as opportunistically. Regardless of how Brack conceived of the program in October 1939, "euthanasia" soon engulfed other categories of illnesses, along with those who, for whatever reason, were identified by the person doing the selecting as a burden on the economy, and some were killed as undesirable for other reasons.[21] The Nazi style of seeking out victims was opportunistic rather than legalistic, allowing room for either moving faster or more moderately toward Nazi goals, depending on circumstances.

Like other instances of free, popular mobilization of dissent in public, the Catholic Church struggle to retain crucifixes in its schools has received relatively little attention. Jeremy Noakes's 1978 study of the 1936 crucifix struggle in Oldenburg is still the most thorough investigation, although more recent work adds important perspective. Nevertheless, historians mention the crucifix struggles in passing; there is no comprehensive study identifying and then comparing these various struggles. Noakes's study concluded that the regime gave way to the protests against the removal of crucifixes only temporarily. "The main effect of the [protests against removing crucifixes] was a delaying one," he wrote. "Thus, whereas in Munich, Württemberg, the Saar-Palatinate and Rhineland areas denominational schools were abolished during 1936 and 1937 . . . in Oldenburg the authorities evidently felt obliged to move more circumspectly and waited until 1938. But the end result was the same." Noakes wrote that by 1938 the dictatorship "felt sufficiently strong" to simply issue an order declaring that all church schools were "thenceforth terminated."[22] This conclusion, despite Hitler's intentions, suggests that the regime did not care much about whether popular opinion had moved any closer to Nazi policy, but only whether it believed itself to be in a "sufficiently strong" position relative to the people to issue and presumably enforce a policy in the face of sustained popular protests.

The resurgence of church attendance during the war does show that Christianity and the observance of its important rituals could not be eliminated by decree if popular support was to be sustained. Further, as this book argues, the regime did not measure its success only by whether it had issued a policy in line with its ideology. As Noakes suggested, more study is necessary to reveal the sets of circumstances that prompted the regime "to move more circumspectly" in a variety of settings. Comparisons reveal motivations for protest as well: Bishop Maximilian Kaller's community in East Prussia shared a quality Noakes found among Oldenburg Catholics: "strong ties of solidarity" forged in "a tradition of resisting the dominance of Protestant[s]" surrounding them.[23]

ENDANGERED HISTORY? THE WITTEN PROTEST

The Witten and Rosenstrasse protests, examined in chapters VII and VIII, have attracted little attention in comparison with the popular opposition to euthanasia. The archetypal story that any mobilization of popular opposition was futile is consonant with the conclusion that parents had no choice about whether to send their children off on the dicta-torship's KLV evacuations. The interpretation finding that parents were "powerless," because noncompliance was met with state force, extended into the 1990s before being rebutted by research that took account of parents who refused, with impunity, to send their children away.[24]

An interpretive turn against an earlier consensus that Hitler and his circle backed away when confronted with popular opposition is il-lustrated by the changing portraits of the Witten events in the work of Richard J. Evans. In 1976, Evans began to interpret the Witten protests in a way that could cast light on the nature of power and resistance in the Third Reich, in line with his conclusion that year that Hitler backed down in response to popular resistance. "The regime gave in to the women's protests," he wrote, because it feared that "open resistance might have become very difficult to suppress without alienating not only the general populace but also the soldiers at the front." He explained that Nazi authorities feared the "rule-breaking" of women more than men and "kept a particularly close watch on the morale of women during the war." Further, "Women could be much more easily provoked into open resistance than men." Evans continued that histories of Nazi Ger-many had a "common feature" of "almost total neglect of the larger part of the population—the female part. . . . Yet no explanation of any fea-ture of German social history—least of all the rise of Hitler—that leaves out of consideration the larger part of the population can be considered adequate; and there are now [1976], at last signs that the realization of this fact is starting to make an impact at least on historians in Britain and the United States, though it has still to find widespread acceptance in Germany."[25]

In 2008, by contrast, Evans portrayed the Witten protest narrowly and in passing, rather than as anything that could shed light on overall conceptions of resistance and the regime, as he had done in 1976. There is no identification of the protest with women's or Catholic history in his 2008 work; certainly there is no description of the protest as successful resistance in the vein of the earlier Evans. Three decades after his first treatment of this event, he has dropped any mention of its significance with the suggestion that the protesters were not wiped from the square by armed force because the Witten police refused to follow directives to impose order.[26]

This police refusal reveals a degree of freedom, surprising in the context of the overall conclusions in Evans's recent works that the regime's terror intimidated the Germans into meek obedience. As the Witten protest shows, not only the local police but also the civilians did go against the regime's will, even during this waning phase of war. "The truth is that far from Nazi terror being leveled against small and despised minorities," Evans wrote in 2008, "the threat of arrest, prosecution and incarceration in increasingly brutal and violent conditions loomed over everyone in the Third Reich. . . . The regime intimidated Germans into acquiescence, visiting a whole range of sanctions upon those who dared to oppose it."[27] Evans's revised view of the Witten protest, in line with this general assessment of how the regime ruled, ignores recent scholarship that backs up his 1976 conclusion that this women's protest caused the regime to back down.

Since 2006 Julia Torrie has argued on the basis of context and sources that "the public action in Witten and elsewhere convinced policymakers that coercive measures could not be used to separate families and control civilian evacuations. . . . It confirmed that in some circumstances, public protests could make the leaders of the Third Reich change their minds. . . . Even a relatively spontaneous, small-scale protest was taken seriously by National Socialist leaders."[28] In 2015 Nicholas Stargardt wrote that the women protesting at Witten succeeded because they pointed out to the regime that it was not following the law. The women "expected the state to abide by the law and recognize the justice of their claims, and it indeed did," he wrote, identifying the Witten protest with "most kinds of wartime social conflicts" in which "people generally wanted the authorities to step in and put other categories of 'national comrades,' whom they accused of behaving unfairly, firmly in their place." Yet Nazi "authorities" played a range of conflicting, competing roles, just as the law in Nazi Germany often served different purposes beyond restricting the options of these authorities. The women were not concerned about the law, as their refusal to remain in their assigned evacuation shows, but about their families. The theme about strict Nazi regard for the law is illustrated in a further conclusion that the regime's refusal to promulgate a law to annul intermarriages "was key to Victor Klemperer's survival." After hearing about the problems of intermarriage at the Wannsee Conference, Interior Secretary Wilhelm Stuckart also thought that solving the intermarriage problem was as easy as writing a law. But the idea of a law was immediately brushed away by Nazi heavyweights, who pointed out that the issue was how to separate the persons in intermarriage without causing a disturbance and drawing attention to them. A law would not help.[29]

The use of the law for the Nazis is illustrated by Hitler's repeated rejection of all measures to codify euthanasia in law while also using the force of his authority to make sure it was carried out. He wanted to "euthanize" hundreds of thousands, but he did not want this to be codified in law during the war because that would reveal the facts too quickly to a public not yet ready to accept them.

Popular protest, brought to a head by Galen, stopped Hitler from achieving what he wanted. But whether protest brought Nazi practice into alignment with Nazi law is irrelevant. The written codes were transitory because the Nazi goal was to transfer the content and enforcement of law from codes to the normative behavior of the people. Thus under Hitler the law and the appearance of legality were used opportunistically. This characterized Hitler's dictatorship as well as his leadership before 1933. For Hitler's dictatorship, the written law was another tactic among many, to be deployed at particular times and places when it was the best method for building and sustaining the party's momentum toward the ultimate goal of embodying the law in the practice of the people.

Nazi theory allotted the people a fundamental role in politics, and Julia Torrie shows how popular protest slowed Nazi progress. Still such a thesis goes against the trend discounting the significance of the people's consent.[30] The "documentation" published in the early 1990s by the Workshop for Witten Women's History is painfully modest about the 1943 Witten protest, neglecting even to mention that the women got what they demanded. The workshop's call for eyewitnesses or information about the protest has not returned a single echo, as though it were too "daring," in the face of overwhelming popular and official opinion, to claim to have protested openly in Hitler's Germany in late 1943. In June 2007, Ralph Klein, a German historian from Witten, explained this reception:

> I have never, either in private or in public, heard about or read
> in the newspapers any discussion or report [on the Witten

protest in 1943]. Everything possible has been discussed: about the situation in the evacuation sites, about the bomb attacks, about how the war tore families apart. Also in my interviews with women, this topic was never broached. Because I myself first heard of [the protest] about four years ago, from Meldungen aus dem Reich [a collection of Nazi secret police reports], I was also of course unable to ask specifically about it. I would think that the protest of the women is not generally known, and in case it is, it would not be seen as particularly special. . . . I can't imagine that either the protesting women of October 1943, or the public, saw this as something extraordinary. The extraordinary is an interpretation imposed after the fact, because of the general perspective and claim that in National Socialism protests in such forms were not possible.[31]

By August 2015 Klein had still found no further archival traces of this Witten protest and no one in Witten who would talk about it. He had begun to question whether the SD had not fabricated its report of November 18, 1943, which described the Witten protest in detail. But of all the SD reports, those that go against what the dictatorship wanted to hear are most credible. Hitler read these biweekly reports regularly,[32] and if there was any falsification of records in an attempt to please Hitler, they would have hardly produced reports of hundreds of women protesting toward the end of the war. A much more likely explanation for the lack of traces on this incident is that the regime wished to cover up all signs of dissent, especially public protests against an unpopular program of evacuation, and after the war there were few if any receptive ears when anyone talked of bravely protesting, in the context of a belief that public protest was always met with imprisonment or execution.

Why would German historians concerned about the German past not hear about an SD report on the Witten Protest until 2003? The challenge now is to take unexamined documents into account so that we can explain how the regime operated in a way that provides a context for understanding these protests, rather than rejecting documents if they do not fit our perceptions.[33] Keeping an open mind keeps history alive and relevant.

ROSENSTRASSE AND PROTEST AMONG THE HISTORIANS
AND THE MEMORIALS

A clue to the lack of interest in the Witten protest comes from the observation by Ekehard Klausa on the Rosenstrasse protest. "It is a daring but
defensible thesis," he wrote, that "dependent on compliance especially
during war, the regime responded carefully to open and half-open criticism of its Jewish policies and may have even had to react by pulling
back. . . . It actually did this in response to Galen's sermons and the
women's protest on Rosenstrasse."[34] In an atmosphere where it is daring
to claim that a protest had an impact on the regime, who needs the additional challenge? Like the test subject in a Solomon Asch experiment, it
is much more expedient to agree with the crowd, regardless of what actually happened. Anyone who claimed to have gone on the streets in
protest during the Nazi years could be taken as a slap in the face by the
vast masses that collaborated or did nothing. Those who said they had
actually helped to influence the dictatorship through a street protest
would represent a reproach and be seen as troublemakers. They would
also be challenging the common wisdom passed down through the generations in the Federal Republic of Germany that public opposition was
futile, leading to punishment.

No German protest during the Nazi era has stirred more controversy than the one by German women for their Jewish husbands during
the late winter of 1943 in central Berlin.[35] After the war, a woman in
Berlin struggled to explain to her family that some "Aryan" women had
gathered on Berlin's Rosenstrasse to protest the imminent deportation
of their Jewish husbands. Many women had joined together, she said,
defiantly calling out together, despite repeated threats that they would
be shot if they did not clear the street. Five decades later, when this story
finally reached a widespread audience, the woman's nephew recalled that
he had silently scoffed at his aunt's story.

After all, the story ran against common and comforting perspectives, like those of soldiers in Hitler's army who were convicted by the
Nazis of army desertion and undermining morale. These objectors, who
in some cases had earned the enmity of the regime by helping Jews,
endured decades of difficulties in postwar society until the Bundestag
finally rehabilitated them in 2002. That parliament, however, refused to
rehabilitate those soldiers whom the Nazis had convicted of treason,

reasoning that they had perhaps actually harmed other Germans. This gave the benefit of the doubt to the Nazi regime's justice and was thrown into question in 2007 by a book suggesting that most had actually earned the regime's enmity by resisting.[36]

After 1945, many millions of Germans agreed that unarmed persons could not have protested openly. For decades after the war, even Germans who were extraordinarily concerned with Germany's World War II history had never heard of the protest on Berlin's Rosenstrasse in February and March 1943. Gerhard Schumm, filmmaker and professor emeritus at Germany's Babelsberg Film School, recalled that he and his friends first heard of the protest in an article published in 1989, with "astonishment and bafflement about our lack of knowledge. . . . For the first time something was extensively represented [from Nazi history] about which we had never heard or read anything."[37] For many postwar years, only very rare voices, in memoirs, diaries, or historical accounts, raised a muted signal in a sentence or short paragraph about the Rosenstrasse events. The strongest emerged immediately following the war.[38] At least four respected authors and historians writing during the 1960s and 1970s, however, briefly described the protest, and each made an uncontested conclusion that the protest had caused the Gestapo to release rather than deport the intermarried Jews arrested and imprisoned at the Jewish administration building at Rosenstrasse 2–4.[39]

In neither East nor West Germany did this conclusion fit into the dominating narrative framework about Nazi terror and the possibilities of resistance. Only the initiative of private persons and organizations brought the events on Rosenstrasse to light. In 1988, East German historian Konrad Kwiet departed from previous work by drawing conclusions about what a protest that had rescued Jews in 1943 could mean for understanding Nazi power and German society: "The successful result of the public protest suggests the assumption that similar actions could have directed the course of the National Socialist Jewish policies in other directions," Kwiet wrote.[40] This conclusion could hardly be reconciled with popular and scholarly portraits of the Nazi dictatorship, and it raised the question about what could be done with the interpretation that the protest had caused the Gestapo to temporarily change its course.

Kwiet had raised a logical challenge to mainstream interpretations about the possibilities of resistance and the regime's response. In July

1989, Germany's weekly, *Die Zeit,* published a seven-thousand-word "dossier" on the events that reached a broader audience. Several Germans launched documentary films, and, more important, a grassroots initiative, the Berlin History Workshop, increased interest.[41] Much of the passion resided in the fact that some ordinary Germans had actually stood up publicly and made demands, indicating that acts of opposition had not been only conspiratorial like the effort of the elite to kill Hitler, officially commemorated as the "German Resistance." In 1995, the diaries of Victor Klemperer were published, becoming an instant classic and drawing attention to another sometimes awkward truth: nearly all of the German Jews who had survived the war without being deported or going into hiding were married to non-Jews.

Confronted with the Rosenstrasse protest decades after it occurred, some historians responded with "easily detectible errors" and "inconsistencies in narrative," as though there were no established facts or "results of research," observed Antonia Leugers in 2005. In his 1988 history of German Jews, Wolfgang Benz identified the street protest as a topic of Jews surviving while in hiding, although two years later he enthused that the open protest was a "stunning success of resistance," but soon thereafter labeled as "legend" any conclusion that credited the protest with the release of Jews. Was the story so difficult to reconcile with existing accounts that it had to be pushed under the carpet or brandished as an indication that the Germans had really resisted after all? It continued to flummox historians, who categorized it in various ways. Gerd Ueberschär, as Leugers pointed out, identified the collectivity of the women with trade-union-like solidarity and placed the protest under the category of "Resistance in SPD and KPD Circles during the War!" Still today this history is misjudged when the "results of research" are overlooked. "Gerhard Beck was initially saved from deportation by the Rosenstrasse Protests," Nicholas Stargardt wrote.[42] But these results of protest were not just the initial ones. All but a very few of the Jews who were "saved from deportation by the Rosenstrasse protests" were never deported. Gad Beck was also never deported.

Wolf Gruner has undertaken a more serious effort to examine the Rosenstrasse protest in context. In 1995, he grounded his initial assessment that the protest could not have influenced the Gestapo in a concept of Nazi power. Protests were "obviously not the cause for the release of the Jews," he wrote, since "interpretations that such demonstrations could have hindered the deportation plans of the RSHA certainly do not hold up within the historical context." In a scholarly exchange in 2004, Gruner identified this apprehension further: considering the protest as influential carries "a danger of dramatically underestimating the supremacy *[Herrschaft]* of the Nazi regime." Beatte Meyer added in the same exchange that seeing the protest as influential leaves us with the question of "how the murder of Jews could actually happen, if it really only took seven days of standing fast *[Standhaftigkeit]* to hinder it."[43] In 1996 and 1997, Richard J. Evans hailed a new book arguing that the protest had caused the Gestapo to release the Jews with non-Jewish family members locked up on Rosenstrasse.[44] In 2002, Joschka Fischer, foreign minister for a German government with initiatives to teach the virtues of civil society, wrote an essay in praise of the protesters' courage and achievement.[45]

In 2005, in the context of what *Die Zeit* called a small historians' controversy about the Rosenstrasse events, historians published two books on the Rosenstrasse events with contrasting interpretations. Relying largely on evidence from his dissertation, Wolf Gruner adjusted his interpretation of the leeway in the Frankfurt/Oder decree of February 1943, at the center of his argument. Earlier he had concluded that this directive gave the Gestapo "carte blanche" to arrest intermarried Jews. Now in 2005, he wrote that this Frankfurt/Oder decree showed that the regime and its Gestapo had not intended to deport a single Jew during the massive roundups it called the "Elimination of Jews from the Reich," after which Goebbels hoped to declare Berlin "free of Jews." Rather, the Gestapo had merely intended, "very explicitly," to confirm the "racial" status of the Jews imprisoned and also to select 225 Jews to replace workers from the Jewish administration who had just been deported.[46]

An edited collection from Antonia Leugers, also in 2005, on the other hand, argued that the protest caused the Gestapo to release the intermarried Jews, and it introduced a considerable amount of new evidence. While some had written that the protests of church leaders deserved the credit, Leugers showed that the release of intermarried Jews was not due to their intervention. Also, already in 1943, well-informed church officials had attributed the release to the street protest. Joachim

Neander argued that while studies of the event had focused on Berlin and efforts there to push Jews from the Reich, there was also a pull by the SS in Auschwitz for the transfer of skilled German Jewish workers to meet the supply of workers because Himmler had promised IG Farben sufficient workers in exchange for building Auschwitz's "Camp IV." He demonstrated that in March 1943 the SS was expecting to receive Jewish workers from Berlin in a quantity that could only have been met by the deportation of some intermarried Jews.[47]

No one seriously denies that the regime's goal was to remove from Germany anyone wearing the Jewish Star, and it is hard to imagine any reason why Hitler—as well as the RSHA and not just Goebbels—would have preferred to wait to deport the Jews imprisoned at Rosenstrasse until some later point if they could move them at the present. But the stakes for the interpretation of these events were significant. In 2003, during a peak of controversy about it, the East German historian Kurt Pätzold backed the earlier conclusion of his colleague Kwiet. An argument that the protest had influence, he wrote, "strikes at the center of the historical perception of the character of the Nazi regime and the way it functioned and weighs on judgments about the possibilities for resistance."[48]

One possible obstacle to the development of study of public dissent in Nazi Germany is the dearth of sources. Is it possible that a protest the regime neither repressed nor wrote much about (so far as we know) could have significance? In this case the absence of evidence is not the same as evidence of absence, especially regarding the Holocaust and the matter of "racial" intermarriages; the regime wanted to hide the fact that such marriages existed, and deporting German Jews married to German Gentiles threatened the hiding of this fact, as well as the regime's ability to control conversations about the fate of the Jews.[49]

One criticism about work on the Rosenstrasse protest is that it relies on oral history rather than documents with a Gestapo stamp. Yet it is hardly possible to take the other staple sources of Third Reich history—Nazi documents—at face value or read a Gestapo directive as if events unfolded as they were ordered. Christopher Browning recently demonstrated the importance of using oral history to write an otherwise missing story of victims, perpetrators, and others. Just as we would be misled by official records of the October 7, 1944, "Sonderkommando uprising" at Auschwitz if we had no unofficial eyewitness reports, we are also often dependent on eyewitnesses for a picture of events of social protest.[50]

Since those who oppose the long-acknowledged interpretation of the Rosenstrasse demonstration cite Gruner's book of 2005, leaving to his critics any intensive engagement with the complete record of sources and arguments, it is possible to challenge the critics by critiquing Gruner's arguments.[51] Notions that public protests had rescued intermarried Jews were postwar inventions, Gruner wrote, and are "legends based on reports from survivors and subjective impressions."[52]

Gruner's interpretation has been widely criticized for various reasons.[53] Given Hitler's as well as Goebbels's desire to make Berlin free of Jews at this time, the burden of proof is high for any argument that the regime did not wish to deport Jews that it arrested and held for a week at Rosenstrasse. Why would the regime release these Jews once it had them locked up, in an arrest aiming to make Berlin free of Jews? If the Gestapo had planned only to check the "race" status of Berlin's intermarried Jews, why would it have checked only those it imprisoned—some two thousand, a figure that was less than one-quarter of the intermarried Jews living in Berlin? How could checking "racial" status and changing work assignments satisfy the regime's craving to clear Germany of Jews at that time? Gruner does not address such critical questions.

There is neither any precedent for—nor later examples of—thousands of Jews arrested during deportation roundups who were held for a week or more before being released in such large numbers. If imprisoning thousands at Rosenstrasse was the "simplest" way to select 225 persons for work, as Gruner writes, why was this approach not followed every time replacements were needed at the Jewish Community? Why were children and the elderly kept so long in the suffocating misery at Rosenstrasse if the regime was carefully searching out the best workers and if the Gestapo had not planned to deport a single intermarried Jew it had arrested?[54] Gruner writes that the Gestapo took children to the Rosenstrasse so they could be imprisoned with their parents. Joining the image of a Gestapo caring for the "half-Jewish" children in the midst of what it considered the final roundups in its historic mission to eradicate Jews is the claim that the Gestapo strictly forbade the deportation of every intermarried Jew at this point. This line that the Gestapo held everything in its grip and did exactly as it intended has led to the conclusion that the Gestapo itself is to be thanked for sparing the lives of persons it considered Jews and imprisoned at the Rosenstrasse.[55]

This legalistic interpretation of the dictatorship clashes with more common perspectives; the regime was especially opportunistic rather than fastidious about regulations when dealing with the Jews. The replacement of Jewish workers after deportations could hardly be the reason for a massive arrest and weeklong detention in horrible conditions that spurred a street protest since this was a routine matter handled by the Jewish authorities themselves, and it was repeated deportation after deportation—all amid intense pressure to reduce the number of Jewish employees.[56] Given its commitment to diverting attention away from its mass murder, as well as from the existence of intermarried couples, why did Nazi authorities not reassure the women as soon as they began protesting that their family members were going to be released, rather than attempting repeatedly to intimidate their protest with weapons and threats? Why didn't the regime punish the protesters for publicly protesting on behalf of Jews or, for that matter, merely for assembling in a crowd publicly, an act that was also forbidden? Above all, who or what was responsible for the regime's decision to defer the deportation of these Jews temporarily in the first place if not the "Aryans" married to Jews?[57]

The arguments to discredit long-held postwar interpretations come at the expense of the eyewitness victims, including Jews and their partners from intermarriages. If these interpretations comprise a "legend" that arose *after the war,* as Gruner has stated, what are we to make of the reports that connected protest and the release of Jews already in 1943, including those from Goebbels, Interior Minister Frick, Bishop Theophil Wurm, Dr. Margarete Sommer, and Dr. Gerhard Lehfeldt, not to mention the American OSS? Similarly perplexing is the allegation that the customary interpretation of events is "almost completely based on the statements of survivors." Given the regime's scrupulous attention to prohibiting and destroying records of collective public dissent, it is a wonder that even this documentation has survived, but not surprising that it did not survive in the form of SD reports.[58]

Critically, the documents showing that the Jewish Community employed prisoners from Rosenstrasse are merely descriptive; neither they nor any other documents show that the regime intended to imprison Jews for a week in order to check their status and select a fraction for promotions to white-collar jobs. The documents Gruner uses to argue that the regime wanted to register rather than deport these Jews simply describe what happened rather than saying this is what the regime intended. There is a chronological connection between the documents and events but not one of cause and effect. In fact, the job reassignments probably make more sense as an improvised response to circumstances, especially considering Goebbels's criticism on March 6, 1943, that those pressing for deportation, despite the protest, were slavishly following orders (Schema F) rather than adapting pragmatically to circumstances. This version of the events sees the regime as driven by preexisting plans written into orders and carried through flawlessly. Further, official documents are viewed as reflecting the authentic intentions of a regime infamous for exploiting deception as a primary means to achieve its ends. But Nazi trickery specifically within deportation directives is reflected in euphemisms as well as specific attempts to deceive.[59]

In 2013 Gruner published a book condensing his theses in eighty-eight generously illustrated pages. It came out under the auspices of Germany's Topography of Terror Memorial with a preface from the managing director, Rabbi Andreas Nachama, who wrote that his great-aunt had also protested on Rosenstrasse and had also believed that protesters had rescued their Jewish family members.[60] Citing "newer" work stating the regime did not want to deport any intermarried Jews at that time, Rabbi Nachama dismisses her interpretation. Nachama does agree that the fate of the Jews was in the hands of their marriage partners, however. He writes that the partners of Jews that "allowed themselves to be pressured into a divorce by the Gestapo made possible [the deportation of their Jewish partners]" because the Gestapo deported Jews if their non-Jewish partners agreed to divorce. Especially since 1938, the Gestapo had been attempting to intimidate these partners into a separation by summoning them to Gestapo offices one by one to threaten and humiliate them. Elsa Holzer remembered being left to sweat fearfully in the Gestapo office after she had rebuffed their demands, and only a sudden, terrible fear that the Gestapo was perhaps arresting her husband while she was away caused her to rush home without waiting for her interrogators to dismiss her.[61]

We have seen the repeated evidence that only the intermarried Gentiles stood between the Gestapo and their Jewish partners, as Nachama wrote. Given the historical context of so many efforts to intimidate these Aryans into agreeing to abandon their Jewish partners, it seems likely that the arrest and internment of Jewish family members at Rosenstrasse was yet another test, under a yet more heightened and imminent threat, to see whether these wives would finally relent and abandon their Jewish family members, in a building ringed by armed guards who repeatedly threatened that they would shoot if they did not leave the street. The brutal arrests on February 27 and 28 under the SS, which by some reports also guarded the building at Rosenstrasse 2–4 during those first two days that Jews were imprisoned there, however, were met by protesters showing that they were willing to put their own lives on the line.

The difference between the Gruner opinion in 2005 and the one in 2013 is that the later one is now guarded by Berlin's Topography of Terror, posing as official history, among a handful of publications prominently displayed for sale.[62] This status represents an enormous difference from the status of the protest seven years earlier: according to Gruner's 2005 book, the "majority of available statements today" are ambivalent about the Rosenstrasse events.[63] Perhaps ambivalence explains the obscurity of the Rosenstrasse events in Germany before the 1980s. But if this ambivalence endured at least until 2005, what can possibly explain the new utterly non-ambivalent status of the protest in the work of German historians—and Germany's most popular memorial and keeper of official memory, Berlin's Topography of Terror?

Apparently the interpretation of events at Rosenstrasse is so significant that it must be taken under the wing of a public site of memory, and it would be important to know what led to this new, resolutely unambiguous face of the past. There has not been much mention in the exhibits or public presentations of this custodian of German memory that alternative views about the Rosenstrasse events exist, and the testimonies from those wonderful Germans who protested have been absent. What discussions transpired between officials at Germany's war memorials and German historians to replace the ambivalent perspective with a single, sharply focused perspective? In fact, there is a flat denial that there has ever been a significant discussion about the interpretation

of the Rosenstrasse events, with an implication that it was proper to ignore the history for decades.[64]

But there is a plurality of understandings among Germans about
the Rosenstrasse events, including the young generation of Germans
from the Berlin History Workshop, whose dedication to the facts of events
led them to start a project that is now the Topography of Terror Memorial.[65] Why not allow debate instead of asserting that "newer" research
(based on a dissertation from 1995) has upended all previous interpretations? That would probably have been the preference of the great German philosopher Karl Jaspers. Speaking in 1946 of the Nazi past, he
suggested that it would be better to regard differences of opinion as starting points of conversation rather than as "finalities." "We must seek out
rather than shun attacks on us, because they enable us to check up on
our own thought. Our inner attitude will stand the test."[66]

These cooperative public protests by ordinary persons before and during
the war in Nazi Germany show that public opposition in some forms
pushed the regime into compromises and that public dissent also shaped
Hitler's decision making. These protesters pose the legitimate question
of whether more could have been done from within the Reich to stop
Hitler. This is a question no one can answer with certainty, but a usable
past from this dark period is expected to be challenging. The idea that
no German could exercise choice because of Gestapo terror should not
become so firmly entrenched that documents themselves are selected or
edited to match this false perspective. Five decades ago, young German
historians were beginning to challenge the comforting views about the
Nazis because they exculpated virtually everyone but Hitler. History is
always reexamined and rewritten, but a return to a less rich perspective
of seven decades ago would not be excusable now as it was then; following the war, guilt could only be acknowledged gradually as time carried
societies away from the war and the sharpest pangs of acknowledging
culpability. Today we can face the challenges.

NOTES

PREFACE

1. Richard Breitman, *Official Secrets: What the Nazis Planned, What the British and Americans Knew* (New York: Farrar, Straus, and Giroux, 1998), 61, 62; Raul Hilberg, *The Destruction of the European Jews* (New York: Holmes and Meier, 1985), 1008; Henry Friedlander, *The Origins of Nazi Genocide: From Euthanasia to the Final Solution* (Chapel Hill: University of North Carolina Press, 1995), 86.
2. Himmler speeches to SS leaders in Posen, October 4 and 6, 1943, Bundesarchiv (Berlin), NS 19/4010; International Military Tribunal (IMT), *Trial of the Major War Criminals: Proceeding Volumes*, 42 vols. (Nuremberg, November 14, 1945–October 1, 1946), 29:110–173, Document PS-1919 (Himmler's Posen speech to SS leaders).
3. Cited in Thomas Harding, *Hanns and Rudolf: The German Jew and the Hunt for the Kommandant of Auschwitz* (New York: Random House, 2013), 139, 302.
4. Cited in Maike Winters and Anne-Ruth Schüssler, "Führer's Bodyguard: Last Witness to Hitler's Final Hours Dies," *Der Spiegel*, September 6, 2013. http://www.spiegel.de/international/germany/hitler-bodyguard-rochus-misch-dies-at-the-age-of-96-a-920883.html (accessed September 7, 2013).
5. Himmler speeches to SS leaders in Posen, October 4 and 6, 1943.

INTRODUCTION

Epigraph: William L. Shirer, *Berlin Diary: The Journal of a Foreign Correspondent* (New York: Knopf, 1942), 17–19.
1. Early postwar explanations of the dictatorship emphasized terror: Hitler alone, or with a handful of henchmen to help, had forced the Germans to

follow against their will. Although the theme that Hitler ruled his own people primarily by force continued, subsequent explanations emphasized German support for the dictatorship. Totalitarian theory, dominating the 1950s, viewed Hitler and his circle as the seat of all power, and this theory also served to limit the visibility of oppositional mobilizations and the regime's response. Wolfgang Schieder surveys totalitarian historiography, tracing it back to the beginning of fascism in Italy, in "The Historian's Approach to Germany's National Socialist Past," in *Totalitarian and Authoritarian Regimes in Europe: Legacies and Lessons from the Twentieth Century*, ed. Jerzy W. Borejsza and Klaus Ziemer (New York: Berghahn Books, 2006), 140–144.

Hans Mommsen first used the description "weak dictator" in *Beamtentum im Dritten Reich* (Stuttgart: Deutsche Verlags-Anstalt, 1966), 98n2. Mommsen observed that the Nazi dictatorship initiated what he called a "cumulative radicalization," presented briefly in "Cumulative Radicalization and Self-Destruction of the Nazi Regime," in *Nazism*, ed. Neil Gregor (Oxford: Oxford University Press, 2000), 191–194. In this view, Hitler did not exert much effort to escalate anti-Jewish policies to genocide; internal structures pushed Hitler forward in a direction he signaled vaguely. Examples in this book, on the other hand, show Hitler intervening to preempt punishments against German-blooded persons for offenses or to de-escalate a course of punishment suggested by or begun by various Gauleiters (regional party leaders), the Reich Bishop, the Gestapo, Martin Bormann, and others. German labor policies during the late 1930s also showed a "partial de-radicalization of policy" that went "hand in hand with an accelerating, cumulative radicalization toward all 'community aliens.' . . . Precisely because the quasi-utopian visions of society were not pursued further in regard to the Volksgenossen, the regime was able to focus its energies on the persecution and destruction" of outsiders (see Kiran Klaus Patel, *Soldiers of Labor: Labor Service in Nazi Germany and New Deal America, 1933–1945* [Cambridge: Cambridge University Press, 2005], 403). Patel identifies several other examples of this de-radicalization in domestic policies, although these were not due to Hitler's direct intervention.

2. Vice Chancellor Franz von Papen, cited in Joachim C. Fest, *Plotting Hitler's Death: The Story of German Resistance* (New York: Metropolitan Books, 1996), 27.

3. Hitler's hero, Mussolini, was committed to a transformation of society from the inside, based on new myths. Emilio Gentile, *The Origins of Fascist Ideology 1918–1925* (New York: Enigma, 2005), 352–353; Gerhard L. Weinberg, *Germany, Hitler, and World War II: Essays in Modern German and World History* (Cambridge: Cambridge University Press, 1996), 45.

4. Hans Mommsen, "National Socialism—Continuity and Change," in *Fascism, a Reader's Guide: Analyses, Interpretations, Bibliography*, ed. Walter Laqueur (Berkeley: University of California Press, 1976), 200.

5. Popular denunciations illustrate one bottom-up practice that fueled the regime. A recent book advances the position that by the turn of the new millennium, interpretations from the "bottom up" had been pushed too far relative to "top down" perspectives: Paul Corner, ed., *Popular Opinion in Totalitarian Regimes: Fascism, Nazism, Communism* (Oxford: Oxford University Press, 2009). See especially Ian Kershaw's contribution in this collection, "Consensus, Coercion, and Popular Opinion in the Third Reich: Some Reflections," 33–46, esp. 36.

6. Robert Rhodes James, ed., *Churchill Speaks: Winston S. Churchill in Peace and War: Collected Speeches, 1897–1963* (New York: Chelsea House, 1980), 909.

7. On Hitler's role in propaganda, see Jeffrey Herf, *The Jewish Enemy: Nazi Propaganda during World War II and the Holocaust* (Cambridge, MA: Belknap Press of Harvard University Press, 2006), 13, 14. A basic principle for Hitler was that the people must always be propelled forward by the party, with a momentum that never ceased. Jeremy Noakes, "Leaders of the People? The Nazi Party and German Society," *Journal of Contemporary History* 39, no. 2 (April 2004): 192. Adolf Hitler, *Speeches and Proclamations*, 4 vols., ed. Max Domarus (Wauconda, IL: Bolchazy-Carducci, 1990), 2:702.

8. On Stalin, see Stephen Kotkin, *Stalin*, vol. 1: *Paradoxes of Power, 1878–1928* (New York: Penguin Press, 2014), 424–425, 568, 724–727. Political scientist Daniel Treisman elaborates on the concept of "soft authoritarianism" in *The Return: Russia's Journey from Gorbachev to Medvedev* (New York: Free Press, 2011), 352. "Above all, the new autocrats use violence sparingly. This is their key innovation" (Sergei Guriev and Daniel Treisman, "The New Dictators Rule by Velvet Fist," *New York Times*, May 25, 2015, A19). The definition of "soft" in this case is used to distinguish it from the "realist" identification of power with brute force. The concept is related to "soft power," a theory now prevalent in political science (international relations). Joseph S. Nye Jr., *Soft Power: The Means to Success in World Politics* (New York: Public Affairs, 2004). No doubt some historians will be dismayed by the introduction of a theory from political science. I agree that it is analytically weak and that historians should continue to rely heavily on a close examination of primary sources and lightly on theories. (See the last section of the conclusion for more on this position.) However, as a category, the "soft dictator" is not as complicated as Hans Mommsen's "weak dictator," nor does it play down Hitler's role and Nazi ideology. Rather the "soft" designation is judged by a mere examination of tactics.

9. SA prisons killed at least 500–600 during 1933. Ian Kershaw, *Hitler, 1889–1936: Hubris* (New York: W. W. Norton, 2000), 501. Robert Gellately and Nathan Stoltzfus, "Social Outsiders and the Construction of the Community of the People," and Nicholaus Wachsmann, "From Indefinite Confinement to Extermination: 'Habitual Criminals' in the Third Reich," in *Social Outsiders in Nazi Germany,* ed. Robert Gellately and Nathan Stoltzfus (Princeton: Princeton University Press, 2001), 165; M. Wildt, *Hitler's Volksgemeinschaft and the Dynamics of Racial Exclusion* (New York: Berghahn, 2012).

10. Adolf Hitler, *Mein Kampf, Complete and Unabridged, Fully Annotated*, ed. John Chamberlain, Sidney B. Fay, et al. (New York: Reynal and Hitchcock, 1939), 80–81.

11. On the need for majority support as a prerequisite for using force to stabilize support, see ibid., 764–765. The extent to which *Mein Kampf* is a trustworthy source is debated. Ian Kershaw concluded that "Hitler was frequently inaccurate or careless with detail in the autobiographical parts of *Mein Kampf*" (*Hubris*, 7). In this book I refer to sections of *Mein Kampf* if they are verified by Hitler's practices between 1925 and 1945. Hitler made notoriously inconsistent statements, and his mind did shift in some ways over the course of his dictatorship. He is well known for his violent mood swings, which increased under the strains of war. He also increasingly believed that he was predestined to be a history-shaping leader, even as he also feared a premature death that would rob him of a monumental impact. His hypochondria increased as his health deteriorated, beginning in 1941, and after another turn for the worse in 1943, he had become very ill by 1944. His daily doses of pills and injections must have affected his judgment as well, although his "mental capacity" probably remained unimpaired even through the last phase of the war. Ian Kershaw, *Hitler, 1936–1945: Nemesis* (New York: W. W. Norton, 2000), 612. Through it all, until some point in his bunker late in the war, he retained his need for adulation, along with a fundamental belief that his fortunes rested on the efforts of the German people.

   On Gauleiters, see Walter Ziegler, "Gaue und Gauleiter im Dritten Reich," in *Nationalsozialismus in der Region: Beiträge zur regionalen und lokalen Forschung und zum internationalen Vergleich*, ed. Horst Möller, Andreas Wirsching, and Walter Ziegler (Munich: Oldenbourg, 1996), 139. On rival Gauleiter definitions of "race purity" that Hitler tolerated despite Himmler's entreaties, see Catherine Epstein, *Model Nazi: Arthur Greiser and the Occupation of Western Poland* (New York: Oxford University Press, 2010).

12. Michael Wildt, *An Uncompromising Generation: The Nazi Leadership of the Reich Security Main Office* (Madison: University of Wisconsin Press, 2009). On World War II, see Hannes Heer and Klaus Naumann, eds., *War of Extermination: The German Military in World War II, 1941–1944* (New York: Berghahn Books, 2000). Jacques Semelin, *Purify and Destroy: The Political Use of Massacre and Genocide* (London: Hurst, 2007), 170. Michael Thad Allen, *The Business of Genocide: The SS, Slave Labor, and the Concentration Camps* (Chapel Hill: University of North Carolina Press, 2002). On conquered territories, see Mark Mazower, *Hitler's Empire: How the Nazis Ruled Europe* (New York: Penguin Press, 2008).

13. The Gestapo valued an image of professionalism over brute force, and Heydrich ordered his men to exercise restraint in dealing with Germans. J. Ryan Stackhouse, "Gestapo Interrogations: Myths and Realities," in *Interrogation in War and Conflict: A Comparative and Interdisciplinary Analysis,* ed. Christopher Andrew and Simona Tobia (New York: Routledge, 2014), 79, 82–83, 87.

14. On Hitler's image, see Kershaw, *Hubris,* 484. Hitler and the leadership preferred propaganda to prevent dissent but could compromise if propaganda
did not work. As Hitler observed, it was "clever" to evade "a struggle where it
can be avoided," rather than confronting head on with force (cited in H. R.
Trevor-Roper, ed., *Hitler's Table Talk, 1941–1944* [New York: Enigma Books,
2007; orig. 1953], 47, entry for October 14, 1941).

15. "Currently we are on the best path to bending the will of the state to the will
of the people. . . . The state may never, against its better insight, give in to
the pressure of the street," since each time the state gave in, it lost more
power. Joseph Goebbels, *Die Tagebücher von Joseph Goebbels,* ed. Elke
Fröhlich (Munich: K. G. Saur, 1993–1996), part II, 10:222, entry for November 2, 1943. (See chapter VII below.)

16. This mechanism of popular displacement of blame on Hitler in order to protect the people's belief in Hitler is a theme in Ian Kershaw, *The "Hitler
Myth": Image and Reality in the Third Reich* (New York: Oxford University
Press, 1987). My research does not change the basic paradigm of the "Hitler
Myth" as defined by Kershaw but adds perspective by examining the dimen-
sion of Hitler's willingness to compromise in ruling his people due to a recognition of the limits of brute force. See also 336n75.

17. As I learned from one student exam, a number of editions of "Just the Facts,
E-Study Guide" assure students that "The historian Richard J. Evans translated the term *[Gleichschaltung]* as 'forcible coordination' in his most recent
work on Nazi Germany." An online search showed this definition was repeated
in nine different "e-study" guides (available online for $14.95) that promised
"just the facts" for students facing a test the next day. Each had a publication
date of 2012. I referred the students instead to definitions in line with those
from Ian Kershaw, reflecting other contemporaneous and scholarly sources:
"[Gleichschaltung] was for the most part undertaken voluntarily and with
alacrity" (Kershaw, *Hubris,* 435).

18. Hitler, *Speeches,* 2:717, October 8, 1935, inaugurating the October 1935 Winter
Relief program. On "living practice," see Dagmar Reese, *Growing Up Female
in Nazi Germany* (Ann Arbor: University of Michigan Press, 2006), 8. From
the beginning the regime did not aim simply to "suppress opposition and
dissent" but to "encourage active acceptance of the regime's policies and
their implementation in daily life" (Jill Stephenson, *Women in Nazi Germany*
[Harlow, England: Longman, 2001], 89). On promiscuity, see Dagmar Herzog, "Hubris and Hypocrisy, Incitement and Disavowal," in *Sexuality and
German Fascism,* ed. Dagmar Herzog (New York: Berghahn Books, 2005),
8–9. Nazi sexual ethics went against traditional opinion, as some in charge
at camps run by the Hitler Youth demonstrated, by binding the hands of
masturbating boys in thick gloves. Michael H. Kater, *Hitler Youth* (Cambridge, MA: Harvard University Press, 2004), 47. The "national conscience"
quote is from Joseph Goebbels, "Kriegsweihnacht," in *Der steile Aufstieg. Reden und Aufsätze aus den Jahren 1942/43* (Munich: Franz Eher, 1944), 90. On

the peculiar Nazi perspective on sacrificial death late in the war, see Michael Geyer, " 'There Is a Land Where Everything Is Pure: Its Name Is Land of Death': Some Observations on Catastrophic Nationalism," in *Sacrifice and National Belonging in Twentieth-Century Germany,* ed. Greg Eghigian and Matthew Paul Berg (College Station: Texas A&M University Press, 2002), 118–147.

19. Hitler, *Speeches,* 2:636, January 30, 1935. At various points Hitler spoke of phases and stages of Nazi development. See ibid., 1:403, December 31, 1933, and 2:644, March 1, 1935. Others in Hitler's circle, including Himmler, also spoke of a "transitory period" (Thomas Kühne, *Belonging and Genocide: Hitler's Community, 1918–1945* [New Haven: Yale University Press, 2010], 33, 35). On Gürtner, see Claudia Koonz, *The Nazi Conscience* (Cambridge, MA: Harvard University Press, 2003), 174.

20. Even as his party condemned Weimar's parliamentary system, Hitler put aside or marginalized some parts of the Nazi program to gain a foothold in power within that system. Robert Paxton, *Anatomy of Fascism* (New York: Knopf, 2004), 18–19. Hitler made opportunistic compromises with German conservatives and then broke away from this alliance after the conservatives were no longer important as partners. Wolfgang Schieder, *Geschichte: Faschismus-Leibeigenschaft* (Freiburg: Herder and Herder, 1974), 41–42; Hitler pursued goals in war and foreign policy set by ideology, but his methods for achieving these goals have been viewed as very flexible. Schieder, "The Historian's Approach to Germany's National Socialist Past," 145. During the war, Jewish soldiers served in armies affiliated with the Reich, and Hitler maintained alliances with countries that refused to surrender their Jews. As German victories turned to defeat, the dictatorship traded Jews in exchange for war supplies, and during 1945 Jews were spared execution as potential forces in Germany's desperate cause. Gerhard L. Weinberg, *Hitler's Foreign Policy, 1933–1939,* rev. ed. (New York: Enigma Books, 2005), 38, 42n100, 102, 636–637. See also Gerhard L. Weinberg, *A World at Arms: A Global History of World War II* (Cambridge: Cambridge University Press, 2005), 672, 783, 839–840. On foreign labor, see Ulrich Herbert, *Geschichte der Ausländer, Beschäftigung in Deutschland, 1880 bis 1980: Saisonarbeiter, Zwangsarbeiter, Gastarbeiter* (Berlin: J. H. W. Dietz, 1986), 135–141. When the German drive to capture Moscow ground to a halt by December 1941, Hitler authorized the conscription of Soviet civilians and prisoners of war by early November 1941—in the face of the lengthy opposition of ideologues arguing that Nazi racial ideals could not be compromised in this way. The German debacle at Stalingrad unleashed a brutal conscription of some 2.5 million more *Ostarbeiter.* Foreign laborers violated its ideology but allowed the regime to fulfill the Nazi political-ideological goal of maintaining living standards along with the loyalty of the German people.

21. H. R. Trevor-Roper, "The Mind of Adolf Hitler," in Trevor-Roper, *Hitler's Table Talk,* xxxi. The dictatorship sought to change the way the Volk

thought. Yehuda Bauer, "Overall Explanations, German Society, and the Jews or: Some Thoughts about Context," in *Probing the Depths of German Anti-Semitism: German Society and the Persecution of the Jews, 1933–1941,* ed. David Bankier (New York: Berghahn Books, 2000), 16. See also Hitler, *Speeches,* 1:517, August 6, 1934.

22. Kershaw, *Nemesis,* 94, 273.

23. "This process of transformation and approach will not be finished in ten or twenty years, but experience shows that it will take many generations." Hitler, *Mein Kampf,* 472. Hans V. Kaltenborn and Adolf Hitler, "An Interview with Hitler, August 17, 1932," *Wisconsin Magazine of History* 50, no. 4, Unpublished Documents on Nazi Germany from the Mass Communications History Center (Summer 1967): 288. An "inner regeneration" of Prussians had taken more than a century. "It took more than 150 years until Prussia, the germ cell of a new Empire, arose out of the old disintegrated Empire to fulfill its historic mission. And believe me: the question of the inner regeneration of a Volk is no different in the least" (Hitler's speech before the Industry Club in Düsseldorf, January 27, 1932; Hitler, *Speeches,* 1:110).

24. Dietrich Orlow, *The Nazi Party, 1919–1945: A Complete History* (New York: Enigma, 2008), 425.

25. Hess to Reich leaders and Gauleiters, Memorandum 82/37, June 30, 1937, Bundesarchiv, R 187/245, 153. Ernst Helmreich, *The German Churches under Hitler: Background, Struggle, and Epilogue* (Detroit: Wayne State University Press, 1979), 24, 213. The Hess memo was circulated by the head of the SS Main Office on July 15, 1937. On Rosenberg, see Hitler's speech to the Gauleiters, February 2, 1934; cited in Jeremy Noakes and Geoffrey Pridham, eds., *Nazism, 1919–1945,* vol. 2: *State, Economy and Society, 1933–1939* (Exeter: University of Exeter Press, 2000), 40–42. Trevor-Roper, *Hitler's Table Talk,* 418–419, entry for July 4, 1942. On Rosenberg: "I still think it was a great mistake that Rosenberg ever let himself be drawn into a battle of words with the Church. He had absolutely nothing to gain from it; the hesitant Catholics of their own free will regarded the Church with a critical eye and from the truly devout not only could he expect no fair hearing for his 'heretical outpourings,' but must also have realized that the opposition propaganda would condemn him for his meddling in matters of faith and successfully point to him as a man of moral sin" (Trevor-Roper, *Hitler's Table Talk,* 418–419, entry for July 4, 1942).

26. Hitler, *Mein Kampf,* 366; Trevor-Roper, *Hitler's Table Talk,* 49, entry for October 14, 1941. Hitler's table talks too must be checked against the record of his actions. Richard C. Carrier, "Hitler's Table Talk—Troubling Finds," *German Studies Review* 26, no. 3 (October 2003): 563.

27. Goebbels, *Tagebücher,* part II, 3:545–546, entry for March 25, 1942.

28. Andrew Wackerfuss gives a new account of "backlash" against SA bullying in *Stormtrooper Families: Homosexuality and Community in the Early Nazi*

Movement (New York: Harrington Park Press, 2015), 303–310. I do not closely examine the motivations and milieus of popular unrest. Milieu studies of churches, becoming prominent in the 1990s, have directed attention toward motivations and definitions of resistance and away from the regime's response. On Catholicism, see Markus Huttner, "Milieukonzept und Widerstandsdebatte in der deutschen zeitgeschichtlichen Katholizismusforschung—ein kritischer Kommentar," in *The Challenge of Dictatorship/Die Herausforderung der Diktaturen: Catholicism in Germany and Italy from 1918 to 1943/45/Katholizismus in Deutschland und Italien 1918–1943/45*, ed. Wolfram Pyta et al. (Berlin and New York: Walter de Gruyter–Max Niemeyer Verlag, 2009), 233–248.

29. Noakes and Pridham, *Nazism, 1919–1945*, 2:40–42. Hitler, *Mein Kampf*, 223. On "people leadership," historians have likened Nazism's appeal to that of religion. See Michael Burleigh, *The Third Reich: A New History* (New York: Hill and Wang, 2000). "National Socialism is in fact not a religion, but it can become one someday under the impact of very powerful national experiences," Goebbels wrote. "But one can't decree this from a writing desk; it must instead spring from the creative energies of the people itself" (*Tagebücher*, part II, 2:500, entry for December 13, 1941). In Hitler's thinking, war also had the benefit of facilitating popular unity. Two ways for "uniting a people" were "common ideals and common crime," Hitler said in 1923 (quoted in Thomas Kühne, *Belonging and Genocide: Hitler's Community, 1918–1945* [New Haven: Yale University Press, 2010], v). Hitler aimed to entangle the Germans with a sense of complicity.

30. Peter Longerich, *Heinrich Himmler: A Life* (Oxford: Oxford University Press, 2012), 262, 265–269. "We must persuade our people [in cases to] have sons [because without this] moral anchoring we will not be able to overcome Christianity" (Heinrich Himmler, *Geheimreden 1933 bis 1945 und andere Ansprachen* [Berlin: Ullstein, 1974], 160–161). Even agencies of Himmler's SS itself used "tactical moderation," and Nazi policy regarding the churches was "flexible and always determined by tactical necessity," according to Elias Füllenbach, "Shock, Renewal, Crisis: Catholic Reflections on the Shoah," in *Antisemitism, Christian Ambivalence, and the Holocaust*, ed. Kevin P. Spicer (Bloomington: Indiana University Press, 2007), 222. John S. Conway, *The Nazi Persecution of the Churches, 1933–34* (Toronto: Ryerson Press, 1968), 225.

31. Trevor-Roper, *Hitler's Table Talk*, 484, entry for August 20, 1942. On Gürtner, see Koonz, *Nazi Conscience*, 172–177. The popular acceptance of the Night of the Long Knives murders illustrates the early progress the party had made in its ability to claim that law was expressed simply by the "healthy sentiment of the Volk" (Kershaw, *Hubris*, 501, 520). The National Socialist concept of law posited that these "healthy sentiments" themselves would form "the true and unique source of legitimate law" (Frank Caestecker and David Fraser, "The Extraterritorial Application of the

Nuremberg Laws: *Rassenschande* and 'Mixed' Marriages in European Liberal Democracies," *Journal of the History of International Law* 10, no. 1 [2008]: 40).

32. Hitler's speech to the Gauleiters, February 2, 1934; an English translation of a summary is cited in Noakes and Pridham, *Nazism, 1919–1945*, 2:40–42. See the German original in Martin Broszat, *The Hitler State: The Foundation and Development of the Internal Structure of the Third Reich* (London: Routledge, 1981), 209–210. On Wagner, see Orlow, *The Nazi Party, 1919–1945*, 425.

33. See chapter III, 77.

34. "Stenographic Report for a Meeting on the Jewish Question under Goering at the Reich Aviation Ministry on November 12, 1938," in International Military Tribunal (IMT), *Trial of the Major War Criminals: Proceeding Volumes*, 42 vols. (Nuremberg, November 14, 1945–October 1, 1946), 28:534, Document 1816-PS. Relatively widespread awareness of mass murder did little to dim admiration for Hitler, according to Eric Johnson and Karl-Heinz Reuband, *What We Knew: Terror, Mass Murder and Everyday Life in Nazi Germany* (New York: Basic Books; London: John Murray, 2005).

35. See chapter VII, 209–211.

36. Protests increased during the war but were not treated more harshly than before the war. Jill Stephenson, "Women and Protest in Wartime Nazi Germany," in *Protest in Hitler's "National Community": Popular Unrest and the Nazi Response*, ed. Nathan Stoltzfus and Birgit Maier-Katkin (New York: Berghahn Books, 2015), 20–21, 33. William Sheridan Allen, *The Nazi Seizure of Power: The Experience of a Single German Town, 1930–1935* (Chicago: Quadrangle Books, 1965), 301, found that even during "the depths" of Nazi rule, popular opinion forced Nazi leaders "to accept the reality" of existing attitudes.

37. Robert Paxton stresses that populism—in particular ultranationalist populism—is a core characteristic of fascism as an "ideal type" (*Anatomy of Fascism*, 21). On mobilization, see Alexander Watson, *Ring of Steel: Germany and Austria-Hungary in World War I* (New York: Basic Books, 2014), 3–4, 78. Hitler's worlds: "If it is said that a man's world is the State . . . a woman's world is a smaller one. . . . The large world is built upon this small world! This greater world cannot survive if the small world is not firm. Providence assigned to woman the care of this, her very own world, and it is only on this foundation that the man's world can be formed and can grow" (Hitler, *Speeches*, 1:534, September 8, 1934).

38. Hitler, *Mein Kampf*, 246.

39. Richard Bessel, "Catastrophe and Democracy: The Legacy of the World Wars in Germany," in *Working towards the Führer: Essays in Honour of Sir Ian Kershaw*, ed. Anthony McElligott and Tim Kirk (Manchester: Manchester University Press, 2003), 22.

40. Goebbels was concerned that the churches, by holding ceremonies for Germans who had died on the war front, were winning converts. The churches should not receive the credit since, after all, "those who fell did not die for a

Church but for Germany" (Bundesarchiv, NS 18/112, to all Gauleiters, August 13, 1940). See also Guenter Lewy, *The Catholic Church and Nazi Germany* (Cambridge, MA: Da Capo Press, 2000), 253.

41. Hitler, *Speeches*, 3:2087. Shelley O. Baranowski, *Strength through Joy: Consumerism and Mass Tourism in the Third Reich* (New York: Cambridge University Press, 2004); Götz Aly, *Hitlers Volksstaat: Raub, Rassenkrieg und nationaler Sozialismus* (Frankfurt am Main: Fischer, 2005).

42. On army retreat, see R. A. C. Parker, *Struggle for Survival: The History of the Second World War* (Oxford: Oxford University Press, 1989), 107–108. Hitler's belief that the home front was of such fundamental concern is confirmed by the account of Hitler's valet: "Goebbels was much more firm and committed on this [total war] than Hitler. If Hitler had given in, total war would certainly have begun in the winter of 1941" (Heinz Linge, *With Hitler to the End: The Memoirs of Adolf Hitler's Valet,* trans. Geoffrey Brooks [New York: Skyhorse Publishing, 2009], 86).

43. Alan Milward's conclusion that Hitler repressed total war measures due to anxiety about the popular reaction to their effect on the economy holds even if other centers of power in the Reich were planning for "total war" as early as 1939 or even 1936 (*The German Economy at War* [London: Athlone Press, 1965], 8–11). Despite the high levels of mobilization in Germany, Hitler's refusal to mobilize women stands out in contrast to the stance of Germany's democratic enemies.

44. Gerhard L. Weinberg, "Comments on the Papers by Friedlander, Breitman, and Browning," *German Studies Review* 17, no. 3 (October 1994): 509.

45. On Galen and Catholic statements supporting the war in September 1941, see chapter VI. For a study of the exercise of power by a withholding of the resort to force in England two centuries earlier, see Douglas Hay, "Property, Authority and the Criminal Law," in *Albion's Fatal Tree: Crime and Society in Eighteenth-Century England,* ed. Douglas Hay, Peter Linebaugh, John G. Rule, E. P. Thompson, and Cal Winslow (New York: Pantheon Books, 1976), 17–64.

46. On strikes, see Timothy W. Mason, "Massenwiderstand ohne Organisation: Streiks in faschistischen Italien und NS-Deutschland," in *Aufstieg Nationalsozialismus, Untergang der Republik, Zerschlagung der Gewerkschaften,* ed. Ernst Breit (Cologne: Bund-Verlag, 1984), 202. The global history of mass extermination shows that because genocide itself frequently stirs unrest, perpetrators exempt certain persons from the targeted group: "To defuse dissent, divide opposition, or concentrate maximum force, selected members of groups from a targeted community may be spared, singled out for preferential treatment, or even enlisted in the cause" (Ben Kiernan, *Blood and Soil: A World History of Genocide and Extermination from Sparta to Darfur* [New Haven: Yale University Press, 2008], 34).

47. On death penalties, see Richard J. Evans, *Rituals of Retribution: Capital Punishment in Germany, 1600–1987* (Oxford: Oxford University Press, 1996),

917; Marlis G. Steinert, *Hitler's War and the Germans: Public Mood and Attitude during the Second World War,* trans. T. E. J. de Witt (Athens: Ohio University Press, 1977), 229.

48. Hitler, *Mein Kampf,* 129. A number of public demonstrations, not examined here, occurred during the last several months of 1945, whether in opposition to the demands of the newly created Volkssturm militia or to convince local leaders to surrender a city rather than face utter destruction at the hands of the Soviet Army.

   On escalating violence: the Nazi leadership reacted ferociously against "disobedience or dissent, especially in later wartime Germany" (Stephenson, *Women in Nazi Germany,* 109). Martin Broszat wrote that there was "an acceleration of violence and terror" as the war advanced ("A Social and Historical Typology of the German Opposition to Hitler," in *Contending with Hitler: Varieties of German Resistance in the Third Reich,* ed. David Clay Large [Cambridge: Cambridge University Press, 1992], 26). Broszat classified the German resistance in three stages to support a claim that "acts and attitudes of opposition . . . were often dependent upon the rule played by the Nazi authorities at a particular time" and that "significant and fundamental resistance arose only in the initial and final phases of Nazi rule."

49. "Now a fanatical fight begins, which recalls our struggle for power," Hitler said on April 16. "However great the superiority of our enemies may be at this moment, it will in the end break" (cited in Albert Speer, *Inside the Third Reich: Memoirs by Albert Speer* [New York: Macmillan, 1970], 405, 440). In early March 1945, Hitler said that "If the war is lost, the people will also be lost," according to Speer; Hitler repudiated all thoughts of defeat (Hitler, *Speeches,* 4:2907, July 3, 1944, and 4:2992, January 1, 1945). "There is a tremendous difference between the Germany of 1920 and that of 1945. Back then, it was a nation completely paralyzed—today, it is a military Volk fighting with the utmost fanaticism" (Hitler, *Speeches,* 4:3015, February 24, 1945); Hitler to Karl Holz, deputy to Gauleiter Julius Streicher, April 16, 1945 (Hitler, *Speeches,* 4:3041).

   A date for Hitler's surrender of a belief in a possible German victory cannot be established. Ideological training for soldiers in 1944 stressed repelling all thoughts of defeat, while the creation of the Volkssturm in October 1944 marked the culmination of the drive for total war accompanied by an expectation that the people would sacrifice everything they still had for the regime. But Hitler continued to solicit the people's sacrifice rather than turning to coercion; perhaps acknowledging defeat, he abandoned plans in March 1945 to evacuate Germany's western borders when the people began to greet rather than fight Allied armed forces.

50. SD report, July 8, 1943, vol. 14, 5448. This was printed in "Der Führer darf das gar nicht wissen: Aus den Stimmungs-Analysen des nationalsozialistischen Sicherheitsdienstes von 1939 bis 1943," *Der Spiegel* 51 (December 15, 1965), 83. Press coverage of crucifix struggles was also banned (see chapter

V). On the credibility of SD reports: generally, SD reports that are negative about Germany's situation are considered to be more credible than those that are positive, especially toward the end of the war. Hitler was unwilling to acknowledge the full extent of the souring popular mood as Germany's situation in the war grew more dire, so SD reports may have abandoned objectivity in order to please the Leader. See Kershaw, "Consensus, Coercion, and Popular Opinion," 38.

51. Concessions to workers are well established by historians focusing on the working class. Nazi labor policy was "an anxious attempt to diminish the risks of political disaffection among workers by making social and welfare concessions" (Detlev Peukert, *Inside Nazi Germany: Conformity, Opposition, and Racism in Everyday Life* [New Haven: Yale University Press, 1987; orig. 1982], 31). Some historians have concluded that the regime's willingness to make concessions to the workers was unique. Hitler's concessions to the laborers prevented a larger revolt by that class, argued Timothy Mason, since the dictatorship's anxiety about alienating workers limited its willingness to coerce their cooperation with force (*Nazism, Fascism and the Working Class* [New York: Cambridge University Press, 1995], 23, 119–120). It constituted "an entirely different order of importance" for the regime because it "potentially endangered the stability of the regime and the accomplishment of its aims." Thus "the sensitivity shown towards the working class was not matched by similar regard for opinion in other social groups" (Kershaw, "Consensus, Coercion, Popular Opinion," 375, 380). Some have argued that the dictatorship responded to crimes by German women more leniently than to crimes by men, although the evidence for this claim does not take account of the kind of mass, open dissent under discussion here, which is a different phenomenon from that of other "crimes" for which Germans were punished in a regime so sensitive to public representations.

52. "Why should I nationalize the industries? I will nationalize the people" (cited in John Lukacs, *The Hitler of History* [New York: Vintage Books, 1997], 92, noting that this quote attributed to Hitler by former Nazi Hermann Rauschning reflects Hitler's thinking).

53. Although structural conditions facilitated Hitler's charismatic rule, Hitler was indispensable for the Nazi dictatorship, and Hitler's sense of mission and his perceived basis of authority correspond to an extent with Max Weber's terms, which identify "charisma" as inherently unstable and according to which Hitler's dictatorship was bound to remain unstable and finally fail because it did not develop structures to routinize his leadership, such as an accepted successor (Max Weber, "Charisma and Its Transformation," in *Economy and Society*, vol. 2, ed. Guenther Roth and Claus Wittich [Berkeley: University of California Press, 1978], 1114, 1121). For a consideration of why Germans fought right up until collapse and terrible destruction, see Ian Kershaw, *The End: The Defiance and Destruction of Hitler's Germany, 1944–1945* (New York: Penguin Press, 2011).

CHAPTER I. THE STRATEGY OF HITLER'S "LEGAL COURSE"
TO POWER

Epigraph: Cited in H. R. Trevor-Roper, ed., *Hitler's Table Talk, 1941–44* (New York: Enigma Books, 2007 [orig. 1953]), 375.

1. Richard Bessel, *Nazism and War* (New York: Modern Library, 2004), 15, 19. Bruce Campbell, *The SA Generals and the Rise of Nazism* (Lexington: University of Kentucky Press, 1998), 20. On demands for a putsch, see Stefan Kley, "Hitler and the Pogrom of November 9–10, 1938," *Yad Vashem Studies on the European Jewish Catastrophe and Resistance* (Jerusalem: Yad Vashem, 2000), 28:87–88. Kley concludes that Hitler's concessions decreased in proportion to his rising popularity so that by November 1938, "on the basis of his most recent successes, Hitler was at a new high point in public popularity and had less reason for concessions to the more radical elements in the party and the SA than ever before" (96).

2. Hitler, *Mein Kampf, Complete and Unabridged, Fully Annotated*, ed. John Chamberlain, Sidney B. Fay, et al. (New York: Reynal and Hitchcock, 1939), 263, 265. Hitler falsified his biography when it was self-serving, although this statement is quite plausible.

3. On the German Left, see Ruth Fischer, *Stalin and German Communism: A Study in the Origins of the State Party* (Cambridge, MA: Harvard University Press, 1948), 121–123, 133–134. In Berlin the young Sebastian Haffner remembered the five days of the attempted coup as something like a row of Sundays: no one went to work, there was no transportation, no newspapers, and very little commerce (*Defying Hitler: A Memoir*, trans. Oliver Pretzel [London: Weidenfeld and Nicolson, 2002], 44). On KPD losses, see Dirk Schumann, *Political Violence in the Weimar Republic, 1918–1933: Fight for the Streets and Fear of Civil War* (New York: Berghahn Books, 2009), 241. On Weimar resistance, see Fischer, *Stalin and German Communism*, 252; Shelley O. Baranowski, *Nazi Empire: German Colonialism and Imperialism from Bismarck to Hitler* (Cambridge: Cambridge University Press, 2010), 136.

4. Hitler, *Mein Kampf*, 122. Hitler's statement to Held: Kurt Bauer, *Nationalsozialismus: Ursprünge, Anfänge, Aufstieg und Fall* (Vienna: Böhlau, 2008), 127–130. The "legal course" was already embraced by the Bavarian Volkish Block but was contrary to the direction of the Great German National Community, an organization Alfred Rosenberg established as an ersatz continuation of the Nazi Party when it was banned following its failed putsch.

5. On the problems of the Weimar Constitution, particularly the emergency powers allotted to the president under Article 48, see Otto Kirchheimer, "Weimar—and What Then? An Analysis of a Constitution," in *Politics, Law, and Social Change: Selected Essays*, ed. Otto Kirchheimer (New York: Columbia University Press, 1969), 33–74. For a study of public SA violence that does not take account of Hitler's "legal course," see Stefan Hördler, ed., *SA-Terror als Herrschaftssicherung: "Köpenicker Blutwoche" und öffentliche Gewalt*

im Nationalsozialismus (Berlin: Metropol, 2013); cf. the essay by Irene von Götz, "Terrornetz in Berlin: Haft- und Fölterstätten," 60.

6. On Luxemburg, see Eric Weitz, *Creating German Communism, 1890–1990: From Popular Protests to Socialist State* (Princeton: Princeton University Press, 1997), 180. Hitler's statement is taken from a letter from Hitler dated November 1, 1926, in Jeremy Noakes and Geoffrey Pridham, eds., *Nazism 1919–1945*, vol. 1: *The Nazi Party, State and Society 1919–1939* (New York: Schocken Books, 1990), 56.

7. German streets were used heavily by pedestrians because Germany attained only in 1936 the number of automobiles that were already present in England ten years earlier, and a similar difference existed between France and Germany. Jeffrey Herf, *The Jewish Enemy: Nazi Propaganda during World War II and the Holocaust* (Cambridge: Belknap Press of Harvard University Press, 2006), 29. Germany had only twenty-five motor vehicles per one thousand persons in 1939, a ratio that was less than one-tenth that of the United States, and car ownership in Germany was also lower than that in France and Britain. Dorothee Hochstetter, *Motorisierung und "Volksgemeinschaft": Das Nationalsozialistische Kraftfahrkorps (NSKK), 1931–1945* (Munich: Oldenbourg, 2005), 186. On radio, see Florence Feiereisen and Alexandra Merley Hill, eds., *Germany in the Loud Twentieth Century: An Introduction* (Oxford: Oxford University Press, 2012), 18, 165.

8. Alfred Döblin, "May the Individual Not Be Stunted by the Masses," in *The Weimar Republic Sourcebook*, ed. Anton Kaes et al. (Berkeley: University of California Press, 1994), 386–392, and M. M. Gehrke and Rudolf Arnheim, "The End of the Private Sphere," 613–615, in the same volume.

9. Hitler appreciated the power of collective actions in Socialist demonstrations and trade unions. Hitler, *Mein Kampf,* 54–66.

10. Hitler, "Fundamental Thoughts on the Meaning and the Organization of the Storm Troop," *Mein Kampf,* 764–765. Hitler's statement about legislative majorities is from 1930, although his statements as well as the program for the SA after the Beer Hall Putsch indicate that this was his aim before as well. In early 1935, two years after taking power, Hitler identified the army and the Nazi Party as "the two pillars of the state," declaring his faith in the army to be "unshakeable." Ernest R. May, *Strange Victory: Hitler's Conquest of France* (New York: Hill and Wang, 2000), 30. But he thought the loyalty of the "Volk's army" to Nazism was rooted in the widespread popular allegiance to the dictatorship; speeches of September 10, 1935, and November 8, 1936, in Adolf Hitler, *Speeches and Proclamations,* 4 vols., ed. Max Domarus (Wauconda, IL: Bolchazy-Carducci, 1990), 2:525, 624. Thus when his conscription order in early 1935 swelled the army from some 100,000 to 550,000 men, he was convinced that it would be unswervingly loyal since it now represented the Volk itself. Trevor-Roper, *Hitler's Table Talk,* 375, entry for May 21, 1942; Gordon A. Craig, *The Politics of the Prussian Army: 1640–1945* (New York: Oxford University Press, 1955), 481.

11. Detlef Mühlberger, *Hitler's Voice: The Völkischer Beobachter: 1920–1933* (New York: Lang, 2004), 107; Thomas D. Grant, *Stormtroopers and Crisis in the Nazi Movement* (New York: Routledge, 2004), 68, 69. On the myth, see Ian Kershaw, *Hitler, 1889–1936: Hubris* (New York: W. W. Norton, 2000), 251.

12. On the new SA mandate, see Kershaw, *Hubris*, 265. On the testimony of Ohlendorf, see *The United States of America v. Otto Ohlendorf et al.* Einsatzgruppen Trial Transcript, October 8, 1947, National Archives Microfilm Publication M895, roll 2, 478–479.

13. "In so far as the members undergo physical training the main emphasis must be not on military drill but far more on sports activities. Boxing and Ju-Jitsu have always seemed to me far more important than any ineffective (because incomplete) shooting practice. . . . [The SA] must not meet in secret but should march in the open air and thereby . . . conclusively destroy all legends of a 'secret organization.' . . . It must from the very beginning be initiated into the great idea of the movement and be trained in the task of representing this idea to such a degree that the . . . individual SA man does not see his mission in the elimination of some crook or other, whether big or small, but in helping to build a new National Socialist racialist state." Hitler's directives to the SA leader, former Freikorps leader Franz Pfeffer von Salomon, from SABE (SA Befehle) 1, November 1, 1926, in Bärbel Dusik, ed., *Hitler: Reden, Schriften, Anordnungen: Februar 1925 bis Januar 1933* (Munich: K. G. Saur, 1992), 83ff., vol. 2, part 1, July 1926–July 1927; translated in Noakes and Pridham, *Nazism, 1919–1945*, 1:56. See also Hitler, *Mein Kampf*, 801.

14. The quote is from Hitler, *Mein Kampf*, 798. Hitler reiterated the SA directive in a September 1931 speech to SA officers, for example. Othmar Plöckinger, *Geschichte eines Buches: Adolf Hitlers "Mein Kampf": 1922–1945* (Munich: Oldenbourg, 2011), 117; Eleanor Hancock, *Ernst Röhm: Hitler's SA Chief of Staff* (New York: Palgrave Macmillan, 2008), 106. On SA violence, Hitler boasted, for example, that during the party's early days his men forced a gang of Communists to flee and thus "we were greeted with cheers from all the windows." Even the police were grateful for the thrashing the Nazis dealt those Communist "dogs" (Trevor-Roper, *Hitler's Table Talk*, 136–137, entry for November 30, 1941).

15. On Goebbels in Berlin, see Jay Baird, *To Die for Germany: Heroes in the Nazi Pantheon* (Bloomington: Indiana University Press, 1990), 104. On the 1928 election, see Russel Lemmons, *Goebbels and Der Angriff* (Lexington: University Press of Kentucky, 1984), 89.

16. On the SA ban, see Lemmons, *Goebbels and Der Angriff*, 19–20. On the masses, see "Wille und Weg," *Wille und Weg* (later *Unser Wille und Weg*) 1 (1931): 2–5, http://www.calvin.edu/academic/cas/gpa/wille.htm (accessed June 20, 2013).

17. Cited from Goebbels, *Kampf um Berlin* (1934), in Hochstetter, *Motorisierung und "Volksgemeinschaft,"* 40. Within weeks of his arrival, according to Goebbels, 280 SA men made a determined "march through the red stronghold of

Berlin-Neukölln." His account stresses the steadfastness of the SA in reaching its propaganda goal by avoiding a frontal assault on the stronger Communists. While the KPD's paramilitary "Red Front" harassed and bullied the SA men, the SA men continued unfalteringly to their destination at the Hallesches Tor. Regardless of whether Goebbels's account is accurate, it does reflect the priorities of Hitler's November 1926 order. Lemmons, *Goebbels and Der Angriff,* 112, 113.

18. Hilton Tims, *The Last Romantic: A Life of Erich Maria Remarque* (New York: Carroll and Graf, 2003), 71.

19. Goebbels on power: Joseph Goebbels, "Isidor," *Der Angriff,* August 15, 1927. While Goebbels associated Weiss (and other Jews) with the Weimar democracy that many Germans saw as a miserable failure, police efforts to restrain the Nazi Party were used to cast the Nazis as martyrs for the German cause. The NSDAP scolded Weiss for violating the constitution with its ban on the party in May 1927; "Violations of the Constitution by the Jewish-Marxist Berlin Police," *Völkischer Beobachter,* May 8–9, 1927; Norbert Finzsch and Dietmar Schirmer, eds., *Identity and Intolerance: Nationalism, Racism, and Xenophobia in Germany and the United States* (Cambridge: Cambridge University Press, 2002), 279.

20. Elisabeth Beck-Gernsheim, "Namenspolitik: Zwischen Assimilation und Antisemitismus—zur Geschichte jüdischer Namen im 19. und 20. Jahrhundert," in *Der Begriff des Politischen: Sonderheft der Sozialen Welt,* ed. Armin Nassehi and Markus Schroer (Baden-Baden: Nomos, 2003), 580; Joachim Rott, *"Ich gehe meinen Weg ungehindert geradeaus": Dr. Bernhard Weiss (1880–1951)* (Berlin: Frank and Timme, 2010), 95, 96. In April 1932, when Weiss was the keynote speaker at a campaign rally for the German State Party (successor of the German People's Party), Nazi activists stirred up the crowd, attempting to provoke Weiss with catcalls and choruses. Weiss, according to reports in the press, reacted sharply to the provocations and had to interrupt his speech due to the rising tumult, continuing only after the hecklers had been removed.

21. According to Goebbels, the graphic artist Hans Schweitzer (known as Mjölner) "had the great gift of being able to make a vital point with a few lines" (Joseph Goebbels, *Die Tagebücher von Joseph Goebbels,* ed. Elke Fröhlich [Munich: K. G. Saur, 1993–1996], part I, vol. 1/III, entry for September 15, 1929); Lemmons, *Goebbels and Der Angriff,* 27, 115, 120–123. In mid-September 1929, as the Nazi Party was still marginal but growing fast, Goebbels commented that Weiss was "small and inaccessible. He can counter us only with power. But we'll get him alright." In 1928 Goebbels authored the *Book of Isidor* with the help of Mjölner, who illustrated Nazi posters and anti-Semitic works and was later appointed by Hitler to represent Nazi ideology in "artistic form" (Herf, *The Jewish Enemy,* 29).

22. Rott, *"Ich gehe meinen Weg ungehindert geradeaus,"* 55, 62–63.

23. Hans Mommsen, *The Rise and Fall of Weimar Democracy* (Chapel Hill: University of North Carolina Press, 1996), 318. For Germans the Nazi Party became "first and foremost an anti-Marxist Party" that could crush class warfare. William Sheridan Allen, *The Nazi Seizure of Power: The Experience of a Single German Town, 1922–1945* (New York: F. Watts, 1984), 34, 134.

24. On the Nazi anthem, see Baird, *To Die for Germany*, 77ff. On Wessel and Communists, see Anthony Read, *The Devil's Disciples: Hitler's Inner Circle* (New York: W. W. Norton, 2004), 188. Goebbels on Wessel: Goebbels, *Tagebücher*, part I, vol. 1/III, entry for January 16, 1929.

25. Robert B. Kane, *Disobedience and Conspiracy in the German Army, 1918–1945* (Jefferson, NC: McFarland, 2002), 73.

26. Cited in Thomas Friedrich, *Hitler's Berlin: Abused City* (New Haven: Yale University Press, 2012), 157; Geoffrey Pridham, *Hitler's Rise to Power* (New York: Harper and Row, 1972), 213; Alice Gallin, *Midwives to Nazism: University Professors in Weimar Germany, 1925–1933* (Macon, GA: Mercer University Press, 1986), 69, 76–77.

27. On Stennes, see Timothy Scott Brown, *Weimar Radicals: Nazis and Communists between Authenticity and Performance* (New York: Berghahn Books, 2009), 61, and Kershaw, *Hubris*, 347. On the attraction violence held for SA men, see Richard Bessel, *Political Violence and the Rise of Nazism: The Storm Troopers in Eastern Germany, 1925–1934* (New Haven: Yale University Press, 1984), 49–53, 75–96. See also Hancock, *Ernst Röhm*, 107, 109; Pamela E. Swett, *Neighbors and Enemies: The Culture of Radicalism in Berlin, 1929–1933* (Cambridge: Cambridge University Press, 2004), 169–170.

28. Lemmons, *Goebbels and Der Angriff*, 82, 88.

29. On the 1930 election, see Mommsen, *The Rise and Fall of Weimar Democracy*, 315. On Nazi momentum, see William Patch, *Heinrich Brüning and the Dissolution of the Weimar Republic* (Cambridge: Cambridge University Press, 1998), 98. Chancellor Heinrich Brüning was eclipsed as the nation's most influential political figure, according to one eyewitness, since the recurrent question in political discussions was not whether Brüning would remain in power but whether Hitler would *come* to power (Haffner, *Defying Hitler*, 87).

30. Hitler's testimony on September 25, 1930, is excerpted and translated in Benjamin C. Sax and Dieter Kuntz, *Inside Hitler's Germany: A Documentary History of Life in the Third Reich* (Lexington, MA: D. C. Heath, 1992), 105, 109. As if appealing to a tradition of law, Hitler claimed that the constitution had set up a make-believe system in which the mob ruled while traditional parties fought for liberty. As he often did, he presented the SA as a defensive formation organized to protect the party with force *only* when attacked with force. Reporting on the trial, the *New York Times* of September 26, 1930, ran a story on page 1 titled "Hitler Would Scrap Versailles Treaty and Use Guillotine."

31. Hitler's testimony in Sax and Kuntz, *Inside Hitler's Germany*, 105–109. On the legal process, see Heinrich August Winkler, *Germany: The Long Road*

West, vol. 1: *1789–1933* (New York: Oxford University Press, 2006), 440. "Magnificent echo" is in Goebbels, *Tagebücher*, part I, vol. 2/I, entry for September 26, 1930.

32. On a putsch, see Patch, *Heinrich Brüning and the Dissolution of the Weimar Republic*, 136–137. On President Hindenburg, see Irene Strenge, *Kurt von Schleicher: Politik im Reichswehrministerium am Ende der Weimarer Republik* (Berlin: Duncker and Humblot, 2006), 76–90.

33. On the army, see Mommsen, *The Rise and Fall of Weimar Democracy*, 425. On "cultural bolshevism," see Patch, *Heinrich Brüning and the Dissolution of the Weimar Republic*, 138–139.

34. Brown, *Weimar Radicals*, 17; Kershaw, *Hubris*, 337.

35. Patch, *Heinrich Brüning and the Dissolution of the Weimar Republic*, 194.

36. Excerpted and translated in Noakes and Pridham, *Nazism, 1919–1945*, 1:90.

37. T. Friedrich, *Hitler's Berlin*, 191; Brown, *Weimar Radicals*, 60. That month Hitler issued SA guidelines identifying "special tasks" for the SA in bringing the party to power legally. Although he opposed smoking, Hitler did not object to the introduction of a special Sturm brand of cigarettes that SA men were encouraged to smoke (Kershaw, *Hubris*, 348).

38. Goebbels, *Tagebücher*, part I, vol. 2/I, 26–27, entry for February 24, 1931.

39. Cited in Brown, *Weimar Radicals*, 18, 21.

40. Schumann, *Political Violence in the Weimar Republic*, 305.

41. KPD as army: Eve Rosenhaft, *Beating the Fascists? The German Communists and Political Violence, 1929–1933* (Cambridge: Cambridge University Press, 1983), 3, 21, 142.

42. Michael Burleigh, *The Third Reich: A New History* (New York: Hill and Wang, 2000), 131. See also Rosenhaft, *Beating the Fascists?* 21, 53, 77, 142. Statistics in November 1931 showed that the Communists were responsible for more murders than the Nazis, according to police reports. The Red Front by 1932 was planning raids and attacks aimed at eliminating individual Nazis.

43. Reinhard R. Doerries, *Hitler's Intelligence Chief: Walter Schellenberg* (New York: Enigma, 2009), 48n112.

44. Hancock, *Ernst Röhm*, 113, 115, 116.

45. On Stegmann, see Henry Ashby Turner, *Hitler's Thirty Days to Power: January 1933* (Reading, MA: Addison-Wesley, 1996), 73, and Brown, *Weimar Radicals*, 76. On mutiny, see Brown, *Weimar Radicals*, 62.

46. On party structures, see Lemmons, *Goebbels and Der Angriff*, 83. The SA men, however, proved ingenuous at inventing contraptions of pipes and steel weights they could swing as weapons, or they carried brass knuckles. Furthermore, decentralized control of the SA allowed the Storm Troopers at least in some parts to continue as a brutal force, sometimes with military training, at the service of regional or local party leaders. W. S. Allen, *Nazi Seizure of Power*, 78.

47. Dietrich Orlow, *The Nazi Party, 1919–1945: A Complete History* (New York: Enigma, 2008), 148. The common designation of violence-prone SA men

who sought armed confrontation with the state as "radicals," in contrast to Hitler's position, is not precise, considering that Hitler, in his far-reaching vision, was more radical.

48. On SA violence, see Grant, *Stormtroopers and Crisis in the Nazi Movement,* 56. On Goebbels, see Patch, *Heinrich Brüning and the Dissolution of the Weimar Republic,* 147.

49. Cited in *Völkischer Beobachter,* March 31, 1931, in Grant, *Stormtroopers and Crisis in the Nazi Movement,* 72.

50. Ibid.

51. On Stennes in the press, see Patch, *Heinrich Brüning and the Dissolution of the Weimar Republic,* 148–149; Mühlberger, *Hitler's Voice,* 432. There were intrigues around the revolt of Stennes, some by leading government officials hoping to repress Nazism, others by party leaders attempting to gain the upper hand. Joseph Goebbels, "National Socialists! Party Comrades and SA Men!" *Völkischer Beobachter,* April 4, 1931.

52. On Stennes's refusal, see Mühlberger, *Hitler's Voice,* 424–425. Mühlberger points out that "not surprisingly, reference to the Stennes revolt is limited in the accounts"; officials limited reports even within their own documents on events they did not want others to hear about—i.e., actions that rejected National Socialism. On the SA and Goebbels, see Lemmons, *Goebbels and Der Angriff,* 85.

53. On loyalty to Hitler, see Hancock, *Ernst Röhm,* 109. On Goebbels, see "Wille und Weg" 1 (1931): 2–5, http://www.calvin.edu/academic/cas/gpa/wille.htm (accessed June 20, 2014).

54. Orlow, *The Nazi Party, 1919–1945,* 161. Hitler had just joined his party with Hugenberg's "national opposition" to review a huge demonstration at Bad Harzburg on October 12. It was the same coalition that had opposed the Young Plan, an initiative to clear debts that Germany had accrued in the peace settlement at the end of World War I, but now Hitler's party, the one that had burgeoned in numbers, truly represented the base of mass support that the others at Harzburg didn't have. Mühlberger, *Hitler's Voice,* 426.

55. The state officials retorted that the Storm Troopers committed murder as often as the KPD's Red Front and insisted that Berlin must ban the wearing of uniforms by all paramilitary groups, the NSDAP as well as the KPD. Patch, *Heinrich Brüning and the Dissolution of the Weimar Republic,* 227. In late November 1931, the discovery of sensational reports known as the "Boxheim documents" called into question the credibility of Hitler's legality pledge. The documents disclosed a plan for the abolition of the current legal order in case of a destructive Communist uprising, plotted by Werner Best and the SA in Hesse, where Best was a Nazi legal adviser. But once again officials lacked evidence that Hitler even knew of the plan. Patch, *Heinrich Brüning and the Dissolution of the Weimar Republic,* 225–226.

56. Cited in Hancock, *Ernst Röhm,* 98, 105.

57. Grant, *Stormtroopers and Crisis in the Nazi Movement*, 73. A number of high-ranking Nazi officials publicly and sometimes repeatedly declared allegiance to legality, including Goebbels, Wilhelm Frick, Fritz Saukel, and others.

58. Brüning, quoted in Patch, *Heinrich Brüning and the Dissolution of the Weimar Republic*, 228.

59. Otto Wagener, *Hitler: Memoirs of a Confidant*, ed. Henry Ashby Turner, trans. Ruth Hein (New Haven: Yale University Press, 1985), 184. The Nazi press did assault Hindenburg, as did Goebbels, in the Reichstag.

60. On Hitler's loss, see Mommsen, *The Rise and Fall of Weimar Democracy*, 410, 411. On SA violence, see Grant, *Stormtroopers and Crisis in the Nazi Movement*, 75.

61. On the new decree, see Swett, *Neighbors and Enemies*, 291.

62. Mommsen, *The Rise and Fall of Weimar Democracy*, 420. Although the ban signaled that the SA posed a threat of treason, some thought such a threat was due only to those Nazi leaders who opposed Hitler. Winkler, *Germany: The Long Road West*, 1:449; Patch, *Heinrich Brüning and the Dissolution of the Weimar Republic*, 246–252.

63. On the conservatives, see Campbell, *The SA Generals and the Rise of Nazism*, 92; on rescinding the ban, see Grant, *Stormtroopers and Crisis in the Nazi Movement*, 75, 78. Winkler, *Germany: The Long Road West*, 1:449; Patch, *Heinrich Brüning and the Dissolution of the Weimar Republic*, 246–252.

64. Grant, *Stormtroopers and Crisis in the Nazi Movement*, 78.

65. Mommsen, *The Rise and Fall of Weimar Democracy*, 339. The party turned to Twentieth-Century Fox for quality outdoor audio.

66. Heinrich August Winkler, *Auf ewig in Hitlers Schatten?: über die Deutschen und ihre Geschichte* (Munich: Beck Verlag, 2007), 90.

67. In his diary, Goebbels declared this to be a victory: Weiss "must now be finished. Six long years I have fought against him. He is for every Berlin National Socialist the representative of the system. If he falls, then the system will also not hold much longer" (*Tagebücher,* part I, vol. 2/II, entry for July 24, 1932); Hermann Beck, *The Fateful Alliance: German Conservatives and Nazis in 1933: The Machtergreifung in a New Light* (New York: Berghahn Books, 2008), 102; Rott, *"Ich gehe meinen Weg ungehindert geradeaus,"* 105.

68. Cited in Grant, *Stormtroopers and Crisis in the Nazi Movement*, 66, 80.

69. Hancock, *Ernst Röhm*, 117, citing Röhm's confidant, Sefton Delmer.

70. Schumann, *Political Violence in the Weimar Republic*, 305.

71. Beck, *The Fateful Alliance*, 81.

72. Report on Sentiment, SA Group Southwest to the SA Chief of Staff in Munich, September 21, 1932, National Archives, Record Group 242, Reel 81, 105058–105245. SA morale reports were sent for review to both Ernst Röhm and Rudolf Hess.

73. On SA problems, see Grant, *Stormtroopers and Crisis in the Nazi Movement*, 81–82. Mommsen, *The Rise and Fall of Weimar Democracy*, 483.

74. Turner, *Hitler's Thirty Days to Power*, 15; Anna von der Goltz, *Hindenburg: Power, Myth, and the Rise of the Nazis* (New York: Oxford University Press, 2009), 169.

75. Some expressed faith that President Hindenburg would continue to refuse Hitler's demands, as he had done in August, before the Nazi electoral and propaganda losses in November. Grant, *Stormtroopers and Crisis in the Nazi Movement*, 87.

76. Julius Elbau, editor in chief of the *Vossische Zeitung*, commented that current signs indicated that the "looming Putsch," threatened by the Nazis since the September 1930 election, was now a subsiding risk. Cited by Eberhard Kolb, "Was Hitler's Seizure of Power on January 30, 1933, Inevitable?" (Washington, DC: German Historical Institute, 1997), 11, Occasional Paper No. 18; von der Goltz, *Hindenburg*, 167–168.

77. Hitler holds to legal way: Mommsen, *The Rise and Fall of Weimar Democracy*, 482. *Der deutsche Weg*, December 2, 1932, 3; cited in Grant, *Stormtroopers and Crisis in the Nazi Movement*, 9.

78. Eberhard Kolb, *The Weimar Republic*, 2nd ed. (London: Routledge, 2005), 127. Compare Kolb's argument to arguments that by declaring a state of emergency, the government might have held Hitler off. Dirk Blasius, *Weimars Ende: Burgerkrieg und Politik 1930–1933* (Göttingen: Vandenhoeck and Ruprecht, 2006).

79. Turner, *Hitler's Thirty Days to Power*, 110.

80. This is according to historian Henry Turner, *Hitler's Thirty Days to Power*, 110.

81. Alan Bullock, *Hitler: A Study in Tyranny* (New York: Harper and Row, 1962), 182. Wolfram Pyta, *Hindenburg: Herrschaft zwischen Hohenzollern und Hitler* (Berlin: Siedler, 2007), 846.

82. Turner, *Hitler's Thirty Days to Power*, 16, 43, 88, 157. In Nazi lore, Hitler's accession to power completed the time of struggle that Nazi leaders would refer to as evidence that the party would prevail, despite the odds and the daunting outlook, as Hitler's power waned during the war.

83. Official reports show that the Volk generally greeted the new police state measures positively, as a step toward the repression of communism and a restoration of order, and the parliament fell in line. Ian Kershaw, *Popular Opinion and Political Dissent in the Third Reich: Bavaria 1933–1945* (New York: Oxford University Press, 2002 [orig. 1983]), 247.

84. On violence against Jews, see Stefan Hördler, introduction to *SA-Terror als Herrschaftssicherung*, 13; See in general *SA-Terror als Herrschaftssicherung* on SA violence after Hitler took power. William E. Dodd, *Ambassador Dodd's Diary, 1933–1938*, ed. William E. Dodd Jr. and Martha Dodd (New York: Harcourt, Brace, 1941), 26, 27. SA group leader Karl Ernst of Berlin apologized to the ambassador, reportedly bent to American demands that the SA offender be imprisoned, and promised "that such a thing would not happen again." Despite Ernst's clicking boots, Prussian bow, and Hitler salute (which Dodd

returned "as best I saw fit"), American consul general George Messer-schmidt assured Dodd that the "incidents will go on."

85. Kershaw, *The "Hitler Myth": Image and Reality in the Third Reich* (New York: Oxford University Press, 1987), 52; Harold Marcuse, *Legacies of Dachau: The Uses and Abuses of a Concentration Camp, 1933–2001* (New York: Cambridge University Press, 2001), 21; Robert Gellately, *Backing Hitler: Consent and Co-ercion in Nazi Germany* (Oxford: Oxford University Press, 2001), 2, 21.

86. Bullock, *Hitler: A Study in Tyranny*, 288. Claudia Koonz, *The Nazi Conscience* (Cambridge, MA: Harvard University Press, 2003), 84. Kershaw, *Hubris*, 502.

87. Kershaw, *Hubris*, 437.

88. English translation of a summary of Hitler's speech to the Gauleiters on the role of the NSDAP, February 2, 1934, in Noakes and Pridham, *Nazism, 1919–1945*, 2:40–42. See German original in Broszat, *Hitler State*, 209–210.

89. Kershaw, *Hubris*, 52, 501, 520.

90. Ibid., 436, 518–519.

91. Koonz, *Nazi Conscience*, 97, 98.

92. Trevor-Roper, *Hitler's Table Talk*, 375. See chapter V below for Hitler's rela-tionship to the army and his consolidation of power in 1938.

CHAPTER II. CONTESTED MOBILIZATIONS

1. Cited in Otto Wagener, *Hitler: Memoirs of a Confidant*, ed. Henry Ashby Turner, trans. Ruth Hein (New Haven: Yale University Press, 1985), 18–22 (emphasis added).

2. A national church in fact had been an idea prevalent in segments of Protes-tant opinion dating back at least to 1863 and the German Protestant Association. Shelley O. Baranowski, *The Sanctity of Rural Life: Nobility, Protestantism, and Nazism in Weimar Prussia* (New York: Oxford University Press, 1995), 181; Ian Kershaw, *Hitler, 1889–1936: Hubris* (New York: W. W. Norton, 2000), 489. On Henry VIII as Hitler's model, see Albert Speer, *Inside the Third Reich: Memoirs by Albert Speer* (New York: Macmillan, 1970), 95.

3. The history of the independence asserted by Bishops Hans Meiser (in Ba-varia) and Theophil Wurm (in Württemberg) has often been written as church history, while here it is examined through the eyes of the dictator-ship, as part of its efforts to transform German attitudes. Christiane Kuller, "The Demonstrations in Support of the Protestant Provincial Bishop Hans Meiser: A Successful Protest Against the Nazi Regime?" in Stoltzfus and Maier-Katkin, *Protest in Hitler's "National Community,"* 38–39.

4. Doris L. Bergen, *Twisted Cross: The German Christian Movement in the Third Reich* (Chapel Hill: University of North Carolina Press, 1996), 15; Jona-than R. C. Wright, *Über den Parteien: Die politische Haltung der evangelischen Kirchen Führer 1918–1933* (Göttingen: Vandenhoeck and Ruprecht, 1977), 217. Both Meiser and Wurm were concerned with creating and maintaining

good relationships with the new regime, as well as with the German Christians, in the spring of 1933. Wurm expressed an intention that the church adapt to the new state. Part of the reason for this hope in the new government was based on statements made by Nazi officials. For example, Hans Schemm as Bavarian culture minister used the slogan "Our religion is named Christ and our politics is named Germany." Thus it was possible for church leaders to claim that at least "part of the NSDAP" wished the church well and that the church should stand behind the party. Hitler thought that a mass movement might succeed in achieving a religious reformation but that this could not be done by the "roundabout way of political organization" (Adolf Hitler, *Mein Kampf, Complete and Unabridged, Fully Annotated,* ed. John Chamberlain, Sidney B. Fay, et al. [New York: Reynal and Hitchcock, 1939], 147).

5. Hitler, *Mein Kampf,* 223.

6. On Christianity's demise: Trevor-Roper, ed., *Hitler's Table Talk, 1941–1944* (New York: Enigma Books, 2007 [orig. 1953]), 48, entry for October 14, 1941. Robert P. Ericksen and Susannah Heschel, eds., *Betrayal: German Churches and the Holocaust* (Minneapolis: Fortress Press, 1999), 10. Throughout the twelve Nazi years the Protestant as well as Catholic Churches remained institutions officially recognized by the state, with the state collecting a church tax and funding church expenses. State universities too continued to fund theological faculties. Chaplains continued to serve in the military, and of course the regime continued to welcome any blessing of the war church leaders might offer. For Hitler's statement, see Hitler and Catholic Church Services, March 21, 1933, in Carsten Nicolaisen, ed., *Dokumente zur Kirchenpolitik des Dritten Reiches,* vol. 1: *Das Jahr 1933* (Munich: C. Kaiser, 1971), 23–24.

7. Meiser cited in Matthew D. Hockenos, *A Church Divided: German Protestants Confront the Nazi Past* (Bloomington: Indiana University Press, 2004), 17. Meiser continued: "With gratitude and joy the Church takes note that the new state bans blasphemy, assails immorality, establishes discipline and order, with a strong hand, while at the same time calling upon man to fear God, espousing the sanctity of marriage and Christian training for the young, bringing into honor again the deeds of our fathers and kindling in thousands of hearts, in place of disparagement, an ardent love of Volk and Fatherland." For the daily practice of Nazism, see Jill Stephenson, *Women in Nazi Germany* (Harlow, England: Longman, 2001), 89.

8. For Wurm's praise of Nazism, see Paul Sauer, *Württemberg in der Zeit der Nationalsozialismus* (Ulm: Süddeutsche Verlagsgesellschaft, 1975), 181. Like Hans Meiser and Michael von Faulhaber, Wurm had greeted the rise of Nazism and Hitler with open enthusiasm. Robert P. Ericksen, *Complicity in the Holocaust* (Cambridge: Cambridge University Press, 2012), 171. Peter Hoffmann, *The History of the German Resistance, 1933–1945,* trans. Richard Barry (London: Macdonald and Jane's, 1977), 13. For an overview of the range of expressions of this opinion by Protestants, see David Sikkink and Mark Regnerus, "For God and the Fatherland: Protestant Symbolic Worlds and the

322 NOTES TO PAGES 56–57

Rise of National Socialism," in *Disruptive Religion: The Force of Faith in Social Movement Activism*, ed. Christian Smith (Abingdon: Routledge, 1996), 156–157.

9. A national church had been an idea prevalent in segments of Protestant opinion dating back at least to 1863 and the German Protestant Association. Article 24 of the 1920 platform also suggested such a union as a step toward the Leader's efforts to collect loyalties behind his movement. Article 24 professed the attractive-sounding yet nebulous "positive Christianity" as the foundation of the German state. Heinz-Gerhard Haupt and Dieter Langewiesche, *Nation und Religion in der deutschen Geschichte* (Frankfurt am Main: Campus Verlag, 2001), 564. On efforts to unify the Protestant Church under Müller, see Kyle Jantzen, *Faith and Fatherland: Parish Politics in Hitler's Germany* (Minneapolis: Fortress Press, 2008), 5. On Niemöller and the Confessing Church, see Kershaw, *Hubris*, 490. Ian Kershaw, *Popular Opinion and Political Dissent in the Third Reich: Bavaria 1933–1945* (New York: Oxford University Press, 2002 [orig. 1983]), 159. On the conservativeness of Meiser, as well as Wurm and Hannover bishop August Marahrens, the three bishops who refused to join their churches with the Reich Church, see Manfred Gailus and Hartmut Lehmann, *Nationalprotestantische Mentalitäten: Konturen, Entwicklungslinien und Umbrüche eines Weltbildes* (Göttingen: Vandenhoeck and Ruprecht, 2005), 264ff.; Bergen, *Twisted Cross*, 113; Richard Steigmann-Gall, *The Holy Reich: Nazi Conceptions of Christianity, 1919–1945* (Cambridge: Cambridge University Press, 2004), 157. The German Christians lost momentum due to disputes among church leaders over whether to voluntarily introduce the "Aryan paragraph," the dictatorship's April 1933 measure that eliminated Jews from all civil service positions. While the Protestant leaders had agreed on the need for renewal, some sought to reform Christianity completely, while others wished only to make adjustments. Ericksen, *Complicity in the Holocaust*, 101. Jantzen, *Faith and Fatherland*, 5.

10. Hitler is cited in Steigmann-Gall, *The Holy Reich*, 167–168. The meeting is recounted in Nicolaisen, *Dokumente zur Kirchenpolitik des Dritten Reiches*, 2:20–33.

11. Cited in Steigmann-Gall, *The Holy Reich*, 169.

12. Conway, *The Nazi Persecution of the Churches*, 75–76.

13. On "blood and race," see Klaus Scholder, *Die Kirchen und das Dritte Reich*, vol. 2: *Das Jahr der Ernüchterung 1934* (Berlin: Siedler, 1985), 96ff. Meiser's response is in Helmut Baier, "Die bayerische Landeskirche im Umbruch 1931–1934," in *Kirche und Nationalsozialismus. Zur Geschichte des Kirchenkampfes*, ed. Paul Rieger and Johann Strauss (Munich: Claudius, 1969), 64.

14. Cited in Thomas Martin Schneider, *Reichsbischof Ludwig Müller: Eine Untersuchung zu Leben, Werk und Persönlichkeit* (Göttingen: Vandenhoeck and Ruprecht, 1993), 146.

15. Kershaw, *Popular Opinion*, 164; Steigmann-Gall, *The Holy Reich*, 166. By some accounts it was his henchman August Jäger who encouraged Müller to resort more quickly to the use of force. Schneider, *Reichsbischof Ludwig Müller*, 185. Jantzen, *Faith and Fatherland*, 5. For Wurm's appeal to unity, see Sauer, *Württemberg*, 188.

16. Later Müller presided over the baptism of Göring's daughter (Schneider, *Reichsbischof Ludwig Müller*, 168, 221). On Jäger's use of the SA, see Otto Büsch and Wolfgang Neugebauer, *Vom Kaiserreich zum 20. Jahrhundert und grosse Themen der Geschichte Preussens*, vol. 3: *Handbuch der preussischen Geschichte* (Berlin: De Gruyter, 2001), 4, 5, 15, 664, 667. President Hindenburg to Reichs Chancellor, June 30, 1933, in Nicolaisen, *Dokumente zur Kirchenpolitik des Dritten Reiches*, 1:83. On Granzow's termination of Rendtorff, see Heinrich Holze, *Die Theologische Fakultät Rostock unter zwei Diktaturen: Studien zur Geschichte 1933–1989* (Münster: LIT Verlag, 2004), 33. Nazi ideologue Walter Bohm made a gesture toward stirring grassroots support in the style of Nazi politics by announcing in the local newspaper that the Volk must resist the "domination" of bishops and "take over the government of the church for [themselves] along with all functions of church government down to community level" (Steigmann-Gall, *The Holy Reich*, 157–158). For Rendtorff's reinstatement, see Scholder, *Die Kirchen und das Dritte Reich*, 1:380–381. Müller had promised Rendtorff that he would intervene personally on his behalf with Hitler, but he did nothing. Cf. Schneider, *Reichsbischof Ludwig Müller*, 149. Rendtorff had, after all, like bishops around Germany, lent his authority to Hitler's vision with an appeal for an "unconditional 'Yes' to the Nazi movement."

17. Scholder, *Die Kirchen und das Dritte Reich*, 2:271.

18. Ericksen, *Complicity in the Holocaust*, 101; Helmut Baier, *Die Deutschen Christen Bayerns im Rahmen des bayerischen Kirchenkampfes* (Nuremberg: Verein für Bayerische Kirchengeschichte, 1968), 145; Schneider, *Reichsbischof Ludwig Müller*, 188, 209; Scholder, *Die Kirchen und das Dritte Reich*, 2:317.

19. Helmut Baier, *Kirchenkampf in Nürnberg 1933–1945* (Nuremberg: Korn and Berg, 1973), 5–6.

20. Report of the Ansbach District President, Hans Dippold, Ansbach, May 20, 1934, in Helmut Witetschek, *Die kirchliche Lage in Bayern nach den Regierungspräsidentenberichten, 1933–1943*, vol. 2: *Regierungsbezirk Ober- und Mittelfranken* (Mainz: Matthias-Grünewald, 1967), 26; Scholder, *Die Kirchen und das Dritte Reich*, 2:319; Kershaw, *Popular Opinion*, 165.

21. Report of the Ansbach District President, Hans Dippold, Ansbach, May 20, 1934, in Witetschek, *Die kirchliche Lage in Bayern*, 2:26, 30–31; Scholder, *Die Kirchen und das Dritte Reich*, 2:319. Dippold perceived dangers to the Nazi movement, and Hitler's response shows that he agreed.

22. On rejecting union with the Reich Church, see Kershaw, *Popular Opinion*, 165. Further news that party leaders found somewhat distasteful arrived

with the results of the national plebiscite from August 19 following the death
of President Hindenburg. The president's son, Oskar Hindenburg, had campaigned for Hitler by announcing that "my now immortalized father himself saw Adolf Hitler as his immediate successor." Purveying the core Nazi
message of unity, he appealed for Germans to demonstrate "that an un-
breakable bond firmly encompasses the German Volk in a single will."
Despite this call for unity, many Germans had either voted "no" or spoiled
their ballots, something of a surprise after the almost uniform vote of "yes"
in the plebiscite of November 12, 1933. Officially 89.9 percent voted for Hitler.
Two future national plebiscites were scheduled to directly follow spectacular
feats of the Führer—the 1936 remilitarizing of the Rhineland and the annexation of Austria two years later. Both were also preceded by weeks of propaganda and yielded invalid and negative ballots totaling only 1–2 percent.
Adolf Hitler, *Speeches and Proclamations*, 4 vols., ed. Max Domarus (Wauconda, IL: Bolchazy-Carducci, 1990), 1:524–525.

23. Bans quoted in Witetschek, *Die kirchliche Lage in Bayern*, 2:31n1. Jäger's announcement is in Ericksen, *Complicity in the Holocaust*, 102.

24. Witetschek, *Die kirchliche Lage in Bayern*, 2:31 and 31n1, quoting Reich Governor Epp to the interior minister, September 20, 1934.

25. Ian Kershaw, *The "Hitler Myth": Image and Reality in the Third Reich* (New
York: Oxford University Press, 1987), shows Hitler's appeal despite lower ex-
pectations for his Nazi Party. Report of the Ansbach District President,
Hans Dippold, Ansbach, November 9, 1934, in Witetschek, *Die Kirchliche
Lage in Bayern*, 2:40.

26. Scholder, *Die Kirchen und das Dritte Reich*, 2:310–111.

27. For Jäger's charges against Wurm, see Ericksen, *Complicity in the Holocaust*,
102–103. The judiciary acquitted Wurm in late November; Scholder, *Die
Kirchen und das Dritte Reich*, 2:246. On Hitler at the Party Rally, see Baier,
Deutschen Christen Bayerns, 145; Schneider, *Reichsbischof Ludwig Müller*, 188,
209; Scholder, *Die Kirchen und das Dritte Reich*, 2:317. A handshake was a
very public but also ambiguous sign of support allowing Hitler to backtrack
if the people were not yet ready to accept his message.

28. Conway, *The Nazi Persecution of the Churches*, 99; Ericksen, *Complicity in the
Holocaust*, 102–103; Heinrich Hermelink, *Kirche im Kampf* (Tübingen: R.
Wunderlich, 1950), 136–137, 139–142; Ernst C. Helmreich, "The Arrest and
Freeing of the Protestant Bishops of Württemberg and Bavaria, September–
October 1934," *Central European History* 2, no. 2 (June 1969): 160nn2–5.

29. David Blackbourn, "Apparitions of the Virgin Mary in Bismarckian Germany," in *Society, Culture, and the State in Germany, 1870–1930*, ed. Geoff
Eley, 189–219 (Ann Arbor: University of Michigan Press, 1996), 194–195. See
chapter IV below.

30. Hermelink, *Kirche im Kampf*, 142; Scholder, *Die Kirchen und das Dritte Reich*,
2:315–316, 331. Scholder opines that the government had reduced options for
subjugating the Bavarian church through police force due to the popular

support for Bishop Meiser. Helmreich, "The Arrest and Freeing of the Protestant Bishops of Württemberg and Bavaria," 160.

31. Scholder, *Die Kirchen und das Dritte Reich,* 2:316; Helmreich, "The Arrest and Freeing of the Protestant Bishops of Württemberg and Bavaria," 160; Baier, *Kirchenkampf in Nürnberg,* 11.

32. Cited in Baier, *Kirchenkampf in Nürnberg,* 12.

33. Ibid., 12–13. Helmreich, "The Arrest and Freeing of the Protestant Bishops of Württemberg and Bavaria," 160.

34. Hermelink, *Kirche im Kampf,* 156; Report of the Ansbach District President, Hans Dippold, Ansbach, October 9, 1934, in Witetschek, *Die kirchliche Lage in Bayern,* 2:34–36; Baier, *Kirchenkampf in Nürnberg,* 13–14.

35. Scholder, *Die Kirchen und das Dritte Reich,* 2:317; Baier, *Kirchenkampf in Nürnberg,* 14–15. Baier says that Protestant loyalists were turned away from the square by the police at seven o'clock and that they then collected in the other churches. Scholder says that Protestant loyalists heard that the SA was making its way to the square at 6:30 and that they then responded by beginning to collect in the churches. Ericksen, *Complicity in the Holocaust,* 103.

36. Helmreich, "The Arrest and Freeing of the Protestant Bishops of Württemberg and Bavaria," 160–161; Scholder, *Die Kirchen und das Dritte Reich,* 2:320.

37. Helmreich, "The Arrest and Freeing of the Protestant Bishops of Württemberg and Bavaria," 161; Müller's demand for "a Rome-free church" is in Scholder, *Die Kirchen und das Dritte Reich,* 2:320–322.

38. Baier, *Kirchenkampf in Nürnberg,* 13–14.

39. Report of the Ansbach District President, Hans Dippold, Ansbach, October 9, 1934, in Witetschek, *Die kirchliche Lage in Bayern,* 2:35–36.

40. Scholder, *Die Kirchen und das Dritte Reich,* 2:314.

41. Baier, *Kirchenkampf in Nürnberg,* 15. Sermons were based on passages from the Book of Acts with texts such as "Pay heed to yourselves," "Pay heed to the earth," and "Pay heed to your faith!"

42. Cited in Kershaw, *Popular Opinion,* 166–167. Baier, *Kirchenkampf in Nürnberg,* 15.

43. Kershaw, *Popular Opinion,* 168.

44. Cited in Baier, *Deutschen Christen Bayerns,* 141–142. Schemm proposed to establish a Nazi Party Church that would serve as a substitute for, and eventually displace altogether, the traditional churches.

45. Scholder, *Die Kirchen und das Dritte Reich,* 2:329; Baier, *Bayerischen Kirchenkampfes,* 128, 132.

46. Helmreich, "The Arrest and Freeing of the Protestant Bishops of Württemberg and Bavaria," 167, 169; Meiser cited in Carsten Nicolaisen and Gerhart Herold, eds., *Hans Meiser, 1881–1956: Ein lutherischer Bischof im Wandel der politischen Systeme* (Munich: Claudius Verlag, 2006), 43.

47. Scholder, *Die Kirchen und das Dritte Reich,* 2:330.

48. On communication after Meiser's arrest, see Baier, *Deutschen Christen Bayerns*, 138; Anne Lore Bühler, *Der Kirchenkampf im evangelischen München: Die Auseinandersetzung mit dem Nationalsozialismus und seinen Folgeerscheinungen im Bereich des Evang.-Luth. Dekanates München, 1923–1950* (Nuremberg: Selbstverlag des Vereins für Bayerische Kirchengeschichte, 1974), 85. On witnessing Meiser's arrest, see Paul Kremmel, *Pfarrer und Gemeinden im evangelischen Kirchenkampf in Bayern bis 1939: Mit besonderer Berücksichtigung der Ereignisse im Bereich des Bezirksamts Weissenburg in Bayern* (Lichtenfels: Kommissionsverlag Schulze, 1987), 366. For the impact in Bavaria see Baier, *Deutschen Christen Bayerns*, 136.

49. Report of the Ansbach District President, Hans Dippold, for October, dated November 9, Ansbach, in Witetschek, *Die Kirchliche Lage in Bayern*, 2:38. On the "muzzle decree," see Baier, *Deutschen Christen Bayerns*, 128, 131, 133–134. On continued protests, see Scholder, *Die Kirchen und das Dritte Reich*, 2:376.

50. Government report in Witetschek, *Die kirchliche Lage in Bayern*, 2:37. Meiser's declaration is cited in Scholder, *Das Jahr der Ernüchterung, 1934*, 2:331.

51. Report of the Ansbach District President, Ansbach, November 9, in Witetschek, *Die kirchliche Lage in Bayern*, 2:39. The two citations from *Die kirchliche Lage in Bayern* come from different documents, but both are from Ansbach and dated November 9, 1934. The first has the heading "Lagebericht der Regierung" and the second has the heading "Lagesonderbericht der Regierung." On grassroots support, see Kershaw, *Popular Opinion*, 167.

52. On Epp and protest, see Baier, *Deutschen Christen Bayerns*, 137–139. Schemm is quoted in Franz Kühnel, *Hans Schemm: Gauleiter und Kultusminister, 1891–1935* (Nuremberg: Korn und Berg, 1985), 338. Schemm is also quoted as saying, "I warned the pastors who spoke out against the Reich Church government last Sunday that we know your struggle is aimed not so much against the Reich Bishop as against National Socialism!" (quoted in Steigmann-Gall, *The Holy Reich*, 172). On Bolshevism and the SA, see Kershaw, *Popular Opinion*, 172. On sacrifice, see Report of the Ansbach District President, Hans Dippold, Ansbach, November 9, in Witetschek, *Die Kirchliche Lage in Bayern*, 2:37–38.

53. Kershaw, *Popular Opinion*, 170–171.

54. Baier, *Deutschen Christen Bayerns*, 135. Pastors cited in Baier, *Kirchenkampf in Nürnberg*, 19 (emphasis added).

55. Cited in Baier, *Kirchenkampf in Nürnberg*, 22.

56. Cited in Kershaw, *Popular Opinion*, 170–171 (emphasis added).

57. Baier, *Kirchenkampf in Nürnberg*, 22.

58. Kershaw, *Popular Opinion*, 171–172; Scholder, *Die Kirchen und das Dritte Reich*, 2:328, 331, 332.

59. Report of the Ansbach District President, Ansbach, November 9, in Witetschek, *Die kirchliche Lage in Bayern*, 2:37. The expansion of the National Socialist movement depended somewhat on visual representations of unified support, together with the lack of public cues that opposition existed. The regime was well aware that any number of Germans were secretly dissatisfied, but the willingness of specific persons to identify themselves publicly with a position of dissent when this was multiplied by thousands and displayed day after day in public places threatened Nazi propaganda of German unity. On Hitler's role, see Helmreich, "The Arrest and Freeing of the Protestant Bishops of Württemberg and Bavaria," 164.

60. Baier, *Deutschen Christen Bayerns*, 148–149, 151.

61. Witetschek, *Die Kirchliche Lage in Bayern*, 2:39.

62. Kershaw, *Popular Opinion*, 171–172.

63. Scholder, *Die Kirchen und das Dritte Reich*, 2:331; *Deutschen Christen Bayerns* Baier, 153, 154; Nicolaisen and Herold, *Hans Meiser*, 44.

64. Use of "*Widerstand*" in government report in Witetschek, *Die kirchliche Lage in Bayern*, 2:39. On the role of the foreign press, see Helmreich, "The Arrest and Freeing of the Protestant Bishops of Württemberg and Bavaria," 160, 166. Schemm's response is in Witetschek, *Die kirchliche Lage in Bayern*, 2:37, 39.

65. Scholder, *Die Kirchen und das Dritte Reich*, 2:312, 320, 331, 333. Helmreich, "The Arrest and Freeing of the Protestant Bishops of Württemberg and Bavaria," 166–167.

66. Scholder, *Die Kirchen und das Dritte Reich*, 2:332–334.

67. Nicolaisen, *Dokumente zur Kirchenpolitik des Dritten Reiches*, 2:193n38.

68. Ibid., 2:189.

69. Joseph Goebbels, *Die Tagebücher von Joseph Goebbels*, ed. Elke Fröhlich (Munich: K. G. Saur, 1993–1996), part I, vol. 3/I, entry for October 25, 1934. Schneider, *Reichsbischof Ludwig Müller*, 185, 211. Victoria Barnet, *For the Soul of the People: Protestant Protest against Hitler* (Oxford: Oxford University Press, 1992), 64. On the day that Meiser and Wurm were released Goebbels wrote of the "real tumult in Bavaria" and suggested that the "Reibi [Reich Bishop] completely failed" (Goebbels, *Tagebücher*, part I, vol. 3/I, entry for October 27, 1934). Looking back on the whole affair the next day, Goebbels reflected, "This is a new [Ernst] Röhm or [Theodor] Habicht catastrophe. Why does one meet this with untimely countermeasures? Must it always end with shooting? Pfeffer and Jäger resigned. And Reibi propped up by the authority of the Leader alone" (Goebbels, *Tagebücher*, part I, vol. 3/I, entry for October 29, 1934).

70. Hitler's previous condemnation of Meiser and Wurm is in Kershaw, *Hubris*, 575. As Goebbels said on the topic of the Reich Church, "In a time when the whole Reich is unifying itself twenty-eight provincial churches can[not] persist. In the interpretation of the Gospel one may hold the command of God

higher than human commands. In the interpretation of political realities we consider ourselves to be God's instrument" (quoted in Steigmann-Gall, *The Holy Reich*, 178–179). On Kerrl's task, see Jantzen, *Faith and Fatherland*, 8. On unifying with force see Hitler, *Speeches*, 2:744, January 25, 1936.

71. Jantzen, *Faith and Fatherland*, 5.

72. Gailus and Lehmann, *Nationalprotestantische Mentalitäten*, 244; Jantzen, *Faith and Fatherland*, 8; Steigmann-Gall, *The Holy Reich*, 186–187.

73. Hess to Gauleiters and Reich leaders, Memorandum 82/37, June 30, 1937, Bundesarchiv, R 187/245, 153. See also Ernst C. Helmreich, *The German Churches under Hitler: Background, Struggle, and Epilogue* (Detroit: Wayne State University Press, 1979), 24, 213. The memo was circulated by the "Chef des SS Hauptamtes" on July 15, 1937.

74. On Hitler's decision to arrest Niemöller, see James Bentley, *Martin Niemöller, 1892–1984* (New York: Free Press, 1984), 127. Public reaction to Niemöller's arrest is in Newsletter 61, July 15, 1937, in Richard Bonney, *Confronting the Nazi War on Christianity: The Kulturekampf Newsletters, 1936–1939* (Oxford: Peter Lang, 2009), 213. Speer, *Inside the Third Reich*, 98. Despite the international protests that his arrest raised, Niemöller remained in custody from 1937 until the defeat of Nazism; Scholder, *Die Kirchen und das Dritte Reich*, 1:75.

75. Jill Stephenson, *Hitler's Home Front: Württemberg under the Nazis* (New York: Hambledon Continuum, 2006), 238. Kyle Jantzen, "Propaganda, Perseverance, and Protest: Strategies for Clerical Survival amid the German Church Struggle," *Church History* 70, no. 2 (June 2001): 297–305.

76. Nicolaisen and Herold, *Hans Meiser*, 45.

CHAPTER III. GERMANY'S CONFESSIONAL DIVIDE
AND THE STRUGGLE FOR CATHOLIC YOUTH

1. Streicher's statement is in Winfried Müller, *Schulpolitik in Bayern im Spannungsfeld von Kultusbürokratie und Besatzungsmacht 1945–1949* (Munich: Oldenbourg, 2009), 193. On confessional schools and Volksgemeinschaft, see Christoph Wagner, *Entwicklung, Herrschaft und Untergang der nationalsozialistischen Bewegung in Passau 1920 bis 1945, Geschichtswissenschaft* (Berlin: Frank and Timme, 2007), 217. Hess's statement is in John S. Conway, *The Nazi Persecution of the Churches* (Toronto: Ryerson Press, 1968), 177.

2. Of the 1933 German population of sixty-five million, there were forty-one million Protestants and twenty-one million Catholics, settled roughly along lines defined by the Peace of Westphalia, ending the Thirty Years' War. Between 1872 and 1875, Bismarck had led an effort to subject all Prussian schools to state authority. R. S. Alexander, *Europe's Uncertain Path, 1814–1914: State Formation and Civil Society* (Malden, MA: John Wiley and Sons, 2012), 175; Lisa Pine, *Education in Nazi Germany* (Oxford: Berg, 2010), 30.

3. Martin Broszat, *The Hitler State* (New York: Longman, 1981), 229.

4. On Nazism, "political Catholicism," and Protestant standards, see Ralf Meindl, *Ostpreussens Gauleiter: Erich Koch—eine politische Biographie*, Einzelveröffentlichungen des Deutschen Historischen Instituts Warschau (Osnabrück: Fibre Verlag, 2007), 140, citing Klaus Scholder, *The Churches and the Third Reich* (Philadelphia: Fortress Press, 1988), 137–139; Franz Kühnel, *Hans Schemm*, 241. By the end of 1933, 1.2 million Protestant youth had already been assimilated into the Hitler Youth. Heinrich August Winkler, *Germany: The Long Road West*, vol. 2: *1933–1990* (New York: Oxford University Press, 2006), 26. For the deterioration of Protestant identity, see Meindl, *Ostpreussens Gauleiter*, 222; Herbert Wagner, *Die Gestapo war nicht allein: Politische Sozialkontrolle und Staatsterror im deutsch-niederländischen Grenzgebiet 1929–1945* (Münster: LIT Verlag, 2004), 309–310.

5. See Walter Ziegler, "Gaue und Gauleiter im Dritten Reich," in *Nationalsozialismus in der Region: Beiträge zu regionalen und lokalen Forschung und zum internationalen Vergleich*, ed. Horst Möller, Andreas Wirsching, and Walter Ziegler (Munich: Oldenbourg, 1996), 139–160. The role of the Gauleiters in transforming Nazi ideology into policy in their regions was not uniform and is sometimes difficult to distinguish from that of other officials. See Suzanne Heim, "Kommentar: Regionalpotentaten oder Akteure auf Reichsebene," in *Die NS-Gaue: Regionale Mittelinstanzen im zentralistischen "Führerstaat,"* ed. Jürgen John, Horst Möller, and Thomas Schaarschmidt (Munich: Oldenbourg, 2007), 136–137. Much of a Gauleiter's power in his region was exercised through prerogatives over personnel decisions. Jeremy Noakes, "'Viceroys of the Reich'? Gauleiters 1925–45," in *Working towards the Führer: Essays in Honour of Sir Ian Kershaw*, ed. Anthony McElligott and Tim Kirk (Manchester: Manchester University Press, 2003), 132. On whether the multiple offices many Gauleiters held largely forced them to abandon the role of leading the party in their regions, see Ziegler, "Gaue und Gauleiter im Dritten Reich," 139–144.

6. For Hitler on the Gauleiters, see H. R. Trevor-Roper, ed., *Hitler's Table Talk, 1941–1944* (New York: Enigma Books, 2007 [orig. 1953]), 416, entry for July 4, 1942. Germany's Catholic leaders identified the Gauleiters as the authorities behind Nazi attacks on denominational schools. See Meindl, *Ostpreussens Gauleiter*, 139. For an overview of agencies supervising the churches, see Heinz Boberach, "Organe der nationalsozialistischen Kirchenpolitik. Kompetenzverteilung und Karrieren in Reich und Ländern," in *Staat und Parteien: Festschrift für Rudolf Morsey zum 65. Geburtstag*, ed. Karl Dietrich Bracher, Paul Mikat, and Rudolf Repgen (Berlin: Dunker and Humblot, 1992), 305–331; Manfred Gailus and Wolfgang Krogel, *Von der babylonischen Gefangenschaft der Kirche im Nationalen: Regionalstudien zu Protestantismus, Nationalsozialismus und Nachkriegsgeschichte 1930 bis 2000* (Berlin: Wichern, 2006); Peter Huettenberger, *Die Gauleiter. Studie zum Wandel des Machtgefueges in der NSDAP* (Stuttgart: Deutsche Verlags-Anstalt, 1969), 149. The Law for the Reorganization of the Reich of January 30, 1934, disempowered the state parliaments, including their authority over schools, but remained only

partly implemented since the Reich ministries in Berlin still depended on the work of local ministries. In March 1934, Bernhard Rust became head of the newly founded Reich Ministry for Education, although this new ministry did not lead to a unified school policy since it did not have its own means to carry out policies independent of local state ministries. Daniel Böhme, *Nationalsozialistische Schulpolitik 1933–1945: Von Hitlers pädagogischen Maximen bis zur praktisch-politischen Umsetzung und mit einem Exkurs zu Dresden* (Munich: Grin Verlag, 2007), 29.

7. Hitler on the Gauleiters is in Trevor-Roper, *Hitler's Table Talk*, 416, entry for July 4, 1942. The boundaries of each Gau were delineated around what were seen as coherent cultural and social units, consisting on average of about 2.5 million people and broken down further into one to two dozen counties, or *Kreise*. Heinz Jürgen Priamus, "Regionale Aspekte in der Politik des nordwestfälischen Gauleiters Alfred Meyer," in *Nationalsozialismus in der Region*, ed. H. Möller, A. Wirsching, and W. Ziegler (Munich: Oldenbourg, 1996), 177. Hitler allowed the Gauleiters of the Reich's newly conquered eastern territories discretion in the way they "Germanized" their regions. Gauleiter Albert Forster identified some persons as Germans whose family members Gauleiter Arthur Greiser, in his neighboring Gau, expelled as non-Germans. Catherine Epstein, *Model Nazi: Arthur Greiser and the Occupation of Western Poland* (New York: Oxford University Press, 2010).

8. On Hitler's intervention in regional governance, Rudolf Jordan recalls in his postwar memoir the moment in 1931 when Hitler named him Gauleiter for Halle-Merseberg; see Ziegler, "Gaue und Gauleiter im Dritten Reich," 139. On Gauleiter independence, see Noakes, "'Viceroys of the Reich'?" 135–136. Favoritism and access to Hitler, as Epstein argues in the duel between Gauleiters Forster and Greiser, helped determine a Gauleiter's power and independence (*Model Nazi*, 7). See also Martin Broszat, *The Hitler State: The Foundation and Development of the Internal Structure of the Third Reich* (London: Routledge, 1981), 118–119, on competition among Gauleiters. During the Final Solution, competition developed among the Gauleiters in the race to declare various regions *"judenfrei,"* and as the Forster-Greiser competition shows, although each Gauleiter used dramatically different methods to determine who was "Aryan," Hitler did not interfere. For variations in the Nazification of schools, see Pine, *Education in Nazi Germany*, 24; Elizabeth Harvey, *Women and the Nazi East: Agents and Witnesses of Germanization* (New Haven: Yale University Press, 2003), 242–243.

9. Kühnel, *Hans Schemm*, 211.

10. For Schemm's rally, see Winfried Müller, "Gauleiter als Minister: Die Gauleiter Hans Schemm, Adolf Wagner, Paul Giesler und das Bayerische Staatsministerium für Unterricht und Kultus 1933–1945," *Zeitschrift für bayerische Landgeschichte* 60 (1997): 979. On shared goals, see Jeremy Noakes, "Leaders of the People? The Nazi Party and German Society," *Journal of Contemporary History* 39, no. 2 (April 2004): 190, 203. Schemm began

to receive such a flood of requests that Cardinal Faulhaber intervened to re-press the volume of Catholic entreaties (Kühnel, *Hans Schemm*, 23, 30, 322). Norbert Frei, *Nationalsozialistische Eroberung der Provinzpresse: Gleichschaltung, Selbstanpassung und Resistenz in Bayern* (Munich: Oldenbourg, 1980), 88ff; Adolf Hitler, Klaus A. Lankheit, and Christian Hartmann, *Reden, Schriften, Anordnungen: Oktober 1932–Januar 1933* (Munich: K. G. Saur Verlag, 1998), 372n1. For an account of Schemm's release of Catholic bishops, despite Wagner with all his firepower as head of the Bavarian Interior Ministry and the police, see Kühnel, *Hans Schemm*, 322.

11. Kühnel, *Hans Schemm*, 284, 289–291, 326. Schemm's program reflected the deceptions achieved in the Reich Concordat, which warmed church leaders and laity alike to Nazism and put them on record as solid supporters early on.

12. Kühnel, *Hans Schemm*, 327.

13. Joachim Kuropka, *Meldungen aus Münster 1924–1944. Geheime und vertrauliche Berichte von Polizei, Gestapo, NSDAP und ihren Gliederungen, staatlicher Verwaltung Gerichtsbarkeit und Wehrmacht über die politische und gesellschaftliche Situation in Münster* (Münster: Regensberg, 1992), 347.

14. Kühnel, *Hans Schemm*, 263, 291.

15. Verein für Hamburgische Geschichte, Uwe Schmidt, and Rainer Hering, eds., *Hamburger Schulen im "Dritten Reich,"* Beiträge zur Geschichte Hamburgs (Hamburg: Hamburg University Press, 2010), 382.

16. Kuropka, *Meldungen aus Münster*, 355, citing an activity report of the NSLB to the Gauamtleitung Westphalia-North for the second quarter of 1935.

17. The "struggle of the church against National Socialism has reached an unprecedented level," declared an April 1935 report of the NSLB to Gauleiter Alfred Meyer's office. "From every corner incidents are reported of incitements by the Catholic clergy and its organizations. . . . Among the staff of teachers are still some who with sophisticated deceptions in league with chaplains and vicars agitate against everything under the name of National Socialism" (cited in Kuropka, *Meldungen aus Münster*, 359–360).

18. Stefan Klemp, *Richtige Nazis hat es hier nicht gegeben. Eine Stadt, eine Firma, der vergessene mächtigste Wirtschaftsführer und Auschwitz*, Geschichte 14 (Münster: LIT Verlag, 2000), 225.

19. As of 1936 leading Reich offices in Berlin began to direct the party initiatives at regional levels, mostly through secret channels. At the same time the Gestapo became more independent in its own initiatives. Lothar Wettstein, *Josef Bürckel: Gauleiter Reichsstatthalter Krisenmanager Adolf Hitlers* (Norderstedt: Books on Demand, 2010), 323, 326. Kuropka, *Meldungen aus Münster*, 349; for local control over schools, see W. Müller, *Schulpolitik in Bayern*, 193.

20. On Wagner's efforts to secularize schools, see Ulrich von Hehl, *Priester unter Hitlers Terror: Eine biographische und statistische Erhebung* (Paderborn: Schöningh, 1996), 1:140, 193–194. In 1933 89 percent of Bavarians voted for

the continuance of the Catholic school system, but by 1936 in Munich, a mere 35 percent of children were enrolled in denominational schools while 65 percent were not. By January 30, 1937, less than 5 percent of Bavarian parents reportedly wished to enroll their children in church schools. Richard Bonney, *Confronting the Nazi War on Christianity: The Kulturekampf Newsletters, 1936–1939* (Oxford: Peter Lang, 2009), 145; Conway, *The Nazi Persecution of the Churches*, 179; James Donohoe, *Hitler's Conservative Opponents in Bavaria, 1930–1945: A Study of Catholic, Monarchist, and Separatist Anti-Nazi Activities* (Leiden: Brill, 1961), 57. The statement by the League for the Defense of Christianity is in Bonney, *Confronting the Nazi War on Christianity*, 145–146. On party efforts to build unity, see Hehl, *Priester unter Hitlers Terror*, 47–48, 142.

21. On the emergence of Catholic resistance, see Kuropka, *Meldungen aus Münster*, 357. On the secularizing trend in Germany, see Franz-Josef Luzak, "Die Lutherbildaffäre in Oldenburg: Die Evangelische-Lutherische Kirche im Kampf um Kreuz und Lutherbild," in *Zur Sache—das Kreuz! Untersuchungen zur Geschichte des Konflikts um Kreuz und Lutherbild in den Schulen Oldenburgs, zur Wirkungsgeschichte eines Massenprotests und zum Problem nationalsozialistischer Herrschaft in einer agrarisch-katholischen Region*, ed. Joachim Kuropka (Vechta: Vechtaer Druckerei und Verlag, 1986), 82–100. For the situation in Bavaria, see C. Wagner, *Entwicklung, Herrschaft und Untergang*, 218. Lothar Wettstein writes that due to Gestapo pressures, the solidarity among clergy began to break down. (*Josef Bürckel*, 326). Wagner's order in W. Müller, *Schulpolitik in Bayern*, 193–194.

22. By some accounts there was a marked resurgence in support for denominational schools beginning during the summer of 1936, led by parents (C. Wagner, *Entwicklung, Herrschaft und Untergang*, 217). Heydrich's instructions are in Hehl, *Priester unter Hitlers Terror*, 50–51, 54, 136. Bormann's order is in Kuropka, *Meldungen aus Münster*, 349.

23. On Austrian protest, see Evan Burr Bukey, *Hitler's Austria: Popular Sentiment in the Nazi Era, 1938–1945* (Chapel Hill: University of North Carolina Press, 2000), 118. For techniques used to remove crucifixes, see Ursula Dluhosch and Ralph Rotte, "Das Kultusministerium als Machtfaktor in der NS-Schulpolitik Bürokratische Friktionen am Beispiel Bayerns," *Paedagogica Historica: International Journal of the History of Education* 37, no. 2 (2001): 334.

24. Bureaucrats in the Bavarian Culture Ministry were able to thwart the wishes of the regional Nazi elite on personnel matters, at least in two cases. "Das Kultusministerium als Machtfaktor in der NS-Schulpolitik: Bürokratische Friktionen am Beispiel Bayerns," *Paedagogica Historica: International Journal of the History of Education* 37, no. 2 (2001): 317–340.

25. Heinz Jürgen Priamus, "Regionale Aspekte in der Politik des nordwestfälischen Gauleiters Alfred Meyer," in *Nationalsozialismus in der Region: Beiträge zur regionalen und lokalen Forschung und zum internationalen Vergleich*,

ed. H. Möller, A. Wirsching, and W. Ziegler (Munich: Oldenbourg, 1996), 175–195. See H. Priamus and S. Goch, *Macht der Propaganda oder Propaganda der Macht?* (Essen: Klartext, 1992), 48–66.

26. H. W. Koch, *The Hitler Youth: Origins and Development, 1922–1945* (New York: Cooper Square Press, 2000), 133, 134; Robert Anthony Krieg, *Catholic Theologians in Nazi Germany* (New York: Continuum, 2004), 75.

27. Report of the state police office for the Münster government area, April 1935, in Kuropka, *Meldungen aus Münster*, 153, 163–164. For general information on Catholic discord with National Socialism in this area, see ibid., 154–164 and also chapter 13.

28. Cited in Priamus, "Regionale Aspekte," 186.

29. Kuropka, *Zur Sache—das Kreuz!*, 31.

30. Cited in Priamus, "Regionale Aspekte." 186.

31. Jeremy Noakes's study, "The Oldenburg Crucifix Struggle of November 1936: A Case of Opposition in the Third Reich," in *The Shaping of the Nazi State*, ed. Peter D. Stachura (London: Croom Helm, 1978), foreshadowed prominent themes in important works of the following decade but concluded that Catholics failed to mount a resistance against Hitler's regime itself because it lacked its own "alternative political ideology" (p. 229).

32. Ibid., 213–216, 297–306; Kuropka, *Meldungen aus Münster*, 353.

33. Willi Baumann, "Franz Vorwerk: Der 'Offizial des Kreuzkampfes,'" in Kuropka, *Zur Sache—das Kreuz!*, 298–303.

34. Willi Baumann and Peter Sieve, "Konflikte zwischen Kirche und Nationalsozialismus in Friesoythe 1936/37," in Kuropka, *Zur Sache—das Kreuz!*, 165–175, 299, 300. It is not clear whether Vorwerk's superior, Bishop Galen, also encouraged this instigation to protest.

35. Cited in Baumann, "Franz Vorwerk," 300, 301.

36. Noakes, "The Oldenburg Crucifix Struggle," 218–219. The decree is printed in Johann Neuhäusler, *Kreuz und Hakenkreuz: Der Kampf des Nationalsozialismus gegen die katholische Kirche und der kirchliche Widerstand* (Munich: Katholische Kirche Bayerns, 1946), 116.

37. Kuropka, *Zur Sache—das Kreuz!*, 28.

38. Noakes, "The Oldenburg Crucifix Struggle," 219. Vorwerk's pastoral letter is in Baumann, "Franz Vorwerk," 301. Joachim Kuropka, *Geistliche und Gestapo: Klerus zwischen Staatsallmacht und kirchlicher Hierarchie* (Münster: LIT Verlag, 2004), 220ff.

39. Vorwerk's reflections on his letter are in Joachim Kuropka, *Für Wahrheit, Recht und Freiheit—gegen den Nationalsozialismus*, Dokumente und Materialien zur Geschichte und Kultur des Oldenburger Münsterlandes (Vechta: Oldenburgische Volkszeitung, 1983), 91. Mayor Prüllage's report is in Kuropka, *Zur Sache—das Kreuz!*, 15. On conferences of priests, see Maria Anna Zumholz, "'Nein, Herr Minister, das machen wir nicht mit, das lassen wir uns nicht gefallen!' Kreuzkampf in Molbergen, Vorgeschichte und Folgen," in Kuropka, *Zur Sache—das Kreuz!*, 120.

40. Heinrich Hachmöller, "Der Kreuzkampf im Löningen: Auswirkung der nationalsozialistischen Schulpolitik," in Kuropka, *Zur Sache—das Kreuz!*, 137–142; Kuropka, " 'Das Volk steht auf,' " in Kuropka, *Zur Sache—das Kreuz!*, 16.

41. Willi Baumann, "Franz Uptmoor: 'Der Prediger des Kreuzkampfes,' ": in Kuropka, *Zur Sache—das Kreuz!*, 314–316; Noakes, "The Oldenburg Crucifix Struggle," 220–221; Noakes writes that the event took place on November 10.

42. In a 1962 memoir, a Cloppenburg administrator recalled the dissension that the crucifix decree caused among local and area officials (August Münzebrock, *Amtshauptmann in Cloppenburg, 1933–1945* [Cloppenburg: Janssen, 1962]). On the belief in Pauly's ignorance, see Martina Bahl, "Essen (Oldgb.) Im Zeichen des Kreuzkampfes," in Kuropka, *Zur Sache—das Kreuz!*, 194.

43. Noakes, "The Oldenburg Crucifix Struggle," 219. On the Esseners, see Bahl, "Essen (Oldgb.)," 194.

44. Cited in Bahl, "Essen (Oldgb.)," 194.

45. Ibid., 195.

46. Noakes, "The Oldenburg Crucifix Struggle," 221–222.

47. Ibid., 222.

48. Ibid., 221, 222.

49. Niermann had the help of the local farm director *(Ortsbauernführer)*, Josef Holters, who would have had practice in negotiating on behalf of local farmers with the Reich organization regulating food production (Reichsnährstand). Bahl, "Essen (Oldgb.)," 200; Daniela Münkel, *Nationalsozialistische Agrarpolitik und Bauernalltag* (Frankfurt am Main: Campus Verlag, 1996), 370.

50. Cited in Bahl, "Essen (Oldgb.)," 196. This statement was signed by eight or nine respected men of the community, including businessmen and two politicians whom the Nazi Party had replaced, even though they had won election by popular vote. Half were farmers, some of whom held official party positions.

51. Ibid., 197.

52. Noakes, "The Oldenburg Crucifix Struggle," 221.

53. Zumholz, "Nein, Herr Minister," 116. The story of Molbergen is absent in Noakes, "The Oldenburg Crucifix Struggle"; cf. 222.

54. Zumholz, "Nein, Herr Minister," 121, 122.

55. Ibid.

56. Ibid., 123.

57. Kuropka, "Das Volk," 23, 35.

58. Joseph Goebbels, *Die Tagebücher von Joseph Goebbels*, ed. Elke Fröhlich (Munich: K. G. Saur, 1993–1996), part I, vol. 3/II, 352, entry for January 30, 1937. Baumann, "Franz Vorwerk," 302; Kuropka, *Zur Sache—Das Kreuz!*, 25. A ban on press coverage of the Frankenholz crucifix struggle the following year was applied immediately. ZSg. 101/91/173/Nr. 314, March 3, 1937, in Gabriele Toepser-Ziegert, ed., *NS-Presseanweisungen der Vorkriegszeit: Edition und Dokumentation* (Munich and New York: K. G. Saur, 1984–2001), 549.

59. Jürgen John, Horst Möller, and Thomas Schaarschmidt, *Die NS-Gaue: Regionale Mittelinstanzen im zentralistischen "Führerstaat"* (Munich: Oldenburg Verlag, 2007), 251; Georg Kretschmar et al., *Dokumente zur Kirchenpolitik des Dritten Reiches*, vol. 3: *1935–1937, Von der Errichtung des Reichsministeriums für die kirchlichen Angelegenheiten bis zum Rucktritt des Reichskirchenausschusses, Juli 1934–Februar 1937* (Munich: C. Kaiser, 1994), 256; Goebbels, *Tagebücher*, Part I, 4:69, entry for March 26, 1937.

60. Noakes, "The Oldenburg Crucifix Struggle," 224; Zumholz, "Nein, Herr Minister," 124.

61. On the dissemination of information about Oldenburg, see Rudolf Willenborg, "Zur Rezeptionsgeschichte des Kreuzkampfes im Deutschen Reich und im Ausland," in Kuropka, *Zur Sache—das Kreuz!*, 341, 345. Reactions from Galen and the police are in Geheimes Staatsarchiv Preussischer Kulturbesitz, PK, I. HA Rep. 90 Staatsministerium, Annex P Geheime Staatspolizei, Nr. 86/2, Lagebericht des Geheimen Staatspolizeiamts (Gestapa) Berlin für den Zeitraum vom 1. Oktober bis zum 28. Februar 1937 (no date).

62. Zumholz, "Nein, Herr Minister," 124.

63. Kuropka, *Zur Sache—das Kreuz!*, 24; Oldenburg Protestants encouraged Vorwerk to organize protests because "people in south Oldenburg [Catholics] can be mobilized better than those in the north." Luzak, "Die Lutherbildaffäre," 88, 89. On Röver's rescission order, see Luzak, "Die Lutherbildaffäre," 96, 97.

64. The replacement of Molbergen crucifixes is in Zumholz, "Nein, Herr Minister," 123–125. Hitler and the party routinely used pressures of social conformity to repress dissent and drive the Volk in the direction they wanted. But in this case officials brought in someone who would be immune to the immediate surrounding social pressures.

65. "Die Zeit des Kreuzes ist nun vorbei," *Pariser Tageblatt* 3, no. 499 (November 25, 1935): 2; Kuropka, *Zur Sache—das Kreuz!*, 37.

66. Baumann, "Franz Vorwerk," 304–305; Walter Schultze, "Kreuzkampf und Schulkampf in der Gemeinde Goldenstedt," in Kuropka, *Zur Sache—das Kreuz!*, 129–136.

67. Noakes, "The Oldenburg Crucifix Struggle," 225–226.

68. Many if not all Catholic bishops prior to March 1933 issued some kind of warning against the Nazis.

69. Richard Steigmann-Gall has argued that leading Nazis identified their movement in "specifically Christian terms" (*The Holy Reich: Nazi Conceptions of Christianity, 1919–1945* [Cambridge: Cambridge University Press, 2004], 3). Koch's position on religion is in Meindl, *Ostpreussens Gauleiter*, 79, 169–172, 341, 487. According to postwar assessments of Protestants, Koch did not even attempt to change the beliefs of the church. He was eventually forced by the party to distance himself from Protestants and left the church in 1943 (Meindl, *Ostpreussens Gauleiter*, 165, 169, 171).

70. Meindl, *Ostpreussens Gauleiter*, 142–144, 164; Guenter Lewy, *The Catholic Church and Nazi Germany* (Cambridge, MA: Da Capo Press, 1964), 28–29.

71. On Kaller's procession to Dittrichswalde and reactions to these processions from the church and state, see David Blackbourn, *Marpingen: Apparitions of the Virgin Mary in Bismarckian Germany* (Oxford: Clarendon Press, 1993), 339; Andreas Kossert, *Ostpreussen: Geschichte und Mythos* (Munich: Siedler, 2005), 295. Kaller as an "enemy of the state" is in Michael Phayer, *The Catholic Church and the Holocaust, 1930–1965* (Bloomington: Indiana University Press, 2000), 18.

72. The Gestapo took action to intimidate or ban some clergy from preaching, as in the case of Jesuit priest Rupert Mayer. Neuhäusler, *Kreuz und Haken-kreuz: Der Kampf des Nationalsozialismus gegen die katholische Kirche und der kirchliche Widerstand*, 46–51. Only in February 1945, just before the Soviet army swept through the area, did the SS force Kaller to leave his position and his diocese. Gerhard Reifferscheid, *Das Bistum Ermland und das Dritte Reich* (Cologne: Böhlau, 1975), 164–165, 172.

73. Reifferscheid, *Das Bistum*, 177, 178. See also Noakes, "The Oldenburg Crucifix Struggle," 213.

74. Walter Adolph, *Geheime Aufzeichnungen aus dem nationalsozialistischen Kirchenkampf: 1935–1943*, ed. Ulrich von Hehl, Veröffentlichungen der Kommission für Zeitgeschichte, Reihe A: Quellen, Bd. 28 (Mainz: Matthias Grünewald Verlag, 1979), 220. Adolph saw Kaller as "a nature much too simple and unbending, to understand the complicated church-political game, replete with tactics and intrigue." Hans-Jürgen Karp and Joachim Köhler, *Katholische Kirche unter nationalsozialistischer und kommunistischer Diktatur: Deutschland und Polen 1939–1989* (Cologne: Böhlau, 2001), 236. For Heydrich's suspension of the ban, see "Express Letter from the Chief of Security Police to the Reich Minister and Chief of the Reich Chancellery," February 19, 1938, Berlin; reproduced in Reifferscheid, *Das Bistum*, 304.

75. "I have attempted to warn the former rulers in Austria not to continue on this route of theirs. Only a lunatic could believe that suppression and terror can permanently rob people of their love for their ancestral Volkstum. European history has proven that such cases serve to breed an even greater fanaticism. This fanaticism then compels the oppressor to resort to ever harsher methods of violation, and these in turn increase the loathing and hatred of the objects of those methods." Hitler's proclamation of March 12, read by Göring and broadcast on all German and Austrian radio stations; Adolf Hitler, *Speeches and Proclamations*, 4 vols., ed. Max Domarus (Wauconda, IL: Bolchazy-Carducci, 1990), 2:1047, March 12, 1938.

76. Cited in Kossert, *Ostpreussen: Geschichte und Mythos*, 296. Kaller, leading his fifty thousand to the apparition site in Dittrichswalde in 1936, did recognize the Polish people who had just suffered pastoral restrictions, but that was before the war. Blackbourne, *Marpingen*, 339.

NOTES TO PAGES 106–111   337

77. Lewy, *The Catholic Church and Nazi Germany*, 214–217.

78. Memorandum partially reproduced in Reifferscheid, *Das Bistum*, 305–306, and cited as Generalstaatsanwalt Kapeller to the Reich Justice Ministry (for State Secretary Hans Schlegelberger), 1941, Königsberg.

79. Noakes, "The Oldenburg Crucifix Struggle," 228. On the necessity of replacing the Christian morality among Germans with a Nazi worldview so they could meet the "epochal struggle," see Peter Longerich, *Heinrich Himmler: A Life* (Oxford: Oxford University Press, 2012), 265.

80. Verein für Hamburgische Geschichte, Uwe Schmidt, and Rainer Hering, eds., *Hamburger Schulen im "Dritten Reich,"* Beiträge zur Geschichte Hamburgs (Hamburg: Hamburg University Press, 2010), 2:111, 587. By May 20, 1943, Bormann's Party Chancellery concluded that orders from Berlin to the Gauleiters were useless since "the Gauleiters in the end simply do what they want." Akten der Partei-Kanzlei, II 4, pp. 516ff., Regest Nr. 44 378, in Möller, Wirsching, and Ziegler, *Nationalsozialismus in der Region*, 152.

CHAPTER IV. STREET DEMONSTRATIONS

1. Guenter Lewy, *The Catholic Church and Nazi Germany* (Cambridge, MA: Da Capo Press, 1964), 101; Kevin P. Spicer, *Hitler's Priests: Catholic Clergy and National Socialism* (DeKalb, IL: Northern Illinois University Press, 2008), 53–56; 80–87; Derek Hastings, *Catholicism and the Roots of Nazism: Religious Identity and National Socialism* (Oxford: Oxford University Press, 2010), 129, 132.

2. Spicer, *Hitler's Priests*, 35, 47, 54–57.

3. Newspaper account titled "Enormous Protest Rally for Alban Schachleiter," excerpted in *Dokumente zur Kirchenpolitik des Dritten Reiches*, vol. 1: *Das Jahr 1933*, ed. Carsten Nicolaisen (Munich: C. Kaiser, 1971), 25, 26; Lewy, *The Catholic Church and Nazi Germany*, 101; Hastings, *Catholicism and the Roots of Nazism*, 172.

4. English translation of a summary of Hitler's speech to the Gauleiters on the role of the NSDAP, February 2, 1934, in Jeremy Noakes and Geoffrey Pridham, eds., *Nazism 1919–1945*, vol. 2: *State, Economy and Society, 1933–1939* (Exeter: University of Exeter Press, 2000), 40–42. Adolf Hitler, *Speeches and Proclamations*, 4 vols., ed. Max Domarus (Wauconda, IL: Bolchazy-Carducci, 1990), 1:285, 452, March 23, 1933, May 1, 1934.

5. Thomas Nipperdey, *Deutsche Geschichte 1866–1918*, vol. 1: *Arbeitswelt und Bürgergeist* (Munich: C. H. Beck, 1991), 434; Christoph Kösters, "Demonstrationskatholizismus im Bistum Münster 1933–1945," in *Zwischen Loyalität und Resistenz: Soziale Konflikte und politische Repression während der NS-Herrschaft in Westfalen*, ed. Rudolf Schlögl and Hans-Ulrich Thamer (Münster: Aschendorff, 1996), 161, 168; Joachim Kuropka, *Meldungen aus Münster 1924–1944. Geheime und vertrauliche Berichte von Polizei, Gestapo, NSDAP und ihren Gliederungen, staatlicher Verwaltung Gerichtsbarkeit und Wehrmacht über die politische und gesellschaftliche Situation in Münster* (Münster: Regensberg, 1992), 435.

6. On Nazi warnings about protest, see Kösters, "Demonstrationkatholismus," 167–169, 177. On demonstrations in Münster, see Rottenburg Landrat (district chairman) Alfred Chormann to Sproll, April 13, 1938, in Paul Kopf and Max Miller, eds., *Die Vertreibung von Bischof Joannes Baptista Sproll von Rottenburg 1938–1945: Dokumente zur Geschichte des kirchlichen Widerstands* (Mainz: Matthias Grunewald, 1971), 91. Additional accounts of events are in Paul Kopf, *Joannes Baptista Sproll, Leben und Wirken* (Sigmaringen: Thorbecke, 1988), and Bernhard Hanssler, *Bischof Johannes Sproll* (Sigmaringen: Thorbecke, 1984).

7. Staatspolizeistelle für den Reigierungsbezirk Köln to Geheime Staatspolizeiamt in Berlin, Köln, 13 August 1935, Betr. Zusammenstoesse zwischen Angehoerigen des katholischen Jugendverbandes in Siegburg-Wolsdorf und der Hitler Jugend, 20 Juli 1935, Bundesarchiv, R58/57006. This is the written statement of the Landrat in Siegburg, transmitted from the Gestapo in Cologne to Gestapo headquarters in Berlin on August 13, 1935. The report indicates that at least in this particular Gau only the Gauleiters or Kreisleiters were authorized to organize demonstrations.

8. Preussische Politische Polizei Bericht, Berlin 11.03.1933, YVA; 0.51/331, in Otto Kulka and Eberhard Jäckel, eds., *Die Juden in den geheimen NS-Stimmungsberichten 1933–1945* (Düsseldorf: Droste Verlag, 2004), 45, 46.

9. David Bankier, *The Germans and the Final Solution: Public Opinion under Nazism* (Cambridge, MA: Blackwell, 1992), 37. Staatspolizeistelle für den Reigierungsbezirk Köln to Geheime Staatspolizeiamt in Berlin, Köln, 13 August 1935, Betr. Zusammenstoesse zwischen Angehörigen des katholischen Jugendverbandes in Siegburg-Wolsdorf und der Hitler Jugend, 20 Juli 1935, Bundesarchiv, R58/57006.

10. Otto Dov Kulka, "Popular Opinion in Nazi Germany as a Factor in the Policy of the 'Solution of the Jewish Question': The Nuremberg Laws and the Reichskristallnacht," in *Popular Opinion in Totalitarian Regimes: Fascism, Nazism, Communism*, ed. Paul Corner, 81–106 (Oxford: Oxford University Press, 2009). On the treatment of racial defilement *(Rassenschande)*, see Patricia Szobar, "Telling Sexual Stories in the Nazi Courts of Law: Race Defilement in Germany, 1933 to 1945," in *Sexuality and German Fascism*, ed. Dagmar Herzog, 131–163 (New York: Berghahn Books, 2005). In the Baltic states, "Nazi-incited pogroms, followed by more organized and systematic mass shootings," were the pattern. Richard Breitman et al., *U.S. Intelligence and the Nazis* (Cambridge: Cambridge University Press, 2005), 23–24. Hitler to Adolf Gemlich, September 16, 1919, in Eberhard Jäckel and Axel Kuhn, eds., *Hitler: Sämtliche Aufzeichnungen, 1905–1924* (Stuttgart: Deutsche Verlags-Anstalt, 1980), 88–90, 119, 176–177.

11. David Bankier, "Hitler and the Policy-Making Process on the Jewish Question," *Holocaust and Genocide Studies* 3, no. 1 (1988): 4. Michael Wildt, "The Boycott Campaign as an Arena of Collective Violence against Jews in Ger-

many, 1933–1938," in *Nazi Europe and the Final Solution,* ed. David Bankier and Israel Gutman (Jerusalem: Yad Vashem, 2003), 56.

12. On the 1933 Jewish boycott, see the Prussian Political Police Report, March 11, 1933, in Kulka and Jäckel, *Die Juden,* 45ff. Public reactions in Jessnitz and the case of Max Gumpel are from Staatsministerium Anhalt, "Bericht über die politische Lage," Bericht für August und September 1935, Dessau, 29 Oktober 1935, Bundesarchiv, R 58/3625. Breslau police report, August 3, 1935, in Kulka and Jäckel, *Die Juden,* 149.

13. Stefan Hördler, introduction to *SA-Terror als Herrschaftssicherung "Köpenicker Blutwoche" und öffentliche Gewalt im Nationalsozialismus* (Berlin: Metropol, 2013), 13; Hans Bernd Gisevius, *To the Bitter End* (Boston: Houghton Mifflin, 1947), 308. Hermann Beck, *The Fateful Alliance: German Conservatives and Nazis in 1933: The Machtergreifung in a New Light* (New York: Berghahn Books, 2008), 103. Götz Aly and Wolf Gruner, eds., *Die Verfolgung und Ermordung der europäischen Juden durch das national sozialistisches Deutschland,* vol. 1: *Deutsches Reich 1933–1937* (Munich: Oldenbourg, 2008), 34.

14. On Heydrich, see Michael Wildt, "Before the 'Final Solution': The Judenpolitik of the SD, 1935–1938," *Leo Baeck Institute Yearbook* 43, no. 1 (1998): 244–245. For police and popular anti-Semitism, see Michael Wildt, *Hitler's Volksgemeinschaft.* Wildt treats spectator and crowd actions as forceful accomplices in Nazi oppression.

15. On Hitler's toleration of rioting, see Alan E. Steinweis, *Kristallnacht 1938* (Cambridge, MA: Belknap Press, 2009), 11. On Helldorf and marriage, see Aly and Gruner, *Die Verfolgung,* 1:462–464. On street demonstrations against Jews turning violent, see Kulka, "Popular Opinion." Heydrich's statement is in Lothar Gruchmann, *Justiz im Dritten Reich 1933–1940* (Oldenburg: Wissenschaftsverlag, 2010), 430. On intermarriage: Wildt, *Judenpolitik des SD, 1935 bis 1938* (Munich: Oldenbourg, 1995), 248.

16. Best to Darre, September 1935, Document 195, in Aly and Gruner, *Die Verfolgung,* 1:486–487. On the Nuremberg Laws' definition of Jewishness, see Manfred Berg and Martin H. Geyer, eds., *Two Cultures of Rights: The Quest for Inclusion and Participation in Modern America and Germany* (Cambridge: Cambridge University Press, 2002), 89. Hitler's stance on this definition is in Michael Mayer, *Staaten als Täter: Ministerialbürokratie und "Judenpolitik" in NS-Deutschland und Vichy-Frankreich* (Oldenburg: Wissenschaftsverlag, 2010), 169–170. For Hitler's prohibition of *Einzelaktionen,* see Gruchmann, *Justiz im Dritten Reich,* 876–877.

17. Streicher on *Einzelaktionen* is in Nachman Blumenthal, "Action," in *Yad Vashem Studies on the European Jewish Catastrophe and Resistance,* ed. Shaul Esh (Jerusalem: Yad Vashem, 1960), 4:58, 59. Hitler's statement is in Saul Friedländer, *Das Dritte Reich und die Juden: Die Jahre der Verfolgung 1933–1939* (Munich: Beck, 1998), 159–160. For Best's recommendation of a gradual

approach, see Gestapo Berlin, Dr. Werner Best (Acting Director of the Prussian Gestapo), December 19, 1935, in Aly and Gruner, *Die Verfolgung*, 1:541. Heydrich's support for this approach is in International Military Tribunal (IMT), Document 1816-PS, Stenographische Niederschrift der Besprechung über die Judenfrage bei Göring am 12 Nov. 1938, in *Nazi Conspiracy and Aggression*, 8 vols., and Supplements A and B (Washington, D.C.: Government Printing Office, 1946–1948), 4:425; IMT, *Trial of the Major War Criminals: Proceeding Volumes*, 42 vols. (Nuremberg, November 14, 1945–October 1, 1946), 28:534; Eric Johnson and Karl-Heinz Reuband, *What We Knew: Terror, Mass Murder and Everyday Life in Nazi Germany: An Oral History* (New York: Basic Books; London: John Murray, 2005). According to Johnson and Reuband, relatively widespread awareness of mass murder did little to dim admiration for Hitler.

18. David Clay Large, *Nazi Games: The Olympics of 1936* (New York: W. W. Norton, 2007), 127; Ian Kershaw, *Hitler, 1889–1936: Hubris* (New York: W. W. Norton, 2000), 57; Aly and Gruner, *Die Verfolgung*, 1:559.

19. On the construction of restaurants, see Heydrich to the Brown House, February 1, 1937, Document 264, in Aly and Gruner, *Die Verfolgung*, 1:635. Eichmann and Heydrich on riots is in Wildt, *Judenpolitik des SD*, 33, 41.

20. "Characteristically" the police "exploited the existing pogrom climate" to make massive arrests. Wildt, *Judenpolitik des SD*, 41, 263 and *Hitler's Volksgemeinschaft*, 233–238; Steinweis, *Kristallnacht*, 13, 19, 20, 24.

21. Joseph Goebbels, *Die Tagebücher von Joseph Goebbels*, ed. Elke Fröhlich (Munich: K. G. Saur, 1993–1996), part I, vol. 6, 177–181, entries for November 9 and 10, 1938. Evidence substantiates Goebbels's claims that Hitler decided for the pogrom during his conversation with Goebbels. Steinweis, *Kristallnacht*, 6, 43, 45.

22. Stefan Kley, "Hitler and the Pogrom of November 9–10, 1938," *Yad Vashem Studies on the European Jewish Catastrophe and Resistance* (Jerusalem: Yad Vashem, 2000), 28:88; cf. Ian Kershaw's extended discussion of the relationship between Hitler's charismatic power and the radicalization of Nazi policies in "'Working Towards the Führer': Reflections on the Nature of the Hitler Dictatorship," *Contemporary European History* 2, no. 2 (July 1993): 103–118. Steinweis, *Kristallnacht*, 50–53; Richard J. Evans, *Lying about Hitler: History, Holocaust, and the David Irving Trial* (New York: Basic Books, 2001). Steinweis argues that Kristallnacht can be seen as a "nationalization of a series of localized anti-Jewish actions" as much as an atrocity initiated and orchestrated from the top (*Kristallnacht*, 3–6, 23). See the security police report for a description of the origins and evolution of the Kassel riot, summarized in Steinweis, *Kristallnacht*, 24.

23. Nathan Stoltzfus, *Resistance of the Heart: Intermarriage and the Rosenstrasse Protest in Nazi Germany* (New York: Norton, 1996), 98; Steinweis, *Kristallnacht*, 54–55, 58.

24. Hitler approved a statement Goebbels planned to issue calling a halt to the violence (Steinweis, *Kristallnacht*, 99). For the popular reception of Kristallnacht, see Ian Kershaw, *Hitler, 1936–1945: Nemesis* (New York: W. W. Norton, 2000), 142–144. The people generally blamed Goebbels. Hitler expressed his disappointment by saying, "The party stood behind me, even in times of set-back and dismay. . . . This is precisely what we must bring the Volk to do. It must learn to fanatically believe in the *Endsieg* [ultimate victory]." Hitler, *Speeches*, 2:1252, November 10, 1938; on the restoration of quiet, see 2:1244ff., November 10, 1938. Goebbels, *Tagebücher*, part I, vol. 6, 183–186, entries for November 12 and 13, 1938.

25. On the Jewish Star, see David Bankier, "Hitler and the Policy Making Process on the Jewish Question," *Holocaust and Genocide Studies* 3, no. 1 (1988): 6. Jeffrey R. Smith, "The First World War and the Public Sphere in Germany," in *World War I and the Cultures of Modernity*, ed. Douglas Mackaman and Michael Mays (Jackson: University of Mississippi Press, 2000), 80; Henry Friedlander, *The Origins of Nazi Genocide: From Euthanasia to the Final Solution* (Chapel Hill: University of North Carolina Press, 1995), 23.

26. On Bismarck and "social boycotts," see John C. G. Röhl, *Germany without Bismarck: The Crisis of Government in the Second Reich, 1890–1900* (Berkeley: University of California Press, 1967), 18; George Herbert Perris, *Germany and the German Emperor* (London: A. Melrose, 1912), 456. Heeringen's statement is in Röhl, *Germany without Bismarck*, 18; Perris, *Germany and the German Emperor*, 456.

27. Adam Roberts, ed., *The Strategy of Civilian Defence: Non-Violent Resistance to Aggression* (London: Faber, 1967), 122; E. P. Thompson, "The Moral Economy of the English Crowd in the Eighteenth Century," *Past and Present* 50 (1971): 98, 113. Gene Sharp, *The Politics of Nonviolent Action*, vol. 2: *The Methods of Nonviolent Action* (Boston: P. Sargent, 1973), 189. English and colonial American societies more readily associated with early democracy and civil disobedience than Germany—and also provided precedents for crowds imposing their will while claiming to act on behalf of the commonwealth and in place of the law. In England, popular consensus expressed as riots prevailed at times in matters of the distribution and sale of bread. Direct actions by aggrieved crowds acting both upon customary social norms and intervening against official rulings are also richly documented in early American history, where crowds acting on behalf of a shared sense of justice frequently claimed lawful status. The American "patriot movement" responded to British policies beginning in the 1760s, with crowds that set aside class, beliefs, and geography in order to join the common cause of justice as the collective perceived it—including one notable incident in Wethersfeld, Connecticut, after the passage of the unpopular Stamp Act of 1765. In it, a town stamp master was required to resign publicly by an

enraged crowd. When assemblymen asked whether it would not be best to wait "for the sense of the government," they were told that the crowd itself "is the sense of government" (Barbara Clark Smith, *The Freedoms We Lost: Consent and Resistance in Revolutionary America* [New York: New Press, 2010], 94).

28. Fear of public disorder and even warnings that the "fanatical mob" might be concealing a "revolutionary upheaval" were heightened by rumors of a French plot with pilgrims acting as enemies within. David Blackbourn, *Marpingen: Apparitions of the Virgin Mary in Bismarckian Germany* (Oxford: Clarendon Press, 1993), 194–195, 206, 211–213, 216, 218.

29. Sproll's Pastoral letter, September 8, 1939, in Lewy, *The Catholic Church and Nazi Germany*, 226. Hitler banned "every action against the Catholic or Protestant Churches for the duration of the war," explicitly in order to preempt unrest. NO-1392, Staatsarchiv Nürnberg, Reich Führer SS, gez. Paucke, September 8, 1939; unpublished Nuremberg Trial Document NO-1392. Cf. John Conway, *The Nazi Persecution of the Churches* (Toronto: Ryerson Press, 1968), 435n1 (cited as NG-1392).

30. On Sproll's developing capacity for resistance by practicing it, see Dominik Burkart, *Joannes Baptista Sproll: Bischof im Widerstand* (Stuttgart: Kohlhammer, 2013), 87–89. German bishops spoke out against the sterilization law but compromised this position in practice lest they endanger the Concordat and other Catholic priorities. Jill Stephenson, *Hitler's Home Front: Württemberg under the Nazis* (New York: Hambledon Continuum, 2006), 122, 230, 241; Friedlander, *The Origins of Nazi Genocide*, 113. For Sproll's statements about Rosenberg, see the accusations in the Report of the Attorney General for the Special Court for Greater Stuttgart Region to the Reich Minister of Justice, February 1, 1938, in Kopf and Miller, *Bischof Sproll*, 60–61.

31. The indictment is printed as the "Report of the Attorney General for the Special Court for Greater Stuttgart Region to the Reich Minister of Justice," February 1, 1938, in Kopf and Miller, *Bischof Sproll*, 54–63.

32. The song Sproll decried was about Horst Wessel. Hubert Wolf, *Pope and Devil: The Vatican's Archives and the Third Reich* (Cambridge, MA: Harvard University Press, 2010), 228. SA Sturmführer Horst Wesel became a Nazi Party hero after his murder on February 23, 1930, by Communist opponents.

33. Prosecutor's Indictment, February 1, 1938, in Kopf and Miller, *Bischof Sproll*, 58. The state welfare assistance refers to the Winterhilfswerk program.

34. Cited in Kopf and Miller, *Bischof Sproll*, 58.

35. Lewy, *The Catholic Church and Nazi Germany*, 213; Kopf and Miller, *Bischof Sproll*, ix.

36. Kopf and Miller, *Bischof Sproll*, ix.

37. The only German bishop known to have approved of the pope's suggestion that the church sacrifice Sproll as an unambiguous step toward relaxing tensions with the regime was Michael von Faulhaber. Like the pope, Faulha-

ber was committed to a diplomatic game that could include the sacrifice of a single person for the perceived advantages of improved relations with the regime. Kopf and Miller, *Bischof Sproll*, 108, 179, 241, 242. On bishops and appeasement, see Wolfgang Schieder, "Pius XII im II Weltkrieg," *Historische Zeitschrift* 207, no. 2 (October 1968): 356; Josef Matthias Görgen, *Pius XII: Katholische Kirche und Hochhuths "Stellvertreter"* (Buxheim: Martin Verlag, 1964), 143. Pacelli on Sproll is in Wolf, *Pope and Devil*, 52. Bergen to the Foreign Ministry, June 10, 1938, is in Kopf and Miller, *Bischof Sproll*, 146–147.

38. H. R. Trevor-Roper, ed., *Hitler's Table Talk, 1941–1944* (New York: Enigma Books, 2007 [orig. 1953]), 418–419.

39. Winfried Süss, *Der "Völkskörper" im Krieg: Gesundheitspolitik, Gesundheitsverhältnisse und Krankenmord im nationalsozialistischen Deutschland 1939–1945* (Munich: Oldenbourg, 2003), 143, 144.

40. Kopf and Miller, *Bischof Sproll*, 108, 179, 241, 242. After consulting with the attorney general in Stuttgart, the Tübingen prosecutor declined to bring charges against anyone who had damaged Sproll's belongings because the bishop's "un-German" behavior was to blame for the "extraordinary excitement among the people" (Burkart, *Joannes Baptista Sproll*, 98).

41. Kopf and Miller, *Bischof Sproll*, 87–89.

42. See Kopf and Miller, *Bischof Sproll*, for the following: on the "showdown" with Nazism, 122; for the removal of the flag, 88; State Secretary Weizsäcker, memorandum, May 10, 1938, 127; Galen sermon on May 10, 1938, 122–124; Rottenburg Landrat Alfred Chormann to Sproll, April 13, 1938, 91.

43. Prosecutor's Indictment, in Kopf and Miller, *Bischof Sproll*, 59–61.

44. On Kottmann and the Rottenburg demonstration, April 22, 1938, see Kopf and Miller, *Bischof Sproll*, 94–95; see also 69, 100.

45. Kopf and Miller, *Bischof Sproll*, 100; Galen sermon on May 10, 1938, in ibid., 122–124. The Gestapo warned in writing that the bishop himself was at fault for the agitation of the people of the region of Württemberg.

46. Kottmann on the Bishop Sproll matter reported that there was still unrest as of May 2, 1938; ibid., 99; see also 111–113.

47. Ibid., 104, 105

48. Ibid., 111–113, 118.

49. Cited in ibid., 126.

50. Ibid., 112, 118.

51. Ibid., 120–121.

52. Wienken informed the Gestapo that the church would agree to the replacement of the three pastors the police had arrested in Waldstetten. Kopf and Miller, *Bischof Sproll*, 124–126, report that the German bishops had recently agreed to the Gestapo's requests that three German priests be replaced. The Allmendingen priest's statement is in ibid., 112.

53. Cited in ibid., 119.

54. Galen sermon on May 10, 1938, in ibid., 122–124. Galen's words were the public expression of the struggle in the context of a series of private communications.

55. Gerhard Ritter notes that no bishop was more effective than Galen in resisting because no one else spoke out so "courageously, so popularly." Ritter opines that although bishops were too important as popular figures to the people for the regime in its cost-benefit calculations to punish, hundreds of chaplains and pastors were sent to camps and some executed. (*The German Resistance: Carl Goerdeler's Struggle against Tyranny* [New York: Frederick A. Praeger, 1958], 55, 56). Bishop Galen to Archbishop Gröber, May 30, 1938, in Kopf and Miller, *Bischof Sproll*, 143–144.

56. Kopf and Miller, *Bischof Sproll*, 70–72, citing Ludwig Volk, "Die Fuldaer Bischofskonferenz von der Enzyklika 'Mit brennender Sorge' bis zum Ende der NS-Herrschaft," in L. Volk, *Katholische Kirche und Nationalsozialismus. Ausgewählte Aufsätze*, ed. Dieter Albrecht (Mainz: Kommission für Zeitgeschichte, 1987), B/46, 247ff.

57. Kopf and Miller, *Bischof Sproll*, 69, 100, 103.

58. Ibid., 116. The district leadership of Rottweil (Kreisleitung Rottweil) instructed all its Ortsgruppenleiter on July 7, 1938.

59. The official attack on the Bavarian bishops in 1934 had also included a defamation campaign but had shown that a bishop might command loyalties stronger than even those of his regional Nazi Party counterparts, the Gauleiters. Murr was following directives from Berlin, but it was up to him to win the crowd to his side. A copy of Murr's article is in ibid., 107–110; Murr to Weizsäcker, May 25, 1938, is in ibid., 143.

60. Heydrich (signed Karl Werner Best) to SS-Brigadeführer Julius Schaub (Hitler's personal adjutant, 1925–1945), July 23, 1938, is in ibid., 191, 192; Michael Kissener and Joachim Scholtyseck, *Die Führer der Provinz: NS-Biographien aus Baden und Württemberg* (Constance: UVK, Universitätsverlag Konstanz, 1999), 477, 492.

61. Kopf and Miller, *Bischof Sproll*, 69, 100, 170–172.

62. Report of the bishopric, July 17, 1938, in ibid., 159.

63. See ibid. for the following: Kerrl's explanation, 126; Ambassador Bergen to Foreign Ministry, August 1, 1938, 159, 226–228; Murr to Kerrl, July 16 and 20, 1938, 169–170.

64. Pacelli's statement is in ibid., 169–170; report of the bishopric, July 19, 1938, is on 160–162. A diocesan report put the number of demonstrators at between 1,500 and 2,000, adding that their protest lasted from 10:00 until 11:30 p.m.

65. Report of the bishopric, July 19, 1938, in ibid., 160–162. For Bertram's appeal to Hitler, see ibid., 168.

66. See ibid. for the following: Bergen's reaction, 230; Deputy State Secretary Woermann to Bergen, memorandum of July 25, 1938, on July 21, 1938, visit by Der Nuntius, 175; Bergen to foreign ministry, memorandum, July 26, 1938, 177.

67. Bergen to Foreign Ministry, memorandum, July 26, 1938, in ibid., 177; German Foreign Ministry, *Documents on German Foreign Policy, 1918–1945* (Washington, D.C.: Government Printing Office, 1949), xcvi; Richard Bonney, *Confronting the Nazi War on Christianity: The Kulturkampf Newsletters, 1936–1939* (Oxford: Peter Lang, 2009), 421; Kopf and Miller, *Bischof Sproll*, 186–188.

68. IMT, Document PS-849, Kerrl to the Minister of State and Chief of the Praesidium Chancellery, Berlin, July 23, 1938, *Nazi Conspiracy and Aggression*, 3:614–616; IMT, *Trial of the Major War Criminals: Proceeding Volumes*, 4:61–63.

69. IMT, Document 848-PS, Gestapo Nurnberg-Fuerth Office Teletype Section, July 24, 1938, in *Nazi Conspiracy and Aggression*, 3:613; IMT, *Trial of the Major War Criminals: Proceeding Volumes*, December 17, 1945, 4:49. Gröber said he now wanted "to turn to the Fuehrer and to Reich Minister of the Interior Dr. Frick, anew," indicating that Gröber may well have protested personally more than once.

70. Anonymous report on another demonstration, July 23, 1938, in Kopf and Miller, *Bischof Sproll*, 186–188. This report is from the documents of Monsignor Stauber, who was present at Sproll's palace during the demonstrations. According to Kopf and Miller, his other reports are so detailed that this report too should be trustworthy.

71. Heydrich's claim is found in Kritzinger Notes, July 25, 1938, in ibid., 204. "I was always proud of my Fatherland," an SA man wrote the bishop. "But on Saturday I was ashamed for the first time to be a German. And just as I experienced this, so did many comrades from my troop" (SA man to Sproll, July 23, 1938, in ibid., 189).

72. SA man to Sproll, July 23, 1938, in ibid., 189; Senior Prosecutor of Tübingen to Stuttgart General Prosecutor Wagner, July 26, 1938, in ibid., 202.

73. Senior Prosecutor of Tübingen to Stuttgart General Prosecutor Wagner, July 26, 1938, in ibid., 202. In October, two months later, the dictatorship crushed a rebellion by Catholics who launched physical attacks at the "Rosary Festival" while at Vienna's St. Stephen's Cathedral. When thousands of Catholic youth expressed opposition to Hitler's rule and some turned violent, party mobs went on a spree of violent anti-church rioting that punished the church for a week. Evan Burr Bukey, *Hitler's Austria: Popular Sentiment in the Nazi Era, 1938–1945* (Chapel Hill: University of North Carolina Press, 2000), 102–103. On October 7, 1938, thousands of Catholic youth expressed opposition, saying "Christ is our Führer," and "Archbishop, command; we follow thee," while some physically attacked a sentry of the Hitler Youth. In response, the Nazis unleashed their own mobs of Hitler Youth, party militants, and Storm Troopers. They stormed the cardinal's palace, smashed property, and hurled a curate from a window, breaking both his hips. Party mobs continued anti-church rioting for a week before this culminated in a party rally of two hundred thousand at Heroes' Square; the rally was

addressed by Vienna's Gauleiter Josef Bürckel, who spoke in ominous tones of a church clergy attempting to dominate power in the state.

74. Report of Landrat Chormann, July 28, 1938, is in Kopf and Miller, *Bischof Sproll*, 197–201; Chormann and the Stuttgart Gestapo reporter rendered similar reports on these demands. This was a controlled representation of popular opinion in a style mirrored by women demonstrating their limited opposition in Witten and Berlin in 1943. (See chapters VII and VIII below.)

75. On the rift of opinion, see Kopf and Miller, *Bischof Sproll*, 195. The Kritzinger Notes, July 25, 1938, are in ibid., 204; IMT, Document 848-PS, cited in Robert Jackson's opening address for the United States, Nuremberg Trial, *Nazi Conspiracy and Aggression*, 1: chapter 5.

76. Lammers's personal assistant, Hermann von Stutterheim, to SS Brigade Leader Schaub, July 29, 1938, in Kopf and Miller, *Bischof Sproll*, 205; IMT, Document 849-PS, Reich Minister for Church Affairs, Kerrl, to the Minister of State and Chief of the Praesidium Chancellery, Berlin, July 23, 1938, *Nazi Conspiracy and Aggression*, 3:614. The letter of Minister Kerrl, dated July 23, 1938, ahead of the crippling violence that evening, identifies Gauleiter Murr as the instigator of the demonstrations, although he himself took credit for having the Foreign Ministry ask the Vatican to secure Bishop Sproll's resignation. Heydrich (signed. Karl Werner Best) to SS-Brigadeführer Julius Schaub (Hitler's personal adjutant, 1925–1945), July 23, 1938, in Kopf and Miller, *Bischof Sproll*, 191–192. Cf. Burkart, *Joannes Baptista Sproll*, 95–132.

77. IMT, Document PS-849, Reich Minister for Church Affairs, Kerrl, to the Minister of State and Chief of the Praesidium Chancellery, Berlin, July 23, 1938, *Nazi Conspiracy and Aggression*, 3:614–616; IMT, *Trial of the Major War Criminals: Proceeding Volumes*, 4:61–63. On the turning away of Stuttgart demonstrators, see Kopf and Miller, *Bischof Sproll*, 195.

78. Seeger to Murr, in Kopf, *Bischof Sproll*, 196.

79. Ibid., 228–229.

80. Sproll's statement is in ibid., 201. On the reconciliation of church and state, see ibid., 195.

81. Nathaniel Micklem, *National Socialism and the Roman Catholic Church* (Oxford: Oxford University Press, 1939), 219; German Foreign Ministry, *Documents on German Foreign Policy*, 1057, Reich Minister Kerrl's missive to Goebbels with a note to be published.

82. Katholisches Amts-Blatt für die Diözese Rottenburg of September 8, 1939, cited in Rainer Bendel, *Die katholische Schuld? Katholizismus im Dritten Reich zwischen Arrangement und Widerstand* (Münster: LIT Verlag, 2002), 157.

83. Forcibly exiled from his position, Sproll represents the "tip of the iceberg" of "innumerable" Catholic conflicts with the dictatorship. W. Süss, *Der "Völkskörper,"* 143–144; Bendel, *Die katholische Schuld?* 30. On the severity of Sproll's punishment, see Paul Kopf, "Kirche im Nationalsozialismus,"

in *Rottenburger Jahrbuch für Kirchengeschichte,* ed. Geschichtsverein der Diözese Rottenburg-Stuttgart (Sigmaringen: J. Thorbecke Verlag, 1984), 115, 123.

84. Lewy, *The Catholic Church and Nazi Germany,* 217 (emphasis added), 101, 194, 225, 234. The widespread backing for Volkish nationalism that the Reich enjoyed was hardly abridged by church leaders, who at critical junctures had done their part, and sometimes their utmost, to promote Hitler's successes and his image. See Faulhaber's intervention on the regime's side in the case of Schachleiter and the promise of the bishop of Trier, Franz Bornewasser, to do his "utmost for the return of the Saar to the German Reich." They taught their flocks to praise Hitler's foreign policy and to get behind his expansionist war. They seemed to have overlooked the mass killings of innocents in the war.

85. Gerhart Binder, *Irrtum und Widerstand: Die deutschen Katholiken in der Auseinandersetzung mit dem Nationalsozialismus* (Munich: Pfeiffer, 1968), 306–309; Kommission für Geschichtliche Landeskunde in Baden-Württemberg, *Lebensbilder aus Schwaben und Franken* (Stuttgart: Kohlhammer, 1977), 464.

86. Binder, *Irrtum und Widerstand,* 306–309; Kommission für Geschichtliche Landeskunde in Baden-Württemberg, *Lebensbilder aus Schwaben und Franken,* 464. As Germany lost one battle after another, the possibility of national defeat fostered a belief among Germans that their cruelties had brought about a heavenly retribution, a foreboding accompanied by a new sense of guilt, as displayed by Bishop Wurm in August 1943. Theodore S. Hamerow, *On the Road to the Wolf's Lair: German Resistance to Hitler* (Cambridge, MA: Harvard University Press, 1997), 301.

CHAPTER V. FÜHRER POWER AND THE 1938
MILITARY CONSPIRACY AGAINST HITLER

1. William L. Shirer, *Berlin Diary: The Journal of a Foreign Correspondent* (New York: Knopf, 1942), 41–43.

2. Hitler before the Party Congress, in Adolf Hitler, *Speeches and Proclamations,* 4 vols., ed. Max Domarus (Wauconda, IL: Bolchazy-Carducci, 1990), 2:836, September 12, 1936. Ernest R. May, *Strange Victory: Hitler's Conquest of France* (New York: Hill and Wang, 2000), 31, 39.

3. On Locarno, see Gerhard L. Weinberg, *Hitler's Foreign Policy 1933–1939,* rev. ed. (New York: Enigma Books, 2005), 187. On the Stresa Front, see Ian Kershaw, *Hitler, 1889–1936: Hubris* (New York: W. W. Norton, 2000), 583; Weinberg, *Hitler's Foreign Policy,* 188, 196, 200. On Hitler's comments at the Olympics, see David Clay Large, *Nazi Games: The Olympics of 1936* (New York: W. W. Norton, 2007), 148–149; Helmut-Dieter Giro, *Die Remilitarisierung des Rheinlands 1936: Hitler's Weg in den Krieg?* (Essen: Klartext Verlag, 2006), 67. French ambassador André François-Poncet claimed that the whole world "was in ecstasy" about the organization and spirit of the Olympics held in Germany (Karen Fiss, *Grand Illusion: The Third Reich, the Paris*

Exposition, and the Cultural Seduction of France [Chicago: University of Chicago Press, 2009], 230n48).

4. On the Prussian military, see Hans Mommsen, *The Rise and Fall of Weimar Democracy* (Chapel Hill: University of North Carolina Press, 1996), 2. On Blomberg's support for Hitler, see May, *Strange Victory*, 33; John Wheeler-Bennett, *The Nemesis of Power: The German Army in Politics, 1918–1945* (New York: St. Martin's Press, 1954), 296; Gerald Reitlinger, *The SS: Alibi of a Nation, 1922–1945* (New York: Viking Press, 1957), 91; Gordon A. Craig, *The Politics of the Prussian Army, 1640–1945* (New York: Oxford University Press, 1955), 472, 473, 476.

5. The Law for the Reorganization of the Reich was not immediately enforced throughout the Reich because national agencies continued to depend on state agencies. Hermann Beck, *The Fateful Alliance: German Conservatives and Nazis in 1933: The Machtergreifung in a New Light* (New York: Berghahn Books, 2008), 257. On the wide acceptance of the Night of the Long Knives, see Peter Hoffmann, *The History of the German Resistance, 1933–1945*, trans. Richard Barry (London: Macdonald and Jane's, 1977), 55. Goerdeler willingly accepted reappointment as Reich Price Commissioner. Hindenburg's congratulations to Hitler and Göring, July 2, 1934, are in Hitler, *Speeches*, 2:480. The army readily agreed that no one would succeed Hindenburg as president, recognizing Hitler's new extra-constitutional and personal power as Führer (Kershaw, *Hubris*, 535). On Hitler's attitudes toward mass conscription, see H. R. Trevor-Roper, ed., *Hitler's Table Talk, 1941–1944* (New York: Enigma Books, 2007 [orig. 1953]), 375, entry for May 21, 1942; Craig, *The Politics of the Prussian Army*, 481; Aristotle A. Kallis, *Fascist Ideology: Territory and Expansionism in Italy and Germany, 1922–1945* (New York: Routledge, 2000), 112.

6. On Hitler's diversion of resources to purchase food, see Kershaw, *Hubris*, 576–579. On "Guns or Butter," see Weinberg, *Hitler's Foreign Policy*, 192. Goebbels adopted this slogan in an attempt to persuade Germans to forgo luxuries in favor of rearmament.

7. On the importance for the regime of the new pleasures within the reach of workers, see Shelley O. Baranowski, *Strength through Joy: Consumerism and Mass Tourism in the Third Reich* (New York: Cambridge University Press, 2004), 1–9.

8. Notes of State Secretary von Bülow about a conversation with Beck, Berlin, December 1, 1934, in Klaus-Jürgen Müller, *General Ludwig Beck: Studien und Dokumente zur politisch-militärisch Vorstellungswelt und Tätigkeit des Generalstabschefs des deutschen Heeres 1933–1938* (Boppard am Rhein: Harald Boldt Verlag, 1980), 395–398. Not until 1939 or 1940, Beck calculated, would Germany have a force strong enough to resist France, and it would not be able to prevail in a longer conflict since it was encircled by enemies. Peter Hoffmann, "Ludwig Beck: Loyalty and Resistance," *Central European History* 14, no. 4 (December 1981): 337–339.

9. Recent work argues against the "legend" that the generals were less willing than Hitler to remilitarize the Rhineland in early March 1936 by shedding "new light" on Hitler's relationship with senior members of the officer corps—without, however, taking account of Hitler's relationship to the German people. Benoît Lemay, "La remilitarisation de la Rhénanie en 1936: Une réévaluation du rôle des généraux allemands (1933–1936)," *Guerres mondiales et conflits contemporains*, no. 224 (October 2006): 35–36. On von Neurath's position, see Kallis, *Fascist Ideology*, 82, 83. For Goebbels's conversion to Hitler's line, see Joseph Goebbels, *Die Tagebücher von Joseph Goebbels*, ed. Elke Fröhlich (Munich: K. G. Saur, 1993–1996), part I, vol. 3/I, 575–576, entry for February 29, 1936, and part I, vol. 3/II, 577, entry for March 2, 1936; Kershaw, *Hubris*, 585–587.

10. Ambassador Ulrich von Hassell concurred with von Neurath. Ian Kershaw, "Social Unrest and the Response of the Nazi Regime, 1934–1936," in *Germans against Nazism: Nonconformity, Opposition, and Resistance in the Third Reich: Essays in Honor of Peter Hoffmann*, ed. Francis Nicosia and Lawrence Stokes (New York: Berg, 1990), 169. The "timing and character" of the remilitarization "were Hitler's. They bore his hallmark at all points" (Kershaw, *Hubris*, 583).

11. Weinberg, *Hitler's Foreign Policy*, 164, 246. Hans-Adolf Jacobsen, *Ausgewählte Dokumente zur Geschichte des Nationalsozialismus, 1933–1945* (Bielefeld: Verlag Neue Gesellschaft, 1961), Document 14.II.–15.III. Giro, *Die Remilitarisierung des Rheinlands*, 67–69. For operational plans, see Weinberg, *Hitler's Foreign Policy*, 196.

12. Instructions regarding proper coverage of the reoccupation of the Rhineland originated from press directives of the Propaganda Ministry released the day of the remilitarization. Gabriele Toepser-Ziegert and Hans Bohrmann, eds., *NS-Presseanweisungen der Vorkriegszeit: Edition und Dokumentation* (Munich: K. G. Saur, 1993), 1:252. On the respective strength of the Germans and the French in the region, see Kershaw, *Hubris*, 588.

13. Wheeler-Bennett, *Nemesis of Power*, 352. Testimony of Field Marshal von Manstein is in International Military Tribunal (IMT), *Trial of the Major War Criminals: Proceeding Volumes*, 42 vols. (Nuremberg, November 14, 1945–October 1, 1946), 20:608, August 10, 1946.

14. Weinberg, *Hitler's Foreign Policy*, 190.

15. For the rapid de-escalation from crisis, see Weinberg, *Hitler's Foreign Policy*, 201–203. Hitler's comments on the possibility of failure to Frank are in Kershaw, *Hubris*, 588–589; Wheeler-Bennett, *Nemesis of Power*, 353.

16. Trevor-Roper, *Hitler's Table Talk*, 378, entry for May 21, 1942.

17. On Hitler's increased prestige and capacity for risk, see Weinberg, *Hitler's Foreign Policy*, 204. Hitler's March 14 statement is in Richard Bessel, *Nazism and War* (New York: Modern Library, 2004), 54; Alan Bullock, *Hitler: A Study in Tyranny* (New York: Harper and Row, 1962), 375. Dietrich on Hitler's confidence is in Kershaw, *Hubris*, 542.

18. Marie-Corentine Sandstede-Auzelle, *Clemens August Graf von Galen, Bischof von Münster im Dritten Reich* (Münster: Aschendorff, 1986), 32. Marc Steinhoff, *Widerstand gegen das Dritte Reich: Im Raum der katholischen Kirche* (Frankfurt am Main: Peter Lang, 1997), 82.

19. Police reports of Germans' reactions are in Bernhard Vollmer, *Volksopposition im Polizeistaat. Gestapo-und Regierungsberichte 1934–1936* (Stuttgart: Deutsche Verlags-Anstalt, 1957), 370ff.; Heinrich August Winkler, *Germany: The Long Road West*, vol. 2: *1933–1990* (New York: Oxford University Press, 2006), 2:46. Hitler declared the swastika flag Germany's national flag on September 15, 1935. On reactions within the party, see W. E. Hart [pseud.], *Hitler's Generals* (Garden City, NY: Doubleday, 1944), 19.

20. Goebbels, *Tagebücher*, part I, vol. 3/II, 36, entry for March 8, 1936. On Hitler's use of plebiscites, see Kershaw, *Hubris*, 542. The sloganeering of Hitler, Göring, and Goebbels is in William E. Dodd, *Ambassador Dodd's Diary, 1933–1938*, ed. William E. Dodd Jr. and Martha Dodd (New York: Harcourt, Brace, 1941), 322.

21. Quoted in Richard Bonney, *Confronting the Nazi War on Christianity: The Kulturekampf Newsletters, 1936–1939* (Oxford: Peter Lang, 2009), 40; Guenter Lewy, *The Catholic Church and Nazi Germany* (Cambridge, MA: Da Capo Press, 1964), 203, 204.

22. Dodd, *Ambassador Dodd's Diary*, 21–27. Ambassador Dodd thought that Economics Minister Hjalmar Schacht had never appeared so optimistic; he was expecting now a quick return of Germany's colonies. The results of the plebiscite represented a strong rebound for the regime since support in the most recent plebiscite of August 1934 had fallen nearly 5 percent relative to the regime's plebiscite in late 1933, representing "a sobering decrease" for the regime, according to Winkler, *Germany: The Long Road West*, 2:49.

23. Dodd, *Ambassador Dodd's Diary*, 21–27; Victor Klemperer, *I Will Bear Witness*, vol. 1: *1933–1941*, trans. Martin Chalmers (New York: Modern Library, 1999), 41, entry for November 14, 1933.

24. Hitler had notoriously indulgent work habits, but he was very careful and disciplined about preserving his image as the Leader among the Germans, avoiding controversy as well as appearances that could undermine his image as Germany's most powerful and benevolent servant. He appeared in public only as the hero of an orchestrated setting, preferred not to be on record as supporting a particular position in a controversy between hard-line ideologues and those willing to make compromises, and sought grounds for plausible deniability such as giving oral rather than written orders. Nonetheless, Hitler was a "master opportunist," and "neither the time nor the detail nor even the sequence of events was defined [by Hitler] long before hand," (Wheeler-Bennett, *Nemesis of Power*, 345). For Hitler's belief regarding the consequence of a German attitude change, see the speech by Hitler on May

1, 1935, at Tempelhofer Field to an assembled multitude of 1.5 million in Hitler, *Speeches*, 664; cited in Max Domarus, ed., *The Essential Hitler* (Wauconda, IL: Bolchazy-Carducci, 2007), 137.

25. Goebbels, *Tagebücher*, part I, 5:117, entry for January 27, 1938.

26. Kallis, *Fascist Ideology*, 87, 88. Adolf Hitler, *Mein Kampf, Complete and Unabridged, Fully Annotated*, ed. John Chamberlain, Sidney B. Fay, et al. (New York: Reynal and Hitchcock, 1939), 953.

27. On the Hössbach Conference, see Weinberg, *Hitler's Foreign Policy*, 311. For the January 1938 meeting, see Harold C. Deutsch, *Hitler and His Generals* (Minneapolis: University of Minnesota Press, 1974), 38, 40.

28. Beck's remarks of November 12, 1937, regarding Hitler's military adjutant, Colonel Friedrich Hössbach's protocol of the meeting in the Reich Chancellery on November 5, 1937, are in K.-J. Müller, *General Ludwig Beck*, 498–501; Gerhard L. Weinberg, "The German Generals and the Outbreak of War, 1938–1939," in Gerhard L. Weinberg, *Germany, Hitler, and World War II: Essays in Modern German and World History* (Cambridge: Cambridge University Press, 1995), 136; Ian Kershaw, *Hitler, 1936–1945: Nemesis* (New York: W. W. Norton, 2000), 50; Weinberg, *Hitler's Foreign Policy*, 311; Kallis, *Fascist Ideology*, 82–83.

29. Wolfram Wette, *The Wehrmacht: History, Myth, Reality*, trans. Deborah Lucas (Cambridge, MA: Harvard University Press, 2006), 72, 73; Klaus-Jürgen Müller, *Das Heer und Hitler: Armee und nationalsozialistisches Regime 1933–1940* (Stuttgart: Deutsche Verlags-Anstalt, 1969), 79, 84. See also the recent popular biography of Manstein: Benoît Lemay, *Erich von Manstein: Hitler's Master Strategist*, trans. Pierce Heyward (Havertown, PA: Casemate Publishers, 2010). Beck to Major Schöder on local conditions, October 27, 1937, is in K.-J. Müller, *General Ludwig Beck*, 497–498. Fritsch's comments on propriety are in Wette, *The Wehrmacht*, 84, 85. The April 7, 1933, Law for the Restoration of the Professional Civil Service excluded all Jews from civil service jobs with the exception of Jews who had served on the war front or whose sons or fathers had fallen in battle.

30. General Beck did not wish to surrender the army's position as a partner in making military-political decisions; Deutsch, *Hitler and His Generals*, 38, 40. For the acquiescence of others, see Kershaw, *Nemesis*, 50, 51.

31. Dorothy Rowe, *Representing Berlin: Sexuality and the City in Imperial and Weimar Germany* (Aldershot: Ashgate, 2003), 137.

32. Friedrich Hössbach, *Zwischen Wehrmacht und Hitler, 1934–1938* (Wolfenbüttel: Wolfenbüttel Verlagsanstalt, 1949), 122; Kershaw, *Nemesis*, 52; Karl-Heinz Janssen and Fritz Tobias, *Der Sturz der Generäle: Hitler und die Blomberg-Fritsch-Krise 1938* (Munich: Beck, 1994); Alan Bullock, *Hitler and Stalin: Parallel Lives* (New York: Knopf, 1992), 555. Bullock writes that Fritsch told Hitler to fire Blomberg. Janssen and Tobias present the idea as Hitler's, with later encouragement from the army.

33. Beck's statement cited in Robert B. Kane, *Disobedience and Conspiracy in the German Army, 1918–1945* (Jefferson, NC: McFarland, 2002), 125. Leeb's and List's reactions are in Weinberg, "The German Generals," 132.

34. The reliable source on the Blomberg-Fritsch events is Harold Deutsch, *Hitler and His Generals*, according to Gerhard Weinberg ("The German Generals," 138n26) and Geoffrey Magargee and Williamson Murray (*Inside Hitler's High Command* [Lawrence: University of Kansas Press, 2000], 252n12). The secondary source preferred by Ian Kershaw in *Nemesis* is Janssen and Tobias, *Der Sturz der Generäle*, who have written something of a rejoinder to Deutsch, who relies on more than six dozen interviews he conducted and numerous published and unpublished memoirs, including the Keitel Memoir. Janssen and Tobias have found additional sources since Deutsch published. Magargee and Murray write that arguments in *Sturz der Generäle* "have some merit but are not completely convincing" (*Inside Hitler's High Command*, 252).

35. Weinberg, *Hitler's Foreign Policy*, 577. The dictatorship had such respect for the power of rumors to influence popular opinion that it planted many but also pursued those who spread rumors like they were resisters. Wheeler-Bennett, *Nemesis of Power*, 357–358.

36. Goebbels's diaries and the use of the media indicate his assistance. The role of Goering in exposing the Blomberg story is not clear, with some accounts portraying the field marshal as having urged Blomberg into marriage only to spring a trap as soon as the vows were said. Others see in Göring only a rather passive servant of Hitler in this matter. Deutsch, *Hitler and His Generals*, 79ff.; Kershaw, *Nemesis*, 51ff. See also two immediate postwar memoirs: Wilhelm Keitel, *The Memoirs of Field Marshal Keitel*, ed. W. Görlitz (New York: Stein and Day, 1966), 45, 46, and Hössbach, *Zwischen Wehrmacht und Hitler*, 124.

37. On the origin of the case against Fritsch, see Kane, *Disobedience and Conspiracy*, 125–126. Beck's objections are in ibid., 126.

38. A more empathetic interpretation of the source of Fritsch's silence could see a combination of factors: his conception of military, the expectation that an officer be taken at his word; willingness to wait for the judgment of an objective evaluation; etc. See Wheeler-Bennett, *Nemesis of Power*, 362; Deutsch, *Hitler and His Generals*, 167, 240–241. Fritsch's observations are excerpted in Jeremy Noakes and Geoffrey Pridham, eds., *Nazism, 1919–1945*, vol. 3: *Foreign Policy, War and Racial Extermination* (Exeter: University of Exeter Press, 2001), 37–38. Kershaw, *Nemesis*, 50, 51.

39. Weinberg, *Hitler's Foreign Policy*, 322–323.

40. Goebbels, *Tagebücher*, part I, 5:128, entry for February 1, 1938.

41. *Frankfurter Zeitung*, February 5, 1938.

42. "Germany's No. 1 Soldier Quits His Job for a Wife," *Life*, February 14, 1938, 68.

43. IMT, *Trial of the Major War Criminals: Proceeding Volumes*, 9:290, Testimony of Hermann Göring, March 14, 1946. Göring is hardly a trustworthy

witness, but there is little reason to doubt this testimony. William L. Shirer, *The Rise and Fall of the Third Reich* (New York: Touchstone, 1990), 319.

44. Weinberg, *Hitler's Foreign Policy*, 319, 320; Hans Bernd Gisevius, *To the Bitter End* (Boston: Houghton Mifflin, 1947), 243; Deutsch, *Hitler and His Generals*, 184–186.

45. Weinberg, *Hitler's Foreign Policy*, 138. Earlier, Hitler acknowledged that he might, through a miscalculation, sometime suffer a major setback. See Hitler's statement on the death of Hans Schemm that he might lose Germany, but if he did, he was certain that he knew how to win it back again. In Hitler, *Speeches*, 1:649, March 5, 1935. Hitler, however, was pressed for time.

46. Hitler's plans for a coup in Austria are in Weinberg, *Hitler's Foreign Policy*, 321. Negotiations with Schuschnigg are in Kershaw, *Nemesis*, 86. Weinberg considers multiple factors that triggered Hitler's decision to annex Austria (*Hitler's Foreign Policy*, 506–507). Hitler may have been more apt to take action in response to Schuschnigg to drown out opposition within the military, considering the influence of Schuschnigg's plebiscite on Hitler's action.

47. Kallis, *Fascist Ideology*, 88.

48. For an excellent early account of this emerging personal alliance, see F. W. Deakin, *The Brutal Friendship: Mussolini, Hitler and the Fall of Italian Fascism* (London: Weidenfeld and Nicolson, 1962). For Hitler's conciliatory approach, see Weinberg, *Hitler's Foreign Policy*, 499.

49. Weinberg, *Hitler's Foreign Policy*, 499–500.

50. Kershaw, *Nemesis*, 45.

51. George O. Kent, "Franz von Papen and the Anschluss," in *Essays in European History: Selected from the Annual Meetings of the Southern Historical Association, 1988–1989*, ed. June K. Burton and Carolyn W. White (Lanham, MD: University Press of America, 1989), 2:22.

52. Ambassador Papen was to be assassinated if this would serve as an excuse for a German invasion; see Norbert Schausberger, *Der Griff nach Österreich. Der Anschluss* (Vienna: Jugend und Volk, 1978), 508ff.; Kent, "Franz von Papen and the Anschluss," 23. Hitler would adopt the same model in Czechoslovakia the following year (Domarus, *The Essential Hitler*, 86, 87). For Hitler's instructions to Forster regarding a coup in Austria, see Weinberg, *Hitler's Foreign Policy*, 505.

53. Weinberg, *Hitler's Foreign Policy*, 508; Hitler, *Speeches*, 2:1024, February 20, 1938.

54. Kane, *Disobedience and Conspiracy*, 128.

55. Weinberg, *Hitler's Foreign Policy*, 511–513. For Cardinal Innitzer's order, see Arthur Stuart Duncan-Jones, *The Struggle for Religious Freedom in Germany* (London: V. Gollancz, 1938), 237.

56. On Hitler's tracking of subordinates' offenses, see Hjalmar Schacht, *76 Jahre meines Lebens* (Bad Woerishofen: Kindler und Schiermeyer Verlag, 1953), 463. On the belief in Hitler's infallibility among the elite, see Gisevius, *To the Bitter End*, 46. Following his resignation and acquittal, Fritsch

was interested in challenging Himmler to a duel—an effort to force a showdown between the army and the SS and retake the initiative, according to Deutsch, *Hitler and His Generals*, 210, 365–368.

57. Kershaw, *Nemesis*, 50, 51. Hitler's replacement of Blomberg, Fritsch, and the others, including the foreign and finance ministers, increased the number of those who asked no questions among those surrounding him, although it is not clear that the war would have unfolded differently otherwise. Kallis, *Fascist Ideology*, 90.

58. The most prominent among those considering rebellion included Lieutenant General Paul von Hase, Ambassador Friedrich-Werner Graf von der Schulenburg, Major General Hans Oster, Hans Bernd Gisevius, Finance Minister Hjalmar Schacht, General Field Marshal Erwin von Witzleben, and Colonel General Franz Halder (Hoffmann, *History of the German Resistance*, 69, 89, 90). Beck, notes on the crisis of trust in the government, July 29, 1938, is in K.-J. Müller, *General Ludwig Beck*, 561. Beck appears to have had an eye on popular sentiment. On Hitler's fear that Beck would lead a revolt, see Kane, *Disobedience and Conspiracy*, 127.

59. Beck, notes about Hitler's speech that day regarding action against Czechoslovakia, May 28, 1938, is in K.-J. Müller, *General Ludwig Beck*, 516; Kershaw, *Nemesis*, 100, 107–109, 112, 115.

60. Beck memorandum concerning the conditions and possibilities of success of a military action against Czechoslovakia, on the instructions of the commander in chief of the army, June 3, 1938, is in K.-J. Müller, *General Ludwig Beck*, 528–537. The response to Hitler's proclamations of May 28, 1938, regarding the political and military conditions of an action against Czechoslovakia, May 29, 1938, is in ibid., 521–528. Beck imagined that the French and British leaders thought in patterns similar to his (Kallis, *Fascist Ideology*, 156).

61. Others who questioned Operation Green included Four-Year Plan director Hermann Göring, Hitler's adjutant Fritz Wiedemann, and Joseph Goebbels; see Kallis, *Fascist Ideology*, 90, 135. Brauchitsch's refusal to hear objections is in Weinberg, "The German Generals," 142. Schmundt's statement is in Kane, *Disobedience and Conspiracy*, 132. For the National Socialist approach to war, see Bessel, *Nazism and War*.

62. Hoffmann, *History of the German Resistance*, 90; Gisevius, *To the Bitter End*, 291, 296–297, 309–311.

63. Joachim C. Fest, *Plotting Hitler's Death: The Story of German Resistance* (New York: Metropolitan Books, 1996), 91; Gerhard Ritter, *The German Resistance: Carl Goerdeler's Struggle against Tyranny* (New York: Frederick A. Praeger, 1958), 104, 148, 148n2; Gisevius, *To the Bitter End*, 296–297, 309–311.

64. Beck to Brauchitsch, memorandum about the military pointlessness of a war against Czechoslovakia, July 15, 1938, is in K.-J. Müller, *General Ludwig Beck*, 538; Weinberg, "The German Generals," 142. Gisevius, *To the Bitter End*, 404.

65. Beck's notes for a lecture, July 29, 1938, are in K.-J. Müller, *General Ludwig Beck*, 558.

66. Marian Zgórniak, *Europa am Abgrund—1938* (Münster: LIT Verlag, 2002), 149; Beck cited in Kane, *Disobedience and Conspiracy*, 132.

67. Beck, notes for a speech, July 16, 1938, is in ibid., 551–554 (emphasis added).

68. For the people as a check to militancy, see Beck to Brauchitsch, memoranda, July 15 and 16, 1938, in K.-J. Müller, *General Ludwig Beck*, 538–539, 544–545, 553. For Beck's slogans, see Beck, notes for a speech, July 19, 1938, in ibid., 555–556 (emphasis in original). The absence of plans for transferring their slogans into opinion illustrates how far Beck and the others had to go (Deutsch, *Hitler and His Generals*, 89).

69. On the feelings of the conspirators regarding the SS, see Noakes and Pridham, *Nazism, 1919–1945*, 3:37–38. Beck on radicals and war plans is in Ritter, *The German Resistance*, 92. Beck on big shots and communism is in Beck, notes for a speech, July 19, 1938, in K.-J. Müller, *General Ludwig Beck*, 555. For Beck's praise of Hitler's accomplishments, see Beck, notes on the crisis of trust in the government, July 29, 1938, in K.-J. Müller, *General Ludwig Beck*, 561; Beck, notes for an address by the commander in chief of the army, is on p. 576.

70. For Guse's positioning of the conspirators as protectors of Hitler, see Forster, cited in Hoffmann, *History of the German Resistance*, 76; K.-J. Müller, *General Ludwig Beck*, 316–317. On Beck's resignation, see Forster, cited in Hoffmann, *History of the German Resistance*, 79. (The resignation was for reasons of "foreign policy," according to Hoffmann.) On Beck's promotion, see Holtzmann, notes from his visit with Beck on November 16, 1938, in K.-J. Müller, *General Ludwig Beck*, 582, 582nn12–13.

71. Fabian von Schlabrendorff, *The Secret War against Hitler* (New York: Pitman Publishing, 1965), 72. Gisevius, *To the Bitter End*, 292, 305.

72. Gisevius, *To the Bitter End*, 46, 299, 309, 310, 312, 314.

73. Ibid., 292, 293, 305.

74. Wheeler-Bennett, *Nemesis of Power*, 428–429.

75. Gisevius, *To the Bitter End*, 300. See also Hoffmann, *History of the German Resistance*, 86.

76. Beck, Holtzmann's notes about his visit, November 16, 1938, is in K.-J. Müller, *General Ludwig Beck*, 580; Beck to his son Wilhelm, September 21 and 22, 1939, is in ibid., 588, 590. "Fritsch lived another year and a half, an embittered and broken man. When the war started, he went along as chief of a regiment. This was a courtesy title and did not involve a position of command. The death he sought found him during a battle in the Polish campaign. False accusations, which had broken him during his life, continued to pursue Fritsch even after his death" (Schlabrendorff, *The Secret War*, 76).

77. Peter Hoffmann, *Carl Goerdeler and the Jewish Question, 1933–1942* (Cambridge: Cambridge University Press, 2011), 93.

78. Shirer, *Berlin Diary*, 124, September 9, 1938. The SD wrote that "There exists in the broadest sections of the population the earnest concern that in the long or short run a war will put an end to the economic prosperity and have a terrible end for Germany" (cited in Kershaw, *Nemesis*, 107–108).

79. For Hitler's speech, see Hitler, *Speeches*, 2:1183–1193, September 26, 1938. For Shirer's response, see Shirer, *Berlin Diary*, 141–142, September 26, 1938. The following day, September 27, Hitler maintained his bravado, shouting at Chamberlain's adviser, Sir Horace Wilson, that "If France and England strike, let them do so. It's a matter of complete indifference to me!" (cited in Neville Henderson, *Failure of a Mission: Berlin, 1937–1939* [New York: G. P. Putnam's Sons, 1940], 165).

80. Shirer, *Berlin Diary*, 142–143, September 27, 1938; Henderson, *Failure of a Mission*, 160–162. Reports on the Berlin response to the Second Division and its impact on Hitler: Shirer, *Berlin Diary*, Sept. 27, 142f., and Paul Schmidt, *Hitler's Interpreter* (New York: Macmillan, 1951), 105. For Hitler's speech and his response to this incident, see Hitler, *Speeches*, 2:1200–1202.

81. Randall L. Bytwerk, *Landmark Speeches of National Socialism* (College Station: Texas A&M University Press, 2008), 51. Hitler, *Mein Kampf*, 460.

82. On Hitler's acquiescence to negotiation, see Kershaw, *Nemesis*, 119. The decision to hold the Munich conference is in Niall Ferguson, "Realism and Risk in 1938: German Foreign Policy and the Munich Crisis," in *History and Neorealism*, ed. Ernest R. May, Richard Rosecrance, and Zara Steiner, 155–184 (Cambridge: Cambridge University Press, 2010), 173. On the results of the Munich Agreement, see Kallis, *Fascist Ideology*, 120.

83. Goerdeler on naked force is in Hoffmann, *History of the German Resistance*, 17, 59 (emphasis added). The reaction of the general staff is in Kane, *Disobedience and Conspiracy*, 136.

84. Hitler's speech at the Munich Führerbau, November 10, 1938, *Vierteljahreshefte für Zeitgeschichte* 6, no. 2 (1958): 182. Hitler continued: "This means, therefore, to shed light on certain circumstances so that the conviction is gradually, totally automatically, awakened in the brain of the vast masses of the Volk that if one can't put an end to it peacefully, then one must do it with force." Perhaps Hitler was also influenced to negotiate in 1938 because of poor popular support for war.

85. Following the German attack on the Soviet Union, the German Catholic episcopacy called upon the people to fulfill the "difficult duties of our time" since they served not only the Fatherland, but also the "holy will of God." Galen prayed for what he called the "new crusade" against the "plague of Bolshevism" and proclaimed in September 1941 that for their "heroic sacrifice," God allows Christian soldiers to be rewarded with "eternal glory, quite similar to [that for] the Holy Martyrs" (Hans Günter Hockerts, "Kreuzzugsrhetorik, Vorsehungsglaube, Kriegstheologie: Spuren religiöser Deutung in Hitler's 'Weltanschauungskrieg," in *Heilige Kriege: Religiöse Begründungen militärischer Gewaltanwendung: Judentum, Christentum und Islam im Ver-*

gleich, ed. Klaus Schreiner and Elizabeth Müller-Luckner ([Munich: Olden-bourg, 2008], 243); Joachim Maier, "Von Gott reden in einer zerrissenen Welt: Beobachtungen zu einer 'Theologie' Clemens August Graf von Ga-lens in seinen Predigten und Hirtenbriefen," in *Clemens August Graf von Galen: Neue Forschungen zum Leben und Wirken des Bischofs von Münster,* ed. Joachim Kuropka (Münster: Verlag Regensberg, 1992), 285.

CHAPTER VI. CHALLENGES ON THE HOME FRONT

1. Bishop Galen's sermon of August 3, 1941, translated in Anson Rabinbach and Sander L. Gilman, eds., *Third Reich Sourcebook* (Berkeley: University of California Press, 2013), 346–347.
2. On the still unripe opinion, see Lothar Gruchmann, "Euthanasie und Justiz im Dritten Reich," *Vierteljahrshefte für Zeitgeschichte* 3 (July 1972): 237. On the churches, see Albert Hartl postwar testimony, in Ernst Klee, *Dokumente zur "Euthanasie"* (Frankfurt am Main: Fischer Taschenbuch Verlag, 1985), 147, and Henry Friedlander, *The Origins of Nazi Genocide: From Euthanasia to the Final Solution* (Chapel Hill: University of North Carolina Press, 1995), 113, 154. On polycracy and Hitler's charismatic leadership as the engine of radicalization in Nazi eugenic practices, see Hans-Walter Schmuhl, "Sterili-sation, 'Euthanasie,' 'Endlösung': Erbgesundheitspolitik unter den Bedin-gungen charismatischer Herrschaft," in *Medizin und Gesundheitspolitik in der NS-Zeit,* ed. Norbert Frei (Munich: Oldenbourg, 1991), 295–308.
3. Gruchmann, "Euthanasie und Justiz," 235, 236.
4. *Das Schwarze Korps,* excerpt from March 18, 1937, in Jeremy Noakes and Geoffrey Pridham, eds., *Nazism, 1919–1945,* vol. 3: *Foreign Policy, War, and Racial Extermination* (Exeter: University of Exeter Press, 2001), 395–396. Jill Stephenson, *Hitler's Home Front: Württemberg under the Nazis* (New York: Hambledon Continuum, 2006), 126; Hitler's claim: Gruchmann, "Euthana-sie und Justiz," 239.
5. The psychiatrist's report is in Noakes and Pridham, *Nazism, 1919–1945,* 3:396.
6. Joseph Goebbels, *Die Tagebücher von Joseph Goebbels,* ed. Elke Fröhlich (Munich: K. G. Saur, 1993–1996), part I, vol. 3/I, entries for August 19 and September 6, 1935; quote from entry for September 6, 1935; Hitler to Brandt: Norbert Frei, "Medizin und Gesundheit im Spannungsfeld von Politik, Ide-ologie und wissenschaftlichem Fortschritt," in Frei, *Medizin und Gesund-heitspolitik,* 28; Hans-Walter Schmuhl, *Rassenhygiene, Nationalsozialismus, Euthanasie: Von der Verhütung zur Vernichtung "lebensunwerten Lebens," 1890–1945* (Göttingen: Vandenhoeck and Ruprecht, 1987), 181.
7. Donald J. Dietrich, *Catholic Citizens in the Third Reich: Psycho-Social Princi-ples and Moral Reasoning* (New Brunswick, NJ: Transaction Press, 1988), 156–158.
8. Rudolf Willenborg, "Zur Rezeptionsgeschichte des Kreuzkampfes im Deutschen Reich und im Ausland," in *Zur Sache—das Kreuz! Untersuchungen*

zur Geschichte des Konflikts um Kreuz und Lutherbild in den Schulen Olden-
burgs, zur Wirkungsgeschichte eines Massenprotests und zum Problem national-
sozialistischer Herrschaft in einer agrarisch-katholischen Region, ed. Joachim
Kuropka (Vechta: Vechtaer Druckerei und Verlag, 1986), 341.

9. Preysing's appeal to Bertram and the Fulda Bishops' Conference, October 10, 1937, is printed in Vera Bücker, Bernhard Nadorf, and Markus Pot-
thoff, eds., *Nikolaus Gross: Arbeiterführer-Widerstandskämpfer-Glaubenszeuge:*
Wie sollen wir vor Gott und unserem Volk bestehen?: Der politische und soziale
Katholizismus im Ruhrgebiet 1927 bis 1949 (Münster: LIT Verlag, 2001), 208,
209; see also Walter Adolph, *Geheime Augzeichnungen aus dem nationalsozi-*
alistischen Kirchenkampf: 1935–1943, ed. Ulrich von Hehl, Veröffentlichungen
der Kommission für Zeitgeschichte, Reihe A: Quellen, Bd. 28 (Mainz: Matthias Grünewald Verlag, 1979), 170ff.

10. Adolf Hitler, *Speeches and Proclamations,* 4 vols., ed. Max Domarus (Wauconda,
IL: Bolchazy-Carducci, 1990), 2:979–980, November 23, 1937 (emphasis added).

11. "Military necessity" was cited for a variety of official wartime acts, including
the confiscation of church property. See, for example, LeRoy Walters, "Paul
Braune Confronts the National Socialists' 'Euthanasia' Program," *Holocaust*
and Genocide Studies 21, no. 3 (2007): 454–487.

12. For the economic necessity of war, see Adam Tooze, *The Wages of Destruc-*
tion: The Making and Breaking of the Nazi Economy (New York: Penguin,
2006). Hitler's belief in his own importance is in Ian Kershaw, *Hitler, 1936–*
1945: Nemesis (New York: W. W. Norton, 2000), 207–208, citing Hitler's address to Wehrmacht leaders on August 22, 1939. On the source of this
address, see Winfried Baumgart, "Zur Ansprache Hitlers vor den Führern
der Werhmacht am 22. August 1939: Eine quellenkiritische Untersuchung,"
Vierteljahrshefte für Zeitgeschichte 16, no. 2 (1968): 120–149.

13. Nuremberg trial document NO 1392, Reich Führer SS, signed, aucke, September 8, 1939, Staatsarchiv Nürnberg; cf. John Conway, *The Nazi Persecu-*
tion of the Churches (Toronto: Ryerson Press, 1968), 435n1 (where the
document is cited as NG-1392).

14. Hitler on January 19, 1940, is quoted in E. D. R. Harrison, "The Nazi Dissolution of the Monasteries: A Case-Study," *English Historical Review* 109, no.
431 (April 1994): 326. On the restoration of holidays and rates, see Timothy
Mason, "Some Origins of the Second World War," in Timothy Mason, *Na-*
zism, Fascism and the Working Class (New York: Cambridge University Press,
1995), 49. Hitler, *Speeches,* 3:1957, March 11, 1940. On Ribbentrop, see
Guenter Lewy, *The Catholic Church and Nazi Germany* (Cambridge, MA: Da
Capo Press, 1964), 252, citing NG-1755, Minister of Interior to Governing Officials, July 24, 1940.

15. Michael Burleigh, *Death and Deliverance: "Euthanasia" in Germany, 1900–*
1945 (New York: Cambridge University Press, 1994), 171, 173. E. Klee, *Doku-*
mente zur "Euthanasie," 143, 144. Theodore Hamerow identified a related
behavior: "The great majority of clergymen failed to oppose the Nazi regime,

not only for fear of reprisal but out of expediency or even conviction. The higher their position, moreover, the more reluctant were they to challenge the authority of the state" (Theodore S. Hamerow, "Cardinal Faulhaber and the Third Reich," in *From the Berlin Museum to the Berlin Wall: Essays on the Cultural and Political History of Modern Germany,* ed. David Wetzel [Westport, CT: Praeger, 1996], 147).

16. For an overview of Kreyssig's history, see Hans Döring, ed., *Lothar Kreyssig: Aufsätze, Autobiografie und Dokumente* (Leipzig: Evangelische Verlagsanstalt, 2011); Burleigh, *Death and Deliverance,* 171. Complaints against Kreyssig during 1935 in Bericht des Oberlandesgerichtspriasidenten in Dresden an den Reichsjustizminister, October 15, 1935, are in Lothar Gruchmann, *Justiz im Dritten Reich 1933–1940* (Oldenburg: Wissenschaftsverlag, 2010), 477–480. For the charges against Kreyssig, see Bericht des Amtsgerichtsdirektors Dr. D. an den Leiter der Personalabteilung im Reichsjustizministerium, November 1935, in Gruchmann, *Justiz im Dritten Reich,* 480–482; for Freisler's reluctance to punish Kreyssig, see 464–466. The Reich Justice Ministry identified Kreyssig's offenses as motivated by religious belief rather than a base attitude, a consideration for handling his case with more leniency. Antrag des Reichsjustizministeriums an den Chef der Reichskanzlei, 10 Mai 1941, auf Versetzung Dr. Kreyssigs in den Ruhestand, in Gruchmann, *Justiz im Dritten Reich,* 485–488.

17. The impact of the war on the publicity of "euthanasia" is in Lewy, *The Catholic Church and Nazi Germany,* 256; Goebbels's order to the Gauleiters, August 13, 1940, Bundesarchiv, NS 18/112. On the German willingness to sacrifice, see Eckhard Hansen, *Wohlfahrtspolitik im NS-Staat. Motivationen, Konflikte und Machtstrukturen im "Sozialismus der Tat" des Dritten Reiches* (Augsburg: Maro-Verlag, 1991), 41.

18. Gruchmann, *Justiz im Dritten Reich,* 470–471, 511–512. Friedlander, *The Origins of Nazi Genocide,* 121.

19. Gruchmann, "Euthanasie und Justiz," 241, 253; Gruchmann, *Justiz im Dritten Reich,* 512.

20. On Kreyssig's retirement, see Aktenvermerk des Ministerialrats S. im Reichsjustizministerium, December 2, 1940, in Gruchmann, *Justiz im Dritten Reich,* 471, 484. Gruchmann states that Hitler's personal assistant, Reichsleiter Bormann, undoubtedly saw the complete list of Kreysigg's offenses, listed by the Justice Ministry in May 1941 (473).

21. Douglas Hay, "Property, Authority and the Criminal Law," in *Albion's Fatal Tree: Crime and Society in Eighteenth-Century England,* ed. Douglas Hay, Peter Linebaugh, John G. Rule, E. P. Thompson, and Cal Winslow (New York: Pantheon Books, 1976), 25, 56. Hay writes primarily about eighteenth-century British criminal law and hangings relative to popular food riots as "organized and often highly disciplined popular protest."

22. On popular discontent, see Stephenson, *Hitler's Home Front,* 127–130; Winfried Süss, " 'Dann ist keiner von uns seines Lebens mehr sicher.' Bischof

von Galen, der katholische Protest gegen die 'Euthanasie' und der Stopp der 'Aktion T4,'" in *Skandal und Diktatur: Formen öffentlicher Empörung im NS-Staat und in der DDR*, ed. Martin Sabrow (Göttingen: Wallstein, 2004), 105. For discontent regarding "euthanasia," see Kurt Nowak, "Widerstand, Zustimmung, Hinnahme: Das Verhalten der Bevölkerung zur 'Euthanasie,'" in Frei, *Medizin und Gesundheitspolitik*, 241.

23. Gruchmann, "Euthanasie und Justiz," 250.

24. Galen wrote to Bertram on July 28, 1940, and Bertram responded on August 5. Ludwig Volk, *Akten deutscher Bischöfe über die Lage der Kirche 1933–1945*, vol. 5: *1940–1942* (Mainz: Matthias Grünewald Verlag, 1983). Wolfgang Schieder, "Pius XII. im II. Weltkrieg," *Historische Zeitschrift* 207, no. 2 (October 1968): 355. On the position of the bishops, see Joseph A. Biesinger, "The Reich Concordat of 1933: The Church Struggle against Nazi Germany," in *Controversial Concordats: The Vatican's Relations with Napoleon, Mussolini, and Hitler*, ed. Frank J. Copp (Washington, D.C.: Catholic University of America Press, 1999), 162.

25. Gruchmann, "Euthanasie und Justiz," 236–237; Johann Neuhäusler, *Kreuz und Hakenkreuz, der kampf des Nationalsozialismus gegen die Katholische Kirche und der kirchliche Widerstand* (Munich: Katholische Kirche Bayerns, 1946), Faulhaber to Gürtner, November 6, 1940, 359–363. Numerous documents and eyewitness reports attest to this panic and anger. See Noakes and Pridham, *Nazism, 1919–1945*, 3:415–433.

26. Noakes and Pridham, *Nazism, 1919–1945*, 3:415–423. Also in Neuhäusler, *Kreuz und Hakenkreuz*, 359–363.

27. On Catholic bishops and unrest, see Marlis G. Steinert, *Hitler's War and the Germans: Public Mood and Attitude during the Second World War*, trans. T. E. J. de Witt (Athens: Ohio University Press, 1977), 78. For Protestant dissent, see Correspondence of General Prosecutor in Stuttgart to Reich Minister of Justice, October 12, 1940, in E. Klee, *Dokumente zur "Euthanasie,"* 210–212; Nowak, "Widerstand, Zustimmung, Hinnahme," 245. Wurm's intervention is in Stephenson, *Hitler's Home Front*, 131–132.

28. Braune's statements are in Nowak, "Widerstand, Zustimmung, Hinnahme," 242; Walters, "Paul Braune Confronts the National Socialists' 'Euthanasia' Program," 454, 458.

29. Bodelschwingh to Frick, September 28, 1940, in E. Klee, *Dokumente zur "Euthanasie,"* 173–176.

30. Paul Braune, "Der Kampf der Inneren Mission gegen die Euthanasie," a 1949 article in *Evangelische Dokumente: Zur Ermordung der "unheilbar Kranken" unter der nationalsozialistischen Herrschaft in den Jahren 1939–1945*, ed. Hans Christoph von Hase (Stuttgart: Innere Mission und Hilfswerk der EKD, 1964), 109. Braune is quoted in Walters, "Paul Braune Confronts the National Socialists' 'Euthanasia' Program," 474–475.

31. Walters, "Paul Braune Confronts the National Socialists' 'Euthanasia' Program," 457, 475–476; Friedlander, *The Origins of Nazi Genocide*, 114. The

memorandum of Pastor Paul Gerhard Braune for Hitler of July 9, 1940, is in E. Klee, *Dokumente zur "Euthanasie,"* 151–162.

32. On Holzhäuer, see E. Klee, *Dokumente zur "Euthanasie,"* 208. Gruchmann, "Euthanasie und Justiz," 251; Schlegelberger to Lammers, March 4, 1941, is in E. Klee, *Dokumente zur "Euthanasie,"* 213–216. For a detailed overview of the German judiciary's efforts to legalize euthanasia and Hitler's steadfast refusal, see Gruchmann, *Justiz im Dritten Reich,* 505–534.

33. On the closing of the Brandenburg operation, see Friedlander, *The Origins of Nazi Genocide,* 88. On legality, see Burleigh, *Death and Deliverance,* 171–172; Gruchmann, "Euthanasie und Justiz," 249–250; Goetz Aly, "Das 'Gesetz über die Sterbehilfe bei Unheilbar Kranken' Protokolle der Diskussion über die Legalisierung der nationalsozialisitischen Anstaltsmorde in den Jahren 1938–1941," in *Erfassung zur Vernichtung: Von der Sozialhygiene zum "Gesetz über Sterbehilfe,"* ed. Karl Heinz Roth (Berlin: Verlagsgesellschaft Gesundheit, 1984), 101–179; William L. Shirer, *Berlin Diary: The Journal of a Foreign Correspondent* (New York: Knopf, 1942), 423, entry for November 25, 1941.

34. Gruchmann, "Euthanasie und Justiz," 255, 256n60.

35. Nuremberg Military Tribunal (NMT), NO-001, Else von Loewiss to Frau Buch Concerning the Treatment of Incurably Insane Persons, November 25, 1940. NMT, NO-002, Buch to Himmler, December 7, 1940 (Nuremberg trial document NO-002), Harvard Law School Library Item No. 465.

36. Reichsführer-SS Heinrich Himmler to Oberdienstleiter Viktor Brack, December 19, 1940, Nuremberg trial document NO-018; Gruchmann, "Euthanasie und Justiz," 277; Friedlander, *The Origins of Nazi Genocide,* 107–108; Nowak, "Widerstand, Zustimmung, Hinnahme," 242.

37. On Grafeneck, see Stephenson, *Hitler's Home Front,* 127. Some otherwise excellent histories do not take note of this correspondence on the closing of Grafeneck due to agitation and conclude that "Grafeneck had by this time apparently served its purpose of eliminating most of the 'useless eaters' in Württemberg and Baden." The judgment is then made that Hitler's "halt" order of August 24, 1941, was a mere "pretense" since the program had killed the targeted number of "useless eaters" (Stephenson, *Hitler's Home Front,* 133).

38. On the morale effects of Hadamar, see Nowak, "Widerstand, Zustimmung, Hinnahme," 243. On the reduced target, see Peter Longerich, *Holocaust: The Nazi Persecution and Murder of the Jews* (Oxford: Oxford University Press, 2010), 278.

39. International Military Tribunal (IMT), *Trial of the Major War Criminals: Proceeding Volumes,* 42 vols. (Nuremberg, November 14, 1945–October 1, 1946), 906-D, Kreisleiter Gerstner to Franconia Gauleitung (Sellmer), 35:690–692, 695–699, February 24, 1941; NMT, NO-665, Sellmer to Helfelmann, Chancellery of the Führer, March 1, 1941, *United States of America v. Karl Brandt et al.,* Prosecution Document Book XIV, part III, 296–297, National Archives Microfilm Publication M887, roll 17, 0304–0306.

40. NMT, NO-665, Kreisleiter Gerstner to Franconia Gauleitung (Sellmer), February 24, 1941, *United States of America v. Karl Brandt et al.*, Prosecution Document Book XIV, part III, 296–297, National Archives Microfilm Publication M887, roll 17, 0304–0306. For other cases of public solidarity with victims, see Nuremberg trial documents NO-897, NO-520, NO-844.

41. On the irreconcilability of the church and Nazism, see Bormann's memorandum, June 6–7, 1941, Nuremburg trial document 075-D, translated and cited in Conway, *The Nazi Persecution of the Churches*, 383–386; IMT, *Trial of the Major War Criminals: Proceeding Volumes*, 35:9–13. It was natural "that the representatives of Christian ideology speak against the [euthanasia] Commission's measures; it must be equally taken for granted that all Party offices support, as far as necessary, the work of the Commission" (IMT, *Trial of the Major War Criminals: Proceeding Volumes*, 35:681–682, 906-D, Martin Bormann to Gauleitung of Franconia, September 24, 1940); Rosenberg's statement in IMT, *Nazi Conspiracy and Aggression*, 8 vols. and Supplements A and B (Washington, D.C.: Government Printing Office, 1946–1948), 6:408–409, 3701-PS, Tiessler, "Secret Proposal for Reichsleiter Bormann," Berlin, August 13, 1941; English translation in Benjamin C. Sax and Dieter Kuntz, *Inside Hitler's Germany: A Documentary History of Life in the Third Reich* (Lexington, MA: D. C. Heath, 1992), 488; Conway, *The Nazi Persecution of the Churches*, 249–250.

42. IMT, *Trial of the Major War Criminals: Proceeding Volumes*, 35:699ff., 906-D, District Leader in Ansbach to Franconia Gauleitung, March 6, 1941, drawing on a report from the Bruckberg Local Nazi Party Leader (emphasis added).

43. Lewy, *The Catholic Church and Nazi Germany*, 285–287, citing Heydrich's order on "Behandlung der konfessionnellen Gegner" of October 24, 1941, T-175, 409/2932603, National Archives, Washington.

44. On patterns of confidence in war, see Steinert, *Hitler's War*, 75. Winfried Müller, "Gauleiter als Minister: Die Gauleiter Hans Schemm, Adolf Wagner, Paul Giesler und das Bayerische Staatsministerium für Unterricht und Kultus 1933–1945," *Zeitschrift für Bayerische Landesgeschichte* 60 (1997): 1014; Bormann to Gauleiters, April 12, 1939 (Directive 79/39) and early June 1941 (Directive 132/39), translated and cited in Conway, *The Nazi Persecution of the Churches*, 366–369.

45. Ian Kershaw, *Popular Opinion and Political Dissent in the Third Reich: Bavaria 1933–1945* (New York: Oxford University Press, 2002 [orig. 1983]), 345ff.; W. Müller, "Gauleiter als Minister," 1014–1015; Willi Boelcke, *Wollt Ihr den totalen Krieg? Die geheimen Goebbels-Konferenzen, 1939–1943* (Herrsching: Pawlak, 1989), 236.

46. Harrison, "The Nazi Dissolution of the Monasteries," 327. See also Nicholas Stargardt, *The German War: A Nation under Arms, 1939–1945* (New York: Basic Books, 2015), 151. The results of the Fulda conference are in Beth A. Griech-Polelle, *Bishop von Galen: German Catholicism and National Socialism* (New Haven: Yale University Press, 2002), 69–70, 76.

47. Harrison, "The Nazi Dissolution of the Monasteries," 340. For the complete story of the Münsterschwarzach monastery, see Jonathan Düring, *Wir Weichen nur der Gewalt: Die Mönche von Münsterschwarzach im Dritten Reich,* 2 vols. (Münsterschwarzach: Vier-Türme, 1997).

48. Harrison, "The Nazi Dissolution of the Monasteries," 338 (emphasis added). See also Düring, *Wir Weichen nur der Gewalt.*

49. Helmut Witetschek, *Die kirchliche Lage in Bayern nach den Regierungspräsidentenberichten, 1933–1943* (Mainz: Matthias-Grünewald, 1967), 31:xlviii, 22; Harrison, "The Nazi Dissolution of the Monasteries," 339; Irina Seifert, *Matthias Ehrenfried: Bischof von Würzburg* (Norderstedt: Grin Verlag, 2003), 16.

50. Kershaw, *Nemesis,* 366; Boelcke, *Wollt Ihr den totalen Krieg?* 236. David Stahel, *Operation Barbarossa and Germany's Defeat in the East* (Cambridge: Cambridge University Press, 2009), 148.

51. Friedlander, *The Origins of Nazi Genocide,* 115; Harrison, "The Nazi Dissolution of the Monasteries," 348–349. The pastoral letter is in Volk, ed., *Akten,* 5:464–465.

52. The Battle of Smolensk began on July 10, 1941, and dragged on for two months, disrupting the Wehrmacht's Blitzkrieg strategy. Stahel, *Operation Barbarossa,* 279. On unrest on the home front, see E. Klee, *Dokumente zur "Euthanasie,"* 297, 301–302; Kershaw, *Nemesis,* 426; Griech-Polelle, *Bishop von Galen,* 92.

53. Report by the Nazi Party head of indoctrination in Maxfield, April 9, 1943, translated and cited in Jeremy Noakes, ed., *Nazism, 1919–1945,* vol. 4: *The German Home Front in World War II* (Exeter: Exeter University Press, 1998), 542.

54. Griech-Polelle, *Bishop von Galen,* 81–85; Armin Nolzen, "The NSDAP, the War, and German Society," in *Germany and the Second World War: German Wartime Society, 1939–45: Politicization, Disintegration, and the Struggle for Survival,* ed. Jörg Echternkamp (New York: Oxford University Press, 2008), 151.

55. The three sermons by Galen are in Heinrich Portmann, *Der Bischof von Münster: Das Echo eines Kampfes für Gottesrecht und Menschenrecht* (Münster: Verlag Aschendorff, 1946), 123–155; see the translation of Galen's sermon of August 3, 1941, in Griech-Polelle, *Bishop von Galen,* 186–196. For Galen and the Jews, see Griech-Polelle, *Bishop von Galen,* 84–85.

56. Bormann to Gauleiters, July 31, 1941, Bundesarchiv, R 412 II/1271; Harrison, "The Nazi Dissolution of the Monasteries," 351–353, 355; Lewy, *The Catholic Church and Nazi Germany,* 252–254.

57. Sermon on August 3, 1941, in Portmann, *Der Bischof von Münster,* 143–155.

58. Hitler's comments on Galen in Trevor Roper, ed., *Hitler's Table Talk,* 419.

59. The statement by the court president for Westphalia is in Joachim Kuropka, *Meldungen aus Münster 1924–1944. Geheime und vertrauliche Berichte von Polizei, Gestapo, NSDAP und ihren Gliederungen, staatlicher Verwaltung*

Gerichtsbarkeit und Wehrmacht über die politische und gesellschaftliche Situation in Münster (Münster: Regensberg, 1992), 534. On the distribution of Galen's sermons, see Winfried Süss, *Der "Völkskörper" im Krieg: Gesundheitspolitik, Gesundheitsverhältnisse und Krankenmord im nationalsozialistischen Deutschland 1939–1945* (Munich: Oldenbourg, 2003), 137–138; Griech-Polelle, *Bishop von Galen*, 86, 90. Düsseldorf attorney general Franz Hagemann to Schlegelberger, December 1, 1941, is in E. Klee, *Dokumente zur "Euthanasie,"* 196.

60. Pius XII to Bishop von Preysing, September 20, 1941, in *Die Briefe Pius XII. und die deutschen Bischöfe 1939–1944*, translated and cited in Kevin P. Spicer, review of *Bishop von Galen: German Catholicism and National Socialism*, by Beth Griech-Polelle, *Holocaust and Genocide Studies* 18, no. 3 (Winter 2004): 492–495.

61. "The euthanasia programme was not halted because of some local difficulties with a handful of bishops," according to Burleigh, *Death and Deliverance*, 180. The question of "what effective measures could be taken" in response to Galen's sermons was a decision for the Führer, Goebbels said on August 13, 1941. IMT, *Nazi Conspiracy and Aggression*, 6:408–409, 3701-PS, Walther Tiessler, "Proposal for Reichsleiter Bormann Concerning: Sermon of the Bishop of Muenster on 3 August 1941," Berlin, August 12, 1941; English translation in Sax and Kuntz, *Inside Hitler's Germany*, 488.

62. Propaganda Division Chief to Reich Propaganda Minister Goebbels, August 12, 1941, in Kuropka, *Meldungen aus Münster*, 536ff. See the translation in IMT, *Nazi Conspiracy and Aggression*, 6:406–408, 3701-PS, Tiessler, "Division Chief Propaganda to the Reich Minister for Propaganda and Popular Enlightenment, Concerning: Catholic Action," Berlin, August 12, 1941.

63. Goebbels's statement on equality before the law is in Goebbels, *Tagebücher*, part II, 1:232, entry for August 14, 1941. For Goebbels's desire to avoid a breach with the church, see IMT, *Nazi Conspiracy and Aggression*, 6:408–409, 3701-PS, Tiessler, "Secret Proposal for Reichsleiter Bormann," Berlin, August 13, 1941.

64. On the Justice Ministry, see Gruchmann, *Justiz im dritten Reich*, 521; Bormann on Galen and "euthanasia" is in IMT, *Nazi Conspiracy and Aggression*, 6:406–408, 3701-PS, Tiessler, "Division Chief Propaganda to the Reich Minister for Propaganda and Popular Enlightenment, Concerning: Catholic Action," Berlin, August 12, 1941; Sax and Kuntz, *Inside Hitler's Germany*, 489. Hitler on Rosenberg: "I still think it was a great mistake that Rosenberg ever let himself be drawn into a battle of words with the Church. He had absolutely nothing to gain from it; the hesitant Catholics of their own free will regarded the Church with a critical eye and from the truly devout not only could he expect no fair hearing for his 'heretical outpourings,' but must also have realized that the opposition propaganda would condemn him for his meddling in matters of faith and successfully point to him as a man of moral sin" (Trevor-Roper, *Hitler's Table Talk*, 418–419, entry for July 4, 1942).

65. On the broadening distrust of government, see Griech-Polelle, *Bishop von Galen*, 92. Goebbels on avoiding conflict is in Goebbels, *Tagebücher*, part II, 1:298–299, entry for August 23, 1941. On Hitler's halt order, see the testimony of Viktor Brack, Nuremberg Document NO-426. The euthanasia of children continued. Discontinuing the program for adults would have quashed the rumors about wounded soldiers being euthanized.

66. Brack said that after he received an oral order to halt the "euthanasia" program, "in order to preserve the personnel relieved of these duties and to have the opportunity of starting a new Euthanasia Program after the war, Bouler requested, I think after a conference with Hitler, that I send this personnel to Lublin and put it at the disposal of SS Brigadefuehrer Globocnik. . . . Later . . . I found out that they were used to assist in the mass extermination of the Jews." Personnel redeployed to the East are not mentioned here. Testimony of Viktor Brack, Nuremberg Document NO-426. For Hitler's order to stop attacks on church properties, see Ernst C. Helmreich, *The German Churches under Hitler: Background, Struggle, and Epilogue* (Detroit: Wayne State University Press, 1979), 350.

67. Friedlander, *The Origins of Nazi Genocide*, 110, 111; E. Klee, *Dokumente zur "Euthanasie,"* 283–285; Christoph Heinzen, *Medizin und Gewissenhistorische, systematische und aktuelle Perspektiven im Hinblick aud die Euthanasiegesetzgebung* (Munich: Grin Verlag, 2003), 34, 35. On the reduced size and visibility of "wild euthanasia," see Friedlander, *The Origins of Nazi Genocide*, 111. For changes to the location and targets of killing centers, see Kurt Nowak, "Sterilisation und 'Euthanasie' im Dritten Reich: Tatsachen und Deutungen," *Geschichte in Wissenschaft Und Unterricht* 39, no. 6 (1988): 332; Schmuhl, *Rassenhygiene, Nationalsozialismus, Euthanasie*, 230–236.

68. Friedlander, *The Origins of Nazi Genocide*, 154; Hans-Walter Schmuhl, "Die Selbstverständlichkeit des Tötens: Psychiater im Nationalsozialismus," *Geschichte und Gesellschaft* 16, no. 4 (1990): 412–413; E. Klee, *Dokumente zur "Euthanasie,"* 283.

69. Schmuhl, *Rassenhygiene, Nationalsozialismus, Euthanasie*, 223; on deception, see E. Klee, *Dokumente zur "Euthanasie,"* 283.

70. George C. Browder, *Foundations of the Nazi Police State: The Formation of Sipo and SD* (Lexington: University Press of Kentucky, 2004), 95, 313; Dietrich Orlow, *The Nazi Party 1919–1945: A Complete History* (New York: Enigma, 2008), 488; Robert Lifton, *The Nazi Doctors: Medical Killing and the Psychology of Genocide* (New York: Basic Books, 1986), 49. Christian Kuchler, "Bischoflicher Protest gegen nationalsozialistische 'Euthanasie'—Propaganda im Kino: 'Ich Klage An,'" *Historisches Jahrbuch der Görresgesellschaft* 126 (2006): 269–294. Lower classes were more likely to accept the propaganda than intellectuals, according to an SD report, and Catholics objected more than Protestants. David Welch, *Propaganda and the German Cinema, 1933–1945* (New York: St. Martin's Press, 2001), 103, 106.

71. Harrison, "The Nazi Dissolution of the Monasteries," 353; Kershaw, *Hitler, the Germans, and the Final Solution*, 201.

72. Ludwig Volk, *Akten, Kardinal Michael von Faulhabers* (Mainz: Matthias Grünewald Verlag, 1978), 2:997, cited in Harrison, "The Nazi Dissolution of the Monasteries," 353.

73. Pius XII to Bishop von Preysing, September 20, 1941, in *Die Briefe Pius XII. und die deutschen Bischöfe 1939–1944* (Mainz: Matthias Grünewald Verlag, 1966), 155, translated and cited by Kevin P. Spicer, review of *Bishop von Galen: German Catholicism and National Socialism* by Beth Griech-Polelle, *Holocaust and Genocide Studies* 18, no. 3 (Winter 2004): 492–495.

74. On Hitler's suspension of Wagner's decree, see W. Müller, "Gauleiter als Minister," 1016. Epp on Wagner is in Kershaw, *Popular Opinion*, 353, 354.

75. Goebbels, *Tagebücher*, part II, 1:519, entry for September 30, 1941.

76. Ibid., part II, 3:545, entry for March 25, 1942.

77. Ibid. On Goebbels's meeting with Gauleiter Röver, see ibid., part I, vol. 3/II, 352, entry for January 30, 1937. Stargardt, *The German War*, 260.

78. On his fears following the Witten Protest, see Goebbels, *Tagebücher*, part II, 10:222, entry for November 2, 1943.

CHAPTER VII. "THE PEOPLE KNOW WHERE TO FIND THE LEADERSHIP'S SOFT SPOT"

1. Neil Gregor, "A Schicksalsgemeinschaft? Allied Bombing, Civilian Morale, and Social Dissolution in Nuremberg, 1942–1945," *Historical Journal* 43 (2000): 1051–1070; Jörg Friedrich, *Der Brand: Deutschland im Bombenkrieg, 1940–1945* (Berlin: Propyläen, 2002), 437. Thomas Kühne argues that knowledge of the Holocaust created a sense among Germans of a peculiar common fate (*Belonging and Genocide: Hitler's Community, 1918–1945* [New Haven: Yale University Press, 2010]).

2. SD report, July 8, 1943, in Heinz Boberach, *Meldungen aus dem Reich* (Herrsching: Pawlak, 1984), 14:5445–5446.

3. Peter Fritzsche, "Machine Dreams: Air-mindedness and the Reinvention of Germany," *American Historical Review* 98, no. 3 (June 1993): 689–690.

4. Bernd Lemke, *Luftschutz in Grossbritannien und Deutschland 1923 bis 1939: Zivile Kriegsvorbereitungen als Ausdruck der staats und gesellschaftspolitischen Grundlagen von Demokratie und Diktatur* (Munich: Oldenbourg, 2005), 325–326.

5. Birgit Arnold, *Die Freimachung und Räumung der Grenzgebiete in Baden 1939/40* (Heidelberg: C. Winter, 1996), 54–59.

6. International Military Tribunal (IMT), *Trial of the Major War Criminals: Proceeding Volumes*, 42 vols. (Nuremberg, November 14, 1945–October 1, 1946), 28:389, PS-1780, "Excerpts from General Jodl's Handwritten Diary, February 1937–August 1939," September 28, 1938.

7. Julia S. Torrie, *"For Their Own Good": Civilian Evacuations in Germany and France* (New York: Berghahn Books, 2010), 3, 49.

8. Katja Klee, *Im "Luftschutzkeller des Reiches": Evakuierte in Bayern 1939–1953: Politik, soziale Lage, Erfahrungen* (Munich: Oldenbourg, 1999), 29.

9. Arnold, *Freimachung*, 79, 83.

10. Ibid., 79. On August 29 order, see Torrie, *"For Their Own Good,"* 33.

11. Arnold, *Freimachung*, 91. The dictatorship's concern with keeping plans for evacuation secret stretched back to 1934 and 1935, according to Arnold (21, 30); see also K. Klee, *Im "Luftschutzkeller des Reiches,"* 31.

12. Arnold, *Freimachung*, 95; Dietmar Süss, "Wartime Societies and Shelter Politics in National Socialist Germany and Britain," in *Bombing, States and Peoples in Western Europe, 1940–1945*, ed. Claudia Baldoli, Andrew Knapp, and Richard Overy (London: Continuum, 2011), 30.

13. Torrie, *"For Their Own Good,"* 37, 43; Arnold, *Freimachung*, 85. Arnold estimates the number of Germans who took the initiative to move without government stipulations at 370,000.

14. SD report, October 11, 1939, in Boberach, *Meldungen aus dem Reich*, 2:343–345. This was the number according to the SD.

15. Sopade Report, October 24, 1939, in Klaus Behnken, ed., *Deutschland-Berichte der Sopade* (Salzhausen: Nettelbeck, 1980), 6:973; SD report, November 8, 1939, in Boberach, *Meldungen aus dem Reich*, 2:440; SD report, October 11, 1939, in ibid., 2:343–344; Torrie, *"For Their Own Good,"* 75.

16. SD report, October 11, 1939, in Boberach, *Meldungen aus dem Reich*, 2:343. Also on the problem of theft, see Arnold, *Freimachung*, 95.

17. SD report, October 11, 1939, in Boberach, *Meldungen aus dem Reich*, 2:343; reports summarized by Marlis G. Steinert, *Hitler's War and the Germans: Public Mood and Attitude during the Second World War*, trans. T. E. J. de Witt (Athens: Ohio University Press, 1977), 63. When German standards for practicing medicine were extended to the new German territory of Austria (Ostmark), university students collected, and their loud protest turned into a rumpus. In contrast to its report on the angry gathering at Dudweiler, where the protesters represented the angry opinion of many evacuees, the SD reported that in this university case "names have all been registered; measures initiated. It generally holds in Austria," the SD concluded, "that lust for oppositional action is found mainly in Catholic legitimist circles" (SD report, October 9, 1939, in Boberach, *Meldungen aus dem Reich*, 2:332, 333).

18. SD report, November 8, 1939, in Boberach, *Meldungen aus dem Reich*, 2:439. K. Klee, *Im "Luftschutzkeller des Reiches,"* 34, 35; Arnold, *Freimachung*, 116.

19. SD report, November 8, 1939, in Boberach, *Meldungen aus dem Reich*, 2:439; SD report, October 11, 1939, in ibid., 2:343–334.

20. K. Klee, *Im "Luftschutzkeller des Reiches,"* 30.

21. IMT, *Trial of the Major War Criminals: Proceeding Volumes*, 28:389, PS-1780, "Excerpts from General Jodl's Diary," September 28, 1938.

22. Despite the OKW's efforts to suppress the masses of "wild" evacuees, their numbers became so great that it reversed its prohibition and allowed evacuees to return home. K. Klee, *Im "Luftschutzkeller des Reiches,"* 36.

23. Ibid.

24. Hans Mommsen used the term "weak dictator" in *Beamtentum im Dritten Reich* (Stuttgart: Deutsche Verlags-Anstalt, 1966), 98n26.

25. Steinert, *Hitler's War*, 60, summarizing reports from November 10, 13, and 15, 1939.

26. Heiber, *Akten der Partei-Kanzlei*, 1:508, no. 14417.

27. SD report, October 7, 1940, in Boberach, *Meldungen aus dem Reich*, 5:1647–1649; Torrie, *"For Their Own Good,"* 48.

28. SD report, July 22, 1940, in Boberach, *Meldungen aus dem Reich*, 5:1409.

29. SD report, May 16, 1940, in ibid., 4:1139ff.; SD report, June 6, 1940, in ibid., 4:1219; SD report, June 20, 1940, in ibid., 4:1276; SD report, July 4, 1940, in ibid., 5:1335.

30. William L. Shirer, *Berlin Diary: The Journal of a Foreign Correspondent* (New York: Knopf, 1942), 486, August 26, 1940. SD report, September 9, 1940, in Boberach, *Meldungen aus dem Reich*, 5:1549.

31. Cited in Max Domarus, ed., *Hitler: Reden und Proklamationen 1932–1945* (Munich: Suddeutscher Verlag, 1965), 3:1577, September 4, 1940.

32. SD report, September 9, 1940, in Boberach, *Meldungen aus dem Reich*, 5:1549.

33. SD report, October 11, 1939, in Boberach, *Meldungen aus dem Reich*, 2:339.

34. Joseph Goebbels, *Die Tagebücher von Joseph Goebbels*, ed. Elke Fröhlich (Munich: K. G. Saur, 1993–1996), part I, 8:313, entry for September 8, 1940.

35. Ibid., part I, 8:311, entry for September 7, 1940; SD report, September 12, 1940, in Boberach, *Meldungen aus dem Reich*, 5:1563.

36. Baldur von Schirach, *Ich Glaubte an Hitler* (Munich: Mosaik Verlag, 1967), 269–270. This is the postwar claim of Schirach.

37. Torrie, *"For Their Own Good,"* 53.

38. Memo titled "Entsendung Vorschulpflichtiger und Schulpflichtiger Kinder aus Hamburg und Berlin," September 27, 1940, the date of Hitler's order, cited in Herwart Vorländer, *Die NSV: Darstellung und Dokumentation einer nationalsozialistischen* (Boppard am Rhein: Boldt, 1988), 415–416. This memo was issued the same day that Bormann released a mandate from Hitler to remove children from cities threatened by bombing by expanding the Kinderlandverschickung (KLV) program.

39. Nicholas Stargardt, *The German War: A Nation under Arms, 1939–1945* (New York: Basic Books, 2015), 114–115. Gerhard Kock, *"Der Führer sorgt für unser Kinder . . .": Die Kinderlandverschickung im Zweiten Weltkrieg* (Paderborn: Schöningh, 1997), 69, 353. Donald D. Wall, "The Reports of the Sicherheitsdienst on the Church and Religious Affairs in Germany, 1939–1944," *Church History* 40, no. 4 (December 1971): 446. See also 370n63, 386n24.

40. StA Münster, OP 5074, telex from Bormann to all Gauleiters, September 30, 1940; cited in K. Klee, Im *"Luftschtzkeller des Reiches,"* 45. Torrie, *"For Their Own Good,"* 10.

41. Willi Boelcke, ed., *The Secret Conferences of Dr. Goebbels: The Nazi Propaganda War, 1939–43* (New York: E. P. Dutton, 1970), 530.

42. Reichsleitung der NSDAP, R 36/2596; cited in Olaf Groehler, *Bombenkrieg gegen Deutschland* (Berlin: Akademie-Verlag, 1990), 265; K. Klee, Im *"Luftschtzkeller des Reiches,"* 45. See also Vorländer, *Die NSV,* 417.

43. Cited in Kock, *"Der Führer Sorgt für unser Kinder . . . ,"* 75.

44. Clifford Kirkpatrick, *Nazi Germany: Its Women and Family Life* (Indianapolis, IN: Bobbs-Merrill, 1938), 48–51. The sociologist Clifford Kirkpatrick was living in Nazi Berlin during 1936–1937 on a Guggenheim Fellowship to study women and feminism.

45. Unrest "is growing by [the] hour" in Berlin. SD report, September 30, 1940, in Boberach, *Meldungen aus dem Reich,* 5:1622.

46. Cited in Kock, *"Der Führer sorgt für unser Kinder . . . ,"* 74, 136n235.

47. Goebbels, *Tagebücher,* part I, 8:355, entry for October 1, 1940.

48. Torrie, *"For Their Own Good,"* 91. The new Interministerial Air War Damages Committee, under Goebbels, met first in January 1943; Richard J. Evans, *The Third Reich at War* (London: Allen Land, 2008), 453; Jörn Brinkhus and Bernd Lemke, eds., *Luft- und Zivilschutz in Deutschland im 20. Jahrhundert* (Potsdam: Militärgeschichtliches Forschungsamt, 2007), 15.

49. Fritz Hauschild, *Das Ende der Kriegs-kinderlandverschickung: Die Hamburger KLV-Lager im Jahre 1945: Briefe, Tagebücher, Berichte* (Norderstedt: Books on Demand, 2004), 7; K. Klee, Im *"Luftschtzkeller des Reiches,"* 46.

50. Young-Sun Hong, *Welfare, Modernity, and the Weimar State, 1919–1933* (Princeton, NJ: Princeton University Press, 1998), 27.

51. SD report, March 23, 1942, in Boberach, *Meldungen aus dem Reich,* 9:3509–3516; Joseph Goebbels, in the *Berliner Zeitung,* October 1, 1940.

52. Kock, *"Der Führer sorgt für unser Kinder . . . ,"* 184–188.

53. Ibid., 72; K. Klee, Im *"Luftschtzkeller des Reiches,"* 106; SD report, October 7, 1940, in Boberach, *Meldungen aus dem Reich,* 5:1647ff.

54. "Das Problem der Kinderverschikung beschäftigt auch ihn sehr stark. Ich lege ihm meinen Standpunkt dar, der von ihm gebilligt wird: kein Zwang, nur wer will, wer es allein kann, soll das machen" (Goebbels, *Tagebücher,* part I, 8:354–355, entry for October 1, 1940).

55. Boelcke, *The Secret Conferences of Dr. Goebbels,* 103; SD report, September 9, 1940, in Boberach, *Meldungen aus dem Reich,* 5:1549; SD report, October 7, 1940, in ibid., 5:1647–1648.

56. SD report, February 20, 1941, in ibid., 6:2021; SD report, July 8, 1943, in ibid., 14:5446.

57. Michael H. Kater, *Hitler Youth* (Cambridge, MA: Harvard University Press, 2004), 45.

58. Richard Steigmann-Gall, *The Holy Reich: Nazi Conceptions of Christianity, 1919–1945* (Cambridge: Cambridge University Press, 2004), 166. Kater, *Hitler Youth,* 19.

59. Heinz Schreckenberg, *Erziehung, Lebenswelt und Kriegseinsatz der deutschen Jugend unter Hitler: Anmerkungen zur Literatur* (Münster: LIT Verlag, 2001), 211. For some time scholars had portrayed the evacuation of children as a purely humanitarian mission to save lives, a portrayal that removed it and its surviving personnel from the stigma of National Socialism. More recent scholarship has rebutted this position. Kock, *"Der Führer Sorgt für unser Kinder . . . ,"* 41–45, convincingly makes the argument that evacuation measures and plans indicated a desire of the party to take over the responsibilities of education from the state. K. Klee, *Im "Luftschtzkeller des Reiches,"* has substantiated Kock's argument that Schirach, in conjunction with Hitler, initiated and gave initial form to the evacuation of schoolchildren. Klee agrees that the KLV was intended to increase the influence of National Socialist principles on education and increase the Hitler Youth's influence (303). Torrie agrees that authorities exploited the evacuations "to link vulnerable segments of the population to the regime" (*"For Their Own Good,"* 53).

60. Kock, *"Der Führer sorgt für unser Kinder . . . ,"* 87–88.

61. Schirach to regional officials responsible for KLV evacuations, in response to a question from Gauleiter Meyer of Wesphalia-North, July 21, 1941; in ibid., 185.

62. Even when Gauleiter autonomy over evacuations changed somewhat in April 1943 with the introduction of uniform regulations from Berlin, these new orders made no fundamental changes to the improvisations that the Gauleiters had already developed. K. Klee, *Im "Luftschtzkeller des Reiches,"* 117–132.

63. Stargardt, *The German War,* 403–407. Kock, *"Der Führer sorgt für unser Kinder . . . ,"* 117–118, 194. Kock dismisses an argument by historians like Wolfgang Benz that represent the parents as having had no choice. "The worse the air war grew, the more students were affected by KLV evacuations. . . . The parents were powerless if entire school classes were evacuated" (Benz, "Kinder und Jugendliche in der NS-Zeit," in *Sozialisation und Traumatisierung: Kinder in der Zeit des Nationalsozialismus,* ed. Ute Benz and Wolfgang Benz [Frankfurt: Fischer, 1992], 21). Kock, *"Der Führer sorgt für unser Kinder . . . ,"* 188. Gerhard Dabel, the last director of the KLV headquarters who was also the first chairman of the postwar KLV archive, set a course for the portrayal of KLV evacuations as an effort apart from Nazism, concerned purely with child welfare. A former Hitler Youth leader and author of Nazi youth propaganda, Dabel's 1981 book portrayed the KLV as acting on "humanitarian grounds" (*KLV. Die erweiterte Kinder-Land-Verschickung. KLV-Lager 1940–1945* [Freiburg: Schillinger, 1981]).

64. Kater, *Hitler Youth,* 46. Kater argues that despite parental choice, the regime still made progress toward its indoctrination goals through the KLV evacuations.

65. BA Koblenz NS 12/vorl. 942. Bericht ueber eine Arbeitstagung für KLV in Berlin, June 25, 1941; cited in Kock, *"Der Führer sorgt für unser Kinder . . . ,"* 288; Lisa Pine, *Education in Nazi Germany* (Oxford: Berg, 2010), 31. Rundschreiben Schirach, KOV Nr. 9/40, December 4, 1940; cited in Kock, *"Der Führer sorgt für unser Kinder . . . ,"* 289.

66. Pastoral letter from Bishop Galen, October 26, 1941; cited in Heinrich Portmann, ed., *Dokumente um den Bischof von Münster* (Münster: Aschendorff, 1948), 2:273; SD report, March 23, 1942, in Boberach, *Meldungen aus dem Reich,* 9:3515. Rumors in church circles painted KLV living conditions darkly, adding material reasons for concern. Donald J. Dietrich, *Catholic Citizens in the Third Reich: Psycho-Social Principles and Moral Reasoning* (New Brunswick, NJ: Transaction Press, 1988), 280. On church competition, see Armin Nolzen, "The NSDAP, the War, and German Society," in *Germany and the Second World War: German Wartime Society, 1939–45: Politicization, Disintegration, and the Struggle for Survival,* ed. Jörg Echternkamp (New York: Oxford University Press, 2008), 151.

67. SD report, March 23, 1942, in Boberach, *Meldungen aus dem Reich,* 9:3509–3516. Dietrich, *Catholic Citizens in the Third Reich,* 280.

68. Lewy, *The Catholic Church and Nazi Germany* (Cambridge, MA: Da Capo Press, 1964), 254, citing Heydrich Order on "Behandlung der konfessionnellen Gegner," October 24, 1941.

69. K. Klee, *Im "Luftschtzkeller des Reiches,"* 59.

70. Kock, *"Der Führer sorgt für unser Kinder . . . ,"* 185–186.

71. Reich Youth Authority directive, July 4, 1941, *Reich Youth Authority's Handbook of Guidelines for the Hitler Youth;* cited in Kock, *"Der Führer sorgt für unser Kinder . . . ,"* 189.

72. Albert Speer, *Inside the Third Reich* (New York: Macmillan, 1970), 245.

73. Kock, *"Der Führer sorgt für unser Kinder . . . ,"* 184–186. These complete school transfers had been foreseen in Bormann's transmission of Hitler's original order of September 1940 but were approved by Hitler at the end of 1942.

74. Ibid., 189n179, citing Directives of the Hamburg KLV Gau Authorities from November 29, 1943, StA Hamburg, 361–10/34.

75. On Hamburg, see ibid., 185–186; on Berlin, see SD report, September 30, 1943, in Boberach, *Meldungen aus dem Reich,* 15:5827–5832.

76. Gerhard E. Sollbach, *Der Lufterror geht weiter—Mütter schafft eure Kinder Fort: Erweiterte Kinderlandverschickung und Schulevakuierung in der Stadt Dortmund während des Zweiten Weltkriegs* (Bochum: Projekt Verlag, 2001), 11.

77. Goebbels, *Tagebücher,* part II: 10:514–515, entry for December 20, 1943; 10:338, entry for November 23, 1943; and 10:514ff., entry for December 20, 1943.

78. Kock, *"Der Führer sorgt für unser Kinder . . ."* 218; "Kinder, die zu Hause sitzen," *Bochumer Anzeiger,* October 8, 1943; cited in Sollbach, *Der Lufterror,* 11. See also chapter VI above.

79. Dietrich, *Catholic Citizens in the Third Reich,* 279.

80. Dr. A. Meyer to District Presidents in Münster and Minden, December 10, 1943, BA (USHMM) R 55/447; cited in Sollbach, *Der Luftterror*, 11; Dietrich, *Catholic Citizens in the Third Reich*, 279, citing Heinz Boberach, *Berichte des SD und der Gestapo über Kirchen und Kirchenvolk in Deutschland 1934–1943*.

81. SD report, February 10, 1944, in Boberach, *Meldungen aus dem Reich*, 16:6315. Directives of the Hamburg KLV Gau Authorities, November 29, 1943, StA Hamburg, 361–10/34; cited in Kock, *"Der Führer sorgt für unser Kinder . . . ,"* 189–190.

82. On Hamburg, see Kock, *"Der Führer sorgt für unser Kinder . . . ,"* 192–193 (according to guidelines in Hamburg for advising parents); on Trier, see Wall, "The Reports of the Sicherheitsdienst," 447; Dietrich, *Catholic Citizens in the Third Reich*, 280.

83. Directives of the Hamburg KLV Gau Authorities, November 29, 1943, StA Hamburg, 361–10/34; cited in Kock, *"Der Führer sorgt für unser Kinder . . . ,"* 189–190. The children were given the responsibility for telling their parents that visits from them were possible. On chaplains, see Kock, *"Der Führer sorgt für unser Kinder . . . ,"* 300–301.

84. Wall, "The Reports of the Sicherheitsdienst," 447; Dietrich, *Catholic Citizens in the Third Reich*, 280. Before the war, under Nazi leadership, German church membership had declined about 5 percent per year. During the war, however, this trend slowed and reversed. SD report, April 22, 1943, in Boberach, *Meldungen aus dem Reich*, 13:5174.

85. Torrie, *"For Their Own Good,"* 99.

86. Williamson Murray and Allan R. Millett, *A War to Be Won: Fighting the Second World War* (Cambridge, MA: Belknap Press, 2000), 306, 310; Stephen A. Garrett, "The Bombing Campaign: The RAF," in *Terror from the Sky: The Bombing of German Cities in World War II*, ed. Igor Primoratz (New York: Berghahn Books, 2010), 26–28.

87. Garrett, "The Bombing Campaign," 26–28; Harris and Churchill quoted in Murray and Millett, *A War to Be Won*, 320.

88. Kock, *"Der Führer sorgt für unser Kinder . . . ,"* 192. Torrie, *"For Their Own Good,"* 57.

89. Torrie, *"For Their Own Good,"* 51, 56.

90. Michael Burleigh and Wolfgang Wippermann, *The Racial State* (Cambridge: Cambridge University Press, 1991), 68–69.

91. Armin Nolzen, "Kommunale Krisenbewältigung," in *Deutschland im Luftkrieg: Geschichte und Erinnerung*, ed. Dietmar Süss (Munich: Oldenbourg, 2007), 61–65. Nicholas Stargardt shows how the Germans held out and fought on during the last years of war. Germany did not implode due to a "triumph of organization and mass mobilization" (*The German War*, 394).

92. Nolzen, "Kommunale Krisenbewältigung," 62, 63.

93. K. Klee, *Im "Luftschtzkeller des Reiches,"* 54.

94. Torrie, *"For Their Own Good,"* 73–75.

95. SD report, November 18, 1943, in Boberach, *Meldungen aus dem Reich*, 15:6025–6033, Bundesarchiv, R 58/190; Torrie, *"For Their Own Good,"* 100, 219n137; Groehler, *Bombenkrieg gegen Deutschland*, 274.

96. Randall Thomas Wakelam, *The Science of Bombing: Operational Research in RAF Bomber Command* (Toronto: University of Toronto, 2009), 101, 117.

97. Propaganda Minister to the Gauleiters and Members of the Air War Damages Committees, June 14, 1943, Bundesarchiv (USHMM), R 55/447 (emphasis added).

98. K. Klee, *Im "Luftschtzkeller des Reiches,"* 47; SD report, June 17, 1943, in Boberach, *Meldungen aus dem Reich*, 14:5354.

99. SD report, June 17, 1943, in Boberach, *Meldungen aus dem Reich*, 14:5356; SD report, July 22, 1943, in ibid., 14:5515ff.

100. Popular demonstrations during the Third Reich displayed similarities in their practices, with demands made in a collective chorus in variations on the demand here. The common chorus of demonstrations began with "We want," expressing the common desire and avoiding a provocation of the regime and police—e.g., "We want to see our bishop," or "We want Meiser!" or "We want our crucifix back," or "We want our husbands back" on Rosenstrasse, or "Give us our menfolk back!" in Dortmund-Hörde. This was a dominant form of the Nazi-coached demonstrations against Sproll ("We want a German bishop!"), modeled by the German Christian rally in favor of the Reich Church: "We want to become just one church; that is the will of the people." On the Dortmund-Hörde collective action, see SD report, July 8, 1943, in Boberach, *Meldungen aus dem Reich*, 14:5448.

101. Propaganda Ministry (signed Berndt) to the Gauleiters, Members of the Air War Damages Committees, and Directors of Reich Propaganda Offices, July 14, 1943, Bundesarchiv, R 55/447. "Bericht des Gauleiters Grohé über die Luftangriffe in den letzten Wochen," July 22, 1943, Bundesarchiv, R 3001/2328; cited in Torrie, *"For Their Own Good,"* 101.

102. Reich Propaganda Minister Goebbels to the Gauleiters and Members of the Air War Damages Committees, July 27, 1943, and July 10 (signed Berndt), Bundesarchiv, R 55/447.

103. Reich Propaganda Minister Goebbels to the Gauleiters and Members of the Air War Damages Committees, August 15, 1943, Bundesarchiv, R 55/447.

104. Ibid.

105. Propaganda Ministry (signed Ellgering) to the Gauleiters and Members of the Air War Damages Committees, August 4, 1943, Bundesarchiv, R 55/447.

106. Torrie, *"For Their Own Good,"* 101.

107. Ibid., 100; Goebbels to all Gauleiters, January 28, 1944, Bundesarchiv (USHMM), R 55/447.

108. Wilhelm Reeswinkel, "Wittener Kinder in der Kriegsheimat," *Jahrbuch des Veriens für Orts und Heimatkunde in der Grafschaft Mark* 56 (1953); cited in Torrie, *"For Their Own Good,"* 100. Kock, *"Der Führer sorgt für unser Kinder . . . ,"* 186.

109. Daniel Böhme, *Nationalsozialistische Schulpolitik 1933–1945: Von Hitlers pädagogischen Maximen bis zur praktisch-politischen Umsetzung und mit einem Exkurs zu Dresden* (Munich: Grin Verlag, 2007), 66; Sollbach, *Der Luftterror*, 12n30; Hoffmann to local officials responsible for evacuation measures, October 9, 1943; Torrie, *"For Their Own Good,"* 101; Sollbach, *Der Luftterror*, 155. That same day, the spotty enforcement of Hoffmann's order caused Alfred Meyer, Hoffmann's neighboring Gauleiter in Westphalia-North, to complain in writing about the way the order was being managed so loosely. Kock, *"Der Führer sorgt für unser Kinder . . . ,"* 186.

110. Klaus Scholder, *Die Kirchen und das Dritte Reich*, vol. 2: *Das Jahr der Ernüchterung 1934* (Berlin: Siedler, 1985), 376; Paul Kremmel, *Pfarrer und Gemeinden im evangelischen Kirchenkampf in Bayern bis 1939: Mit besonderer Berücksichtigung der Ereignisse im Bereich des Bezirksamts Weissenburg in Bayern* (Lichtenfels: Kommissionsverlag Schulze, 1987), 366–368. SD report, November 18, 1943, in Boberach, *Meldungen aus dem Reich*, 15:6030 (emphasis in original). Goebbels, *Tagebücher*, part II, 4:33, entry for April 1, 1942.

111. Ibid. (emphasis in original). Quotes in the following paragraph are from this same report.

112. Torrie, *"For Their Own Good,"* 104–105. Torrie writes that at the evacuation site in Baden, Reeswinkel might have encouraged protest. SD report, November 18, 1943, in Boberach, *Meldungen aus Dem Reich,* 15:6030 (Bundesarchiv, R 58/190).

113. SD report, November 18, 1943, in Boberach, *Meldungen aus dem Reich*, 15:6027–6028; cited in Elizabeth Heineman, "Whose Mothers? Generational Difference, War, and the Nazi Cult of Motherhood," *Journal of Women's History* 12, no. 4 (Winter 2001): 146.

114. Victoria de Grazia, *How Fascism Ruled Women: Italy, 1922–1945* (Berkeley: University of California Press, 1992), 112–114. In Germany as in Italy under Mussolini, primary relationships of family lay behind incidents of popular opposition. Julia S. Torrie, "Possibilities of Protest in the Third Reich: The Witten Demonstration in Context," in *Protest in Hitler's "National Community": Popular Unrest and the Nazi Response*, ed. Nathan Stoltzfus and Birgit Maier-Katkin (New York: Berghahn, 2015), 88. "Gauleiter Albert Hoffmann bei den Umquartierten in Baden: Neue Massnahmen der Versorgung und Betreuung," *Westfälische landeszeitung (WLZ)*, no. 242 (October 16–17, 1943): 1; "Der Gauleiter brachte die Grüsse der Heimat: Buntes Mosaik von seinem Besuch bei den umquartierten Frauen und Kindern in Baden," *WLZ*, no. 247 (October 22, 1943): 3.

115. Goebbels, *Tagebücher,* part II, 10:222, entry for November 2, 1943.

116. Ibid., 10:330, entry for November 21, 1943. The issue of the "wild evacuees" threatened to interfere with food distribution as authorities struggled to determine where to send winter provisions, and it taxed the already overcommitted transportation lines. Perhaps the regime would have responded

to more protests, at some point, with greater repression although for many protesters this would have challenged a central mechanism underlying Nazi power—the belief that Hitler made things right as soon as he knew about their grievance.

117. Torrie, *"For Their Own Good,"* 100, 101.

118. Goebbels, *Tagebücher,* part II, 10:363, entry for November 26, 1943.

119. Goebbels wrote that Bormann recommended rigorous measures to coerce women and children into following the regime's will and added that he had suggested the same position months earlier (ibid., 10:465, entry for December 12, 1943). Ibid., 11:144, entry for January 23, 1943, and 10:475, entry for December 14, 1943.

120. Ibid., 10:475, entry for December 14, 1943. Kock, *"Der Führer sorgt für unser Kinder . . . ,"* 255.

121. Goebbels, *Tagebücher,* part II, 11:77, entry for January 12, 1944; "Bericht des Gauleiters Grohé über die Luftangriffe und ihre Folgen im Gau Köln-Aachen in den Monaten Januar und Februar 1943," March 5, 1943, Bundesarchiv, R 3001/2308; "Bericht des Gauleiters Grohé über die Luftangriffe in den letzten Wochen," July 22, 1943, Bundesarchiv, R 3001/2328.

122. Goebbels, *Tagebücher,* part II, 11:88–89, entry for January 14, 1944; Kock, *"Der Führer sorgt für unser Kinder . . . ,"* 187n171.

123. See the decision of Oberlandsgerichtspräsident Hamm to Reichsminister der Justiz, Quarterly Report, December 6, 1943, Bundesarchiv, R3001/alt R 22/3367. Express letter from Goebbels to all Gauleiters, January 28, 1944, Bundesarchiv, R 55/447.

124. Letter from Goebbels to all Gauleiters, January 28, 1944, Bundesarchiv, R 55/447.

125. Ibid. Torrie, *"For Their Own Good,"* 111, citing Himmler's and Bormann's order of July 29, 1944, from a document from the Baden interior minister, August 21, 1944; Bormann to Acting Gauleiter Schlessmann, Essen, October 12, 1944; Torrie, "The Possibilities of Protest," 78.

126. Irene Guenther, *Nazi "Chic"?: Fashioning Women in the Third Reich* (Oxford: Berg, 2004), 248.

127. Claudia Koonz, *Mothers in the Fatherland: Women, the Family, and Nazi Politics* (New York: St. Martin's Press, 1987). Arguably, limiting sacrifices and maintaining a sense of normalcy in order to maintain popular good will toward the regime was a principle more fundamental in Hitler's perception than those concerning women and work.

128. Ian Kershaw, *Hitler, 1936–1945: Nemesis* (New York: W. W. Norton, 2000), 568; Guenther, *Nazi "Chic"?* 249.

129. Heineman, "Whose Mothers," 143–144; Burleigh and Wippermann, *The Racial State,* 264. But the representation of women in war-relevant industries remained very low. See Timothy Mason, *Nazism, Fascism and the Working Class* (New York: Cambridge University Press, 1995), 319–320, 425n69. Adam Tooze, *The Wages of Destruction: The Making and Breaking of the Nazi*

Economy (New York: Penguin, 2006), 358–359. "We must record a total failure to mobilize German women for work in the war effort," reported Speer's Armaments Department, December 1943; quoted in Timothy Mason, "Women in Germany, 1925–1940: Family, Welfare, and Work," *History Workshop Journal* 1, no. 2 (1976): 21; Speer, *Inside the Third Reich*, 287.

130. Cited in Burleigh and Wippermann, *The Racial State*, 264. Matthew Stibbe, *Women in the Third Reich* (London: Arnold, 2003), 142; Jill Stephenson, *Women in Nazi Germany* (Harlow, England: Longman, 2001), 51ff.

131. SD report, March 11, 1943, in Boberach, *Meldungen aus dem Reich*, 13:4934.

132. Heineman, "Whose Mothers," 141–143. Heineman shows that more German working-class than middle-class women worked during the war, although Hitler's conscription decree made no distinctions of class. In some cases, including the application of race theory to intermarried Jews and their children, Hitler chose to compromise one ideal in favor of adhering to his ideal for maintaining authority among ethnic Germans in the Reich.

133. Sönke Neitzel and Harald Welzer, *Soldaten: On Fighting, Killing and Dying: The Secret World War II Transcripts of German POWs* (New York: Alfred A. Knopf, 2012), 272.

134. Beth A. Griech-Polelle, *Bishop von Galen: German Catholicism and National Socialism* (New Haven: Yale University Press, 2002), 108.

CHAPTER VIII. GERMANY'S ROSENSTRASSE AND THE FATE OF MIXED MARRIAGES

Epigraphs: Joseph Goebbels, *Die Tagebücher von Joseph Goebbels,* ed. Elke Fröhlich (Munich: K. G. Saur, 1993–1996), 7:369, 7:487, 7:513, 7:515, 8:125–126, entries for February 18, March 6, March 9, and April 18, 1943.

1. Evan Burr Bukey, *Jews and Intermarriage in Nazi Austria* (New York: Cambridge University Press, 2011), 144, 173; Raul Hilberg, *The Destruction of the European Jews* (New York: Holmes and Meier, 1985), 2:417–430. The danger of intermarriage could be seen among the English, who, particularly in higher circles, had been so corrupted by marriages to Jews that they now "hardly carry any English character," wrote Goebbels. "Fortunately, during wartime, an array of possibilities present themselves" for eliminating the Jews (Goebbels, *Tagebücher,* part II, 3:457, entry for March 12, 1942, and 3:561, entry for March 27, 1942). Berger's letter is in Steven E. Aschheim, *Scholem, Arendt, Klemperer: Intimate Chronicles in Turbulent Times* (Bloomington: Indiana University Press, 2001), 82. Bundesarchiv, NS 19/776; Karl-Heinz Roth et al., eds., *Die Daimler-Benz AG 1916–1948: Schlüsseldokumente zur Konzerngeschichte* (Nordingen: Greno, 1987), 139. See 384n24.

2. Nicholas Stargardt, *The German War: A Nation under Arms, 1939–1945* (New York: Basic Books, 2015), 233–267, identifies the extent to which Germans learned about the extermination of the Jews as the war continued.

3. On categories of intermarried Jews, see Hermann Göring to Ministry of the Interior, December 28, 1938. Hilberg, *Destruction*, 2:443–444; Beate Meyer,

"Jüdische Mischlinge": Rassenpolitik und Verfolgungserfahrung 1933–1945 (Hamburg: Dölling and Galitz, 1999), 30; Nathan Stoltzfus, *Resistance of the Heart: Intermarriage and the Rosenstrasse Protest in Nazi Germany* (New York: Norton, 1996), 74, 305n61, 102–105. Victor Klemperer moved to a "Jewish house" with his "Aryan" wife Eva (Klemperer, *I Will Bear Witness*, vol. 1: *1933–1941*, trans. Martin Chalmers [New York: Modern Library, 1999], 339, diary entry for May 26, 1940). Divorce rates among intermarried couples are based on studies of extant documentation from various regions. Ursula Büttner estimated that 7.2 percent of intermarried couples divorced during the Nazi years in Baden Württemberg, while 9.9 percent divorced in Hamburg between 1942 and 1945 (*Die Not der Juden teilen: Christlich-jüdische Familien im Dritten Reich* [Hamburg: Christians, 1988], 57, 298n253). Bukey calculated from available sources that in Vienna following the Anschluss only "5 to 7 percent divorced" (*Jews and Intermarriage in Nazi Austria*, 94, 191).

4. Joseph Goebbels, "Die Juden Sind Schuld!" in Joseph Goebbels, *Das Eherne Herz* (Munich: Eher Verlag, 1943), 87, 91. On general public feelings regarding intermarriage, see SD report, February 2, 1942, in Heinz Boberach, *Meldungen aus dem Reich* (Herrsching: Pawlak, 1984), 9:3245–3248.

5. Marion Kaplan, *Between Dignity and Despair: Jewish Life in Nazi Germany* (New York: Oxford University Press, 1998), 190; Klemperer, *I Will Bear Witness*, 2:91. Instead of deporting non-privileged intermarried Jews to Auschwitz, it sent them to Theresienstadt (which was commonly thought to afford relatively decent living conditions). However, the great majority of mixed couples remained together, so the Führer's principle of deporting this group of Jews circumspectly conflicted with his resolve that none should survive the war. Jews who did not wear the Star of David and whose partners died or divorced them were exempted according to directives from May 1942. Hans Günther Adler, *Der verwaltete Mensch: Studien zur Deportation der Juden aus Deutschland* (Tübingen: Mohr, 1974), 197.

6. Goebbels wrote on November 1, 1938, that Gottschalk "makes a very deep impression on me" (*Tagebücher*, part I, 6:168, entry for November 1, 1938; see also ibid., part II, 2:247, entry for November 7, 1941). According to Veit Harlan, people attending Gottschalk's funeral were filmed by the Gestapo (*Im Schatten meiner Filme* [Gütersloh: Sigbert Mohn, 1966], 146).

7. Goebbels, *Tagebücher*, part II, 2:340–341, entry for November 22, 1941.

8. Ian Kershaw, *Hitler, 1936–1945: Nemesis* (New York: W. W. Norton, 2000), 481. Kaplan, *Between Dignity and Despair*, 190. Gauleiter Arthur Greiser had a free hand in his Wartheland region, like the carte blanche Hitler granted Gauleiter Baldur von Schirach in Vienna. Kershaw, *Nemesis*, 351, 478–479; Peter Longerich, *Holocaust: The Nazi Persecution and Murder of the Jews* (Oxford: Oxford University Press, 2010), 291; Hans-Ulrich Wehler, *Deutsche Gesellschaftsgeschichte*, vol. 4: *Vom Beginn des Ersten Weltkriegs bis zur Gründung der beiden deutschen Staaten 1914–1949*, Deutsche Gesellschaftsgeschichte (Munich: Beck, 2003), 895.

9. Hitler's statement about Jews surviving the war was according to Hans Frank on December 16, 1941, in Werner Prag and Wolfgang Jacobmeyer, eds., *Das Diensttagebuch des deutschen Generalgouverneurs in Polen 1939–1945* (Stuttgart: Deutsche Verlags-Anstalt, 1975), 457–458. Goebbels, *Tagebücher,* part II, 2:498–499, entry for December 13, 1941. On Gauleiter initiative, see Longerich, *Holocaust,* 302–304. Hans Mommsen, "National Socialism—Continuity and Change," in *Fascism, A Reader's Guide: Analyses, Interpretations, Bibliography,* ed. Walter Laqueur (Berkeley: University of California Press, 1976), 199–200, argues that Gauleiters made decisions about deporting Jews from their regions regardless of consequences.

10. For Heydrich on Theresienstadt as a destination for intermarried Jews, see Nuremburg trial document, NG-2586 (G), Record of the Wannsee Meeting. For the overall significance of this conference, see Mark Roseman, *The Wannsee Conference and the Final Solution: A Reconsideration* (New York: McMillan, 2003). On forcing intermarried couples to divorce, see Nuremburg trial document NG-2586 (H), Record of the Conference on the Final Solution of the Jewish Problem in Berlin held on March 6, 1942. Schlegelberger concluded that in cases in which an intermarried couple refused to be forcibly divorced, both partners must be sent to Theresienstad. Schlegelberger to Bormann, April 5, 1942, Nuremberg Document 4055-PS. Hilberg, *Destruction,* 2:446. Uwe Adam, *Judenpolitik im Dritten Reich* (Düsseldorf: Droste Verlag, 1972), 325. Christian Gerlach, "The Wannsee Conference, the Fate of German Jews, and Hitler's Decision in Principle to Exterminate All European Jews," in *The Holocaust: Origins, Implementation, Aftermath,* ed. Omer Bartov (London: Routledge, 2000), 132–133. For Himmler's reaction, see Gerlach, "Wannsee Conference," 126. Wolf Kaiser, "Die Wannsee-Konferenz," in *Täter, Opfer, Folgen: Der Holocaust in Geschichte und Gegenwart,* ed. Heiner Lichtenstein and Otto R. Romberg (Bonn: Bundeszentrale für Politische Bildung, 1995), 29; Nathan Stoltzfus, "Widerstand des Herzens: Der Protest in der Rosenstrasse und die deutsch-jüdische Mischehe," *Geschichte und Gesellschaft* 21 (1995): 227.

11. Peter Longerich, *Goebbels: A Biography* (New York: Random House, 2015), 528–529.

12. On unrest in Berlin in 1942, see Leugers, "The 1943 Rosenstrasse Protest and the Churches," in *Protest in Hitler's "National Community": Popular Unrest and the Nazi Response,* ed. Nathan Stoltzfus and Birgit Maier-Katkin (New York: Berghahn Books, 2015), 150, citing Margarete Sommer's report (after August 5, 1942) in Ludwig Volk, ed., *Akten deutscher Bischöfe über die Lage der Kirche 1933–1945,* vol. 5: *1940–1942* (Mainz: Matthias-Grünewald-Verlag, 1983), 818. The Darmstadt incident is in Antonia Leugers, ed., *Berlin, Rosenstrasse 2–4, Protest in der NS-Diktatur. Neue Forschungen zum Frauenprotest in der Rosenstrasse 1943* (Annweiler: Plöger, 2005), 11.

13. Büttner, *Die Not der Juden teilen,* 57, writes that the plan to deport some intermarried Jews was in the beginning of the summer of 1942. See also Hil-

berg, *Destruction*, 2:447, and Adam, *Judenpolitik im Dritten Reich*, 17, 29, 316. On Schirach, see Bukey, *Jews and Intermarriage in Nazi Austria*, 152, 153. Albert Speer, *Infiltration* (New York: Macmillan, 1981), 248. Goebbels, *Tagebücher*, part II, 5:606, entry for September 30, 1942. Goebbels added that Hitler rejected industrialists' claims that they could not do without the work of Jews they employed.

14. Joachim Neander, "Auschwitz, the 'Fabrik-Aktion,' Rosenstrasse: A Plea for a Change of Perspective," in Stoltzfus and Maier-Katkin, *Protest in Hitler's "National Community,"* 128–129.

15. The Gestapo in Dortmund, as well as the county administrative office (Landsamt) in Meschede, identified the arrests there in late February and early March 1943 as the "Entjudung des Reichsgebietes" (in *Ich Trage Die Nummer 104953: Ein Letztes Zeugnis*, ed. Werner Jacob et al. [Olpe: Der Oberkreisdirektor des Kreises Olpe, Kreisarchiv, 1997], 145); Leugers, *Berlin, Rosenstrasse 2–4*, 182–183. A telegram of January 25, 1943, from the RSHA to all inspectors of the Security Police and the SD, pertaining to the "Entjudung des Reichsgebietes-Arbeitseinsatz," ordered all inspectors to report, by February 3, the number and nationality of Jews who were employed in armaments production as of January 15, 1943. National Archives, Washington, D.C., Stapost Nuernberg Item no. OCC-110, Roll 657, Frame 1, *Entjudung des Reichsgebietes*. See Joachim Neander, "Auschwitz und die Berliner Fabrikaktion Februar/März 1943," *theologie.geschichte* 1 (2006): 1.

16. The timing of the "Elimination of the Jews" arrests was in conjunction with the tenth anniversary of Nazi rule, according to senior Jewish Community authority B. Murmelstein, " 'Der Letzte der Ungerechten': Der 'Judenälteste' Benjamin Murmelstein," in *Filmen 1942–1975*, ed. Ronny Loewy and Katharina Rauschenberger (Frankfurt: Campus Verlag, 2011), 16. In 1951, Walter Stock, former director of the Berlin Gestapo's Jewish Desk, recalled the name of the massive arrests of some ten thousand Berlin Jews, including those interned at Rosenstrasse 2–4, as the Final Roundup *(Schlussaktion)*. Statement of Walter Stock, August 13, 1951, Strafsache gegen Walter Stock, 1 P Kls 3/52, Landesarchiv Berlin.

17. Goebbels, *Tagebücher*, part II, 7:528, entry for March 11, 1943.

18. Ibid., part II, 7:369, entry for February 18, 1943, and part II, 8:125–126, entry for April 18, 1943.

19. Leugers, "The 1943 Rosenstrasse Protest and the Churches," 147.

20. The decree is cited in full in Leugers, *Berlin, Rosenstrasse 2–4*, 221–224, and translated into English in Stoltzfus and Maier-Katkin, *Protest in Hitler's "National Community,"* 230–231.

21. Leugers, "The 1943 Rosenstrasse Protest and the Churches," 145.

22. For Sprenger's deportations, see Kaplan, *Between Dignity and Despair*, 190. Sprenger's actions led at least one person to question why intermarried couples were "separated" in Frankfurt and not in Berlin. Michael Grüttner, "Hochschulpolitik zwishen Gau und Reich," in *Die NS-Gaue: Regionale*

Mittelinstanzen im zentralistischen "Führerstaat," ed. Jürgen John, Horst
Möller, and Thomas Schaarschmidt (Munich: Oldenbourg, 2007), 183. Various officials took a variety of measures against Jews without legal authorization: in 1935 the Gauleiter of Köln-Aachen ejected a teacher because he
was married to a Jew. In his Frankfurt am Main region, Gauleiter Sprenger
also intervened personally to remove Jews from Frankfurt University. Judgment against Georg Albert Dengler (2a Ks 1/49), 26, Hessisches Haupt-
staatsarchiv, Wiesbaden; cited in Irene Sage-Grande et al., eds., *Justiz und
NS-Verbrechen: Sammlung deutscher Strafurteile wegen nationalsozialistischer
Tötungsverbrechen 1945–1966* (Amsterdam: Amsterdam University, 1981),
22:658–682. See also Leugers, "The 1943 Rosenstrasse Protest and the
Churches," 145. On Hamburg, see Neander, "Die Rosenstrasse von aussen
gesehen," 182. On the murder of intermarried Jews in Austria, see Bukey,
Jews and Intermarriage in Nazi Austria, 141–162.

23. The SS men arresting Jews in Berlin "wore a small band with the script
'Leibstandarte SS Adolf Hitler.' Two were officers wearing war medals."
Statement of Karl Hefter, October 28, 1955, in the trial against Josef (Sepp)
Dietrich, Landesarchiv Berlin, I P Js 3767.65. In his report Gerhard Lehfeldt
identified the Leibstandarte with the plans for intermarried Jews and Mischlinge ("Bericht über die Lage von 'Mischlingen,'" in Leugers, *Berlin, Rosenstrasse 2–4,* 237ff.; translated in Stoltzfus and Maier-Katkin, *Protest in Hitler's
"National Community,"* 223–226). A driver for a truck transporting Jews testified that the Leibstandarte made arrests in working-class neighborhoods
where the chance of uprising was considered highest (statement of Erwin
Sartorius, December 13, 1965, B Rep 058, Landesarchiv Berlin). Eyewitness Martha Mosse, as well as H. G. Adler, identified the SS present as
the Leibstandarte (Adler, *Verwaltete Mensch,* 226–227, 340). Wolf Gruner,
*Widerstand in der Rosenstrasse: Die Fabrik-Aktion und die Verfolgung der
"Mischehen" 1943* (Frankfurt am Main: Frisher Taschenbuch Verlag, 2005),
61, writes that Adler is wrong because he relies on Mosse while overlooking
his formidable context for evaluating this source based in his enormous
erudition.

24. Statement of Else Hannach, July 1944, 171–179, I Js 5/65, supporting documents file 30, Landesarchiv Berlin; Hildegard Henschel, "Aus der Arbeit der
jüdischen Gemeinde Berlin während der Jahre 1941–1943," *Zeitschrift für die
Geschichte der Juden* 9 (1972): 41.

25. During the first week of March, groups of protesters also protested outside a
Jewish old people's home on Berlin's nearby Grosse Hamburgerstrasse after
their Jewish family members were imprisoned there.

26. Sommer's report, March 2, 1943, is in Volk, *Akten,* 6:19–21. Cardinal Bertram also received a report on March 1, 1943, "concerning questions about
the evacuation of *Geltungsjuden.*" Sommer to Bertram, March 2, 1943, in
ibid., 6:20. Cf. report of Margarete Sommer about the threat to "Geltungsju-

den" from March 1, 1943, in Leugers, *Berlin, Rosenstrasse 2–4*, 225–228. On the Foreign Ministry's expectation, see Leugers, "The 1943 Rosenstrasse Protest and the Churches," 144, citing *Orsenigo an Maglione*, March 3, 1943, in Pierre Blet, Robert A. Graham, Angelo Martini, and Burkhart Schneider, eds., *Actes et documents du Saint Siège relatifs à la Seconde Guerre Mondiale*, vol. 9: *Le Saint Siège et les victimes de la guerre: Janvier/ décembre 1943* (Vatican City, 1975 [=ADSS IX]). On deportations, see Stoltzfus, *Resistance of the Heart*, 234–236.

27. The translated text of the WVHA telegram is in Stoltzfus and Maier-Katkin, *Protest in Hitler's "National Community,"* 251–254. See also Neander, "Auschwitz, the 'Fabrik-Aktion,' Rosenstrasse, 132–133. In October 1941, 18,700 Berlin Jews worked for the armaments industry. Adler, *Verwaltete Mensch*, 223. Neander shows that the WVHA in Auschwitz calculated that it needed at least 9,000 (although expecting 15,000) and points out that this is the number of Jews Eichmann planned to send to the East, according to Lehfeldt (Neander, "Auschwitz und die Berliner Fabrikaktion Februar/März 1943"). In Berlin at that time 8,800 Jews were living in mixed marriages (Gruner, *Widerstand*, 178).

28. Wienken to Bertram, March 4, 1943, in Volk, *Akten*, 6:25. In support of his argument, Gruner, *Widerstand*, 115, incorrectly dates Wienken's consultation with Eichmann as March 3. Leugers, "The 1943 Rosenstrasse Protest and the Churches," 144, and Leugers, "Widerstand gegen die Rosenstrasse," *theologie.geschichte* 1 (2006): 152. In addition, this plan to return Berlin's intermarried Jews to armaments work directly contradicts the interpretation Gruner gives to the February 24 Frankfurt/Oder decree, but Gruner has omitted the part of Wienken's report stating that Berlin's Jews would be put back to work in the armaments industry. Wolf Gruner, "The Factory Action and the Events at the Rosenstrasse in Berlin: Facts and Fictions about 27 February 1943: Sixty Years Later," *Central European History* 36, no. 2 (2003): 197. (See the original German in *Jahrbuch für Antisemitismusforschung*, vols. 11–12 [Frankfurt and New York: Campus Verlag].) On Gruner's errors, see Leugers, "The 1943 Rosenstrasse Protest and the Churches," 144, and Leugers, "Widerstand gegen die Rosenstrasse," 177–178; Gruner, *Widerstand*, 53.

29. Sartorius statement, December 13, 1965, B Rep 058, Landesarchiv Berlin. Gutterer interview with author, August 1987.

30. Protests also developed outside of the Old People's Home on the Grosse Hamburger Street, and Goebbels referred to them in his diary on March 6, 1943. Ursula von Kardorff wrote that on March 3, 1943, women workers banded together and "loudly protested the deportation of Jews" (*Berliner Aufzeichnungen 1942 bis 1945: Unter Verwendung der Original-Tagebücher*, 2nd ed. [Munich: Dt. Taschenbugh-Verlag, 1997], 72). Kardoff wrote this in 1947. Ruth Andreas-Friedrich, another diarist in Berlin, wrote of women crying

and screaming for their husbands (*Der Schattenmann: Tagebuchaufzeichnungen 1938–1945* [Berlin: Suhrkamp, 1947; 3rd ed., 1984], 108–110, entries for February 28 and March 7, 1943).

31. Goebbels, *Tagebücher,* part II, 7:487, entry for March 6, 1943. Leugers, "Widerstand gegen die Rosenstrasse," 183. Lehfeldt, who described a public "racket" on March 5, 1943, elsewhere in Berlin, concluded that public protests led Goebbels to release the Jews on March 6.

32. These instructions reference the basic instructions Hitler had given Goebbels on November 22, 1941, on the deportation of intermarried Jews, particularly in artists' circles, as well as the regime's efforts to deport intermarried Jews in phases, avoiding the appearance that all intermarried Jews were being deported at any one time. Goebbels, *Tagebücher,* part II, 7:514, entry for March 9, 1943; part II, 7:528, entry for March 11, 1943; and part II, vol. 7, entry for April 18, 1943.

33. Kaltenbrunner to Frick in Leugers, "Widerstand gegen die Rosenstrasse," 199. Wurm to the Ministry of the Reich Church, March 12, 1943, in Leugers, "The 1943 Rosenstrasse Protest and the Churches," 150–151. Any protests by public offices that Berning credited could hardly have been more effective than the feckless protests by the industrialists who were losing workers and profits because of the Final Roundup of Berlin Jews.

34. On the return of 25 Jews from Auschwitz-Monowitz, see Statement of Ferdinand Wolff, Trial of Otto Bovensiepen et al., B Rep 058, 1 Js 9/65, November 14, 1968, Landesarchiv Berlin. The secretary was told that these Jews had been deported by "mistake" *(Fehlgriffes, versehentlich)* and were returned to Berlin on orders of a "high Reich official." Statement of Johanna Heym summarized in the Trial of Otto of Bovensiepen et al., 213. Wolf Gruner sees this official Gestapo explanation from 1943 as the real explanation—even though only 25 of the 120 intermarried Jews deported to Auschwitz were released ("Ein Historikerstreit? Die Internierung der Juden aus Mischehen in der Rosenstrasse 1943. Das Ereignis, seine Diskussion und seine Geschichte," *Zeitschrift für Geschichtswissenschaft* 1 [2004]: 20). OSS intelligence: Harrison to Donovan, Office of Strategic Services, April 1, 1943, National Archives, Washington, D.C., RG 226 (OSS), Entry 134: Washington Registry Office Radio and Cable Files, Box 171, Folder 1079.

 The full text of this document is in appendix 3 of Stoltzfus and Maier-Katkin, *Protest in Hitler's "National Community,"* 233–234.

35. Margarete Sommer, August 22–24, 1943, in Volk, *Akten,* 6:217–219.

36. Author's conversation with Austrian and intermarriage history expert Evan Bukey about the protest Sommer reported, May 13, 2015. On Hitler's order, see Bukey, *Jews and Intermarriage in Nazi Austria,* 164.

37. Ben Kiernan, *Blood and Soil: A World History of Genocide and Extermination from Sparta to Darfur* (New Haven: Yale University Press, 2008), 34.

CONCLUSION

1. "Any resurrection of the German people can take place only by way of . . . the forces of will power. The best arms are dead and useless material as long as the spirit is missing which is ready, willing and determined to use them" (Adolf Hitler, *Mein Kampf, Complete and Unabridged, Fully Annotated*, ed. John Chamberlain, Sidney B. Fay, et al. [New York: Reynal and Hitchcock, 1939], 439).

2. Evan Burr Bukey, *Hitler's Austria: Popular Sentiment in the Nazi Era, 1938–1945* (Chapel Hill: University of North Carolina Press, 2000), 102–103.

3. On Bishop Sproll's growth in capacity for resistance, see Dominik Burkart, *Joannes Baptista Sproll: Bischof im Widerstand* (Stuttgart: Kohlhammer, 2013), 87–89.

4. Heinz Linge, *With Hitler to the End: The Memoirs of Adolf Hitler's Valet*, trans. Geoffrey Brooks (New York: Skyhorse Publishing, 2009), 7.

AFTERWORD ON HISTORICAL RESEARCH

Epigraph: Malcolm Gladwell, "How David Beats Goliath," *New Yorker*, May 11, 2009.

1. Hans Mommsen, "National Socialism—Continuity and Change," in *Fascism: A Reader's Guide: Analyses, Interpretations, Bibliography*, ed. Walter Laqueur (Berkeley: University of California Press, 1976), 200. Works on church history that had a lasting impact include Guenter Lewy, *The Catholic Church and Nazi Germany* (Cambridge, MA: Da Capo Press, 1964), and John S. Conway, *The Nazi Persecution of the Churches 1933–45* (Toronto: Ryerson Press, 1968).

2. Martin Broszat et al., eds., *Bayern in der NS-Zeit*, 6 vols. (Munich: Oldenbourg, 1977–1983); Martin Broszat, "Resistenz und Widerstand: Eine Zwischenbilanz des Forschungsprojekts," in ibid., 4:697. Ian Kershaw's pioneering study of popular opinion and political dissent, originally published in 1983, was limited to Bavaria as well: *Popular Opinion and Political Dissent in the Third Reich: Bavaria 1933–1945* (New York: Oxford University Press, 2002).

3. Timothy Mason, *Nazism, Fascism and the Working Class* (New York: Cambridge University Press, 1995), 23, 119–120. Kershaw, *Popular Opinion*, 33–46, 375, 380.

4. Street protests were critically important for Catholics defending their rights during Bismarck's culture wars or for Social Democrats seeking equal rights for workers under the 1850 three-class electoral system. Above all, street protest was key for women seeking the vote and facing men who would not share power with them unless forced to do so. Excluded from the conventional processes of governance and hardly noticed, German women turned to the streets for attention and presence in politics. The First International "Women's Day" in March 1911 saw women on the streets of Europe's major cities, including Dresden, Düsseldorf, and other German cities, marching by hundreds and thousands, singing and calling out under banners demanding the vote for women and proclaiming a "women's revolution." In Berlin the

Socialist newspaper *Vorwärts* reported, "No one had ever seen anything like it before—women stepping out into public in such masses demanding universal suffrage. Every hall was overflowing, and with, indeed, women. The men had to clear the field and waited patiently, for the most part, on the street until the meeting was over. But the hall wasn't big enough even just for the women alone. . . . Quite a procession of women was still out marching on the street. When the meeting ended and the people streamed out, it was of course very lively on the street. A thousand voices were lifted high in demanding the women's right to vote, which pressured, as it appeared, the delicate disposition of the police" (*Vorwärts* cited in Ludwig-Uhland Institut für empirische Kulturwissenschaft der Universität Tübingen, *Als die Deutschen demonstrieren lernten: Das Kulturmuster "Friedliche Strassendemonstration" im preussischen Wahlrechtskampf 1908–1910* [Tübingen: Ludwig-Uhland Institut für empirische Kulturwissenschaft der Universitäat Tübingen: Tübinger Vereinigung für Volkskunde E.V., 1986], 7, 8). On "street politics" and the political and public sphere, see Belinda David, "Reconsidering Habermas, Gender, and the Public Sphere: The Case of Wilhelmine Germany," in *Society, Culture, and the State in Germany, 1870–1930,* ed. Geoff Eley (Ann Arbor: University of Michigan Press, 1996), 404–411.

5. Articles by Peukert and Evans are discussed below in this chapter. Jill Stephenson, "Women and Protest in Wartime Nazi Germany," in *Protest in Hitler's "National Community": Popular Unrest and the Nazi Response,* ed. Nathan Stoltzfus and Birgit Maier-Katkin (New York: Berghahn Books, 2015), 27–28, 32–34. Jeremy Noakes, "The Oldenburg Crucifix Struggle of November 1936: A Case Study of Opposition in the Third Reich," in *The Shaping of the Nazi State,* ed. Peter D. Stachura (London: Croom Helm, 1978).

6. On the character and motives of conspirators who sacrificed their lives, see Christian Gerlach, "Men of 20 July and the War in the Soviet Union," in *War of Extermination: The German Military in World War II, 1941–1944,* ed. Hannes Heer and Klaus Naumann (New York: Berghahn, 2000), 127–145. Efforts to acknowledge the conspirators as resistance were led by the brilliant Jewish lawyer Fritz Bauer. Claudia Frölich, *Wider die Tabuisierung des Ungehorsams. Fritz Bauers Widerstandsbegriff und die Aufarbeitung von NS-Verbrechen* (Frankfurt am Main: Campus Verlag, 2005).

7. Ian Kershaw has pointed out that interpretations have recently begun to swing away from the "bottom up" to the "top down" paradigm. Efforts to understand Nazi power and the German response to Nazism can be visualized as lying along a spectrum that is traced by a swinging pendulum. Interpretations are now "swinging back again towards coercion," Kershaw wrote, citing Robert Gellately's important *Backing Hitler: Consent and Coercion in Nazi Germany* (Oxford: Oxford University Press, 2001), as the turning point (Ian Kershaw, "Consensus, Coercion, and Popular Opinion in the Third Reich: Some Reflections," in *Popular Opinion in Totalitarian Regimes: Fascism, Nazism, Communism,* ed. Paul Corner [Oxford: Oxford University Press, 2009], 36). But

illustrating that "bottom up" histories have not included popular protest, Gellately argues that public protest did not influence Nazi decision makers, in line with his argument that if forces of society set limits on the dictatorship early on, they evanesced with "the approach of war and especially after its outbreak in 1939," as "the regime cracked down on all forms of noncompliance in order to ensure that the home front not collapse." Gellately, *Backing Hitler*, 103, and "Rethinking the Nazi Terror System: A Historiographical Analysis," *German Studies Review* 14, no. 1 (February 1991): 23–38, 24.

8. Families emerged from the ordeal with a better record of opposition when it came to protecting their own Jews than did the churches. See chapter VIII.

9. The attempt to live in the truth is Václav Havel's concept in "The Power of the Powerless," in *The Power of the Powerless: Citizens against the State in Central Eastern Europe*, ed. John Keane (New York: Routledge, 2009), 10ff.

10. Early works on church history during the 1960s showed that the Catholic Church, to the extent that it disagreed with the dictatorship, had underestimated its capacity to influence the Nazi regime; also seen in retrospect, Nazi policy "was flexible and always determined by tactical necessity" (Conway, *The Nazi Persecution of the Churches*, 225). Some historians argued that foreign opinion also influenced Hitler's decision to order a halt to euthanasia. Henry Friedlander argued that this claim of foreign influence was introduced after the war by "the experts directly involved" in the killings themselves (*The Origins of Nazi Genocide: From Euthanasia to the Final Solution* [Chapel Hill: University of North Carolina Press, 1995], 154).

11. Götz Aly, *Aktion T 4: 1939–1945: Die "Euthanasie"-Zentrale in der Tiergartenstrasse 4* (Berlin: Edition Hentrich Druck, 1989), 90. Aly was lead editor of the seven-volume *Beitrage zur nationalsozialistischen Gesundheits- und Sozialpolitik*, published in Berlin by Rotbuch Verlag.

12. Michael Burleigh, *Death and Deliverance: "Euthanasia" in Germany, 1900–1945* (New York: Cambridge University Press, 1994), 180; Michael Burleigh, *Ethics and Extermination: Reflections on Nazi Genocide* (New York: Cambridge University Press, 1997), 141.

13. Michael Burleigh, "Psychiatry, German Society and the Nazi 'Euthanasia' Programme," in *The Holocaust: Origins, Implementation, Aftermath*, ed. Omer Bartov (London: Routledge, 2000), 55. See also Burleigh, *Ethics and Extermination*, 141, in which Burleigh notes another reason for the timing of Galen's sermon.

14. H. R. Trevor-Roper, ed. *Hitler's Table Talk, 1941–1944* (New York: Enigma Books, 2007 [orig. 1953), 418–419, entry for July 4, 1942.

15. Burleigh, *Death and Deliverance*, 180; Raul Hilberg, *The Destruction of the European Jews* (New York: Holmes and Meier, 1985), 1008.

16. Christopher Browning, *The Origins of the Final Solution* (Lincoln: University of Nebraska Press, 2003), 312–313; Friedlander, *The Origins of Nazi Genocide*, xiii, 63, 86–87, 244.

17. Michael Burleigh, *The Third Reich: A New History* (New York: Hill and Wang, 2000), 385; Peter Longerich, *Holocaust: The Nazi Persecution and Murder of the Jews* (Oxford: Oxford University Press, 2010), 278, 530n1.

18. International Military Tribunal (IMT), *Trial of the Major War Criminals: Proceeding Volumes*, 42 vols. (Nuremberg, November 14, 1945–October 1, 1946), 20:82, July 31, 1946; http://avalon.law.yale.edu/imt/07-31-46.asp (accessed November 12, 2012); Longerich, *Holocaust*, 278, 530n1.

19. Jeremy Noakes and Geoffrey Pridham, eds., *Nazism, 1919–1945*, vol. 3: *Foreign Policy, War and Racial Extermination* (Exeter: University of Exeter Press, 2001), 405–406.

20. Asylum directors were asked to report patients with "schizophrenia, epilepsy . . . senile illnesses, paralysis not responsive to therapy and other Lues illnesses, feeble-mindedness of all kinds, encephalitis, Huntington's chorea and other terminal neurological disorders." Forms were to be completed as well for anyone who had been a patient continuously for at least five years, "criminal lunatics," and anyone without German nationality or "not of German or related blood." Interior Ministry instructions to asylum directors, translated and cited in Jeremy Noakes and Geoffrey Pridham, *Nazism, 1919–1945*, vol. 3: *Foreign Policy, War and Racial Extermination* (Exeter: University of Press, 2001), 404–405; Jill Stephenson, *Hitler's Home Front: Württemberg under the Nazis* (New York: Hambledon Continuum, 2006), 127, 129.

21. Ian Kershaw, *Hitler, the Germans, and the Final Solution* (New Haven: Yale University Press, 2008), 148, 149n3.

22. Noakes, "The Oldenburg Crucifix Struggle," 225–226.

23. Ibid., 227–228. Gerhard Reifferscheid published his documentation of the East Prussian crucifix struggle in *Das Bistum Ermland und das Dritte Reich* (Cologne: Böhlau, 1975).

24. Wolfgang Benz, "Kinder und Jugendliche unter der Herrschaft des Nationalsozialismus," in *Sozialisierung und Traumatisierung: Kinder in der Zeit des Nationalsozialismus,* ed. Ute Benz and Wolfgang Benz (Frankfurt, Main: Fischer, 1992), 21. Kock refuted this in *"Der Führer sorgt für unser Kinder . . . ,"* 184–188. Rather, officials were powerless to stem mass parental noncompliance: "One has to make peace with it," said Stuttgart's mayor. "Further punishment is senseless . . . nothing practicable can be done" (Kock, 219).

25. Richard J. Evans, "German Women and the Triumph of Hitler," *Journal of Modern History* 48, no. 1 (March 1976): 125, 159–161.

26. "The police refused to do anything [when directed to restore order], since they were persuaded that the women were right to protest" (Richard J. Evans, *The Third Reich at War* [London: Allen Land, 2008], 452). Richard Overy, *The Bombers and the Bombed* (New York: Viking Press, 2013), 275, wrote that SD fears of an "inner collapse" in 1943 extended beyond whether the police obeyed orders.

27. Richard J. Evans, *The Third Reich in Power, 1933–1945* (London: Penguin Press, 2005), 117. A number of historians have cited this Witten protest. Mar-

tina Kliner-Lintzen, and Sybil Milton viewed the protest as a sign of women's discontent. Detlev Peukert and Wolfgang Werner interpreted the protest as workers' opposition. Martina Kliner-Lintzen, "Rathaus Witten: Unmut oder Widerstand?" in *Wittener Frauengeschichte(n): Dokumentation anlässlich einer frauengeschichtlichen Stadtrundfahrt,* ed. Beate Brunner and Martine Kliner-Lintzen (Witten: Laube, 1990); Sybil Milton, "Women and the Holocaust: The Case of German and German-Jewish Women," in *When Biology Became Destiny: Women in Weimar and Nazi Germany,* ed. Renate Bridenthal et al. (New York: Monthly Review Press, 1984), 319; Detlev Peukert, *Ruhrarbeiter gegen den Faschismus: Dokumentation über Widerstand im Ruhrgebiet 1933–1945* (Frankfurt am Main: Röderberg, 1976), 310; Wolfgang Franz Werner, *"Bleib übrig!": Deutsche Arbeiter in der nationalsozialistischen Kriegswirtschaft* (Düsseldorf: Schwann, 1983), 272. In his work on children's evacuations, Gerhard Kock links the protest to parents' disapproval of the regime's attempts to make the evacuation of their offspring compulsory *("Der Führer sorgt für unser Kinder . . .": Die Kinderlandverschickung im Zweiten Weltkrieg* [Paderborn: Schöningh, 1997], 186–187). Gerhard Sollbach follows a similar line of reasoning, reconstructing events surrounding the protest with material from the city archives of the *Ruhrgebiet* ("'Mütter—schafft eure Kinder fort!': Kinderlandverschickung im Ruhrgebiet während des Zweiten Weltkriegs," *Geschichte im Westen* 13 [1998]). Olaf Groehler, on the other hand, connects the incident to workers' rejection of evacuations because they found it difficult to pay the extra costs these measures entailed (*Bombenkrieg gegen Deutschland* [Berlin: Akademie-Verlag, 1990], 275). Several other historians have written tersely in JSTOR publications about the protest, all since the late 1990s. Julia Torrie has done a thorough investigation in "'If Only Family Unity Can Be Maintained': The Written Protest and German Civilian Evacuations," *German Studies Review* 29, no. 2 (May 2006): 347–366, and *"For Their Own Good": Civilian Evacuations in Germany and France, 1939–1945* (New York: Berghahn Books, 2010), 94–127. Evans, *The Third Reich at War,* 452, does not take the new scholarship into account or explain why his 1976 conclusions were incorrect.

28. Julia S. Torrie, "The Possibilities of Protest in the Third Reich: The Witten Demonstration in Context," in Stoltzfus and Maier-Katkin, *Protest in Hitler's "National Community,"* 76–77. See chapter II for other examples of police refusing orders to crush public protests.

29. Nicholas Stargardt, *The German War: A Nation under Arms* (New York: Basic Books, 2015), 263, 406. On Stuckart and the regime's consideration of a law forcing the annulment of intermarriages, see 378n10. For more on Hitler's use of law, as illustrated by euthanasia, see the end of chapter VI.

30. See Ekkehard Klausa, "Ganz normale deutsche: Das Judenbild der conservative Widerstands," in *Der vergessene Widerstand: Zu Realgeschichte und Wahrnehmung des Kampfes,* ed. Johannes Tuchel (Göttingen: Wallstein, 2005), 199–200.

31. Wittener Frauengeschichte(n), ed., *Arbeitskreis Frauengeschichte Witten* (Witten: Arbeitskreis Frauengeschichte Witten, 1992), 45, 47. E-mail interview with Ralph Klein, University of Dortmund, June 13, 2007. Klein notes that women from the Ruhr had protested for matters of food and family since at least 1790. Nevertheless, the 1943 protest stands out against the special experience of, and scrutiny given to, life in the Third Reich and the fact that, as he says, all related topics have been much discussed. The perspective that the protests were just part of a tradition hundreds of years old suggests an interesting continuity and a normalcy, but is it possible that the women didn't view their Nazi government as more dangerous? Goebbels claimed this was the case in April 1942 (see chapter VII, p. 235).

32. If Hitler "did not wish to hear or see negative military reports, at least in this respect he wanted to receive the facts" (Heinz Linge, *With Hitler to the End: The Memoirs of Adolf Hitler's Valet,* trans. Geoffrey Brooks [New York: Skyhorse Publishing, 2009], 7).

33. E-mail interview with Ralph Klein, August 4, 2015; Klein agreed to have it cited.

34. Klausa, "Ganz normale deutsche," 199–200.

35. See Antonia Leugers, "The 1943 Rosenstrasse Protest and the Churches," in *Protest in Hitler's "National Community": Popular Unrest and the Nazi Response,* ed. Nathan Stoltzfus and Birgit Maier-Katkin (New York: Berghahn Books, 2015), 149. The lively exchange in 2003 about the Rosenstrasse protest led editors in the German weekly *Die Zeit* to characterize it as a *Historikerstreit,* a controversy among historians. Editorial introduction to Nathan Stoltzfus, "Die Wahrheit jenseits der Akten: Wer nur den NS-Dokumenten vertraut, verkennt den Widerstand der Deutschen," *Die Zeit,* no. 45/30 (October 2003), 48. H-German sponsored an online forum that ran from July through September 2004 with scores of opinions exchanged under the heading "Rosenstrasse Forum" and posted until 2015: http://www.h-net.org/~german/discuss/Rosenstrasse/Rosenstrasse_index .htm. As of September 2015 it had disappeared, although the entries for the Rosenstrasse Forum can be viewed, one by one rather than as a unit, under the discussion logs of H-German at http://h-net.msu.edu/cgi-bin/logbrowse .pl?trx=lm&list=h-german, where entries are listed in the order that they were originally published. The separate entries in this forum can be viewed in the months of July, August, and September 2004. Beatte Meyer's entry is at http://h-net.msu.edu/cgi-bin/logbrowse.pl?trx=vx&list=H-German&month =0407&week=d&msg=oN6p2xHv/wqg9q2hC75dFw&user=&pw=; Wolf Gruner's is at http://h-net.msu.edu/cgi-bin/logbrowse.pl?trx=vx&list=H -German&month=0409&week=b&msg=UMAIiJEoRcI%2bCDoy5xkAyA &user=&pw=; Nathan Stoltzfus's is at http://h-net.msu.edu/cgi-bin /logbrowse.pl?trx=vx&list=H-German&month=0409&week=d&msg =xcSwqBWaTwMa%2bfoY%2bz4HTg&user=&pw=.

36. On Nazi treason, see Wolfram Wette and Detlef Vogel, *Das letzte Tabu: NS-Militärjustiz und "Kriegsverrat"* (Berlin: Aufbau Verlag, 2007).

37. Gerhard Schumm, in the introduction to the website he launched soon after hearing of the protest: http://www.rosenstrasse protest.de/projekt/index _projekt_1993.html (accessed July 18, 2014). The article Schumm mentions was a dossier on the protest in *Die Zeit*, published in July 1989 on the forty-fifth anniversary of the July 20 attempt on Hitler's life. Nathan Stoltzfus, "Jemand war für mich da: Der Aufstand der Frauen in der Rosenstrasse," *Die Zeit*, no. 30/21 (July 1989): 9–13.

38. The exception was a two-page article published in December 1945 by Georg Zivier titled "Aufstand der Frauen," in the postwar women's and human rights publication *Sie*, no. 2 (December 1945): 1–2. Zivier, a journalist, was an intermarried Jew whose wife had protested on the streets outside of the building on Rosenstrasse where he was imprisoned with hundreds of other intermarried Jews. Brief mentions concluding that the Rosenstrasse protest caused the release of some two thousand intermarried Jews include the following: Ruth Andreas-Friedrich, *Der Schattenmann: Tagebuchaufzeich-nungen 1938–1945* (Berlin: Suhrkamp, 1947; 3rd ed., 1984); Martin Riesen-burger, *Das Licht verlöschte nicht. Ein Zeugnis aus der Nacht des Faschismus* (Teetz: Heinrich and Heinrich, 2003); Heinz Ullstein, *Spielplatz meines Leb-ens. Erinnerung* (Munich: Kindler, 1961); Inge Unikower, *Suche nach dem gel-obten Land. Die fragwürdigen Abenteuer des kleinen Gerschon. Bibliographie* (Berlin: Verlag der Nation, 1978); Kurt Jakob Ball-Kaduri, "Berlin wird Ju-denfrei: Die Juden in Berlin in den Jahren 1942/1943," *Jahrbuch für die Ge-schichte Mittel- und Ostdeutschlands* 22 (1973): 212–214; Peter Edel, *Wenn es ans Leben geht. Meine Geschichte* (Frankfurt am Main: Röderberg Verlag, 1979); Georg Zivier, *Deutschland und seine Juden. Ein Buch gegen Vorurteile* (Hamburg: Hoffmann und Campe, 1971); Walter Laqueur, *The Missing Years* (London: Weidenfeld and Nicolson, 1980).

39. Eyewitnesses in a position to know agreed with Dr. Margarete Sommer's and G. Luckner's assessment in 1943. These included Leopold Gutterer, the deputy of Propaganda Minister and Gauleiter Goebbels, and Herbert Titze, the Gestapo officer who was charged with preparing the lists for each depor-tation of Berlin Jews. Jewish Community authorities Martha Mosse and Siegbert Kleemann also said that because of the protest, the regime did not deport the Jews to the East as it had intended. Titze testified: "The mixed marriage partners sent to the Rosenstrasse Collection Center were released a little later. The Aryan wives of these Jews got together back then to protest in front of the center" (Herbert Titze statement, August 1, 1966, B Rep. 058, Nr. 22, 1 JS 9/65, Landesarchiv Berlin). Mosse's testimony from 1958 is cited in Hans Günther Adler, *Der Verwaltete Mensch: Studien zur Deportation der Juden aus Deutschland* (Tübingen: Mohr, 1974), 785. For the statements of Kleemann and Gutterer, see Stoltzfus, *Resistance of the Heart: Intermarriage*

and the Rosenstrasse Protest in Nazi Germany (New York: Norton, 1996), 213, 244–245, 260–261.

Over the decades, the judgment of a variety of experts, historians as well as German prosecutors and judges, has also been that the protest influenced the regime to release rather than deport these Jews. The postwar German judiciary, as well as scholars, has agreed. Christof Dipper wrote in 1996 that up until this point only a few historians had doubted that the protest had caused the Gestapo to release the Jewish prisoners at Rosenstrasse ("Schwierigkeiten mit der Resistenz," Geschichte und Gesellschaft 22 [1996]: 409–416). Some who have made this interpretation, aside from Antonia Leugers and Joachim Neander, as cited here, include the following: Ball-Kaduri, "Berlin wird Judenfrei," 212–14; Doris L. Bergen, War and Genocide: A Concise History of the Holocaust (Lanham, MD: Rowman and Littlefield, 2009), 202; Heinz Boberach, Aemter, Abkuerzungen, Aktionen des NS-Staates: Handbuch für die Benutzung von Quellen der Nationalsozialistischen Zeit (Munich: K. G. Saur, 1997), 379; Paul Bookbinder, "Confronting Resistance in Nazi Germany: An Overview," in Confront! Resistance in Nazi Germany, ed. John Michalczyk (New York: Peter Lang, 2004), 8; Helmut Eschwege and Konrad Kwiet, Selbstbehauptung und Widerstand deutsche Juden im Kampf um Existenz und Menschewuerde 1933–1945 (Hamburg: Christians, 1984), 43; Raul Hilberg, Perpetrators, Victims, Bystanders: The Jewish Catastrophe, 1933–1945 (New York: Aaron Asher Books, 1992), 132; Eric A. Johnson, Nazi Terror: The Gestapo, Jews, and Ordinary Germans (New York: Basic Books, 1999), 25; Marion A. Kaplan, Between Dignity and Despair: Jewish Life in Nazi Germany (New York: Oxford University Press, 1998), 193; Ian Kershaw, Hitler, 1936–45: Nemesis (New York: W. W. Norton, 2000), 936n115; Claudia Koonz, Mothers in the Fatherland: Women, the Family, and Nazi Politics (New York: St. Martin's Press, 1987), 337; Milton, "Women and the Holocaust," 319; Monika Richarz, Jüdisches Leben in Deutschland: Selbstzeugnisse zur Sozialgeschichte, vol. 3: 1918–1945 (Stuttgart: Deutsche Verlags-Anstalt, 1982), 64; Wolfgang Scheffler, Judenverfolgung im Dritten Reich 1933 bis 1945 (Frankfurt am Main: Büchergilde Gutenberg, 1965), 44, 69; Marlis G. Steinert, Hitler's War and the Germans: Public Mood and Attitude during the Second World War, trans. T. E. J. de Witt (Athens: Ohio University Press, 1977), 142. A court judgment rationale of 1969 for the regional court of Berlin stated that "There developed in front of the collection center [Rosenstrasse] an overt protest [Protestkundgebung] of 'Aryan' marriage partners, which led to the result that a part of those arrested were set free again, while others [Jews in intermarriage], by contrast, had to make their way to Auschwitz . . . from which they were, however, returned to Berlin a couple of weeks later." Urteilsgründe, trial against Kurt Venter and Max Graustueck [(500) 1 Ks 2/69 (10/69)], 79, 80. In charges against a former head of the Berlin Gestapo, a postwar German prosecutor made the same conclusion. Trial against Otto Bovensiepen et al., B Rep 058, 1 Js 9/65, Landesarchiv Berlin.

40. Konrad Kwiet, "Nach dem Pogrom: Stufen der Ausgrenzung," in *Die Juden in Deutschland 1933–1945: Leben unter national-sozialistisher Herrschaft,* ed. Wolfgang Benz (Munich: Beck, 1988), 594.

41. Stoltzfus, "Jemand war für mich da." Jenny Wüstenberg, "Vom alternativen Laden zum Dienstleistungsbetrieb: The Berliner Geschichtswerkstatt, A Case Study in Activist Memory Politics," *German Studies Review* 32, no. 3 (October 2009): 590–618. In 1988, the East German Jewish Community organized a commemorative ceremony. The first documentary film dates to 1988, by Roza Berger-Fiedler, *Betrifft Fabrikaktion* (DEFA Studio für Dokumentarfilme Gruppe Chronik). East German artist and sculptor Ingeborg Hunzinger obtained state funding in East Germany for a sculpture, "Block of Women," installed in 1995.

42. Antonia Leugers, "Widerstand gegen die Rosenstrasse," http://aps.sulb.uni -saarland.de/theologie.geschichte/inhalt/2006/11.html. Print version: *theologie.geschichte* 1 (2006): 131–205. Wolfgang Benz, *Herrschaft und Gesellschaft im nationalsozialistischen Staat* (Frankfurt am Main: Fischer, 1990), 190. Gerd R. Ueberschär, *Für ein anderes Deutschland. Der deutsche Widerstand gegen den NS-Staat 1933–1945* (Frankfurt am Main: Fischer, 2005), 8; Stargardt, *The German War,* 264.

43. Wolf Gruner, "Die Reichhauptstadt und die Verfolgung der Berliner Juden 1933–1945," in *Jüdische Geschichte in Berlin: Essays und Studien,* ed. Reinhard Rürup (Berlin: Edition Hentrich, 1995), 253. The scholarly exchange was an H-German forum on Rosenstrasse including the contributions of Gruner and Meyer. http://www.h-net.org/~german/discuss/Rosenstrasse /Rosenstrasse_index.htm. See note 35 for this chapter for the new web addresses.

44. Richard J. Evans, "Wives against the Nazis," *Sunday Telegraph,* November 17, 1996, reviewing Stoltzfus, *Resistance of the Heart,* wrote that "a careful and subtle historian . . . suggests plausibly that Hitler and Goebbels wanted to avoid disturbing Berlin's female population at a time when the Propaganda Minister had just called on them to mobilise for 'total war.'" In "German Questions," *Jewish Chronicle* (London), February 21, 1997, Evans wrote that "In his moving and highly readable book, the American historian Nathan Stoltzfus uses interview material as well as original documentation to trace the sacrifices of 'Aryan' women who had married German Jews. A large group of such 'Aryan' women staged a week-long public protest. . . . Goebbels had imprisoned their husbands in February 1943 prior to an intended deportation to Auschwitz. Their efforts eventually forced their husbands' release. As Stoltzfus convincingly argues, the majority of Germans were indifferent to the fate of the Jews." But within a decade Evans's opinion had been turned on its head, much as in the case of the Witten protest: in the third volume of his trilogy on the Third Reich (*The Third Reich at War,* 271–272, including note 201), Evans changes his representations dramatically, writing that "subsequent legend elevated this incident into a rare public protest that

had secured the internees' release; but there had never been any intention of sending these particular Jews east for extermination, and the crowd had not engaged in any kind of explicit protest. . . . For the legend in its classical form see Nathan Stoltzfus, *Resistance of the Heart: Intermarriage and the Rosenstrasse Protest in Nazi Germany* (New York 1996), 209–258 (relying heavily on oral history interviews)." Naturally Evans has the right to change his mind, and one would like to know why; but he merely cites one page of Gruner's 2005 book (*Widerstand in der Rosenstrasse: Die Fabrik-Aktion und die Verfolgung der "Mischehen" 1943* [Frankfurt am Main: Frisher Taschenbuch Verlag, 2005], and Gruner's 2002 article on the "Fabrik-Aktion" ("The Factory Action and the Events at the Rosenstrasse in Berlin: Facts and Fictions about 27 February 1943: Sixty Years Later," *Central European History* 36, no. 2 [2003]).

45. Joschka Fischer, foreword, in Nathan Stoltzfus, *Widerstand des Herzens* (Hamburg: Deutscher Taschenbuch Verlag, 2002).

46. "Historikerstreit" comment in the editor's introduction to Nathan Stoltzfus, "Die Wahrheit jenseits der Akten," *Die Zeit,* October 30, 2003, an article written in response to Wolfgang Benz, "Kitsch as Kitsch Can," *Die Süddeutsche Zeitung,* September 20, 2003. Gruner, *Widerstand,* 55, 110, 119, 128. According to the Frankfurt/Oder order, "Much would depend on the arbitrary behavior of the officers at each location," Gruner wrote in his 1994 dissertation, "Arbeitseinsatz." "The officials had received a 'carte blanche' to penalize 'impudent behavior' from 'protected' Jews by taking them into protective custody; however, the officials were also told not to overstep their authority." It was not rare for officials at this level to initiate the protective custody of Jews that would send them to a camp, never to return. This Frankfurt/Oder decree, translated in full, appears in Stoltzfus and Maier-Katkin, *Protest in Hitler's "National Community,"* 229–231.

47. Antonia Leugers, "Der Protest in der Rosenstrasse 1943 und die Kirchen," in *Berlin, Rosenstrasse 2–4: Protest in der NS-Diktatur. Neue Forschungen zum Frauenprotest in der Rosenstrasse 1943,* ed. Antonia Leugers (Annweiler: Plöger, 2005), 47–80; translated in Leugers, "The 1943 Rosenstrasse Protest and the Churches," 143–176.

48. Kurt Pätzold, "Der eigentliche Streitwert. Zur Kontroverse um die Rosenstrasse," *Neues Deutschland,* September 27, 2003.

49. The Topography of Terror Memorial's seemingly random choice of ten documents to display at its single exhibit on the Rosenstrasse protest is mystifying for anyone trying to make any sense out of why events unfolded as they did. The selection could have been organized around a hypothesis about what happened. See the documents at http://www.rosenstrasse-protest.de/interviews/index_topo_engl.html (accessed July 15, 2015).

50. Christopher Browning, *Remembering Survival: Inside a Nazi Slave Labor Camp* (New York: W. W. Norton, 2009), 8–12. Of course eyewitness testi-

mony must be assessed judiciously in the context of knowledge about the regime's pertinent processes. On the "Sonderkommando uprising," see Gideon Graif, *We Wept without Tears: Testimonies of the Jewish Sonderkommando from Auschwitz* (New Haven: Yale University Press, 2005 [orig. 1995]).

51. Gruner, *Widerstand*. Wolfgang Benz, for example, wrote that Gruner's work "reconstructed the real history of Rosenstrasse," and he also apparently sees no reason for further discussion (Benz, "Kitsch as Kitsch Can"; see the response, Stoltzfus, "Die Wahrheit jenseits der Akten"). In his latest book, Benz writes off the customary interpretation as legend without citing any source (*Der deutsche Widerstand gegen Hitler* [Munich: Beck, 2014], 65–66). However, this book indicates that he now sees it as necessary to include "Rosenstrasse" in a book on resistance, although his earlier treatments did not (e.g., Wolfgang Benz and Walter H. Pehle, eds., *Encyclopedia of German Resistance to the Nazi Movement* [New York: Continuum, 1997]). Still missing from these overviews on resistance are other significant acts of public protest, including the Witten protest examined by Julia Torrie and others. Torrie, "The Witten Protest and German Civilian Evacuations," *German Studies Review* 29, no. 2 (2006): 347–366.

52. Gruner, *Widerstand*, 32, 202.

53. Wolf Gruner, *Gedenkort Rosenstrasse 2–4. Internierung und Protest im NS-Staat* (Berlin: Topographie des Terrors, 2013). See Antonia Leugers's review at http://universaar.uni-saarland.de/journals/index.php/tg/article /viewArticle/536/575. Examples of the criticisms of Gruner's 2005 book, *Widerstand*, are in Evan Bukey in *Holocaust and Genocide Studies* 21, no. 2 (Fall 2007): 308–312; Antonia Leugers, "Widerstand gegen die Rosenstrasse," *theologie.geschichte* 1 (2006); Joachim Neander, "Rezension zu: Gruner, Wolf: *Widerstand in der Rosenstrasse*," in H-Soz-u-Kult, 02.03.2006, http://hsozkult.geschichte.hu-berlin.de/rezensionen/2006-1-145; Nathan Stoltzfus in *American Historical Review* 1 (2007): 1628–1629.

54. The words "set free" and "released," which the RSHA and other officials used to describe the fate of those at Rosenstrasse, are better suited to captives than they are to persons who are having their identities checked or who are being reviewed for a job selection. Gruner, *Widerstand*, 121. Gruner explained that the Gestapo took children from their homes and locked them up at Rosenstrasse "so they would not be left alone at home when their parents were arrested" (*Widerstand*, 109). On this, see Leugers, "Widerstand gegen Rosenstrasse," 188, and Stoltzfus, *Resistance of the Heart*, 219.

55. Gruner, *Widerstand*, 109. A logical conclusion from Gruner's argument about the importance of one Gestapo directive is the following: "On February 20, 1943, the Reich-wide decree was released, which some Geltungsjuden [those at Rosenstrasse] should thank for their survival" (Maria von der Heydt, " 'Wer fährt den gerne mit dem Judenstern in der Straßenbahn?': Die Ambivalenz des 'geltungsjüdlischen' Alltags zwischen 1941 und 1945," in *Alltag*

im Holocaust: Jüdisches Leben im Grossdeutschen Reich 1941–1945, ed. Andrea Löw, Doris L. Bergen, and Anna Hájková [Munich: Oldenbourg, 2013], 74). Bergen herself concluded that "in the 1943 Rosenstrasse protest, the gentile wives of German Jewish men forced cancellation of plans to transport their husbands to the east to be killed" (*War and Genocide*, 202).

56. In an effort to reduce what the SS considered to be an overgrown number of Jews protected by their employment with the Berlin Jewish Community, Eichmann's deputy, Rolf Günther, had asked the Berlin Community authorities to select some five hundred Berlin Jews employed by the community for deportation to Auschwitz on October 26, 1942. Elisabeth Kraus, *Die Familie Mosse: Deutsch-jüdisches Bürgertum im 19. und 20. Jahrhundert* (Munich: C. H. Beck, 1999), 580; Annagrette Ehmann et al., eds., *Die Grunewald-Rampe: Die Deportation der Berliner Juden* (Berlin: Spiess, 1993), 39.

57. Leugers has shown that the churches were not the prime agents. "The 1943 Rosenstrasse Protest and the Churches," 143–176.

58. The regime kept records assiduously on every possible public dissenter, including "wandering speakers," and the interest in ways to deport the intermarried Jews without drawing attention was acute. The entry under "wandering orators" ("Wanderredner" 38 0396), in Heinz Boberach, ed., *Regimekritik, Widerstand und Verfolgung in Deutschland und den besetzten Gebieten: Meldungen und Berichte aus dem Geheimen Staatspolizeiamt, dem SD-Hauptamt der SS und dem Reichssicherheitshauptamt 1933–1945* (Berlin: K. G. Saur, 2003, in cooperation with the Bundesarchiv), microfiche edition. This recent enormous collection of police reports (Gestapo and SD), pairing resistance with persecution under one title, does identify some incidents of popular "protest" and "demonstrations," although only in other countries. Under these categories for Germany, incidents of public protest and demonstrations are taken from what the regime categorized as "enemy propaganda." But, of course, not all the records of public protests in Germany can be attributed to "enemy propaganda." An SD secret police account of November 18, 1943, for example, covers a public protest staged by three hundred women in Witten on October 11, 1943, in considerable detail, within a report titled "Contemporary Events and the Impact on the Morale and Behavior of Women."

59. Gruner, *Widerstand*, 194. There are many examples of deception in the documents, including Heydrich's decision to order that decorated Jewish veterans be sent not to Auschwitz but to Theresienstadt, and the regime did take the effort to send them there first, before sending them posthaste to Auschwitz. Hilberg, *Destruction*, 2:448–449. Peter Fritzsche, *Life and Death in the Third Reich* (Cambridge, MA: Belknap Press, 2008), 207.

60. For years before this 2013 publication, the Topography of Terror's website had taken the same position as Gruner, stating, despite all the German experts who disagreed, that the Gestapo never intended to deport a single intermarried Jew from Berlin in March 1943. It does not acknowledge the

opinions of other accomplished German historians, such as Joachim Neander and Antonia Leugers, who wrote in 2013 that as a site of public
memory, Topography of Terror had a responsibility to "inform the public of
the complexity of the Rosenstrasse events rather than declaring them settled in a one-sided way and off-bounds to discussion" (Leugers, review of
Wolf Gruner, "Gedenkort Rosenstrasse 2–4," *theologie.geschichte* 8 [2013];
http://universaar.uni-saarland.de/journals/index.php/tg/article
/viewArticle/536/575).

61. Andreas Nachama, foreword to Wolf Gruner, *Gedenkort Rosenstrasse 2–4. Internierung und Protest im NS-Staat* (Berlin: Hentrich and Hentrich, 7–8). For
Holzer, see Stoltzfus, *Resistance of the Heart*, 106–108.

62. The Berlin Memorial to German Resistance, founded in 1983 to commemorate all German resistance, once had a project file on the Rosenstrasse protest, but the commemoration has moved on to the much more popular
Topography of Terror Memorial.

63. The "ambivalence" that Gruner, an East German youth at the time, detected
(Widerstand, 156) was between an article's title and its content, in the newspaper of the East German Socialist Unity Party, *Neues Deutschland*. Inge
Unikower wrote that the women called out together in a chorus demanding
the release of their husbands. The article appeared under the title "Silent
Protest"—a designation likely given by the newspaper editors in 1964 to
suit the party line. Unikower's 1978 book, *Suche nach dem gelobten Land,* is
hardly ambivalent, beginning with, "We wish to establish a historical monu-
ment *[Denkmal]* and a memorial warning future generations *[Mahnmal]*. . . .
When had this ever happened before, that German women rose up against
the leadership, against the Gestapo, for their Jewish husbands, for their
children. . . . Before a few hundred determined women the SS and Gestapo
capitulated."

64. For an account of German historians forming a union around specific interpretations, see Otto Pflanze, "Another Crisis among German Historians?
Helmut Bohme's Deutschlands Weg zur Grossmacht," *Journal of Modern
History* 40, no. 1 (March 1968): 118–129; on the denial of any controversy, see
Wolf Gruner, "Ein Historikerstreit? Die Internierung der Juden aus Mischehen in der Rosenstrasse 1943," *Zeitschrift für Geschichtswissenschaft* 1
(2004): 5–22. Katharina von Kellenbach, concluding that the protest has
not been recognized because it was by women, points out that authors who
have not mentioned the protest before label but do not discuss the relevant
documents and arguments ("The 'Legend' of Women's Resistance in the
Rosenstrasse," in Stoltzfus and Maier-Katkin, *Protest in Hitler's "National
Community,"* 106–124).

65. Many of these workshop Berliners were from the 1968 generation credited
with toppling the lockstep German Historians Bund. Their "Active Museum,"
as it came to be known, held a "symbolic dig" in May 1985 at a Gestapo
building site and later unearthed its ruins. This was done "because it was

part of the new-left consensus concerning how history should be presented in public." A leading expert in German memory wrote that "There is considerable disappointment among the activists that their engagement did not result in more long-term benefits for them in the form of employment or permanent funding. Highly qualified activists were passed over for leading positions at Schöneweide and the [Berlin History Workshop] was maneuvered out of the decision-making committees at the Topography Foundation, retaining only observer status" (Wüstenberg, "Vom alternativen Laden zum Dienstleistungsbetrieb," 605, 610). "Top," as the memorial is now jauntily called, has now earned a spot as probably Germany's most important site of official memory. This memorial's title announces its focus, but a complete view of terror contrasts the extent to which Hitler ruled his people by terror and the way he ruled others. Although it is fully publicly funded and in that sense represents official history, history the way Germans are supposed to know it, many concerned Germans disagree. See, for example, Professor Gerhard Schumm's website, www.rosenstrasse-protest.de.

66. Karl Jaspers, *The Question of German Guilt* (New York: Fordham University Press, 2001), 12, 116.

ACKNOWLEDGMENTS

I HOPE TO give back as much as I have received from the loved ones, friends, and colleagues who have helped me write this book. I would also like to thank institutions. I am grateful to the Deutscher Akademischer Austausch Dienst and Florida State University's CRC Cornerstone Program for research awards. Thanks as well to the FSU Department of Arts and Sciences and the History Department for research and sabbatical semesters, as well as travel funding. Ed Gray, chair *extraordinaire* of the History Department, has been an anchor of support. Thanks to Vicky, Diane, Julie, and Anne, the wonderful department staff, for always being there when needed.

I would especially like to thank Daniel Maier-Katkin for pithy suggestions during our lengthy discussions, as well as for his encouragement that there is still room for another book on Hitler and Nazi Germany, perhaps now more than before. Dan McMillan has also been a remarkable source of insight and perspective. I am grateful to Chris Osmar for writing the index, and for his sharp-eyed, knowledgeable scrutiny as my research assistant and student. Thanks also to Mercedes Krimme and my students Becca Shriver, Kayleigh Whitman, and Danielle Wirsansky. I will always be indebted to Charles S. Maier, Harvey Cox, and Gene Sharp of Harvard University, as well as Karen Colvard of the Harry Frank Guggenheim Foundation for their support and continuing inspiration.

397

I am grateful to Klaus Larres for the opportunity to exchange ideas on the themes of this book at the University of North Carolina's Richard M. Krasno Distinguished Professor Lecture Series, with Gerhard Weinberg and Konrad Jarausch.

Thanks to the experts and archivists Bianca Welzing-Bräutigam, Kristin Hartisch, William Cunliffe, and Martina Kliner-Fruck, who, along with Ralph Klein and Dick de Mildt, found and made sources available. For reading and offering valuable comments on all or parts of the manuscript as it developed, I am very grateful to colleagues Gerhard Weinberg, Robert Beachy, John Connelly, Jeff Richter, Laura Mahrenbach, Hilary Potter, David Clay Large, Hermann Beck, Jeffrey Herf, Mark Roseman, Robert Gellately, and Darrin McMahon. Kevin Spicer read the entire manuscript at a sensitive moment and fielded questions even while conducting his own research. I thank the anonymous readers for Yale University Press; editors Erica Hanson, Annie Imbornoni, and Jenya Weinreb; and my copyeditor, Bojana Ristich. I am especially appreciative of my editor, Christopher Rogers, a lighthouse guiding the manuscript to completion. I dedicate the book to the one most deserving of my appreciation and gratitude, my strong and loving wife, Maria Foscarinis.